Eighth Edition

Writing About Literature

EDGAR V. ROBERTS

*Lehman College
of
The City University of New York*

PRENTICE HALL, Englewood Cliffs, New Jersey 07632

Library of Congress Cataloging-in-Publication Data

Roberts, Edgar V.
  Writing about literature / Edgar V. Roberts. —8th ed.
    p.   cm.
  Rev. ed of: Writing themes about literature. c1991.
  Includes index.
  ISBN 0-13-097585-0
  1. English language—Rhetoric. 2. Literature—History and
criticism—Theory, etc. 3. Criticism—Authorship. 4. Report
writing. I. Roberts, Edgar V. Writing themes about literature.
II. Title.
PE1479.C7R59 1995
808'.0668—dc20   94-27498
                                         CIP

Acquisitions editor: Alison Reeves
Editorial assistant: Kara Hado
Editorial/production supervision: Linda B. Pawelchak
Copy editor: Lois Thompson/Maine Proofreading Services
Cover design: Bruce Kenselaar
Buyer: Lynn Pearlman
Cover photo: Jacques Villon
  Spaces. *1920*
  Oil on canvas
  28 3/4 × 36 1/16 in. (73 × 91.6 cm.)
  The Solomon R. Guggenheim Foundation, New York,
  Peggy Guggenheim Collection, Venice, 1976
  Photograph by Carmelo Guadagno copyright The
  Solomon R. Guggenheim Foundation, New York

© 1995, 1991, 1988, 1983, 1977, 1973, 1969, 1964 by Prentice-Hall, Inc.
A Simon & Schuster Company
Englewood Cliffs, New Jersey 07632

Printed in the United States of America
10 9 8 7 6 5 4 3 2

ISBN 0-13-097585-0

Prentice-Hall International (UK) Limited, *London*
Prentice-Hall of Australia Pty. Limited, *Sydney*
Prentice-Hall Canada Inc., *Toronto*
Prentice-Hall of Hispanoamericana, S.A., *Mexico*
Prentice-Hall of India Private Limited, *New Delhi*
Prentice-Hall of Japan, Inc., *Tokyo*
Simon & Schuster Asia Pte. Ltd., *Singapore*
Editora Prentice-Hall do Brasil Ltda., *Rio de Janeiro*

Contents

12 Writing About a Problem: Challenges to Overcome in Reading

13 Writing for Comparison and Contrast: Learning by Seeing Literary Works Together

14 Writing About Prosody: Rhythm and Sound in Poetry

15 Writing About Rhyme: Line-Ending Sounds That Clinch Ideas

Plays:

To the Instructor

In the eighth edition of *Writing About Literature,* I have kept and strengthened those features that so many of you have valued over the years. As in the past, I base my approach not on genres, with specific assignments to be determined, but rather on topics for full-length essays on texts in any genre. While the constant emphasis is on writing complete essays about literature, the chapters may also be used as starting points for classroom study and discussion and may also be adapted for shorter writing assignments. In a one-semester course the book is extensive enough to offer selective choices for study and writing; whereas in a two- or three-semester sequence, it offers the possibility of complete or close-to-complete use.

Organization

As in each past edition of *Writing About Literature,* the chapters consist of two parts. The first is a discussion of a literary approach, and the second consists of suggestions for writing, together with a sample essay showing how students might deal with the approach.

A major characteristic preserved in this edition is that, after the preliminary discussion in Chapter 1, the chapters are arranged in order of increasing difficulty. Beginning with Chapter 2, which helps students connect their reading with their responses and preferences, the chapters progress from topics relevant to all the genres. The comparison-contrast chapter

(Chapter 13), for example, illustrates the ways in which the earlier techniques may be focused on any of the topics in the book. The later chapters, such as those on prosody, film, and research, are increasingly complex; but they also combine and build on the various techniques of analysis presented in the earlier chapters.

Although you might assign the chapters in sequence throughout your course, you may decide to choose them according to need and objective. One instructor, for example, might pass over the earlier chapters and go directly to the later ones. Another might choose the chapter on comparison-contrast for separate assignments such as comparative studies of imagery, structure, character, and point of view. Still another might use just a few of the chapters, assigning them two or more times until students overcome initial difficulties. No matter how the chapters are used, the two parts—discussion and illustration—enable students to improve the quality of their analytical writing.

The illustrative parts of the chapters—the sample essays—are presented in the belief that the word *imitation* need not be preceded by adjectives like *slavish* and *mere*. Their purpose is to show what *might* be done—not what *must* be done—on particular assignments. Without the samples as guides, students must add the task of creating their own thematic form to the already complex task of understanding new concepts and new works of literature. Some students may follow the samples closely, while others may adapt them or else use them as points of departure. My assumption is that students will become free to go their own ways as they become more experienced as writers.

Because the sample essays are guides, they represent a full treatment of each of the various topics. Nevertheless, in this edition they have been kept within the approximate lengths of most assignments. If students are writing outside of class, they can readily create essays as full as the samples. Even though the samples treat three or more aspects of particular topics, there is nothing to prevent assigning only one aspect, either for an impromptu or for an outside-class essay. Thus, using the chapter on setting, you might assign a paragraph about the use of setting in only the first scene of a story, or a paragraph about interior settings, colors, or shades of light.

Following the sample essays are commentaries, something students recommended that I include in the fourth edition that I have kept ever since. These are designed to connect the precepts in the first parts of the chapters to the sample writing in the second parts.

Changes and Innovations

I have designed all changes in the eighth edition of *Writing About Literature*, as in earlier editions, to guide and help students in reading, studying, thinking, planning, drafting, organizing, and writing. Many chapters are extensively revised; some are almost entirely rewritten. In making the many revisions, alterations, repositionings, and additions (and subtractions), I have tried to improve, sharpen, and freshen the underlying information and examples. Of particular note in the eighth edition, at the requests of numerous readers, is the addition of a new appendix (Appendix C) containing brief descriptions of critical approaches that have proved important in twentieth-century literary studies, such as New Criticism, structuralism, feminism, deconstructionism, and Reader-Response criticism.

Totally new in the eighth edition is the addition of "Special Writing Topics" at the ends of the chapters. These are keyed mainly to the works anthologized in Appendix D, but instructors are encouraged to adapt them to the selections in whatever anthologies they may be using. In a number of the chapters, there are short related topics that are boxed and shaded to set them apart for emphasis. These discussions, such as "A Note on Handwriting and Word Processing" and "Online Computerized Library Services," are designed as short notes to help students think about and develop their own writing.

At the suggestions of readers of the seventh edition, I have reversed Chapters 5 and 6, thus placing the discussion of point of view before setting in the order of chapters. Also, I have emphasized poetry by dividing the previously long chapter on prosody into two chapters, one on prosody and another on rhyme. In addition, I have changed the chapter on close reading (Chapter 16) to emphasize the study of content but not style. Because the extensive chapter on research (Chapter 18) is favored by instructors over the extended comparison-contrast essay in Chapter 13, I have dropped this essay description and have moved the discussion of documenting and footnoting from Appendix B into Chapter 18. This change then enables a change in the name of Appendix B from "A Note on Documentation" to "The Integration of Quotations and Other Important Details, and the Use of Tenses in Writing About Literature."

Aside from the extensive revisions and improvements, the chapters are internally different because of a number of changes in Appendix D ("Works Used for Sample Essays and References"). At the suggestions of readers, Poe's "The Cask of Amontillado" and Bierce's "An Occurrence at Owl Creek Bridge" have been added, in addition to poems by Hayden, Layton, Nye, Piercy, and Wordsworth. Accordingly, a small number of stories and poems have been dropped that were included in the seventh edition. These changes necessarily bring about many alterations in references; I hope these will make the book richer and, within the confines of the short number of selections, timely. With all the changes, the eighth edition of *Writing About Literature* is a useful and comprehensive guide for composition courses in which literature is introduced, and also for literature courses at any level.

An innovation of the sixth edition that is continued in the seventh and eighth is the glossary based on the terms set in boldface in the text. The increasing number of students taking entrance examinations and GREs has justified this continuation. A student may consult the glossary, which contains definitions and page numbers for further reference, and thereby develop full and systematic knowledge of important concepts in the text.

A particular word is in order about the works included in Appendix D. At one time I believed that clarifying references could be drawn from a pool of works commonly known by advanced high school and college students, and I therefore thought that no reference anthology was necessary. I presented a small number of works in the second edition, keyed to some but not all of the sample essays, but reviewers recommended against it for the next editions. Recent commentary, however, has emphasized that references to unknown works, even complete and self-explanatory ones, do not fully explain and clarify. Therefore, after the fifth edition I have made the book almost completely self-contained with the increased number of works in Appendix D (for the chapter on problems, however, I have continued to assume acquaintance with Shakespeare's *Hamlet;* and for the essay on film I have assumed that students might be shown Welles's *Citizen Kane*). The result is that both references and sample essays may be easily verified by a reading of the accompanying works. Experience has shown that the unity and coherence provided by these works help students understand and develop their own assignments.

Writing and Literature

The eighth edition brings into focus something that has been true of *Writing About Literature* since it first appeared in 1964. The book is primarily a practical guide for writing; the stress throughout is on writing. This emphasis is made to help students not only in composition and literature, but in most of their classes. In other subjects such as psychology, economics, sociology, biology, and political science, instructors use texts and ask students to develop raw data, and they assign writing on this basis. Writing is on external, written materials, not on descriptions of the student's own experiences or on opinions. Writing is about reading.

Yet instructors of composition face the problems we have always faced. On the one hand the needs of other departments, recently thrown into renewed focus by studies about "writing across the curriculum," cause wide diversification of subject matter, straining the general knowledge of the staff and also creating a certain topical and thematic disunity. On the other hand, programs stressing internalized subject matter, such as personal experiences or occasional topic materials, have little bearing on writing for other courses. We as English faculty, with a background in literature, have the task of meeting the service needs of the institution without compromising our own disciplinary commitment.

The approach in this book is aimed at this dilemma. Teachers can work with their own discipline—literature—while also fulfilling their primary and often required responsibility of teaching writing that is externally, not internally, directed. The book thus keeps the following issues in perspective:

- The requirement of the institution for composition
- The need of students to develop writing skills based on written texts
- The responsibility of the English faculty to teach writing while still working within their own expertise

It is therefore gratifying to claim that *Writing About Literature* has been offering assistance for many years to meet these needs. The approach works, but it is still novel. It gives coherence to the sometimes fragmented composition course. It also provides for adaptation and, as I have stressed, variety. Using the book, you can develop a virtually endless number of new topics for essays. One obvious benefit is the possibility of entirely eliminating not only the traditional "theme barrels" of infamous memory in fraternity and sorority houses, but also the newer interference from business "enterprises" that provide critical essays to order.

While *Writing About Literature* is designed, as I have said in the past, as a rhetoric of practical criticism for students, it is based on profoundly held convictions. I believe that true liberation in a liberal arts curriculum is achieved only through clearly defined goals. Just to make assignments and let students do with them what they can is to encourage frustration and mental enslavement. If students develop a deep knowledge of specific approaches to subject material, however, they can begin to develop some of that expertness that is essential to freedom. As Pope said:

True Ease in Writing comes from Art, not Chance,
As those move easiest who have learn'd to dance.

It is almost axiomatic that the development of writing skill in one area (in this instance the interpretation of literature) has an enabling effect on skill in other areas. The search for information with a particular goal in mind, the asking of pointed questions, the testing, rephrasing, and developing of ideas—all these and more are transferable skills for students to build on throughout their college years and beyond.

I have one concluding article of faith. Those of us whose careers have been established in the study of literature have made commitments to our belief in its value. The study of literature is valid in and for itself; but literature as an art form employs techniques and creates problems for readers that can be dealt with only through analysis, and analysis means work. Thus the immediate aim of *Writing About Literature* is to help students to read and write about individual literary works. The ultimate objective (in the past I wrote "primary objective") is to promote the pleasurable study and, finally, the love of literature.

Acknowledgments

As I complete the eighth edition of *Writing About Literature,* I renew my deepest thanks to those who have been loyal to all the earlier editions. Your approval of the book is a great honor. As I think about the revisions I am impressed with how much the book has been influenced by the collective wisdom of many, many teachers and students. Those who have been particularly helpful for the eighth edition are Betty Gipson, Southwest Baptist University; Troy D. Nordman, Butler County Community College; Albert E. Wilhelm, Tennessee Technological University. Conversations and discussions with others have influenced my changes in innumerable and immeasurable ways.

I thank Kara Hado, assistant English editor of Prentice Hall, who has guided the eighth edition from beginning to completion. I am also thankful to Alison Reeves, chief English editor of Prentice Hall, for her thoughtfulness and encouragement. Phil Miller of Prentice Hall has given me firm and friendly support over a number of years. I should also like to thank Kate Morgan, formerly of Prentice Hall, for her thoughtful, creative, and thorough assistance. I missed her participation in the development of the eighth edition. Linda Pawelchak of Prentice Hall designed the eighth edition, and for her skill and hard work I am thankful. I should particularly like to thank Lois Thompson, who copyedited the manuscript and who offered many, many improvements. I especially thank Jonathan Roberts for his skilled and unfailing help in preparing the manuscripts and disks of the halting and tentative drafts leading to the final copy.

—*Edgar V. Roberts*

chapter 1

Preliminary:

The Process of Reading, Responding, and Writing About Literature

The following chapters introduce a number of analytical approaches important in the study of literature, along with guidance for writing informative and well-focused essays based on these approaches. The chapters will help you fulfill two goals of composition and English courses: (1) to write good essays, and (2) to understand and assimilate great works of literature.

The premise of the book is that no educational process is complete until you can *apply* what you study. That is, you have not learned something—really *learned* it—until you talk or write about it. This does not mean that you retell a story, state an undeveloped opinion, or describe an author's life, but rather that you deal directly with topical and artistic issues about individual works. The need to write requires you to strengthen your understanding and knowledge through the recognition of where your original study might have fallen short. Thus, it is easy for you to read the chapter on point of view (Chapter 5), and it is also easy to read Bierce's story "An Occurrence at Owl Creek Bridge." Your grasp of point of view as a concept will not be complete, however, nor will your appreciation of the technical artistry of "An Occurrence at Owl Creek Bridge" be complete, until you have *written* about the technique. As you prepare your essay, you need to reread parts of the work, study your notes, and apply your knowledge to the problem at hand; you must check facts, grasp relationships, develop insights, and express yourself with as much exactness and certainty as possible.

Primarily, then, this book aims to help you improve your writing skills through the use of literature as subject matter. After you have finished a number of essays derived from the following chapters, you will be able to approach just about any literary work with the confidence that you can understand it and write about it.

WHAT IS LITERATURE, AND WHY DO WE STUDY IT?

We use the word **literature,** in a broad sense, to mean compositions that tell stories, dramatize situations, express emotions, and analyze and advocate ideas. Before the invention of writing, literary works were necessarily spoken or sung and were retained only as long as living people performed them. In some societies, the oral tradition of literature still exists, with many poems and stories designed exclusively for spoken delivery. Even in our modern age of writing and printing, much literature is still heard aloud rather than read silently. Parents delight their children with stories and poems; poets and storywriters read their works directly before live audiences; and plays and scripts are interpreted on stages and before cameras for the benefit of a vast public.

No matter how we assimilate literature, we gain much from it. In truth, readers often cannot explain why they enjoy reading, for goals and ideals are not easily articulated. There are, however, areas of general agreement about the value of systematic and extensive reading.

Literature helps us grow, both personally and intellectually. It provides an objective base for knowledge and understanding. It links us with the broader cultural, philosophic, and religious world of which we are a part. It enables us to recognize human dreams and struggles in different places and times we would never otherwise know existed. It helps us develop mature sensibility and compassion for the condition of *all* living things—human, animal, and vegetable. It gives us the knowledge and perception to appreciate the beauty of order and arrangement, just as a well-structured song or a beautifully painted canvas can. It provides the comparative basis from which we can see worthiness in the aims of all people, and it therefore helps us see beauty in the world around us. It exercises our emotions through interest, concern, tension, excitement, hope, fear, regret, laughter, and sympathy. Through our cumulative experience in reading, literature shapes our goals and values by clarifying our own identities—both positively, through acceptance of the admirable in human beings, and negatively, through rejection of the sinister. It enables us to develop a perspective on events occurring locally and globally, and thereby it gives us understanding and control. It encourages us to assist creative, talented people who need recognition and support. It is one of the shaping influences of life. Literature makes us human.

TYPES OF LITERATURE: THE GENRES

Literature may be classified into four categories or *genres:* (1) prose fiction, (2) poetry, (3) drama, and (4) nonfiction prose. Usually the first three are classed as **imaginative literature.**

The genres of imaginative literature have much in common, but they also have distinguishing characteristics. **Prose fiction,** or **narrative fiction,** includes **myths, parables, romances, novels,** and **short stories.** Originally, *fiction* meant anything made up, crafted, or shaped, but today the word refers to prose stories based in the author's imagination. The essence of fiction is **narration,** the relating or recounting of a sequence of events or actions. Works of fiction usually focus on one or a few major characters who undergo a change of attitude or character as they interact with other characters and deal with problems. While fiction, like all imaginative literature, may introduce true historical details, it is not real history. Its main purpose is to interest, stimulate, instruct, and divert, not to create a precise historical record.

Poetry expresses a conversation or interchange that is grounded in the most deeply felt experiences of human beings. Poetry exists in many formal and informal shapes, from the brief **haiku** to the extensive **epic.** More economical than prose fiction in its use of words, poetry relies heavily on **imagery, figurative language,** and **sound.**

Drama is literature designed to be performed by actors. Like fiction, drama may focus on a single character or a small number of characters, and it enacts fictional events as if they were happening in the present, to be witnessed by an audience. Although most modern plays use prose dialogue, in the belief that dramatic speech should be as lifelike as possible, many plays from the past, like those of ancient Greece and Renaissance England, are in poetic form.

Nonfiction prose is the literary genre that consists of news reports, feature articles, essays, editorials, textbooks, historical and biographical works, and the like, all of which describe or interpret facts and present judgments and opinions. Major goals of nonfiction prose are to report truth and to present logic in reasoning. Whereas in imaginative literature the aim is to show truth in life and human nature, in nonfiction prose the goal is to reveal truth in the factual world of news, science, and history.

READING LITERATURE AND RESPONDING TO IT ACTIVELY

Do not expect a cursory reading of a literary work to produce full understanding. After a first reading, it may be embarrassingly difficult to answer pointed questions or to say anything intelligent about the work. A more careful, active reading gives us the understanding to develop well-considered answers. Obviously, we must first follow the work and understand its details; but just as importantly we must respond to the words, get at the ideas, and understand the implications of what is happening. We must apply our own experiences to verify the accuracy and truth of the situation and incidents, and we must articulate our own emotional responses to the characters and their problems.

To illustrate such active responding, the following story, "The Necklace" (1884), by the French writer Guy de Maupassant,* is printed with the sorts of marginal annotations that any reader might make during original and follow-up readings. Many observations, particularly at the beginning, are *assimilative*; that is, they do little more than record details about the action. But as the story progresses the comments reflect conclusions about the story's developing meaning. Toward the end, the comments are full rather than minimal; they result not only from first responses, but also from considered thought. Here, then, is Maupassant's "The Necklace."

Guy de Maupassant (1850–1893)

The Necklace

1884

Translated by Edgar V. Roberts

She was one of those pretty and charming women, born, as if by an error of destiny, into a family of clerks and copyists. She had no dowry, no prospects, no way of getting known, courted, loved, married by a rich and distinguished man. She finally settled for a marriage with a minor clerk in the Ministry of Education.

> "She" is pretty but poor. Apparently there is no other life for her than marriage. Without connections, she has no entry into high society, and marries an insignificant clerk.

She was a simple person, without the money to dress well, but she was as unhappy as if she had gone through bankruptcy, for women have neither rank nor race. In place of high birth or important

> She is unhappy.
>
> A view of women that excludes the possibility of a career. In 1884,

---

*Maupassant, an apostle of Gustave Flaubert, was one of the major nineteenth-century French naturalists. He was an especially careful writer, devoting great attention to reality and economy of detail. His stories are focused on the difficulties and ironies of existence among not only the Parisian middle class, as in "The Necklace," but also among both peasants and higher society. Two of his better-known novels are *A Life* (1883) and *A Good Friend* (1885). Among his other famous stories are "The Rendez-vous" and "The Umbrella." "The Necklace" is notable for its concluding ironic twist, and for this reason it is perhaps the best known of his stories.

family connections, they can rely only on their beauty, their grace, and their charm. Their inborn finesse, their elegant taste, their engaging personalities, which are their only power, make working-class women the equals of the grandest ladies.

> women had little else than their personalities to get ahead.

She suffered constantly, feeling herself destined for all delicacies and luxuries. She suffered because of her grim apartment with its drab walls, threadbare furniture, ugly curtains. All such things, which most other women in her situation would not even have noticed, tortured her and filled her with despair. The sight of the young country girl who did her simple housework awakened in her only a sense of desolation and lost hopes. She daydreamed of large, silent anterooms, decorated with oriental tapestries and lighted by high bronze floor lamps, with two elegant valets in short culottes dozing in large armchairs under the effects of forced-air heaters. She imagined large drawing rooms draped in the most expensive silks, with fine end tables on which were placed knickknacks of inestimable value. She dreamed of the perfume of dainty private rooms, which were designed only for intimate tête-à-têtes with the closest friends, who because of their achievements and fame would make her the envy of all other women.

> She suffers because of her cheap belongings, wanting expensive things. She dreams of wealth and of how other women would envy her if she had all these fine things. But these luxuries are unrealistic and unattainable for her.

When she sat down to dinner at her round little table covered with a cloth that had not been washed for three days, in front of her husband who opened the kettle while declaring ecstatically, "Ah, good old boiled beef! I don't know anything better," she dreamed of expensive banquets with shining placesettings, and wall hangings portraying ancient heroes and exotic birds in an enchanted forest. She imagined a gourmet-prepared main course carried on the most exquisite trays and served on the most beautiful dishes, with whispered gallantries which she would hear with a sphinxlike smile as she dined on the pink meat of a trout or the delicate wing of a quail.

> Her husband's taste is for plain things, while she dreams of expensive gourmet food. He has adjusted to his status. She has not.

She had no decent dresses, no jewels, nothing. And she loved nothing but these; she believed herself born only for these. She burned with the desire to please, to be envied, to be attractive and sought after.

> She lives for her unrealistic dreams, and these increase her frustration.

She had a rich friend, a comrade from convent days, whom she did not want to see anymore because she suffered so much when she returned home. She would weep for the entire day afterward with sorrow, regret, despair, and misery.

> She even thinks of giving up a rich friend because she is so depressed after visiting her.

Well, one evening, her husband came home glowing and carrying a large envelope.

> A new section in the story.

"Here," he said, "this is something for you."

She quickly tore open the envelope and took out a card engraved with these words:

> *The Chancellor of Education and Mrs. George Ramponneau request that Mr. and Mrs. Loisel do them the honor of coming to dinner at the Ministry of Education on the evening of January 8.*

An invitation to dinner at the Ministry of Education. A big plum.

10 Instead of being delighted, as her husband had hoped, she threw the invitation spitefully on the table, muttering:

"What do you expect me to do with this?"

"But honey, I thought you'd be glad. You never get to go out, and this is a special occasion! I had a lot of trouble getting the invitation. Everyone wants one. The demand is high and not many clerks get invited. Everyone important will be there."

She looked at him angrily and stated impatiently:

"What do you want me to wear to go there?"

15 He had not thought of that. He stammered:

"But your theater dress. That seems nice to me . . ."

It only upsets her.

She declares that she hasn't anything to wear.

He tries to persuade her that her theater dress might do for the occasion.

He stopped, amazed and bewildered, as his wife began to cry. Large tears fell slowly from the corners of her eyes to her mouth. He said falteringly:

"What's wrong? What's the matter?"

But with a strong effort she had recovered, and she answered calmly as she wiped her damp cheeks:

20 "Nothing, except that I have nothing to wear and therefore can't go to the party. Give your invitation to someone else at the office whose wife will have nicer clothes than mine."

Distressed, he responded:

"Well, all right, Mathilde. How much would a new dress cost, something you could use at other times, but not anything fancy?"

She thought for a few moments, adding things up and thinking also of an amount that she could ask without getting an immediate refusal and a frightened outcry from the frugal clerk.

Finally she responded tentatively:

25 "I don't know exactly, but it seems to me that I could get by on four hundred francs."

He blanched slightly at this, because he had

Her name is Mathilde.
He volunteers to pay for a new dress.

She is manipulating him.

The dress will cost him his next

set aside just that amount to buy a shotgun for Sunday lark-hunts the next summer with a few friends in the Plain of Nanterre.

However, he said:

"All right, you've got four hundred francs, but make it a pretty dress."

summer's vacation. (He doesn't seem to have included her in his plans.)

As the day of the party drew near, Mrs. Loisel seemed sad, uneasy, anxious, even though her gown was all ready. One evening her husband said to her:

"What's the matter? You've been acting funny for several days."

She answered:

"It's awful, but I don't have any jewels to wear, not a single gem, nothing to dress up my outfit. I'll look like a beggar. I'd almost rather not go to the party."

He responded:

"You can wear a corsage of cut flowers. This year it's all the rage. For only ten francs you can get two or three gorgeous roses."

She was not convinced.

"No . . . there's nothing more humiliating than looking shabby in the company of rich women."

But her husband exclaimed:

"God, but you're silly! Go to your friend Mrs. Forrestier, and ask her to lend you some jewelry. You know her well enough to do that."

She uttered a cry of joy:

"That's right. I hadn't thought of that."

The next day she went to her friend's house and described her problem.

Mrs. Forrestier went to her mirrored wardrobe, took out a large jewel box, opened it, and said to Mrs. Loisel:

"Choose, my dear."

She saw bracelets, then a pearl necklace, then a Venetian cross of finely worked gold and gems. She tried on the jewelry in front of a mirror, and hesitated, unable to make up her mind about each one. She kept asking:

"Do you have anything else?"

"Certainly. Look to your heart's content. I don't know what you'd like best."

Suddenly she found a superb diamond necklace in a black satin box, and her heart throbbed with desire for it. Her hands shook as she picked it up. She fastened it around her neck, watched it gleam at her throat, and looked at herself ecstatically.

Then she asked, haltingly and anxiously:

"Could you lend me this, nothing but this?"

"Why yes, certainly."

A new section, the third in the story. The day of the party is near.

30

Now she complains that she doesn't have any nice jewelry. She is manipulating him again.

35

She has a good point, but there seems to be no way out.

He proposes a solution: borrow jewelry from Mrs. Forrestier, who is apparently the rich friend mentioned earlier.

40

Mathilde will have her choice of jewels.

45

A "superb" diamond necklace.

This is what she wants, just this.

50

She jumped up, hugged her friend joyfully, then hurried away with her treasure.

She leaves with the "treasure."

The day of the party came. Mrs. Loisel was a success. She was prettier than anyone else, stylish, graceful, smiling and wild with joy. All the men saw her, asked her name, sought to be introduced. All the important administrators stood in line to waltz with her. The Chancellor himself eyed her.

A new section.

The Party. Mathilde is a huge success.

She danced joyfully, passionately, intoxicated with pleasure, thinking of nothing but the moment, in the triumph of her beauty, in the glory of her success, on cloud nine with happiness made up of all the admiration, of all the aroused desire, of this victory so complete and so sweet to the heart of any woman.

Another judgment about women. Does the author mean that only women want to be admired? Don't men want admiration, too?

She did not leave until four o'clock in the morning. Her husband, since midnight, had been sleeping in a little empty room with three other men whose wives had also been enjoying themselves.

Loisel, with other husbands, is bored, while the wives are having a ball.

55   He threw, over her shoulders, the shawl that he had brought for the trip home—a modest everyday wrap, the poverty of which contrasted sharply with the elegance of her evening gown. She felt it and hurried away to avoid being noticed by the other women who luxuriated in rich furs.

Ashamed of her shabby wrap, she rushes away to avoid being seen.

Loisel tried to hold her back:

"Wait a minute. You'll catch cold outdoors. I'll call a cab."

But she paid no attention and hurried down the stairs. When they reached the street they found no carriages. They began to look for one, shouting at cabmen passing by at a distance.

They walked toward the Seine, desperate, shivering. Finally, on a quay, they found one of those old night-going buggies that are seen in Paris only after dark, as if they were ashamed of their wretched appearance in daylight.

A comedown after the nice evening. They take a wretched-looking buggy home.

60   It took them to their door, on the Street of Martyrs, and they sadly climbed the stairs to their flat. For her, it was finished. As for him, he could think only that he had to begin work at the Ministry of Education at ten o'clock.

"Street of Martyrs." Is this name significant?

Loisel is down-to-earth.

She took the shawl off her shoulders, in front of the mirror, to see herself once more in her glory. But suddenly she cried out. The necklace was no longer around her neck!

SHE HAS LOST THE NECKLACE!

Her husband, already half undressed, asked:

"What's wrong?"

She turned toward him frantically:

65   "I . . . I . . . I no longer have Mrs. Forrestier's necklace."

He stood up, bewildered:

"What! . . . How! . . . It's not possible!"

And they looked in the folds of the gown, in the folds of the shawl, in the pockets, everywhere. They found nothing.

They can't find it.

He asked:

"You're sure you still had it when you left the party?"

70

"Yes. I checked it in the vestibule of the Ministry."

"But if you'd lost it in the street, we would've heard it fall. It must be in the cab."

"Yes, probably. Did you notice the number?"

"No. Did you see it?"

"No."

75

Overwhelmed, they looked at each other. Finally, Loisel got dressed again:

"I'm going out to retrace all our steps," he said, "to see if I can find the necklace that way."

And he went out. She stayed in her evening dress, without the energy to get ready for bed, stretched out in a chair, drained of strength and thought.

He goes out to search for the necklace.

Her husband came back at about seven o'clock. He had found nothing.

But is unsuccessful.

He went to Police Headquarters and to the newspapers to announce a reward. He went to the small cab companies, and finally he followed up even the slightest hopeful lead.

He really tries. He's doing his best.

80

She waited the entire day, in the same enervated state, in the face of this frightful disaster.

Loisel came back in the evening, his face pale and haggard. He had found nothing.

"You'll have to write to your friend," he said, "that you broke a clasp on her necklace and that you're having it fixed. That'll give us time to look around."

Loisel's plan to explain delaying the return. He takes charge, is resourceful.

She wrote as he dictated.

By the end of the week they had lost all hope.

Things are hopeless.

85

And Loisel, looking five years older, declared:

"We'll have to see about replacing the jewels."

The next day they took the case which had contained the necklace and went to the jeweler whose name was inside. He looked at his books:

They hunt for a replacement.

"I wasn't the one, Madam, who sold the necklace. I only made the case."

Then they went from jeweler to jeweler, searching for a necklace like the other one, racking their memories, both of them sick with worry and anguish.

90

In a shop in the Palais-Royal, they found a necklace of diamonds that seemed to them exactly like the one they were looking for. It was priced at

A new diamond necklace will cost 36,000 francs, a monumental amount.

forty thousand francs. They could buy it for thirty-six thousand.

They got the jeweler to promise not to sell it for three days. And they made an agreement that he would buy it back for thirty-four thousand francs if the original was recovered before the end of February.

They make a deal with the jeweler. (Is Maupassant hinting that things might work out for them?)

Loisel had saved eighteen thousand francs that his father had left him. He would have to borrow the rest.

It will take all of Loisel's inheritance...

He borrowed, asking a thousand francs from one, five hundred from another, five louis° here, three louis there. He wrote promissory notes, undertook ruinous obligations, did business with finance companies and the whole tribe of loan sharks. He compromised himself for the remainder of his days, risked his signature without knowing whether he would be able to honor it; and, terrified by anguish over the future, by the black misery that was about to descend on him, by the prospect of all kinds of physical deprivations and moral tortures, he went to get the new necklace, and put down thirty-six thousand francs on the jeweler's counter.

...plus another 18,000 francs that must be borrowed at enormous rates of interest.

95 Mrs. Loisel took the necklace back to Mrs. Forrestier, who said with an offended tone:

"You should have brought it back sooner; I might have needed it."

Mrs. Forrestier complains about the delay.

She did not open the case, as her friend feared she might. If she had noticed the substitution, what would she have thought? What would she have said? Would she not have taken her for a thief?

Is this enough justification for not telling the truth? It seems to be for the Loisels.

Mrs. Loisel soon discovered the horrible life of the needy. She did her share, however, completely, heroically. That horrifying debt had to be paid. She would pay. They dismissed the maid; they changed their address; they rented an attic flat.

A new section, the fifth.

She learned to do the heavy housework, dirty kitchen jobs. She washed the dishes, wearing away her manicured fingernails on greasy pots and encrusted baking dishes. She handwashed dirty linen, shirts, and dish towels that she hung out on the line to dry. Each morning, she took the garbage down to the street, and she carried up water, stopping at each floor to catch her breath. And, dressed in cheap house dresses, she went to the fruit dealer, the grocer, the butchers, with her basket under her arms, haggling, insulting, defending her measly cash penny by penny.

They suffer to repay their debts. Loisel works late at night. Mathilde accepts a cheap attic flat, and does all the heavy housework herself to save on domestic help.

She pinches pennies, and haggles with the local tradesmen.

100 They had to make installment payments

They struggle to meet payments.

louis: a gold coin worth twenty francs.

every month, and, to buy more time, to refinance loans.

The husband worked evenings to make fair copies of tradesmen's accounts, and late into the night he made copies at five cents a page.

And this life lasted ten years.

At the end of ten years, they had paid back everything—everything—including the extra charges imposed by loan sharks and the accumulation of compound interest.

Mrs. Loisel looked old now. She had become the strong, hard, and rude woman of poor households. Her hair unkempt, with uneven skirts and rough, red hands, she spoke loudly, washed floors with large buckets of water. But sometimes, when her husband was at work, she sat down near the window, and she dreamed of that evening so long ago, of that party, where she had been so beautiful and so admired.

What would life have been like if she had not lost that necklace? Who knows? Who knows? Life is so peculiar, so uncertain. How little a thing it takes to destroy you or to save you!

Well, one Sunday, when she had gone for a stroll along the Champs-Elysées to relax from the cares of the week, she suddenly noticed a woman walking with a child. It was Mrs. Forrestier, still youthful, still beautiful, still attractive.

Mrs. Loisel felt moved. Would she speak to her? Yes, certainly. And now that she had paid, she could tell all. Why not?

She walked closer.

"Hello, Jeanne."

The other gave no sign of recognition and was astonished to be addressed so familiarly by this working-class woman. She stammered:

"But . . . Madam! . . . I don't know. . . . You must have made a mistake."

"No. I'm Mathilde Loisel."

Her friend cried out:

"Oh! . . . My poor Mathilde, you've changed so much."

"Yes. I've had some tough times since I saw you last; in fact hardships . . . and all because of you! . . ."

"Of me . . . how so?"

"You remember the diamond necklace that you lent me to go to the party at the Ministry of Education?"

"Yes. What then?"

"Well, I lost it."

Mr. Loisel moonlights to make extra money.

For ten years they struggle, but they endure.
They are successful, and have finally paid back the entire debt.

Mrs. Loisel (how come the narrator does not say "Mathilde"?) is roughened and aged by the work. But she has behaved "heroically" (¶ 98), and has shown her mettle.

A moral? Our lives are shaped by small, uncertain things; we hang by a thread.   105

A scene on the Champs-Elysées. She sees Jeanne Forrestier, after ten years.

110

Jeanne notes Mathilde's changed appearance.

115

Mathilde tells Jeanne everything.

"How, since you gave it back to me?"

120   "I returned another exactly like it. And for ten years we've been paying for it. You understand this wasn't easy for us, who have nothing. . . . Finally it's over, and I'm damned glad."

Mrs. Forrestier stopped her.

"You say that you bought a diamond necklace to replace mine?"

"Yes, you didn't notice it, eh? It was exactly like yours."

And she smiled with proud and childish joy.

125   Mrs. Forrestier, deeply moved, took both her hands.

"Oh, my poor Mathilde! But mine was only costume jewelry. At most, it was worth only five hundred francs! ..."

SURPRISE! The lost necklace was *not* real diamonds, and the Loisels slaved for no reason at all. But hard work and sacrifice probably brought out better qualities in Mathilde than she otherwise might have shown. Is this the moral of the story?

READING AND RESPONDING IN A JOURNAL

The marginal comments demonstrate the active reading–responding process you should apply with everything you read. Use the margins in your text to record your comments and questions, but also keep a **journal** for lengthier responses. Your journal, which may be a notebook or a computer file, will be immeasurably useful to you as you shape your initial impressions into thoughtful analysis.

In keeping your journal, the objective is to learn assigned works inside and out and then to say perceptive things about them. To achieve this goal, you need to read the work more than once. You will need a good note-taking system so that as you read you can develop a "memory bank" of your own knowledge about a work. You can draw from this fund of ideas when you begin to write.

Guidelines for Reading

1. Observations for Basic Understanding

a. Explain words, situations, and concepts. Write down words that are new or not immediately clear. If you find a passage that you do not quickly understand, decide whether the problem arises from unknown words. Use your dictionary and record the relevant meanings in your journal, but be sure that these meanings clarify your understanding. Make note of special difficulties so that you may ask your instructor about them.

b. Determine what is happening. For a story or play, where do the actions take place? What do they show? Who is involved? Who is the major figure? Why is he or she major? What relationships do the characters have with each other? What concerns do the characters have? What do they do? Who says what to whom? How do the speeches advance the action and reveal the characters? For a poem, what is the situation? Who is talking, and to whom? What does the speaker say about the situation? Why does the poem end as it does and where it does?

c. Trace developing patterns. Make an outline or scheme for the story or main idea: What conflicts appear? Do these conflicts exist between people, groups, or ideas? How does the author resolve them? Is one force, idea, or side the winner? Why? How do you respond to the winner, or loser?

d. Use separate cards to write out in full some of the passages that you think are interesting, well written, and important. Keep these passages within easy reach, and when riding public transportation, walking to class, or otherwise not occupying your time, *memorize* them.

e. Always note any questions so that you can use them in class and in your own further study.

2. Notes on First Impressions

a. In your marginal notations, record your first responses to the work. What did you think was funny, memorable, noteworthy, or otherwise striking? Did you laugh, smile, worry, get scared, feel a thrill, learn a great deal, feel proud, find a lot to think about? In your journal, record these responses and explain them more fully.

b. Describe interesting characterizations, events, techniques, and ideas. If you like a character or idea, explain what you like, and do the same for characters and ideas you don't like. Is there anything else in the work that you especially like or dislike? Are parts easy or difficult to understand? Why? Are there any surprises? What was your reaction to them? Be sure to use *your own* words when writing your explanations.

Specimen Journal Entries

The following entries suggest how the guidelines may help you in your first writing attempts. The important issue is not the order of observation, which follows the time sequence of the story, but rather that there are enough observations and responses to be useful later, both for additional study and for a developing essay. Notice that the entries are not only comments but also questions.

Journal Entries on Maupassant's "The Necklace"

Early in the story, Mathilde seems spoiled. She is poor, or at least lower middle class, but is unable to face her own situation.

As a dreamer, she seems harmless. Her daydreams about a fancy home, with all the expensive belongings, are not unusual. Most people dream about being well off.

She is embarrassed by her husband's taste for plain food. The story contrasts her taste for trout and quail with Loisel's cheaper favorites.

Only when the Loisels get the invitation does Mathilde seem especially difficult. Her wish for an expensive dress (the cost of Loisel's entire vacation), and then her wanting the jewelry, are problems.

Her success at the party shows that she has the charm the storyteller talks about in paragraph 2. She seems never to have had any other chance to exert her power.

The worst part of her personality is shown when she hurries away from the party because she is ashamed of her everyday shawl. It is Mathilde's unhappiness and unwillingness to adjust to her modest means that cause the financial downfall of the Loisels. It is her fault.

Borrowing the money to replace the necklace shows that both Loisel and Mathilde have a strong sense of honor. Making up for the loss is good, even if it destroys them financially.

There are some nice touches, like Loisel's seeming to be five years older (paragraph 86), and his staying with the other husbands of women enjoying themselves (paragraph 54). These are well done.

It's too bad that Loisel and Mathilde don't confess to Jeanne that the jewels are lost. Their pride or their honor stops them—or perhaps their fear of being accused of theft.

Their ten years of slavish work (paragraphs 98–102) show how they have come down in life. Mathilde does all her work by hand, so she really does pitch in and is heroic.

Mathilde becomes loud and frumpy when living in the attic flat (paragraph 98), but she also develops strength. She does what she has to. The earlier apartment and the elegance of her imaginary rooms had brought out her limitations.

The setting of the Champs-Elysées also reflects her character, for she feels free there to tell Jeanne about the disastrous loss and sacrifice (paragraph 121), producing the surprise ending.

The narrator's thought about how "little a thing it takes to destroy you or save you" (paragraph 105) is full of thought. The necklace is little, but it makes a huge problem. This creates the story's irony.

Questions: Is this story more about the surprise ending or about the character of Mathilde? Is she to be condemned or admired? Does the outcome stem from the little things that make us or break us, as the narrator suggests, or from the difficulty of rising above one's economic class, or both? What do the speaker's remarks about women's status mean? (Remember, the story was published in 1884.) This probably isn't relevant, but wouldn't Jeanne, after hearing about the substitution, give the full value of the necklace to the Loisels, and wouldn't they then be pretty well off?

These are reasonable, if fairly full, remarks and observations about "The Necklace." Use your journal similarly for *all* reading assignments. If your assignment is simply to learn about a work, general notes like these should be enough. If you are preparing for a test, you might write pointed observations more in line with what is happening in your class and also write and answer your own questions (see Appendix A, "Taking Examinations on Literature"). If you have a writing assignment, these entries can help you focus more closely on your topic—such as character, idea, or setting. Whatever your purpose, always use a journal when you read, and put into it as many details and responses as you can. Your journal will then be invaluable in helping you develop your ideas and refresh your memory.

WRITING ESSAYS ON LITERARY TOPICS

Writing is the sharpened, focused expression of thought and study. It begins with the search for something to say—an idea. Not all ideas are equal; some are better than others, and getting good ideas is an ability that you will develop the more you think and write. As you discover ideas and write them down, you will also improve your perceptions and increase your critical faculties.

Learning to think and write about literature will also prepare you to write about other topics. Because literature itself contains the subject material, though not in a systematic way, of philosophy, religion, psychology, sociology, and politics, learning to analyze literature and to write about it will also improve your capacity to deal with these and other disciplines.

At the outset, it is important to realize that writing is a process that, for most of us, begins in uncertainty. When you read a complete, polished, well-formed piece of writing, you might initially believe that the writer wrote this perfect version in only one draft and never needed to make any changes and improvements in it at all. Nothing could be further from the truth, for writing becomes presentable only by considerable thought and work.

If you could see the early drafts of writing you admire, you would be surprised—but you might also be encouraged—to see that good writers are also human, and that their first versions are messy, uncertain, vague, tangential, tentative, and incomplete. They may not even like these first drafts, but then they build on this first work: They discard some details, add others, chop paragraphs in half, reassemble the parts elsewhere, throw out much (and then maybe recover some of it), revise or completely rewrite sentences, change words, correct misspellings, and add new material to tie all parts together and make them flow smoothly.

For good and not-so-good writers alike, the writing task follows three basic stages. The first—*discovering ideas*—shares many of the qualities of ordinary conversation. Usually, conversation is random and disorganized. It shifts from topic to topic, often without any apparent cause, and it is repetitive. In discovering ideas for writing, your process is much the same, for you jump from idea to idea and do not necessarily identify the connections or bridges between them. By the next step, however—*creating the early, rough draft of a critical paper*—your thought should be less like ordinary conversation and more like classroom discussion. Such discussions generally stick to a point, but they are also free and spontaneous, and digressions often occur. At the final stage—*preparing a finished essay*—your thinking must be sharply focused, and your writing must be concise and highly organized.

If you find that writing a finished essay seems halting and digressive, remember that *it is important just to start*—no matter how unacceptable your first efforts seem. Make the beginning and force yourself to come to grips with the materials. Beginning to write does not commit you to your first ideas. They are not holy and untouchable just because they are on paper or on your computer screen. You may throw them out in favor of new ideas. You may also cross out words or move sections around, as you wish, but if you keep your first thoughts buried in your mind, you will have nothing to work with. It is essential to accept the uncertainties in the writing process and make them work *for* you rather than *against* you.

DISCOVERING IDEAS

Ideas cannot be known and shaped until they take a written form. Thus, the first act of the writing process is to uncover, discover, and drag out of your mind and reading responses all the observations you can make about a particular topic. Write down anything and everything that occurs to you about the work. If you have questions you can't answer, write them down and plan to answer them later. In your attempts to discover ideas, use the following prewriting techniques.

Brainstorming

Brainstorming is an informal way to describe your own written but private no-holds-barred conversation about what you write. The technique is essential in the early writing process. When you begin brainstorming you let your mind play over all the possibilities you generate as you consider the work, or a particular element of the work, or your own earlier responses to it. In effect, you are conversing with yourself to develop ideas by writing down all your thoughts, whether they fall into patterns or seem disjointed, unlikely, or even ridiculous. (This is also sometimes called **freewriting.**) At this time, do not try to organize or criticize your thoughts. Later you can decide which ideas to keep and which to throw out. For now, *the goal is to get all your ideas* *on paper or on the computer screen.* As you develop your essay, you may, at any time, return to the brainstorming process to initiate and develop any new ideas that you think you will need.

Focusing on Specific Topics

DEVELOPING SUBJECTS FROM BRAINSTORMING AND NOTE TAKING. Although the idea of brainstorming is to be totally free about the topics, you will soon need to direct your mind into specific channels. Once you start focusing on definite topics, your thinking becomes analogous to classroom discussion. Let us assume that in brainstorming you produce a topic that you find especially interesting. You might then start to focus on this topic and write as much as you can about it. The following examples show how a writer may zero in on the topic "honor" once the word comes up in freewriting:

> Mathilde could have gone to her friend and told her she lost the necklace. But she didn't. Did her honor stop her?
>
> What is honor? Doing what you think you should even if you don't want to, or if it's hard? Or is it pride? Was she too proud or too honorable to tell her friend? Does having honor mean going a harder way, when either would probably be okay? Do you have to suffer to be honorable? Does pride or honor produce a choice for suffering?
>
> Mathilde wants others to envy her, to find her attractive. Later she tells Loisel that she would feel humiliated at the party with rich women unless she wore jewelry. Maybe M. was more concerned about her own good name than the necklace. Having a good reputation seems to have something to do with honor. So it could be mainly a public thing. When I think of good name, though, I think more of personal qualities than appearance.
>
> Duty. Is it the same as honor? Was her duty to work so hard? In the Middle Ages, it was the duty of knights to defend a lady's honor (her good name?) by fighting or going out to spear dragons . . . or is all this myth?
>
> Honor is a part of myths, I think. They both seem bigger than any one life or person. Honor is just an idea or feeling—can an idea of honor be larger than a life, take over someone's life?

This writer is trying to figure out what honor is and whether Mathilde behaves honorably throughout the story. Although the last two paragraphs depart from the story somewhat, this diversion is perfectly acceptable, for in brainstorming a writer expresses ideas as they arise. If the ideas amount to something, they may be used in the developing essay; but if they don't, they may be discarded. The important principle in brainstorming is to record all ideas—*incomplete thoughts and bad grammar (and spelling) included*—with no initial concern about how they might seem to a reader. The notes are for your use only.

BUILDING ON YOUR ORIGINAL NOTES.   An essential way to focus your mind is to use your journal notes as a mine for likely topics. For example, one of the notes on page 14 brings up the topic of the attic flat in "The Necklace." With this note as a start, you can develop a number of ideas, as in the following:

> The attic flat is important. Before, in her apartment, M. was dreamier and less practical. She was delicate, but after losing the necklace, no way. She becomes a worker when in the flat. She can do a lot more now.

> M. gives up her servant, climbs stairs carrying buckets of water, washes greasy pots, throws water around to clean floors, does all the wash by hand.

> While she gets stronger, she also gets loud and frumpy—argues with shopkeepers to get the lowest prices. She stops caring for herself. A reversal here, from incapable and well groomed to capable and coarse. The attic flat is the location of this reversal.

Notice that just a sentence in an original note can help you discover thoughts that you did not originally have. This act of stretching your mind in the focusing process leads you to put elements of the story together in ways that create support for the assertions that build essays. Even in an assertion as basic as "The attic flat is important," the process itself, which is a form of concentrated thought, leads you creatively forward.

RAISING AND ANSWERING QUESTIONS.   Another major way to discover ideas about a work is to raise questions as you read and then to try answering them. The "Guidelines for Reading" (p. 12) will help you formulate questions, but you may also raise specific questions like these (assuming that you are considering a story):

- What explanations need to be made about the characters? Which actions, scenes, and situations invite interpretation? Why so?
- What assumptions do the characters and speakers reveal about life and humanity generally, about themselves, the people around them, their families, their friends, their work, the economy, religion, politics, and the state of the world?
- What are their manners or customs?
- What kinds of words do they use: formal or informal words, slang or profane ones?
- What literary conventions and devices have you discovered, and how do these add to the work? If an author addresses readers directly, for example, that is a **convention**; if a comparison is used, this is a **device** which might be either a **metaphor** or a **simile**.

Of course you may raise other questions as you reread the piece, or you may be left with one or two major questions that you decide to pursue.

Using the plus–minus, pro–con, or either–or method. A common method of discovering ideas is to develop a set of contrasts: plus–minus, pro–con, either–or. Let us suppose a pro–con method of considering the character of Mathilde in "The Necklace": whether she should be "admired" (pro) or "condemned" (con).

Admired?	Condemned?
After she cries when they get the invitation, she recovers with a "strong effort"—maybe she doesn't want her husband to feel bad.	She only wants to be envied and admired for being attractive (end of first part), not for more important qualities.
She does really score a great victory at the dance. She does have the power to charm and captivate.	She wastes her time in daydreaming about things she can't have and whines about her unhappiness.
Once she lost the necklace, "she did her share . . . completely, heroically" (paragraph 98) to make up for the loss.	She manipulates her husband into giving her a lot of money for a party dress, but they live poorly.
Even when she is poor, she still dreams about that single shining moment. She really gets worse than she deserves.	She assumes that her friend would think she was a thief if she knew she was returning a different necklace.
At the end, she confesses the loss to her friend.	She gets loud and coarse and haggles about pennies, thus undergoing a total cheapening of her character.

Once you begin putting contrasting ideas side by side, new discoveries will occur to you. Filling the columns almost demands that you list as many contrasting positions as you can and that you think about how the story material supports each position. The notes will be useful regardless of how you choose to organize your essay. You may develop either column in a full essay, or you might use the notes to support the idea that Mathilde is too complex to be wholly admired or condemned. You might even introduce an entirely new idea, such as that Mathilde is more to be pitied than either condemned or admired. In short, arranging materials in the either–or pattern is a powerful way to discover ideas that can lead to ways of development that you might not otherwise find.

Tracing developing patterns. You can also discover ideas by making an outline, list, or scheme for the story or main idea. What conflicts appear? Do these conflicts exist between people, groups, or ideas? How does the author resolve them? Is one force, idea, or side the winner? Why? How do you respond to the winner, or loser?

Using this method, you might make a list similar to this one:

Beginning: M. is a fish out of water. Dreams of wealth, but her life is drab and her husband is ordinary.

Fantasies—make her even more dissatisfied—almost punishes herself by thinking of lavish rooms.

Her character relates to the places in the story: the Street of the Martyrs, the dinner party scene, the attic flat. Also the places she dreams of—she fills them with the most expensive things she can imagine.

They get the dinner invitation—she pouts and whines. Her husband feels discomfort, but she doesn't really harm him. She does manipulate him into buying her an expensive party dress, though.

Her dream world hurts her real life when her desire for wealth causes her to borrow the necklace. Losing the necklace is just plain bad luck.

The attic flat brings out her potential coarseness. But she also develops a spirit of sacrifice and cooperation. She loses, but she's actually a winner.

These observations all focus on Mathilde's character; however, you might trace other patterns you find in the work. If you start planning an essay about one of these other patterns, be sure to account for all the actions and scenes that relate to your topic. Otherwise, you may miss a piece of evidence that can lead you to a new viewpoint.

THINKING BY WRITING. No matter what method of discovering ideas you use, it is important to realize that *unwritten thought is incomplete thought.* Make a practice of writing notes about your reactions and any questions that occur to you. They may lead you later to the most startling discoveries you will make about a work

DRAFTING YOUR ESSAY

As you use the brainstorming and focusing techniques for discovering ideas, you are also beginning to draft your essay. Although you will need to revise your ideas—as connections among them become more clear, and as you re-examine the work for support for the ideas you are developing—you already have many of the raw materials you need for developing your topic.

Developing a Central Idea

By definition, an essay is *a fully developed and organized set of paragraphs that are directly connected to a central idea.* Everything in an essay should contribute to the reader's understanding of the idea. To achieve unity and completeness, each paragraph refers to the central idea and demonstrates how selected details from the work relate to it and support it. The central idea helps the writer control and shape the essay, and it provides guidance to the reader.

A successful essay about literature is a brief but thorough (not exhaustive) examination of a literary work in light of a particular element, such as *point of view, imagery,* or *symbolism.* Typical central ideas might be (1) that a character is strong and tenacious, or (2) that the point of view makes the action seem "distant and objective," or (3) that one work is different from or better than another. In essays on these topics, all points must be tied to these ideas. Thus, it is a fact that Mathilde Loisel in "The Necklace" endures ten years of slavish work and sacrifice. This fact is not relevant to an essay on her character, however, unless you connect it by showing how it demonstrates one of her major traits—in this case, her strength or tenacity.

WRITING BY HAND OR BY WORD PROCESSOR

As we have emphasized, *thinking and writing are inseparable processes.* It is therefore essential to get ideas into a *visible form* so that you may develop them further. For many people, *handwriting* is a psychological necessity in this process. In noting handwritten responses to a work, be sure to use *only one side* of your paper or notecards. This will enable you to spread your materials out and overview them when the time comes to begin writing.

Other students prefer word processors. The word processor can help you develop ideas, for it enables you to eliminate unworkable thoughts and replace them with others. You can move sentences and paragraphs tentatively into new contexts, test out how they look, and move them somewhere else if you choose. If you see questionable spellings, you may check them out with a dictionary and make corrections on the screen. (Because spelling is often an element of grading, find out whether your instructor will let you use a spell-check program.)

Studies have shown that errors and awkward sentences frequently are found at the bottoms of pages prepared by hand or with a conventional typewriter. The reason is that writers hesitate to make improvements when they get near the end of a page because they want to avoid the dreariness of starting the page over. Word processors eliminate this difficulty completely. Changes can be made anywhere in the draft, at any time, without damage to the appearance of the final draft.

In addition, with the rapid printers available today, you can print drafts even in the initial and tentative stages. Using your printed draft, you can make additional notes, marginal corrections, and suggestions for further development. With the marked-up draft for guidance, you can go back to the word processor and implement your changes and improvements, repeating this process as often as necessary. This facility makes the machine an additional incentive for improvement, right up to your final draft.

Regardless of your writing method, it is important to realize that *unwritten thought is incomplete thought.* Therefore, somewhere in the composing process, it is vital to prepare a complete draft of what you have written. Even with the word processor's screen, you see only a small part and cannot lay everything out at once. A clean, readable draft permits you to gather everything together and to make even more improvements through the act of revision.

Look through all of your ideas for one or two that catch your eye for development. If you have used more than one prewriting technique, the chances are that you have already discovered at least a few ideas that are more thought-provoking, or important, than the others.

Once you choose one that interests you, write it as a complete sentence. The *complete sentence* is important: A simple phrase, such as "setting and character," does not focus thought the way a sentence does. A sentence moves the topic toward new exploration and discovery because it combines a topic with an outcome, such as "The setting is related to Mathilde's character." You may choose to be even more specific: "Mathilde's strengths and weaknesses are connected to the real and imaginary places in the story."

With a single, central idea for your essay, you have a standard for accepting, rejecting, rearranging, and changing the ideas you have been developing. You may now choose to draft a few paragraphs to see whether your idea seems valid, or you may decide that it would be more helpful to make an outline or list before you attempt to support your ideas in a rough draft. In either case, you need to use your notes for evidence to connect to your central idea. If you need more ideas, use any of the brainstorming–prewriting techniques to discover them. If you need more details, jot them down as you reread the work.

Using the central idea that the story's settings are related to Mathilde's changing character might produce paragraphs such as the following:

The original apartment in the Street of Martyrs and the dream world of wealthy places both show negative sides of her character. The real-life apartment, though livable, is shabby. The furnishings all bring out her discontent. The shabbiness makes her think only of luxuriousness, and her one servant girl makes her dream of many servants. The luxury of her dream life heightens her unhappiness.

Mathilde's character is coarsened during the ten years of repayment. She gives up her domestic help and does all the heavy housework herself. She climbs stairs carrying heavy buckets of water and throws water around to clean floors. She washes greasy and encrusted pots and pans, takes out the garbage, and does the clothes and dishes by hand. She gives up caring for her hair and hands and wears the cheapest clothing possible. She becomes loud and argumentative and spends much time haggling with shopkeepers to save as much money as she can. Whatever delicacy and attractiveness she had, she loses.

Her Sunday walk to the Champs-Elysées is in character. This is a fashionable street, and her walk to it is similar to her earlier daydreams about wealth, since it is on this wide street that wealthy people stroll and flaunt themselves. Her meeting with Jeanne there is accidental, but it also brings out her sense of pride; that is, she confesses to the loss of the necklace, having seen things through to the complete repayment of all indebtedness. The Champs-Elysées thus brings out the surprise and irony of the story, and Mathilde's going there is totally in character and in keeping with her earlier dreams of a luxurious life.

Notice that the first and second paragraphs come directly from earlier notes. The third paragraph was written after the central idea was established. The central idea is not stated, but each paragraph helps to demonstrate how a setting relates to Mathilde's character. No attempt has been made to connect the paragraphs or make the draft read well. Even in this "discovery" draft, however, where the purpose is to write initial thoughts about the central idea, many details from the story are given in support. In the final draft, this support will be essential.

Creating a Thesis Sentence

Using the central idea for guidance, you can now decide which of the earlier observations and ideas can be developed further. Your goal is to establish a number of major topics to support the central idea and to express them in a **thesis sentence**—a sentence that, like a plan, lists the major topics in the order of development in the essay. Suppose you choose three ideas from the discovery stage of development. If you put the central idea at the left and the list of topics at the right, you have the shape of the thesis sentence.

Central Idea	**Topics**
The setting of "The Necklace" reflects Mathilde's character.	1. Real-life apartment
	2. Dream surroundings
	3. Attic flat

This arrangement leads to the following thesis sentence:

Mathilde's character development is related to her first apartment, her dream-life mansion rooms, and her attic flat.

You can revise the thesis sentence at any stage of the writing process if you find you do not have enough evidence from the work to support it. Or perhaps a new topic may occur to you, and you can include it, appropriately, as a part of your thesis sentence.

As we have seen, the central idea is the glue of the essay. The thesis sentence lists the parts to be fastened together—that is, the topics in which the central idea is to be demonstrated and argued. To alert the audience to the essay's structure, the thesis sentence is often placed at the end of the introductory paragraph.

WRITE WITH YOUR READERS IN MIND

In preparing to write, you need to decide how much detail to select and discuss, and this requires that you gauge the needs of your readers. For example, if you assume that they have not read the work you are writing about, you will need to include a short summary as background for them. Otherwise, they may not understand your argument.

Consider, too, any special interests or concerns of your readers. If your readers are especially concerned about politics, sociology, religion, or psychology, you need to select and develop your materials accordingly.

Your instructor will let you know who your audience is. Usually, it will be your instructor or the members of your class. They will be familiar with the work and will not expect you to retell the story but rather will look to you as an explainer or interpreter. Thus, you may introduce details from the work only if they exemplify your central idea and omit details that do not.

WRITING A FIRST DRAFT

To write a first draft, you support the points of your thesis sentence with your notes and discovery materials. You may alter, reject, and rearrange ideas and details as you wish, as long as you change the thesis sentence to account for the changes (a major reason why most writers write their introductions last). The thesis sentence shown earlier contains three topics (it could be two, or four, or more), to be used in forming the body of the essay.

Just as the organization of the entire essay is based on the thesis, the form of each paragraph is based on its **topic sentence**. A topic sentence is an assertion about how a topic from the predicate of the thesis sentence supports the central idea. The first topic in our example is the relationship of Mathilde's character to her first apartment, and the resulting paragraph should emphasize this relationship. If you choose her trait of being constantly dissatisfied, you can then form a topic sentence by connecting the trait with the location, as follows:

Details about the first apartment explain her dissatisfaction and depression.

Beginning with this sentence, the paragraph can show how items in the apartment, such as the furniture, the curtains, and the unwashed tablecloth, feed Mathilde's dissatisfaction.

Usually you will devote a single paragraph to each topic; however, if your topic is difficult, long, and heavily detailed, you may divide it into two or more subtopics, each devoted to single paragraphs. Should you make this division, your topic then is really a section, and each paragraph in the section should have its own topic sentence.

Once you choose your thesis sentence, you can use the statement to focus your observations and conclusions. Let us see how we can sharpen the second paragraph of the discovery draft.

Original Paragraph	**Reshaped Paragraph**
Mathilde's character is coarsened during the ten years of repayment. She gives up her domestic help and does all the heavy housework herself. She climbs stairs carrying heavy buckets of water and throws water around to clean floors. She washes greasy and encrusted pots and pans, takes out the garbage, and does the clothes and dishes by hand. She gives up caring for her hair and hands and wears the cheapest clothing possible. She becomes loud and argumentative and spends much time haggling with shopkeepers to save as much money as she can. Whatever delicacy and attractiveness she had, she loses.	The attic flat reflects the coarsening of Mathilde's character. Maupassant emphasizes the burdens she endures to save money, such as mopping the floors, cleaning greasy and encrusted pots and pans, taking out the garbage, and handwashing clothes and dishes. This work makes her rough and coarse, an effect that is heightened by her giving up care of her hair and hands, her wearing the cheapest dresses possible, and her becoming loud and penny-pinching in haggling with the local shopkeepers. If at the beginning she is delicate and attractive, at the end she is unpleasant and coarse.

Notice that details from the story are substantially the same in each paragraph, but while the paragraph on the left is unfocused, the right-hand paragraph connects the details to Mathilde's housework in the attic flat. The paragraph on the right shows how details from a work may substantiate a unifying central idea.

Developing an Outline

So far we have been developing an *outline*—that is, a skeletal plan of organization for the essay. Some writers never use formal outlines at all, preferring to make informal lists of ideas, but others rely on them constantly. Still other writers insist that they cannot make an outline until they have finished their essays. Regardless of your preference, *your finished essay should have a tight structure*. At some point, therefore, you should create a guiding outline to develop or to shape your essay.

The outline we have been developing here is the **analytical sentence outline**. This type is easier to create than it sounds. It consists of the following:

1. An *introduction*, including the central idea and the thesis sentence. Some instructors require a fusion of the two in the final draft. Therefore, make sure you follow your instructor's directions.

USING THE NAMES OF AUTHORS

For both men and women writers, you should typically include the author's *full name* in the *first sentence* of your essay. Here are a few model first sentences:

> Ambrose Bierce's "An Occurrence at Owl Creek Bridge" is a story featuring both pathos and suspense.

> "An Occurrence at Owl Creek Bridge," by Ambrose Bierce, is a story featuring both pathos and suspense.

For all later references, use only last names, such as *Bierce, Chekhov, Welty,* or *Hardy.* However, for the "giants" of literature, you should use the last names exclusively. In referring to writers such as Shakespeare and Wordsworth, for example, there is no need to include *William.*

In spite of today's informal standards, do not use an author's first name, as in "**Ambrose** skillfully creates pathos and suspense in 'An Occurrence at Owl Creek Bridge.'" Also, do not use a familiar title before the names of dead authors, such as "**Mr.** Bierce's 'An Occurrence at Owl Creek Bridge' is a suspenseful and pathetic story." Use the last name alone.

As with all conventions, of course, there are exceptions. If you are referring to a childhood work of a writer, the first name is appropriate, but shift to the last name when referring to the writer's mature works. If your writer has a professional or a noble title, such as "**Judge** O'Connor," "**Governor** Cross," "**Lord** Byron," or "**Lady** Winchilsea," it is not improper to use the title. Even then, however, the titles are commonly omitted for males, so that most references to Lord Byron and Lord Tennyson should be simply to "Byron" and "Tennyson."

Referring to living authors is somewhat problematic. Some journals and newspapers, such as the *New York Times,* use the respectful titles **Mr.** and **Ms.** in their reviews. Scholarly journals, however, which are likely to remain on library shelves for many decades, follow the general principle of beginning with the entire name and then using only the last name for subsequent references.

2. *Topic sentences* within each paragraph of the body, usually at the beginning. It is also acceptable to include a topic sentence elsewhere in a paragraph, but if you relocate it, be sure that your details make it follow naturally and logically. Usually you may devote a single paragraph to each topic. However, if your topic is difficult, long, and heavily detailed, you may divide it into two or more subtopics, each devoted to single paragraphs.

3. A *conclusion.*

When applied to the subject we have been developing, the outline looks like this:

**TITLE: How Setting in "The Necklace" Is Related to the Character
of Mathilde**

1. **INTRODUCTION**
   a. *Central idea*: Setting is used to show Mathilde's character.
   b. *Thesis sentence*: Her character development is related to her first apartment, her dream-life mansion rooms, and her attic flat.
2. **BODY** *Topic sentences* a, b, and c (and d, e, f, if necessary)
   a. Details about her first apartment explain her dissatisfaction and depression.
   b. Her dream-life images of wealth are like the apartment because they too make her unhappy.
   c. The attic flat reflects the coarsening of her character.
3. **CONCLUSION** *Topic sentence*: All details in the story, particularly the setting, are focused on the character of Mathilde.

The *conclusion* may be a summary of the body; it may evaluate the main idea; it may briefly suggest further points of discussion; or it may be a reflection on the details of the body.

Using the Outline

The sample essays in this book are organized according to the principles of the analytical sentence outline. To emphasize the shaping effect of these outlines, all central ideas, thesis sentences, and topic sentences are underlined. In your own writing, you may underline these "skeletal" sentences as a check on your organization. Unless your instructor requires the underlines, however, remove them in your final drafts.

SAMPLE ESSAY, DRAFT 1

The following essay is a first draft of the topic we have been developing. Although it is relatively advanced, it shows how even working from an outline leaves much yet to do to produce a finished essay. Because the draft omits a topic and some details that will be included in the final draft (pp. 37–38), it reveals the need to make improvements through additional brainstorming and discovery–prewriting techniques. Nevertheless, as it stands, it is an acceptable piece of writing.

How Setting in "The Necklace" Is Related
to the Character of Mathilde Loisel°

[1] In "The Necklace" Maupassant does not give much detail about the setting. He does not even describe the necklace itself, which is the central object in his plot, but he says only that it is "superb" (paragraph 47). Rather, he uses the setting to reflect the character of the central figure, Mathilde Loisel.* All his details are presented to bring out her traits. Her character development is related to her first apartment, her dream-life mansion rooms, and her attic flat.†

[2] Details about her first apartment explain her dissatisfaction and depression. The walls are "drab," the furniture "threadbare," and the curtains "ugly" (paragraph 3). There is only a simple country girl to do the housework. The tablecloth is not changed daily, and the best dinner dish is boiled beef. Mathilde has no evening clothes, only a theater dress that she does not like. These details show her dissatisfaction with life with her low-salaried husband.

[3] Her dream-life images of wealth are like the apartment because they too make her unhappy. In her daydreams, the rooms are large, filled with expensive furniture and bric-a-brac, and draped in silk. She imagines private rooms for intimate talks, and big dinners with delicacies like trout and quail. With dreams of such a rich home, she feels even more despair about her modest apartment on the Street of Martyrs in Paris.

[4] The attic flat reflects the coarsening of Mathilde's character. Maupassant emphasizes the burdens she endures to save money, such as mopping the floors, cleaning greasy and encrusted pots and pans, taking out the garbage, and handwashing dishes and clothes. This work makes her rough and coarse, a fact also shown by her giving up care of her hair and hands, her wearing the cheapest dresses possible, and her becoming loud and penny-pinching in haggling with the local shopkeepers. If at the beginning she is delicate and attractive, at the end she is unpleasant and coarse.

[5] In summary, Maupassant focuses everything in the story, including the setting, on the character of Mathilde. Anything extra is not needed, and he does not include it. Thus he says little about the big party scene, but emphasizes the necessary detail that Mathilde was a great "success" (paragraph 52), because this detail brings out some of her early attractiveness and charm (despite her more usual unhappiness). In "The Necklace," Maupassant uses setting as a means to his end—the story of Mathilde and her needless sacrifice.

Commentary on the Essay

You might notice that several parts of this essay need more thought. For example, paragraph 2 contains a series of short, unconnected comments, and the last sentence of that paragraph implies that Mathilde's dissatisfaction

°See pages 3–12 for this story.
*Central idea.
†Thesis sentence.

relates mainly to her husband, which is not what the writer had intended. Paragraph 4 focuses too much on Mathilde's coarseness and not enough on her sacrifice and cooperation. Finally, there is not enough support in this draft for the contention (in paragraph 5) that *everything* in the story focuses on Mathilde's character. To discover how these issues may be more fully considered, compare this first draft to draft 2 of the essay on pages 37–38.

REVISING THE ESSAY

After finishing your first draft, you may wonder what more you can do. You have read the work several times, discovered ideas to write about through brainstorming techniques, made an outline of your ideas, and written at least one full draft. How can you do better?

The best way to begin is to observe that *a major mistake writers make when writing about literature is to do no more than retell a story or reword an idea.* Retelling a story shows only that you have read it, not that you have thought about it. Writing a good essay requires you to arrange your thoughts into a pattern that can be followed by a perceptive reader.

Using Your Own Order of References

There are many ways to escape the trap of summarizing stories and to set up your own pattern of development. One is to stress *your own* order when referring to parts of a work. Do not treat details as they happen, but rearrange them to suit your own thematic plans. Rarely, if ever, should you begin by talking about a work's opening; it is better to talk first about the conclusion or middle. As you examine your first draft, if you find that you have followed the chronological order of the work instead of stressing your own order, you may use one of the prewriting techniques to figure out new ways to connect your materials. The principle is that you should introduce references to the work only to support the points you wish to make, and only these points.

Using Literary Material as Evidence

Whenever you write, your position is like that of a detective using clues as evidence for building a case, or of a lawyer using evidence as support for an **argument**. Your goal should be to convince your readers of your own knowledge and the reasonableness of your conclusions.

It is vital to use evidence convincingly so that your readers can follow your ideas. Let us look briefly at two drafts of a new example to see how writing may be improved by the pointed use of details. These are from drafts of a longer essay on the character of Mathilde.

1

The major extenuating detail about Mathilde is that she seems to be isolated, locked away from other people. She and her husband do not speak to each other much, except about external things. He speaks about his liking for boiled beef, and she states that she cannot accept the big invitation because she has no nice dresses. Once she gets the dress, she complains because she has no jewelry. Even when borrowing the necklace from Jeanne Forrestier, she does not say much. When she and her husband discover that the necklace is lost, they simply go over the details, and Loisel dictates a letter of explanation, which she writes in her own hand. Even when she meets Jeanne on the Champs-Elysées, she does not say a great deal about her life but only goes through enough details about the loss and replacement of the necklace to make Jeanne exclaim about the needlessness of the ten-year sacrifice.

2

The major flaw of Mathilde's character is that she is withdrawn and uncommunicative, apparently unwilling or unable to form an intimate relationship. For example, she and her husband do not speak to each other much, except about external things such as his taste for boiled beef and her lack of a party dress and jewelry. With such an uncommunicative marriage, one might suppose that she would be more open with her close friend, Jeanne Forrestier, but Mathilde does not say much even to her. This flaw hurts Mathilde greatly, because if she were more open she might have explained the loss and avoided the horrible sacrifice. This lack of openness, along with her self-indulgent dreaminess, is her biggest defect.

A comparison of these paragraphs shows that the first has more words than the second (158 to 120), but that it is more appropriate for a rough than a final draft because the writer is doing little more than retell the story. The paragraph is cluttered with details that do not support any conclusions. If you examine it for what you might learn about Maupassant's actual use of Mathilde's solitary traits in "The Necklace," you will find that it gives you no help at all. The writer needs to consider why these details should be shared and revise the paragraph according to the central idea.

On the other hand, the details in the second paragraph all support the declared topic. Phrases such as "for example," "but even here," and "this lack" show that the writer of paragraph 2 has assumed that the audience knows the story and now wants help in interpretation. Paragraph 2 therefore guides readers *by connecting the details to the topic*. It uses these details *as evidence*, not as a retelling of actions. By contrast, paragraph 1 recounts a number of relevant actions but does not *connect* them to the topic. More details, of course, could have been added to the second draft, but they are unnecessary because the paragraph demonstrates the point with the details used. There are many qualities that make good writing good, but one of the most important is evident here: *In good writing, details are used only as evidence in an original pattern of thought.*

Keeping to Your Point

To show another distinction between writing first and second drafts, let us consider a third example. The following paragraph, in which the writer assumes an audience interested in the relationship of economics and politics to literature, is drawn from an essay on "The Idea of Economic Determinism in 'The Necklace.'" In this paragraph the writer shows how economics are related to a number of incidents from the story. The idea is to assert that Mathilde's difficulties result not from character but rather from financial restrictions:

> More important than chance in governing life is the idea that people are controlled by economic circumstances. Mathilde, as is shown at the story's opening, is born poor. Therefore she doesn't get the right doors opened for her, and her marriage is to a minor clerk. With a vivid imagination and a burning desire for luxury, seeming to be born only for the wealthy life, her poor home brings out her daydreams of expensive surroundings. She taunts her husband, Loisel, when he brings the big invitation, because she does not have a suitable (read "expensive") dress. Once she gets the dress it is jewelry that she lacks, and she borrows that and loses it. The loss of the necklace is the greatest trouble, because it forces the Loisels to borrow deeply and to lead an impoverished life for ten years.

This paragraph begins with an effective topic sentence, indicating that the writer has a good plan. The remaining part, however, shows how easily writers may be diverted from their objective. The flaw is that the material of the paragraph, while accurate, *is not tied to the topic.* Once the second sentence is under way, the paragraph gets lost in a retelling of events, and the fine opening sentence is left behind. The paragraph therefore shows that writers cannot assume that detail alone will make an intended meaning clear. They must do the connecting themselves to make sure that all relationships are explicitly clear. *This point cannot be overstressed.*

Let us see how the problem may be treated. If the ideal paragraph can be schematized with line drawings, we might say that the paragraph's topic should be a straight line, moving toward and reaching a specific goal (explicit meaning). An exemplifying line moves away from the straight line briefly to bring in evidence but returns to the straight line after each new fact to demonstrate the relevance of the fact. Thus, the ideal scheme looks like this, with a straight line touched a number of times by an undulating line:

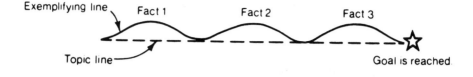

Notice that the exemplifying line, waving to illustrate how documentation or exemplification is to be used, always returns to the topic line. A scheme for the faulty paragraph on "The Necklace," however, would look like this, with the line never returning, but flying out into space:

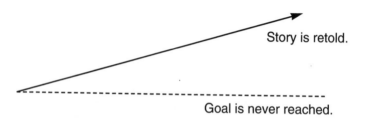

How might the faulty paragraph be improved? The best way is to remind the reader again and again of the topic and to use examples from the text in support.

Consistently with our model diagram, each time the topic is mentioned, the undulating line merges with the straight, or central-idea, line. This relationship of topic to illustrative examples should prevail no matter what subject you write about. If you are analyzing point of view, for example, you should keep connecting your material to the speaker, or narrator, and the same applies to topics like character, theme, or setting. According to this principle, we might revise the paragraph on economic determinism in "The Necklace" as follows. (Parts of sentences stressing the relationship of the examples to the topic of the paragraph are underlined.)

More important than chance in governing life is the idea that people are controlled by economic circumstances. <u>As illustration,</u> the speaker begins by emphasizing that Mathilde, the main character, is born poor. Therefore she doesn't get the right doors opened for her, and her marriage is to a minor clerk. <u>In keeping with the idea,</u> her vivid imagination and burning desire for luxury (she seems to have been born only for the wealthy life) feed on her weakness of character because she feels deep unhappiness and depression with the contrast between her daydreams of expensive surroundings and the poor home she actually has. <u>These straitened economic circumstances</u> inhibit her relationship with her husband, and she taunts him when he brings the big invitation because she does not have a suitable (read "expensive") dress. As a merging of her unrealistic dream life with actual reality, <u>her borrowing of the</u> necklace suggests the impossibility of overcoming economic restrictions. In the context of the idea, the ten-year sacrifice to pay for the lost necklace <u>demonstrates that lack of money keeps people down, destroying their dreams and hopes of a better life.</u>

The paragraph now reaches the goal of the topic sentence. While it has also been lengthened, the length has been caused not by inessential detail but by phrases and sentences that give form and direction. You might object that if you lengthened all your paragraphs in this way, your essays would grow too bulky. The answer to that objection is to reduce the number of your major points and paragraphs. The theory is that *it is better to develop a few topics pointedly than to develop many pointlessly.* Revising for the purpose of strengthening central and topic ideas requires that you either throw out some topics or else incorporate them as subpoints in the topics you keep. To control your writing in this way can result only in improvement.

CHECKING DEVELOPMENT AND ORGANIZATION

One of the first requirements of a good essay, then, is to stick to a point. Another major step toward excellence is to make your central idea expand and grow. The word *growth* is a metaphor describing the creation of new insights, the disclosure of ideas that were not at first noticeable, and the expression of new, fresh, and original interpretations.

An argument against this idea might be that you cannot be original when you are writing about someone else's work. "The author has said everything," might go the argument, "and therefore you can do little more than follow the story." This claim presupposes that you have no choice in selecting material and no opportunity to make individual thoughts and original contributions.

But you *do* have choices and opportunities for originality. One obvious area of originality is the development and formulation of your central idea. For example, a natural first response to "The Necklace" is "It is about a woman who loses a borrowed necklace and endures hardship to help pay for it." Because this response refers only to events in the story and not to any idea, an area of thought might be introduced if the hardship is called "needless." This idea would require an explanation of the differences between needed and unneeded hardships. The application of these differences to the heroine's plight would produce an original essay. Even better and more original insights could result if the topic of the budding essay were to connect the dreamy, withdrawn traits of the main character to her misfortunes and also to general misfortunes. A resulting central idea might be "People themselves create their own difficulties." Such an idea would require the writer to define not only the personal but also the representative nature of Mathilde's experiences, an avenue of exploration that could produce much in the way of a fresh, original essay about "The Necklace."

You can also develop your ability to treat your subject freshly and originally if you plan the body of the essay to build up to what you think is your most important and incisive idea. As examples of such planning, the following brief topic outlines suggest how each central idea may be widened and expanded:[*]

A. **Mathilde as a growing character (***Character, Chapter 4***)**
1. Mathilde has normal daydreams about a better life.
2. She takes a risk to make her daydreams seem real.
3. She develops by facing her mistake and working hard to correct it.

B. **The idea of economic determinism (***Idea or Theme, Chapter 7***)**
1. Mathilde's economic class inhibits her wishes.
2. Her husband's low income is a damper on her character.
3. The ten-year hardship is her punishment for trying to live beyond her means.

C. **The symbolic value of the necklace (***Symbolism and Allegory, Chapter 10***)**
1. The necklace symbolizes economic wealth and ease.
2. Its falseness symbolizes the discrepancy between appearance and reality.
3. Restoring the necklace symbolizes the value of sacrifice and work.

D. **The development of irony in the story (***Tone, Chapter 11***)**
1. Mathilde's dissatisfaction is heightened by her dreams.
2. The loss of the necklace ironically makes the Loisels seem poorer than they really are.
3. Mathilde's failure to confess the loss to Jeanne makes the sacrifice needless.

These outlines indicate how a subject may be enlarged if the exemplifying topics are treated in an increasing order of importance. Outlines A and D, for example, move toward ideas about moral values; outline B moves toward a broad consideration of the story; and outline C suggests a climax based on the story's situational irony. These possible patterns show how two primary standards of excellence in writing—organization and growth—can be met.

Clearly, then, an important goal in writing is the development of your central idea. Constantly adhere to your topic and constantly develop it. Nurture it and make it grow. Admittedly, in a short essay you will be able to move

[*]The critical basis for some of these topics is discussed in Appendix C, on the various critical approaches to literature. Thus the study of character is considered with the description of the psychological approach. The economic topic is described under the category of the Marxian-economic approach. The consideration of irony fits into the formalist category, as does the topic of symbolism.

only a short distance with an idea, but you *should never be satisfied to leave the idea exactly where you found it.* To the degree that you can learn to develop your ideas, you will receive recognition for increasingly superior writing.

USING EXACT, COMPREHENSIVE, AND FORCEFUL LANGUAGE

In addition to being organized and well developed, the best writing is expressed in *exact, comprehensive,* and *forceful* language. At first, sentences and paragraphs are usually weak, and you need to rethink them, reword them, and rearrange them.

Always ask yourself whether your sentences really *mean* what you intend, or whether you can make them more exact and therefore stronger. For example, consider these two sentences from essays about "The Necklace":

> It seems as though the main character's dreams of luxury cause her to respond as she does in the story.

> This incident, although it may seem trivial or unimportant, has substantial significance in the creation of the story; by this I mean the incident that occurred is essentially what the story is all about.

These sentences are inexact and vague and therefore unhelpful; neither of them goes anywhere. The first is satisfactory up to the verb "cause," but then it falls apart because the writer has lost sight of the meaning. It is best to describe *what* that response is, rather than to be satisfied with nothing more than that there *is* a response. To make the sentence more exact, we may make the following revision:

> Mathilde's dreams of luxury make it impossible for her to accept her own possessions, and therefore she goes beyond her means to attend the party.

With this revision, the writer could consider the meaning of the story's early passages and could contrast the ideas there with those in the latter part. Without the revision, it is not clear where the writer might go.

The second sentence is vague because again the writer has lost sight of the topic. If we adopt the principle of aiming toward exactness, however, we may bring the dead sentence to life:

> The accidental loss of the necklace, which is trivial though costly, supports the narrator's claim that major turns in life are produced not by earthshaking events, but rather by minor ones.

In addition to exactness, it is vital to make sentences—all sentences, but particularly thesis and topic sentences—complete and comprehensive. As an example, consider the following sentence, written in a student essay as a central idea about "The Necklace":

> The idea in "The Necklace" is how Mathilde and her husband respond to the loss of the necklace.

This sentence does no more than suggest a summary of the story. It needs additional rethinking and rephrasing to make it more comprehensive, as in these two revisions:

> Maupassant's surprise ending of "The Necklace" symbolizes the need for always being truthful.
>
> In "The Necklace" Maupassant shows that hard work and responsibility are basic and necessary in life.

Like the original sentence, both these revised sentences deal with the Loisels' response to the loss of the necklace. They are more comprehensive than the original sentence, however, and they would therefore be helpful in the creation of thoughtful essays. The first sentence, because it stresses the need for truth, would treat the Loisels' mistake in not confessing their loss; an essay stressing the symbolism of this action would likely emphasize the negative aspects of their characters. The second sentence introduces the moral point that the Loisels create value in their lives because of their years of hard work and sacrifice; an essay treating this idea would likely emphasize their positive traits.

Of course it is never easy to create fine sentences, but as a mode of improvement, you might create some self-testing mechanisms:

- *For responses and impressions.* Do not say simply, "The story's ending left me with a definite impression," but *state* what the impression is: "The story's ending surprised me and also made me sympathetic to Mathilde."
- *For ideas.* Try to make the idea clear and direct. Do not say, "Mathilde is living in a poor household," but rather get at an idea like this one: "The story of Mathilde shows that poor circumstances reduce the quality of life."
- *For critical commentary.* Do not rest with a statement such as "I found 'The Necklace' interesting," but try to describe *what* was interesting and *why* it was interesting: "I found 'The Necklace' interesting because it shows how chance may either make or destroy people's lives."

Good writing begins with attempts, like these, to rephrase sentences to make them really say something. If you always name and pin down descriptions, responses, and judgments, no matter how difficult the task seems, your sentences can be strong because you will be making them exact.

SAMPLE ESSAY, DRAFT 2

The following essay, a revision of the draft on page 28, includes changes that create greater emphasis and unity. Compared to the early draft, it creates more introductory detail, includes another topic, and reshapes each of the paragraphs to stress the relationship of central idea to topic. Within the limits of a short assignment, the essay illustrates all the principles of organization and unity we have been discussing.

Maupassant's Use of Setting in "The Necklace" to Show the Character of Mathilde

---

[1] In "The Necklace" Guy de Maupassant uses setting to reflect the character and development of the main figure, Mathilde Loisel.[*] As a result, his setting is not particularly vivid or detailed. He does not even provide a description of the ill-fated necklace—the central object in the story—but states only that it is "superb" (paragraph 47). He includes only enough description to illuminate his central character, Mathilde. Her changing character may be related to the first apartment, the dream-life mansion rooms, the attic flat, and the public street.[†]

[2] Details about the modest apartment of the Loisels on the Street of Martyrs indicate Mathilde's peevish lack of adjustment to life. Though everything is serviceable, she is unhappy with the "drab" walls, "threadbare" furniture, and "ugly" curtains (paragraph 3). She has domestic help but wants more servants than the simple country girl who does the household chores. Her dissatisfaction is also shown by details of her irregularly cleaned tablecloth and the plain and inelegant boiled beef that her husband adores. Even her best formal, which she wears for the theater, makes her unhappy. All these details of the apartment establish that Mathilde's dominant character trait at the start of the story is maladjustment. She therefore seems unpleasant and unsympathetic.

[3] Like the real-life apartment, the impossibly expensive setting of her daydreams strengthens her unhappiness and her avoidance of reality. All the rooms of her fantasies are large and expensive, draped in silk, and filled with nothing but the best furniture and bric-a-brac. Maupassant gives us the following description of her dream world:

> She imagined a gourmet-prepared main course carried on the most exquisite trays and served on the most beautiful dishes, with whispered gallantries which she would hear with a sphinxlike smile as she dined on the pink meat of a trout or the delicate wing of a quail. (paragraph 4)

With dreams like these filling her mind, her despair is even greater. Ironically, this despair, together with her inability to live with reality, brings about her undo-

[*]Central idea.
[†]Thesis sentence.

[3] ing. It makes her agree to borrow the necklace (which is just as unreal as her daydreams of wealth), and losing the necklace drives her into the reality of giving up her apartment and moving into the attic flat.

[4] Also ironically, the attic flat is related to the coarsening of her character while at the same time it brings out her best qualities of cooperativeness and honesty. Maupassant emphasizes the drudgery of the work she endures to maintain the flat, such as walking up many stairs, washing floors with large buckets of water, cleaning greasy and encrusted pots and pans, taking out the garbage, handwashing clothes, and haggling loudly with local tradespeople. All this reflects her coarsening and loss of sensibility, also shown by her giving up hair and hand care and wearing the cheapest dresses. The things she does, however, make her heroic (paragraph 98). As she cooperates to help her husband pay back the loans, her dreams of a mansion fade and all she has left is the memory of that one happy evening at the Minister of Education's reception. Thus the attic flat brings out her physical change for the worse at the same time that it also brings out her psychological and moral change for the better.

[5] Her walk on the Champs-Elysées illustrates another combination of traits—self-indulgence and frankness. The Champs-Elysées is the most fashionable street in Paris, and her walk to it is similar to her earlier indulgences in her dreams of wealth. She is, in effect, seeing how the upper-class people are living. But it is on this street where she meets Jeanne, and it is Mathilde's frankness in confessing the loss and replacement to Jeanne that makes Mathilde, finally, completely honest. While the walk thus serves as the occasion for the story's concluding surprise and irony, Mathilde's being on the Champs-Elysées is totally in character, in keeping with her earlier reveries about luxury.

[6] Other details in the story also have a similar bearing on Mathilde's character. For example, the story mentions little about the party scene but emphasizes only that she was a great "success" (paragraph 52)—a judgment that shows her ability to shine if given the chance. After she and Loisel accept the fact that the necklace cannot be found, Maupassant includes details about the Parisian streets, the visits to loan sharks, and the jewelry and jewelry-case shops, in order to bring out Mathilde's sense of honesty and pride as she "heroically" prepares to live the life of the poor. Thus, in "The Necklace," Maupassant uses setting to highlight Mathilde's maladjustment, her needless misfortune, her loss of youth and beauty, and finally her growth as a responsible human being.

COMMENTARY ON THE ESSAY

Several improvements to the first draft (p. 28) may be seen here. The language of paragraph 2 has been revised to show more clearly that Mathilde's dissatisfaction does not seem appropriate. In paragraph 3, the irony of the story is brought out, and the writer has connected the details to the central idea in a richer pattern of ideas, showing the effects of Mathilde's despair. In paragraph 6, the fact that Mathilde "shines" at the dinner party is interpreted according to the central idea. Finally, the conclusion is now much more specific, summarizing the change in Mathilde's character rather than saying simply that the setting reveals her "needless sacrifice." In short, the second draft reflects the complexity of "The Necklace" better than the first draft. Because the writer kept thinking about and revising the first-draft ideas about the story, the final essay is insightful, tightly structured, and forcefully written.

ESSAY COMMENTARIES

Throughout this book, the sample essays are followed by short commentaries to show how the essays embody the chapter's instruction and guidelines. For each essay in which a number of possible approaches are suggested, the commentary points out which one is employed; and when a sample essay uses two or more approaches, the commentary makes this fact clear. In addition, each commentary singles out one of the paragraphs for detailed analysis of its strategy and use of detail. It is hoped that the commentaries will help you develop the insight necessary to use the essays as aids in your own study and writing.

To sum up, follow these guidelines whenever you do any kind of writing:

- Keep returning to your points.
- Use material from the work you are studying as evidence to support your argument; do not retell the story.
- Include no details from the work unless you have clearly connected them to your points.
- Develop your topic; make it bigger than it was when you began.
- Always strive to make your statements exact, comprehensive, and forceful.

SPECIAL WRITING TOPICS

1. What effect do the minor characters in "The Necklace" (Loisel and Jeanne Forrestier) have upon your perception of Mathilde?
2. A critic has said that the disaster befalling Mathilde and Loisel results not so much from their losing the necklace as from their not telling Jeanne about the loss. How true is this judgment? Be sure to consider what they themselves think might have happened if they had confessed the loss to Jeanne.
3. Write a brief story of your own in which you show how a chance event has a major impact on the lives of your character or characters. In what ways is your chance event similar to or different from what happens to Mathilde? What view of life and reality do you think is represented by the consequences of the chance event?

chapter 2

Writing About Likes and Dislikes:

Responding to Literature

People read literature because they like it. It is therefore worth considering those qualities that, at the simplest level, produce responses of pleasure and also of displeasure. You either like or dislike a poem, story, or play; but if you say no more than that you have not said much. Writing about likes and dislikes requires you to explain the reasons for your responses. In short, your discussion should be *informed and informative* rather than *uninformed and unexplained*.

Sometimes a first response is that a work is "boring." This reaction is usually a mask covering an incomplete and superficial first reading. It is neither informative nor informed. As you study most works, however, you will be drawn into them and become *interested* and *involved*. To be interested in a work is to be taken into it emotionally; to be involved suggests that your emotions become almost wrapped up in the characters, problems, and outcomes of a work. Both "interest" and "involvement" describe genuine responses to reading. Once you get interested and involved, your reading ceases to be a task or assignment and grows into a pleasure.

USING YOUR JOURNAL TO RECORD RESPONSES

No one can tell you what you should or should not like; liking is your own concern. While your experience of reading is still fresh, therefore, you should use your journal (discussed earlier, pp. 12–15) to record not only your observations about a work but also your responses. Be frank in your judgment. Write down your likes and dislikes, and try to explain the reasons for your responses, even if these are brief and incomplete. If, after later thought and fuller understanding, you change or modify your first impressions, record these changes too. Here is a journal entry that explains a favorable response to Guy de Maupassant's "The Necklace":

> I like "The Necklace" because of the surprise ending. It isn't that I like Mathilde's bad luck, but I like the way Maupassant hides the most important fact in the story until the end. Mathilde does all that work and sacrifice for no reason at all, and the surprise ending makes this point strongly.

This paragraph could be expanded as a part of a developing essay. It is a clear statement of liking, followed by references to likable things in the work. This response pattern, which can be simply phrased as "I like [dislike] this work *because* . . . ," is a useful way to begin journal entries because it always requires that a response be followed with an explanation. If at first you cannot write any full sentences detailing the causes of your responses, at least make a brief list of the things you like or dislike. If you write nothing, you will probably forget your reactions; recovering them later, either for discussion or writing, will be difficult.

Responding Favorably

Usually you can equate your interest in a work with liking it. You can be more specific about favorable responses by citing one or more of the following:

- You like and admire the characters and what they do and stand for.
- You learn something new—something you had never known or thought before.
- You gain new insights into things that you already knew.
- You learn about characters and customs of different places, times, and ways of life.
- You get interested and involved in the outcome of the action or ideas and do not want to put the work down until you have finished it.
- You feel happy or thrilled because of reading the work.
- You are amused and laugh often as you read.
- You like the author's presentation.
- You find that some of the ideas and expressions are beautiful and worth remembering.

Obviously, if you have none of these responses, or find a character or incident that is distasteful, you will not like the work.

Responding Unfavorably

Although so far we have dismissed *boring* and stressed *interest, involvement*, and *liking*, it is important to know that disliking all or part of a work is normal and acceptable. You do not need to hide this response. Here, for example, are two short journal responses expressing dislike for Maupassant's "The Necklace":

1. I do not like "The Necklace" because Mathilde seems spoiled, and I don't think she is worth reading about.
2. "The Necklace" is not an adventure story, and I like reading only adventure stories.

These are both legitimate responses because they are based on a clear standard of judgment. The first stems from a distaste for one of the main character's unlikable traits; the second from a preference for rapidly moving stories that evoke interest in the dangers that main characters face and overcome.

Here is a paragraph-length journal entry that might be developed from the first response. Notice that the reasons for dislike are explained. They would need only slightly more development for use in an essay:

I do not like "The Necklace" because Mathilde seems spoiled and I do not think she is worth reading about. She is a phony. She nags her husband because he is not rich. She never tells the truth. I dislike her for hurrying away from the party because she is afraid of being seen in her shabby coat. She is foolish and dishonest for not telling Jeanne Forrestier about losing the necklace. It is true that she works hard to pay the debt, but she also puts her husband through ten years of hardship. If Mathilde had faced facts, she might have had a better life. I do not like her and cannot like the story because of her.

As long as you include reasons for your dislike, as in this journal paragraph, you can use them again when developing your essay. In further consideration, you will surely also expand thoughts, include new details, pick new topics for development as paragraphs, and otherwise modify your journal entry. You might even change your mind. However, even if you do not, it is better to record your original responses and reasons honestly than to force yourself to say you like something that you do not like.

PUTTING DISLIKES
INTO A LARGER CONTEXT

While it is important to be honest about disliking a work, it is more important to broaden your perspective and expand your taste. For example, a dislike based on the preference for only mystery or adventure stories, if generally applied, would cause a person to dislike most works of literature. This attitude seems unnecessarily self-limiting.

If negative responses are put in a larger context, it is possible to expand the capacity to like and appreciate. For instance, some readers might be preoccupied with their own concerns and therefore be uninterested in remote or "irrelevant" literary figures. However, if by reading about literary characters they can gain insight into general problems of life, and therefore their own concerns, they can find something to like in just about any work of literature. Other readers might like sports and therefore not read anything but the daily sports pages. What probably interests them about sports is competition, however, so if competition or conflict can be found in a literary work, they might discover something to like in that work.

As an example, let us consider again the dislike based on a preference for adventure stories and see if this preference can be widened. Here are some reasons for liking adventures:

1. Adventure has fast action.
2. It has danger and tension and therefore interest.
3. It has daring, active, and successful characters.
4. It has obstacles that the characters work hard to overcome.

No one could claim that the first three points apply to "The Necklace," but the fourth point is promising. Mathilde, the major character, works hard to overcome an obstacle: She pitches in to help her husband pay the large debt. If you like adventures because the characters try to gain worthy goals, then you can also like "The Necklace" for the same reason. The principle here is clear: If a reason for liking a favorite work or type of work can be found in another work, then there is reason to like that new work.

The following paragraph shows a possible application of this "bridging" process of extending preferences. (The sample essay [p. 46] is also developed along these lines.)

> I usually like only adventure stories, and therefore I disliked "The Necklace" at first because it is not adventure. One of my reasons for liking adventure is that the characters work hard to overcome difficult obstacles, like finding buried treasure or exploring new places. Mathilde, Maupassant's main character in "The Necklace," also works hard to overcome an obstacle—helping to pay back the money and interest for the borrowed 18,000 francs used as part of the payment for the replacement necklace. I like adventure characters because they stick to things and win out. I see the same toughness in Mathilde. Her problems get more interesting as the story moves on after a slow beginning. I came to like the story.

In this way, an accepted principle of liking can be applied to another work where it also applies. A person who adapts principles in this open-minded way can redefine dislikes and may consequently expand the ability to like and appreciate many kinds of literature.

An equally open-minded way to develop understanding and widen taste is to put dislikes in the following light: An author's creation of an *unlikable* character, situation, attitude, or expression may be deliberate. Your dislike might then result from the author's *intentions*. A first task of study is therefore to understand and explain the intention or plan. As you put the plan into your own words, you may find that you can like a work with unlikable things in it. Here is a paragraph that traces this pattern of thinking, based again on "The Necklace":

> Maupassant apparently wants the reader to dislike Mathilde, and I do. At first, he shows her being unrealistic and spoiled. She lies to everyone and nags her husband. Her rushing away from the party so that no one can see her shabby coat is a form of lying. I like the story itself, however, because Maupassant makes another kind of point. He does not hide her bad qualities, but makes it clear that she herself is the cause of her trouble. If people like Mathilde never face the truth, they will get into bad situations. This is a good point, and I like the way Maupassant makes it. The entire story is therefore worth liking even though I still do not like Mathilde.

Both of these ways are honest to the original negative reactions. In the first paragraph, the writer applies one of his principles of liking to include "The Necklace." In the second, the writer considers her initial dislike in the context of the work and discovers a basis for liking the story as a whole while still disliking the main character. The main concern in both responses is to keep an open mind despite initial dislike and then to see if the unfavorable response can be more fully and broadly considered.

However, if you decide that your dislike overbalances any reasons you can find for liking, then you should explain your dislike. As long as you relate your response to the work accurately and measure it by a clear standard of judgment, your dislike of even a commonly liked work is not unacceptable. The important issue is not so much that you like or dislike a particular work *but that you develop your own abilities to analyze and express your ideas.*

WRITING ABOUT RESPONSES:
LIKES AND DISLIKES

In writing about your responses, rely on your initial informed reactions. It is not easy to reconstruct your first responses after a lapse of time, so you will need your journal observations to guide the prewriting stage. Develop your essay by stressing those characters, incidents, and ideas that interest (or do not interest) you in the work.

Always relate the details of the work to the point you are making about your ongoing responses. Stress your involvement in the work as you bring out evidence from it. You can show your attitudes by indicating approval (or disapproval), by commenting favorably (or unfavorably) on the details, by indicating things that seem new (or shopworn) and particularly instructive (or wrong), and by giving assent to (or dissent from) ideas or expressions of feeling.

Organizing Your Essay About Likes and Dislikes

INTRODUCTION.   Begin by describing briefly the conditions that influence your response. Your central idea should be why you like or dislike the work. The thesis sentence should list the major causes of your response, which are to be developed in the body.

BODY.   The most common approach is to consider specific details that you like or dislike. The list on page 41 may help you articulate your responses. For example, you may have admired a particular character, or maybe you got so interested in the story that you could not put it down. Also, it may be that a major idea, a fresh insight, or a particular outcome is the major point that you wish to develop. The sample paragraph on page 41 shows a surprise ending as the cause of a favorable response.

A second approach (see p. 43) is to explain any changes in your responses about the work (i.e., negative to positive and vice versa). This approach requires that you isolate the causes of the change, but it does *not* require you to retell the story from beginning to end. (1) One way to deal with such a change—the "bridge" method of transferring preference from one type of work to another—is shown in the sample essay (p. 46). (2) Another way is to explain a change in terms of a new awareness or understanding that you did not have on a first reading. Thus your first response to Poe's "The Cask of Amontillado" might be unfavorable or neutral because the story seems unnecessarily sensational and lurid. Further consideration, however, might lead you to discover new insights that change your mind, such as the needs to overcome personal pride and to stop minor resentments from growing and festering. Your essay would then explain how these new insights have caused you to start liking the story.

CONCLUSION.   Here you might summarize the reasons for your major response. You might also face any issues brought up by a change or modification of your first reactions. For example, if you have always held certain assumptions about your taste but like the work despite these assumptions, you may wish to talk about your own change or development. This topic is personal, but in an essay about likes or dislikes, discovery about yourself is legitimate and worthy.

Sample Essay

Some Reasons for Liking Maupassant's "The Necklace"°

[1]   To me, the most likable kind of reading is adventure. There are many reasons for my preference, but an important one is that adventure characters work hard to overcome obstacles. Because Guy de Maupassant's "The Necklace" is not adventure, I did not like it at first. But in one respect the story is <u>like</u> adventure: The major character, Mathilde, works hard for ten years with her husband, Loisel, to overcome a difficult obstacle. <u>Thus, because Mathilde does what adventure characters also do, the story is likable.</u>* <u>Mathilde's appeal results from her hard work, strong character, sad fate, and also from the way our view of her changes.</u>†

[2]   <u>Mathilde's hard work makes her seem good.</u> Once she and her husband are faced with the huge debt of 18,000 francs, she works like a slave to pay it back. She gives up her servant and moves to a cheaper place. She does the household drudgery, wears cheap clothes, and bargains with shopkeepers for the lowest prices. Just like the characters in adventure stories who do hard and unpleasant things, she does what she has to, and this makes her admirable.

[3]   <u>Her strong character shows her endurance, a likable trait.</u> At first she is nagging and fussy, and she always dreams about wealth and tells lies, but she changes and gets better. She recognizes her blame in losing the necklace, and she has the toughness to help her husband redeem the debt. She sacrifices "heroically" (paragraph 98) by giving up her comfortable way of life, even though in the process she also loses her youth and beauty. Her jobs are not the exotic and glamorous ones of adventure stories, but her force of character makes her as likable as an adventure heroine.

[4]   <u>Her sad fate also makes her likable.</u> In adventure stories the characters often suffer as they do their jobs. Mathilde also suffers, but in a different way, because her suffering is permanent while the hardships of adventure characters are temporary. This fact makes her pitiable, and even more so because all her sacrifices are not necessary. This unfairness about her life invites the reader to take her side.

[5]   <u>The most important quality promoting admiration is the way in which Maupassant shifts our view of Mathilde.</u> As she goes deeper into her hard life, Maupassant stresses her work and not the innermost thoughts he reveals at the beginning. In other words, the view into her character at the start, when she

°See pages 4–12 for this story.
*Central idea.
†Thesis sentence.

dreams about wealth, invites dislike; but the focus at the end is on her achievements, with never a complaint—even though she still has golden memories, as the narrator tells us:

> But sometimes, when her husband was at work, she sat down near the window, and she dreamed of that evening so long ago, of that party, where she had been so beautiful and so admired. (paragraph104)

A major quality of Maupassant's changed emphasis is that these recollections do not lead to anything unfortunate. His shift in focus, from Mathilde's dissatisfaction to her sharing of responsibility and sacrifice, encourages the reader to like her.

[6]   "The Necklace" is not an adventure story, but Mathilde has some of the good qualities of adventure characters. Also, the surprise revelation that the lost necklace was false is an unforgettable twist, and this makes her more deserving than she seems at first. Maupassant has arranged the story so that the reader finally admires Mathilde. "The Necklace" is a skillful and likable story.

COMMENTARY ON THE ESSAY

This essay demonstrates how a reader may develop appreciation by transferring or "bridging" (described on pp. 42–43) a preference for one type of work to a work that does not belong to the type. In the theme, the bridge is an already established taste for adventure stories, and the grounds for liking "The Necklace" are that Mathilde, the main character, shares the admirable qualities of adventure heroes and heroines.

In paragraph 1, the introduction, the grounds for transferring preference are established. Paragraph 2 deals with Mathilde's capacity to work hard, and paragraph 3 considers the equally admirable quality of endurance. The fourth paragraph describes how Mathilde's condition evokes sympathy and pity. These paragraphs hence explain the story's appeal by asserting that the main character is similar to admirable characters from works of adventure.

The fifth paragraph shows that Maupassant, as the story unfolds, alters the reader's perceptions of Mathilde from bad to good. For this reason paragraph 5 marks a new direction from paragraphs 2, 3, and 4: It moves away from the topic material itself—Mathilde's character—to Maupassant's *technique* in handling the topic material.

Paragraph 6, the conclusion, restates the comparison and also introduces the surprise ending as an additional reason for liking "The Necklace." With the body and conclusion together, therefore, the essay establishes five separate reasons for approval. Three of these, derived directly from the main character, constitute the major grounds for liking the story, and two are related to Maupassant's techniques as an author.

Throughout the essay, the central idea is brought out in words and expressions such as "likable," "Mathilde's appeal," "strong character," "she does what she has to," "pitiable," and "take her side." Many of these expressions were first made in the writer's journal; and, mixed as they are with details from the story, they make for continuity. It is this thematic development, together with details from the story as supporting evidence, that shows how an essay on the responses of liking and disliking may be both informed and informative.

SPECIAL WRITING TOPICS
FOR LIKES AND DISLIKES

1. Some readers dislike Poe's "The Cask of Amontillado" because of the speaker's lurid explanation of his revenge. Respond to this view of the work.
2. For what reasons should a reader like Shakespeare's Sonnet 116, "Let Me Not to the Marriage of True Minds"?
3. Explain why a negative response to Glaspell's *Trifles* is not justified by what happens in the play.
4. How can a person like Hawthorne's "Young Goodman Brown" even if that same person dislikes what happens to Brown's character and outlook?

chapter 3

Writing About Plot and Structure:

The Development and Organization of Narratives and Drama

Stories and plays are made up mostly of **actions** or **incidents** that follow each other in chronological order. Finding a sequential or narrative order, however, is only the first step toward the more important consideration—the **plot**, or the controls governing the development of the actions.

The English novelist E. M. Forster, in *Aspects of the Novel*, presents a memorable illustration of plot. To show a bare set of actions, he uses the following: "The king died, and then the queen died." He points out, however, that this sequence does not form a plot because it lacks *motivation* and *causation*. These he introduces in his next example: "The king died, and then the queen died of grief." The phrase "of grief" shows that one thing (grief) controls or overcomes another (the normal desire to live), and motivation and causation enter the sequence to form a plot. In a well-plotted story or play, things precede or follow each other not simply because time ticks away, but more importantly because *effects* follow *causes*. In a good work nothing is irrelevant or accidental; everything is related and causative.

Conflict

The controlling impulse in a connected pattern of causes and effects is **conflict,** which refers generally to people or circumstances a character must face and try to overcome. Conflict brings out the extremes of human energy, causing characters to engage in the decisions, actions, responses, and interactions that make up most stories.

In its most elemental form, a conflict is the opposition of two people. Their conflict may take the shape of envy, hatred, anger, argument, avoidance, gossip, lies, fighting, and many other forms and actions. Conflicts may also exist between groups, although conflicts between individuals are more identifiable and therefore more suitable for stories. Conflicts may also be abstract, such as when an individual opposes larger forces like natural objects, ideas, modes of behavior, or public opinion. A difficult or even impossible *choice*— a **dilemma**—is a natural conflict for an individual person. A conflict may also be brought out in ideas and opinions that may clash. In short, conflict shows itself in many ways.

CONFLICT, DOUBT, TENSION, AND INTEREST.   Conflict is the major element of plot because opposing forces arouse *curiosity,* cause *doubt,* create *tension,* and produce *interest.* The same responses are the lifeblood of athletic competition. Consider which kind of game is more interesting: (1) One team gets so far ahead that the winner is no longer in doubt, or (2) both teams are so evenly matched that the winner is in doubt even in the final seconds. Obviously, every game should be a tense contest between teams of comparable strength. The same applies to conflicts in stories and dramas. There should be uncertainty about a protagonist's success: Unless there is doubt there is no tension, and without tension there is no interest.

PLOT IN OPERATION.   To see a plot in operation, let us build on Forster's description. Here is a bare plot for a story of our own: "John and Jane meet, fall in love, and get married." This is a plot because it shows cause and effect (they get married *because* they fall in love), but with no conflict the plot is not interesting. However, let us introduce conflicting elements in this common "boy meets girl" story:

> John and Jane meet at school and fall in love. They go together for two years and plan to marry, but a problem arises. Jane wants a career first, and after marriage she wants to be an equal contributor to the family. John understands Jane's wishes, but he wants to get married first and let her finish her studies and have her career after they have children. Jane believes that John's plan is not for her because it constitutes a trap from which she will never escape. This conflict interrupts their plans, and they part in regret and anger. Even though they still love each other, both marry other people and build separate lives and careers. Neither is happy even though they like and respect their spouses. The years pass, and, after children and grandchildren, Jane and John meet again. He is now divorced and she is a widow. Because their earlier conflict is no longer a barrier, they marry and try to make up for the past. Even their new happiness, however, is tinged with regret and reproach because of their earlier conflict, their unhappy solution, their lost years, and their increasing age.

Here we have a true plot because our original "boy-meets-girl" story outline contains a major conflict from which a number of related conflicts develop. These conflicts lead to attitudes, choices, and outcomes that make the story interesting. The situation is lifelike; the conflicts rise out of realistic aims and hopes; the outcome is true to life.

WRITING ABOUT PLOT

An essay about plot is an analysis of the conflict and its developments. The organization of the essay should not be modeled on sequential sections and principal events, however, because these invite only a retelling of the story. Instead, the organization is to be developed from the important elements of conflict. Ask yourself the following questions as you look for ideas about plot:

- Who are the protagonist and antagonist, and how do their characteristics put them in conflict? How would you describe the conflict?
- How does the action develop from the conflict?
- If the conflict stems from contrasting ideas or values, what are these, and how are they brought out?
- Does the major character face a dilemma? What is the dilemma? How does the character deal with it?
- How do the major characters achieve (or not achieve) their major goal(s)? What obstacles do they overcome? What obstacles overcome them?
- At the end, are the characters happy or unhappy, satisfied or dissatisfied, changed or about the same, enlightened or ignorant? How has the resolution of the major conflict produced these results?

Organizing Your Essay About Plot

INTRODUCTION. To keep your essay brief, you need to be selective. After you refer briefly to the principal characters, circumstances, and issues of the plot, be sure that your thesis statement includes the topics for fuller development.

BODY. Stress the major elements in the conflicts developed in the work. Rather than detailing everything a major character does, for example, stress the major elements in his or her conflict. Such an essay on Eudora Welty's "A Worn Path" might emphasize Phoenix as she encounters the various obstacles both in the woods and in town. When there is a conflict between two major characters, the obvious approach is to focus equally on both. For brevity, however, emphasis might be placed on just one. Thus, an essay on the plot of "The Cask of Amontillado" might stress the things we learn about the narrator, Montresor, that are important to his being the initiator of the action.

In addition, the plot may be analyzed more broadly in terms of impulses, goals, values, issues, and historical perspectives. Thus, you might emphasize the elements of chance working against Mathilde in Maupassant's "The Necklace" as a contrast to her dreams about wealth. A discussion of the plot of Mansfield's "Miss Brill" might stress the reclusiveness of Miss Brill, the major character, because the plot could not develop without the disclosure of her secret life.

CONCLUSION. The conclusion may contain a brief summary of the points you have made. It is also a fitting location for a brief consideration of the effect or *impact* produced by the conflict. Additional ideas might focus on whether the author has arranged actions and dialogue to direct your favor toward one side or the other, or on whether the plot is possible or impossible, serious or comic, fair or unfair, or powerful or weak.

Sample Essay (on Plot)

The Plot of Eudora Welty's "A Worn Path"°

---

[1]   At first, the complexity of Eudora Welty's plot in "A Worn Path" is not clear. The main character is Phoenix Jackson, an old, poor, and frail woman; the story seems to be no more than a record of her walk to Natchez through the woods from her rural home. By the story's end, however, the plot is clear: It consists of the brave attempts of a courageous, valiant woman to carry on against overwhelming forces.* Her determination despite the great odds against her gives the story its impact. The powers ranged against her are old age, poverty, environment, and illness.†

[2]   Old age as a silent but overpowering antagonist is shown in signs of Phoenix's increasing senility. Not her mind but her feet tell her where to find the medical office in Natchez. Despite her inner strength, she is unable to explain her errand when the nursing attendant asks her. Instead she sits dumbly and unknowingly for a time, until "a flame of comprehension" comes across her face (paragraph 87). Against the power of advancing age, Phoenix is slowly losing. The implication is that she soon will lose entirely.

[3]   An equally crushing opponent is her poverty. She cannot afford to ride to town, but must walk. She has no money and acquires her ten cents for the paper windmill by stealing and begging. The "soothing medicine" she gets for her grandson (paragraph 92) is given to her out of charity. Despite the boy's need for advanced medical care, she has no money to provide it, and the story therefore shows that her guardianship is doomed.

    Closely connected to her poverty is the way through the woods, which dur-

°See page 309–14 for this story.
*Central idea.
†Thesis sentence.

[4]

ing her walk seems to be an almost active opponent. The long hill tires her, the thornbush catches her clothes, the log endangers her balance as she crosses the creek, and the barbed-wire fence threatens to puncture her skin. Another danger on her way is the stray dog, which topples her over. Apparently not afraid, however, Phoenix carries on a cheerful monologue:

> "Out of my way, all you foxes, owls, beetles, jack rabbits, coons and wild animals! . . . Keep out from under these feet, little bob-whites. . . . Keep the big wild hogs out of my path. Don't let none of those come running my direction. I got a long way." (paragraph 3)

She prevails for the moment as she enters Natchez, but all the hazards of her walk are still there, waiting for her to return.

[5]

The force against Phoenix which shows her plight most clearly and pathetically is her grandson's incurable illness. His condition highlights her helplessness, for she is his only support. Her difficulties would be enough for one person alone, but with the grandson the odds against her are doubled. Despite her care, there is nothing anyone can do for the grandson but take the long worn path to get something to help him endure his pain.

[6]

This brief description of the conflicts in "A Worn Path" only hints at the story's power. Welty layers the details to bring out the full range of the conditions against Phoenix, who cannot win despite her determination and devotion. The most hopeless fact, the condition of the invalid grandson, is not revealed until she reaches the medical office, and this delayed final revelation makes one's heart go out to her. The plot is strong because it is so real, and Phoenix is a pathetic but memorable protagonist struggling against overwhelming odds.

COMMENTARY ON THE ESSAY

The strategy of this essay is to explain the elements of plot in "A Worn Path" selectively, without duplicating the story's narrative order. Thus the third aspect of conflict, the woods, might be introduced first if the story's narrative order were to be followed, but it is deferred while the more personal elements of old age and poverty are considered first. It is important to note that the essay does not consider other characters as part of Phoenix's conflict; rather, Phoenix's antagonist takes the shape of impersonal and unconquerable forces, such as the grandson's illness.

Paragraph 1 briefly describes how one's first impressions are changed by the story's end. The thesis sentence anticipates the body by listing the four topics about to be treated. Paragraph 2 concerns Phoenix's old age; paragraph 3 her poverty; paragraph 4 the woods; and paragraph 5, her grandson's illness. The concluding paragraph (6) points out that in this set of conflicts the protagonist cannot win except as she lives out her duty and her devotion to help her grandson. Continuing the idea in the introduction, the last paragraph also accounts for the power of the plot: By building up to Phoenix's personal strength against unbeatable forces, the story evokes sympathy and admiration.

THE STRUCTURE OF NARRATIVES AND DRAMA

Structure describes how the writer arranges and places materials in accord with the general ideas and purpose of the work. While *plot* is concerned with the conflict or conflicts, *structure* defines layout—the way the story, play, or narrative poem is shaped. Structure is about matters such as placement, balance, recurring themes, true and misleading conclusions, suspense, and the imitation of models or forms like reports, letters, conversations, or confessions. Thus a story might be divided up into parts, or it might move from countryside to city, or it might develop relationships between two people from their first introduction to their falling in love. To study structure is to study these arrangements and the purposes for which they are made.

Formal Categories of Structure

Many aspects of structure are common to all genres of literature. Particularly for stories and plays, however, the following aspects form a skeleton, a pattern of development.

EXPOSITION.   **Exposition** is the laying out, the putting forth, of the materials in the story—the main characters, their backgrounds, their characteristics, interests, goals, limitations, potentials, and basic assumptions. It may not be limited to the beginning of the work, where it is most expected, but may be found anywhere. Thus, intricacies, twists, turns, false leads, blind alleys, surprises, and other quirks may be introduced to interest, perplex, intrigue, and otherwise please readers. Whenever something new arises, to the degree that it is new it is a part of exposition.

COMPLICATION.   The **complication** is the *onset* of the major conflict— the plot. The major participants are the protagonist and antagonist, together with whatever ideas and values they represent, such as good or evil, freedom or suppression, independence or dependence, love or hate, intelligence or stupidity, or knowledge or ignorance.

CRISIS.   The **crisis** (Greek for *turning point*) is the separation between what has gone before and what will come after, usually a decision or action undertaken to resolve the conflict. The crisis is that point in which curiosity, uncertainty, and tension are greatest. Usually the crisis is followed closely by the next stage, the *climax*. Often, in fact, the two happen so closely that they are considered to be the same.

CLIMAX. Because the **climax** (Greek for *ladder*) is a consequence of the crisis, it is the story's *high point* and may take the shape of a decision, an action, an affirmation or denial, or an illumination or realization. It is the logical conclusion of the preceding actions; no new major developments follow it. In most stories, the climax occurs at or close to the end. In Chekhov's play, *The Bear,* for example, the climax is that Smirnov, after touching and holding Mrs. Popov when instructing her in how to hold a pistol, impetuously declares his love. This brings their hostility to an unexpected height and also to a sudden reversal. In Lowell's poem "Patterns" the climax is the very last sentence, "Christ, what are patterns for?" This outburst summarizes the speaker's developing sorrow, frustration, and anger.

RESOLUTION, OR DÉNOUEMENT. The **resolution** (a releasing or untying) or **dénouement** (untying) is the finishing of things. Once the untying begins, there is little more tension and uncertainty, and most authors conclude as quickly as possible. Chekhov ends *The Bear* with his two major characters kissing in front of their dumbfounded servants; Welty ends "A Worn Path" with the main character beginning her long walk home; and Twain ends "Luck" with the simple statement that the main character is a fool.

Formal and Actual Structure

The structure just described is a *formal* one, an ideal pattern that moves directly from beginning to end. In practice, however, few narratives and dramas follow this pattern exactly. A mystery story, for example, may hold back crucial details of exposition (because the goal is to mystify); a suspense story may keep the protagonist ignorant but provide readers with abundant details in order to maximize concern and tension about the outcome.

More realistic, less "artificial" stories might also contain structural variations. For example, Welty's "A Worn Path" produces a *double take* because of unique structuring. During most of the story, Phoenix's conflicts are against age, poverty, and environment. At the end, however, we are introduced to an additional difficulty—a new conflict—which enlarges our responses to include not just concern but also heartfelt anguish. "A Worn Path" is just one example of how a structural variation maximizes the impact of a work.

There are many other possible variants in structure. One of these is the **flashback,** in which present circumstances are explained by the selective introduction of past events. The moment at which the flashback is introduced may be a part of the resolution of the plot, and the flashback might lead you into a moment of climax but then go from there to develop the details that are more properly part of the exposition. Let us again consider our brief plot about John and Jane and use the flashback method of structuring the story.

> Jane is now old, and a noise outside causes her to remember the argument that forced her to part with John many years before. They were deeply in love, but their disagreement about her wishes for a career split them apart. Then she pictures in her mind the years she and John have spent happily together after they married. She then contrasts her present happiness with her memory of her earlier, less happy, marriage, and from there she recalls her youthful years of courtship with John before their disastrous conflict developed. Then she looks over at John, reading in a chair, and smiles. John smiles back, and the two embrace. Even then, Jane has tears on her face.

In this structure the action begins and remains in the present. Important parts of the past flood the protagonist's memory in flashback, though not in the order in which they happened. Memory might be used structurally in other ways. The speaker–narrator of Robert Hayden's "Those Winter Sundays," for example, bases the first twelve lines of the poem on the memory of his father's early rising to make life in the house comfortable. The structure of the poem thus takes us, as readers, from the past into the present.

Each narrative or drama has a unique structure. Simple geography, for example, may govern a story's development, as in Irving Layton's poem "Rhine Boat Trip" (from castles observed by a tourist on the Rhine to cattle cars during the Holocaust), or in Welty's "A Worn Path" (a walk from country to town). A work may unfold in an apparently accidental way, with the characters drawing significant conclusions as they make vital discoveries about the major characters, as in Glaspell's *Trifles*. Additionally, parts of a work may be set out as fragments of conversation, as in "A Worn Path"; or as a ceremony, as in "Young Goodman Brown"; or as an announcement of a party, as in "The Necklace." The possible variations are extensive.

WRITING ABOUT STRUCTURE

Your essay should concern arrangement and shape. In form, the essay should not follow the part-by-part unfolding of the narrative or argument. Rather it should explain why things are where they are: "Why is this here and not there?" is the fundamental question you need to answer. Thus it is possible to begin with a consideration of a work's crisis, and then to consider how the exposition and complication have built up to it. A vital piece of information, for example, might have been withheld in the earlier exposition (as in Bierce's "An Occurrence at Owl Creek Bridge" and Welty's "A Worn Path") and introduced only at or near the conclusion; thus the crisis might be heightened because there would have been less suspense if the detail had been introduced earlier. Consider the following questions as you examine the story's structure:

- If spaces or numbers divide the story into sections or parts, what structural importance do these parts have?
- If there are no marked divisions, what major sections can you discover? (You might make divisions according to places where actions occur, to various times of day, to changing weather, or to increasingly important events.)
- If the story departs in major ways from the formal structure of exposition, complication, crisis, climax, and resolution, what purpose do these departures have?
- What variations in chronological order, if any, appear in the story (e.g., gaps in the time sequence, flashbacks)? What effects are achieved by these variations?
- Does the story withhold any crucial details of exposition? Why? What effect is achieved?
- Where does an important action or major section (such as the climax) begin? End? How is it related to the other formal structural elements, such as the crisis? Is the climax an action, a realization, or a decision? To what degree does it relieve the work's tension? What is the effect of the climax on your understanding of the characters involved in it? How is this effect related to the arrangement of the climax?

Organizing Your Essay About Structure

INTRODUCTION.   Most likely you will discuss the structure of an entire work, although you might also discuss the structure of no more than a part of the work, such as the climax or the complication. Your central idea should concern the reasons for the work's structure—to reveal the nature of a character's situation, to create surprise, or to bring out maximum humor. The thesis sentence presents a plan of development for the body.

BODY.   The essay is best developed in concert or agreement with what the work contains. The location of scenes is an obvious organizing element. Thus, an essay on the structure of "A Worn Path" might be based on the countryside, the town, and the medical building, where the actions of the story occur. Hawthorne's "Young Goodman Brown" and Mansfield's "Miss Brill" both take place outside (a dark forest for one and a sunny public park for the other). Maupassant's "The Necklace" begins in interiors and concludes outdoors. The locations of Updike's "A & P" are the aisles and the checkout counter of a supermarket. A structural study of any of these works might be based on these locations and their effect on the plot.

Other ways to consider structure may be derived from a work's notable aspects, such as the growing suspense and horrible conclusion of Poe's "The Cask of Amontillado" or the revelation about the father's loving nature in Hayden's "Those Winter Sundays."

CONCLUSION. The conclusion should highlight the main parts of your essay. You may also deal briefly with the relationship of structure to the plot. If the work you have analyzed departs from chronological order, you might stress the effects of this departure. Your aim should be to focus on the success of the work as it has been brought about by the author's choices in development.

Sample Essay (on Structure)

The Structure of Eudora Welty's "A Worn Path"°

[1] The narrative of Eudora Welty's "A Worn Path" is not difficult to follow. Events occur in sequence. The main character is Phoenix Jackson, an old and poor woman. She walks from her rural home in Mississippi through the woods to Natchez to get a free bottle of medicine for her grandson, who is a hopeless invalid. Everything takes place in just a few hours. This action is only the frame, however, for a skillfully and powerfully structured plot.* The masterly control of structure is shown in the story's locations and in the way in which the delayed revelation produces both mystery and complexity.†

[2] The locations in the story coincide with the increasing difficulties that Phoenix encounters. The first and most obvious worn path is the rural woods with all its natural difficulties. For most people the obstacles would not be challenging, but for an old woman they are formidable. In Natchez, the location of the next part of the story, Phoenix's inability to bend over to tie her shoe demonstrates the lack of flexibility of old age. In the medical office, where the final scene takes place, two major difficulties of the plot are brought out. One is Phoenix's increasing senility, and the other is the disclosure that her grandson is an incurable invalid. This set of oppositions, the major conflicts in the plot, thus coincide with locations or scenes and show the powerful forces opposing Phoenix.

[3] The strongest of these conditions, the revelation about the grandson, makes the story something like a mystery. Because detail about the boy is delayed until the end, the reader wonders for most of the story what bad thing might happen next. In fact, some parts of the story are false leads. For example, the episode with the hunter's dog is threatening, but it leads nowhere: Phoenix, with the aid of the hunter, is unharmed. That she picks up and keeps the nickel dropped by the hunter might seem at first to be cause for punishment. In fact, she thinks it does, as this scene with the hunter shows:

> [H]e laughed and lifted his gun and pointed it at Phoenix.
> She stood straight and faced him.
> "Doesn't the gun scare you?" he said, still pointing it.
> "No, sir, I seen plenty go off closer by, in my day, and for less than what I done," she said, holding utterly still. (paragraphs 55–58)

°See pages 309–14 for this story.
*Central idea.
†Thesis sentence.

[3] But the young hunter does not notice that the coin is missing, and he does not accuse her. Right up to the moment of her entering the medical building, therefore, the reader is still wondering what might happen.

[4] <u>Therefore the details about the grandson, carefully concealed until the end, make the story more complex than it at first seems.</u> Because of this concluding revelation, the reader must do a double take and reconsider what has gone on before. Phoenix's difficult walk into town must be seen not as an ordinary errand but as a hopeless mission of mercy. Her character also bears reevaluation: She is not just a funny old woman who speaks to the woods and animals, but she is also a brave and pathetic woman carrying on against crushing odds. These conclusions are not apparent for most of the story, and the late emergence of the carefully concealed details makes "A Worn Path" both forceful and powerful.

[5] Thus the parts of "A Worn Path," while simple at first, are skillfully arranged. The key to the double take and reevaluation is Welty's withholding of the crucial detail of exposition until the very end. The result is that parts of the exposition and complication, through the speeches of the attendant and the nurse, merge with the climax near the story's end. In some respects, the detail makes it seem as though Phoenix's entire existence is a crisis, although she is not aware of this condition as she leaves the office to buy the paper windmill. <u>It is this complex buildup and emotional peak that make the structure of "A Worn Path" the creation of a master writer.</u>

COMMENTARY ON THE ESSAY

To highlight the differences between essays on plot and structure, the topic of this sample essay on structure in Welty's "A Worn Path" is also analyzed in the sample essay on plot. While both essays are concerned with the conflicts of the story, the essay on plot concentrates on the opposing forces, but the essay on structure focuses on the placement and arrangement of the story's details. Notice that neither essay retells the story, event by event. Instead, these are analytical essays that explain the *conflict* (for plot) and the *arrangement and layout* (for structure). In both essays, the assumption is that the reader has read "A Worn Path"; hence there is no need in the essay to tell the story again.

The introductory paragraph points out that the masterly structure accounts for the story's power. Paragraph 2 develops the topic that the geographical locations are arranged climactically to demonstrate the forces against the major character. Paragraph 3 considers how the delayed exposition about the grandson creates uncertainty about the issues and direction of the story. As supporting evidence, the paragraph cites two important details—the danger from the hunter's dog and the theft of his nickel—as structural false leads about Phoenix's troubles. Paragraph 4 deals with the complexity brought about by the delayed information: the necessary reevaluation of Phoenix's character and her mission to town. The concluding paragraph also considers this complexity, accounting for the story's power by pointing out how a number of plot elements merge near the end to bring things out swiftly and powerfully.

SPECIAL WRITING TOPICS
FOR PLOT AND STRUCTURE

1. What kind of story might "A Worn Path" be, structurally, if the detail about the invalid grandson were introduced at the start, before Phoenix begins her walk to town?

2. Compare the structuring of the interior scenes in "A Worn Path," "The Cask of Amontillado," and "A & P." How do these scenes bring out the various conflicts of the stories? How do characters in the interiors contribute to plot developments? What is the relationship of these characters to the major themes of the stories?

3. Select a circumstance in your life that caused you doubt, difficulty, and conflict. Making yourself anonymous (give yourself a fictitious name and put yourself in a fictitious location), write a brief *story* about the occasion, stressing how your conflict began, how it affected you, and how you resolved it. You might choose to describe the details in chronological order, or you might begin the story in the present tense and introduce details in flashback.

4. Consider those aspects of "A Worn Path" that seem socially and politically significant. You might consider questions such as whether elderly women like Phoenix are living in such remote areas today, whether her grandson should be left entirely in her care, whether she should be near public transportation so that she would not need to walk great distances to attend to her needs. You might also consider her as a representative of a group suffering discrimination and treat her as an example of the need for legislation that would improve her condition.

chapter 4

Writing About Character:
The People in Literature

Literature has flourished along with the study of psychology, which has produced psychological pioneers like Freud, Jung, and Skinner. In this intellectual milieu, writers of fiction and drama have chosen not just to create narratives but also to embody materials that increase the understanding of human nature. Psychologists, in turn, have influenced the study of literature. It is well known that Freud used many literary works, including plays by Shakespeare, to buttress some of his psychological conclusions; and films such as *Spellbound*, *The Snake Pit*, and *Final Analysis* have popularized the relationships between literary character and the science of psychology. Without doubt, the presentation and understanding of character have become a major aim of fiction and drama.

In literature, a **character** may be defined as a verbal representation of a human being. Through action, speech, description, and commentary, authors portray characters who are worth caring about, rooting for, and even loving, although there are also characters you may laugh at, dislike, or even hate.

In a story emphasizing a major character, you may expect that each action or speech, no matter how small, is part of a total presentation of that complex combination of both the inner and outer self that constitutes a human being. Whereas in life things may "just happen," in stories all actions, interactions, speeches, and observations are deliberate. Thus, you read about important actions like a long period of work and sacrifice (Maupassant's "The Necklace"), the taking of a regular journey of mercy (Welty's "A Worn Path"), an act of cruel vengeance (Poe's "The Cask of Amontillado"), or a young man's fanciful dream of freedom (Bierce's "An Occurrence at Owl Creek Bridge"). By making such actions interesting, authors help you understand and appreciate their major characters.

CHARACTER TRAITS

In studying a literary character, begin by determining the character's outstanding traits. A **trait** is a quality of mind or habitual mode of behavior, such as never repaying borrowed money, avoiding eye contact, or always thinking oneself the center of attention. Sometimes, of course, the traits we encounter are minor and therefore negligible, but often a trait may be a person's *primary* characteristic (not only in fiction but also in life). Thus, characters may be ambitious or lazy, serene or anxious, aggressive or fearful, thoughtful or inconsiderate, open or secretive, confident or self-doubting, kind or cruel, quiet or noisy, visionary or practical, careful or careless, impartial or biased, straightforward or underhanded, "winners" or "losers," and so on.

With this sort of list, to which you may add at will, you can analyze and develop conclusions about character. For example, in studying Mathilde in Maupassant's "The Necklace," you would note that at the beginning she dreams of unattainable wealth and comfort, and that she is so swept up in her visions that she scorns her comparatively good life with her reliable but dull husband. It is fair to say that this aversion to reality is her major trait. It is also a major weakness, because Maupassant shows how her dream life harms her real life. By contrast, the narrator of Amy Lowell's poem "Patterns" considers the destruction of her hopes for happiness because of the news of her fiancé's death. Because she faces her difficulties directly, she exhibits strength. By similarly analyzing the actions, speeches, and thoughts in the characters you encounter, you can draw conclusions about their qualities and strengths.

DISTINGUISHING BETWEEN CIRCUMSTANCES AND TRAITS

When you study a fictional person, distinguish between circumstances and character, for circumstances have value *only if they demonstrate important traits*. Thus, if Sam wins a lottery, it is a fortunate circumstance; but the win does not say much about his character—not much, that is, unless we also learn that he has been spending hundreds of dollars each week for lottery tickets. In other words, making the effort to win a lottery *is* a character trait but winning (or losing) *is not*.

Or, let us suppose that an author stresses the neatness of one character and the sloppiness of another. If you accept the premise that people care for their appearance according to choice—and that choices indicate character—you can use these details to make conclusions about a person's self-esteem or the lack of it. In short, when reading about fictional characters, look beyond circumstances, actions, and appearances and *determine what these things show about character.* Always try to get from the outside to the inside, for it is the *internal* quality that determines the *external* behavior.

TYPES OF CHARACTERS: ROUND AND FLAT

No writer can present an entire life history of a protagonist, nor can each character in a story get "equal time" for development. Accordingly, some characters grow to be full and alive, while others remain shadowy. The British novelist and critic E. M. Forster, in his critical work *Aspects of the Novel,* calls the two major types "round" and "flat."

ROUND CHARACTERS. The basic trait of **round characters** is that they *recognize, change with,* or *adjust to* circumstances. The round character—usually the main figure in a story—profits from experience and undergoes a *change* or *alteration;* this may be shown in (1) an action or actions, (2) the realization of new strength and therefore the affirmation of previous decisions, (3) the acceptance of a new condition, or (4) the discovery of unrecognized truths.

Because a round character usually plays a major role in a story, he or she is often called the **hero** or **heroine.** Many main characters are anything but heroic, however, and it is therefore preferable to use the more neutral word **protagonist.** The protagonist is central to the action, moves against an **antagonist,** and exhibits the ability to adapt to new circumstances.

To the degree that round characters are both individual and sometimes unpredictable, and because they undergo change or growth, they are **dynamic.** Minnie Wright, in Glaspell's *Trifles,* is dynamic. We learn that as a young woman she was happy and musical, but she has been deprived and blighted by her marriage of thirty years. Finally, one outrageous action by her husband so enrages her that she breaks out of her subservient role and commits an act of violence. Her action shows her as a character undergoing radical, dynamic change.

FLAT CHARACTERS. In contrast, **flat characters** do not grow. They remain the same because they may be stupid or insensitive or lack knowledge or insight. They end where they begin and are **static,** not dynamic. Flat characters are not worthless, however, for they usually highlight the development of the round characters, as with the male characters in Glaspell's *Trifles.* Usually, flat characters are minor (e.g., relatives, acquaintances, functionaries), although not all minor characters are necessarily flat.

Sometimes flat characters are prominent in certain types of literature, such as in cowboy, police, and detective stories, where the focus is less on character than on performance. Such characters might be lively and engaging, even though they do not develop or change. They must be strong, tough, and clever enough to perform recurring tasks such as solving a crime, overcoming a villain, or finding a treasure. The term **stock character** refers to characters in these repeating situations. To the degree that stock characters have many common traits, they are **representative** of their class or group. Such characters, with variations in names, ages, and sexes, have been constant in literature since the ancient Greeks. Some regular stock characters are the insensitive father, the interfering mother, the sassy younger sister or brother, the greedy politician, the resourceful cowboy or detective, the overbearing or henpecked husband, the submissive or nagging wife, the angry police captain, the lovable drunk, and the town do-gooder.

Stock characters stay flat as long as they merely perform their roles and exhibit conventional and unindividual traits. When they possess no attitudes except those of their class, they are called **stereotype** characters, because they all seem to be cast from the same mold or printing matrix.

When authors bring characters into focus, however, no matter what roles they perform, they emerge from flatness and move into roundness. For example, though most of us would consider the character of a checkout clerk as flat, the clerk Sammy in Updike's "A & P," is a round, not flat, character: An incident at the checkout counter causes him to grow. Minnie Wright in *Trifles*, who has led an ordinary, dull, flat life for most of her years, breaks out of that role through a dynamic process. In sum, the ability to grow and develop and to be altered by circumstances makes characters round; absence of these traits makes characters flat.

HOW IS CHARACTER DISCLOSED IN LITERATURE?

Authors use five ways to present their characters. Remember that you must use your own knowledge and experience to make judgments about the qualities of the characters being revealed.

1. *Actions.* What characters *do* is our best way to understand what they *are.* For example, walking in the woods is recreation for most people, and it shows little about their characters. But Phoenix's walk through the woods (Welty's "A Worn Path") is difficult and dangerous for her. Her walk, seen within the context of her age and her mission, may be taken as an expression of a loving, responsible character.

Actions may also signal qualities such as naiveté, weakness, deceit, a scheming personality, strong inner conflicts, or a realization or growth of some sort. It is not even necessary that fictional characters immediately understand all the implications of their actions. Smirnov in *The Bear*, for example, would be crazy to teach Mrs. Popov to use her dueling pistol, because she has threatened to kill him with it. His change is his sudden realization that he loves her, and his cooperative if potentially self-destructive act shows that his loving nature has overwhelmed his basic instinct of self-preservation. Similarly, a strong inner conflict is seen in the two onstage women in Glaspell's *Trifles*. They have an obligation to the law, but they feel a stronger obligation to the accused killer, Minnie. Hence they remain silent about the incriminating evidence, an action showing their roundness and depth.

2. *Descriptions, both personal and environmental.* Appearance and environment reveal much about a character's social and economic status, of course, but they also tell us more about character traits. A desire for elegance is a trait of Mathilde in Maupassant's "The Necklace." Although her unrealizable taste is destructive, it also brings out her strength of character. In Updike's "A & P," the narrator Sammy devotes great care to the way in which he uses his cash register, and his own self-esteem is suggested by this care.

3. *Dramatic statements and thoughts.* Although the speeches of most characters are functional—essential to keep the action moving along—they provide material from which you can draw conclusions. When the second traveler of "Young Goodman Brown" speaks, for example, he reveals his devious and deceptive nature even though ostensibly he appears friendly. The three men in *Trifles* speak straightforwardly and directly, and these speeches suggest that their characters are similarly orderly. Their constant ridicule of the two women, however, indicates their limitations.

Often, characters use speech to hide their motives, though we as readers should see through such a ploy. The narrator Fortunato in "The Cask of Amontillado," for example, is a vengeful schemer, and we conclude this much from his indirect and manipulative language to the equally unpleasant but gullible Montresor. To Montresor, Fortunato seems friendly and sociable, but to us he is lurid and cynical.

4. *Statements by other characters.* By studying what characters say about each other, you can enhance your understanding of the character being discussed. Thus the two women talking about Phoenix's condition in "A Worn Path" tell us much about her difficult life, but more importantly they provide a basis for conclusions about Phoenix's great strength.

Ironically, the characters doing the talking often indicate something other than what they intend, perhaps because of prejudice, stupidity, or foolishness. Lengel's words about the young women in "A & P," for example, lead us to conclude that they have done nothing unusual by their informal appearance, but more importantly, Lengel also exposes his own rigidity and limited judgment.

5. *Statements by the author speaking as storyteller or observer.* What the author, speaking with the authorial voice, says about a character is usually accurate, and the authorial voice can be accepted factually. However, when

the authorial voice *interprets* actions and characteristics, as in Hawthorne's "Young Goodman Brown," the author himself or herself assumes the role of a reader or critic, and any opinions may be questioned. For this reason, authors frequently avoid interpretations and devote their skill to arranging events and speeches so that readers may draw their own conclusions.

REALITY AND PROBABILITY: VERISIMILITUDE

Characters in fiction should be true to life. That is, their actions, statements, and thoughts must all be what human beings are *likely* to do, say, and think under the conditions presented in the story. The standard is that of **verisimilitude, probability,** or **plausibility.** That is, there may be persons *in life* who perform tasks or exhibit characteristics that are difficult or seemingly impossible (such as always throwing the touchdown pass, getting A+'s on every test, always being cheerful and helpful, or always understanding the needs of others). Such characters *in fiction* would not be true to life, however, because they do not fit within *normal* or *usual* behavior.

One should therefore distinguish between what characters may *possibly* do and what they *most frequently* or *most usually* do. Thus, in "The Necklace," it is possible that Mathilde could be truthful and tell her friend Jeanne Forrestier about the lost necklace. In light of her pride, honor, and respectability, however, it is more in character for her and her husband to hide the loss, borrow money for a replacement, and endure the consequences for ten years. Granted the possibilities of the story (either self-sacrifice or the admission of a fault), the decision she makes with her husband is the more *probable* one.

Probability may also be consistent with exaggeration and surprise. The sudden and seemingly impossible changes concluding *The Bear*, for example, are not improbable because Chekhov early in the play shows that both Mrs. Popov and Smirnov are emotional, somewhat foolish, and impulsive. Even in the face of their unpredictable embraces closing the play, therefore, these qualities of character dominate their lives. For such individuals, surprise may be accepted as a probable condition of life.

There are many ways of rendering probability in character. Works that attempt to mirror life—realistic, naturalistic, or "slice of life" stories like Welty's "A Worn Path"—set up a pattern of everyday probability. Less realistic conditions establish different frameworks of probability, in which characters are *expected* to be unusual. Such an example is Hawthorne's "Young Goodman Brown." Because a major way of explaining this story is that Brown is having a nightmarish psychotic trance, his bizarre and unnatural responses are probable, just as Phoenix Jackson's speeches, influenced as they are by her approaching senility, are probable in "A Worn Path."

You might also encounter works containing *supernatural* figures, such as the second traveler in "Young Goodman Brown." You may wonder whether such characters are probable or improbable. Usually, gods and goddesses embody qualities of the best and most moral human beings, and devils like Hawthorne's guide take on attributes of the worst. However, you might remember that the devil is often given dashing and engaging qualities so that he may deceive gullible sinners and lead them into hell. The friendliness of Brown's guide is therefore not an improbable trait. In judging characters of this or any type, your best criteria are probability, consistency, and believability.

WRITING ABOUT CHARACTER

Usually you will write about a major character, although you might also study a minor character or characters. After your customary overview, begin taking notes. List as many traits as you can, and also determine how the author presents details about the character through actions, appearance, speeches, comments by others, or authorial explanations. If there are unusual traits, determine what they show. The following suggestions and questions will help you get started:

- Describe the importance of the character to the story's principal action. Is the character the protagonist or antagonist?
- How do the protagonist and antagonist interact with each other? How do their qualities produce reactions and changes?
- What actions bring out important traits of the character? To what degree is the character *creating* or just *responding* to events?
- Characterize the protagonist's actions: Are they good or bad, intelligent or stupid, deliberate or spontaneous? How do they help you understand the protagonist?
- Characterize the character's traits, both major and minor. To what extent do the traits permit you to judge the character? What is your judgment?
- What descriptions (if any) of the character's appearance do you discover in the story? What does the appearance demonstrate about the character?
- In what ways is the character's major trait a strength—or a weakness? As the story progresses, to what degree does the trait become more (or less) prominent?
- Is the character round (dynamic)? How does the character recognize, change with, or adjust to circumstances?
- If the character is minor (flat or static), what function does he or she perform in the story (for example, by doing a task or by bringing out qualities of the major character)?
- If a character is a stereotype, to what type does he or she belong? To what degree does the character stay in the stereotypical role or rise above it? How?
- What do any of the other characters do, say, or think to give you insight into the character? What does the character say or think about himself or herself? What

does the storyteller or narrator say? How valid are their comments and insights? How helpful in providing insights into the character?

- Is the character lifelike or unreal? Consistent or inconsistent? Believable or not believable?

Organizing Your Essay About Character

INTRODUCTION.   Identify the character you are studying and refer to noteworthy problems in determining this character's qualities. Use your central idea and thesis sentence to create the form for the body of your essay.

BODY.   Consider one of the following approaches to organize your ideas:

1. *Organization around central traits or major characteristics,* such as "unquestioning devotion and service" (Phoenix of "A Worn Path") or "the habit of seeing the world only on one's own terms" (Miss Brill of "Miss Brill"). This kind of structure would show how the work embodies the trait. For example, in one part a trait may be brought out through speeches that characters make about the major character (as at the end of Mansfield's "Miss Brill"), and in another part through that character's own speeches and actions. Studying the trait thus enables you to focus on the differing ways in which the author presents the character, and it also enables you to focus on separate parts of the work.

2. *Organization around a character's growth or change.* This type of essay describes a character's traits at the story's opening and then analyzes changes or developments. *It is important to stress the actual alterations as they emerge, but at the same time to avoid retelling the story.* Additionally, it is important not only to describe the changing traits but also to analyze how they are brought out within the work (such as the dream of Goodman Brown or Minnie Wright's long ordeal).

3. *Organization around central actions, objects, or quotations that reveal primary characteristics.* Key incidents may stand out, along with objects closely associated with the character being analyzed. There may be important quotations spoken by the character or by someone else in the work. Show how the elements you choose serve as signposts or guides to understanding the character. See the sample essay for an illustration of this type of development.

4. *Organization around qualities of a flat character or characters.* If the character is flat (such as the men in *Trifles* or the servants in *The Bear*), you might develop topics such as the function and relative significance of the character, the group the character represents, the relationship of the flat character to the round ones, the importance of this relationship, and any additional qualities or traits. For a flat character, you should explain the circumstances or defects that keep the character from being round and the importance of these shortcomings in the author's presentation of human character.

CONCLUSION. In the conclusion, show how the character's traits are related to the work as a whole. If the person was good but came to a bad end, does this misfortune make him or her seem especially worthy? If the person suffers, does this fact suggest any attitudes about the class or type of which he or she is a part? Or does it illustrate the author's general view of human life? Or both? Do the characteristics explain why the person helps or hinders other characters? How does your essay help in clearing up first-reading misunderstandings? These and similar questions are appropriate for your conclusion.

Sample Essay

The Character of Minnie Wright in Glaspell's Trifles °

[1] Minnie Wright is Susan Glaspell's major character in *Trifles*. We learn about her, however, not from seeing and hearing her, for she does not act or speak, but rather from the secondhand evidence provided by the major characters. Lewis Hale, the neighboring farmer, tells about Minnie's behavior on the morning when her husband, John, was found strangled in his bed. Mrs. Hale, Hale's wife, tells about Minnie's young womanhood and about how she became alienated from her nearest neighbors because of John's stingy and unfriendly ways. Both Mrs. Hale and Mrs. Peters, the Sheriff's wife, make observations about Minnie based on the condition of her kitchen. From this information we get a full portrait of Minnie, who has changed from passivity to destructive assertiveness.* Her change in character is indicated by her clothing, her dead canary, and her unfinished patchwork quilt.†

[2] The clothes that Minnie has worn in the past and in the present indicate her character as a person of charm who has withered under neglect and contempt. Martha mentions Minnie's attractive and colorful dresses as a young woman, even recalling a "white dress with blue ribbons" (speech 134). Martha also recalls that Minnie, when young, was "sweet and pretty, but kind of timid and—fluttery" (speech 107). In the light of these recollections, Martha observes that Minnie had changed, and changed for the worse, during her twenty years of marriage with John Wright, who is characterized as a "raw wind that gets to the bone" (speech 104). As more evidence for Minnie's acceptance of her drab life, Mrs. Peters says that Minnie asks for no more than an apron and shawl when under arrest in the sheriff's home. This modest clothing, as contrasted with the colorful dresses of her youth, suggests her suppression of spirit.

The end of this suppression of spirit and also the emergence of Minnie's rage are shown by the discovery of her dead canary. We learn that Minnie, who when young had been in love with music, has endured her cheerless farm home

---

°See pages 341–51 for this play.
*Central idea.
†Thesis sentence.

[3]
for thirty years. During this time her husband's contempt has made her life solitary, cheerless, unmusical, and depressingly impoverished. But her buying the canary (speech 87) suggests the reemergence of her love of song, just as it also suggests her growth toward self-assertion. That her husband wrings the bird's neck may thus be seen as the cause not only of immediate grief (shown by the dead bird in a "pretty box" (speech 109) but also of the anger that marks her change from a stock, obedient wife to a person angry enough to kill.

[4]
Like her love of song, her unfinished quilt indicates her creativity. In thirty years on the farm, never having had children, she has nothing creative to do except for needlework like the quilt. Mrs. Hale comments on the beauty of Minnie's log-cabin design (speech 72), and a stage direction draws attention to the pieces in the sewing basket (speech 71 S.D.). The inference is that even though Minnie's life has been bleak, she has been able to indulge her characteristic love of color and form—and also of warmth, granted the purpose of a quilt.

[5]
Ironically, the quilt also shows Minnie's creativity in the murder of her husband. Both Mrs. Hale and Mrs. Peters interpret the breakdown of her stitching on the quilt as signs of distress about the dead canary and also of her nervousness in planning revenge. Further, even though nowhere in the story is it said that John is strangled with a quilting knot, no other conclusion is possible. Both Mrs. Hale and Mrs. Peters agree that Minnie probably intended to knot the quilt rather than sew it in a quilt stitch, and Glaspell pointedly causes the men to learn this detail also, even though they scoff at it and ignore it. In other words, we learn that Minnie's only outlet for creativity—needlework—has enabled her to perform the murder in the only way she can, by strangling John with a slip-proof quilting knot. Even though her plan for the murder is deliberate (Mrs. Peters reports that the arrangement of the rope was "crafty" [speech 65]), Minnie is not cold or remorseless. Her passivity after the crime demonstrates that planning to evade guilt, beyond simple denial, is not in her character. She is not so diabolically creative that she plans or even understands the irony of strangling her husband (he killed the bird by wringing its neck). Glaspell, however, has made the irony plain.

[6]
It is important to emphasize again that we learn about Minnie from others. Nevertheless, Minnie is fully realized, round, and poignant. For the greater part of her adult life, she has patiently accepted her drab and colorless marriage even though it is so cruelly different from her youthful expectations. In the dreary surroundings of the Wright farm, she suppresses her grudges, just as she suppresses her prettiness, colorfulness, and creativity. In short, she had been nothing more than a flat character. The killing of the canary, however, causes her to change and to destroy her husband in an assertive rejection of her stock role as the suffering wife. She is a patient woman whose patience finally reaches the breaking point.

COMMENTARY ON THE ESSAY

The strategy of this essay is to use details from the play to support the central idea that Minnie Wright is a round, developing character. Hence the essay illustrates one of the types in the third approach described on page 68. Other plans of organization could also have been chosen, such as the qualities of acquiescence, fortitude, and potential for anger (first approach), the change in Minnie from submission to vengefulness (second approach), or the reported actions of Minnie's singing, knotting quilts, and sitting in the kitchen on the morning after the murder (another type of the third approach).

Because of the unusual fact that Minnie does not appear in the play, but is described only in the words of the major characters, the introductory paragraph deals with the way information is given about her. The essay thus highlights how Glaspell uses methods 2 and 4 (see pp. 64–66) as the ways of rendering the story's main character but omits methods 1 and 3.

The body of the essay is developed through inferences made from details in the story, namely Minnie's clothing (paragraph 2), her canary (paragraph 3), and her quilt (paragraphs 4 and 5). The last paragraph summarizes a number of these details, and it also considers how Minnie transcends the stock qualities of her role as a farm wife and gains roundness as a result of this outbreak.

As a study in composition, paragraph 3 demonstrates how a specific character trait, together with related details, may contribute to the essay's central idea. The trait is Minnie's love of music (shown by her canary). The connecting details, selected from study notes, are the loss of music in her life, her isolation, her lack of pretty clothing, the contemptibility of her husband, and her grief when putting the dead bird into the box. In short, the paragraph weaves together enough material to show the relationship between Minnie's trait of loving music and the crisis of her developing anger—a change that marks her as the round character described in the introductory paragraph.

SPECIAL WRITING TOPICS
ABOUT CHARACTER

1. Compare the ways in which actions (or speeches or the comments of others) are used to bring out the character traits of Miss Brill of "Miss Brill" and Sammy of "A & P."

2. Write a brief essay comparing the changes or developments of two major or *round* characters in stories or plays included in Appendix D. You might deal with issues such as what the characters are like at the beginning; what conflicts they confront, deal with, or avoid; or what qualities are brought out which signal the changes or developments.

3. Compare the qualities and functions of two or more *flat* characters (e.g., Lengel in "A & P," the men in *Trifles*, the attendants in "A Worn Path"). How do they bring out qualities of the major characters? What do you discover about their own character traits?

4. Topics for brief essays:
   a. What characteristics of the gardener are brought out by Marge Piercy in "A Work of Artifice"? Should the classifications "round" and "flat" even apply to him? Why or why not?

    b. Why does the narrator's father in Robert Hayden's "Those Winter Sundays" get up early on the weekend? What qualities of character does his action reveal?

    c. Consider this proposition: *To friends who haven't seen us for a time, we are round, but to ourselves and most other people, we are flat.*

5. Write a brief story about an important decision you have made (e.g., picking a school, beginning or leaving a job, declaring a major, or ending a friendship). Show how your own qualities of character (to the extent that you understand them), together with your own experiences, have gone into the decision. You may write more comfortably if you give yourself another name and describe your actions in the third person.

chapter 5

Writing About Point of View:
The Position or Stance
of the Work's Narrator
or Speaker

Point of view refers to the position and stance of the **voice** or **speaker** that authors adopt for their works. It supposes a living **narrator** or **persona** who tells stories, presents arguments, or expresses attitudes such as love, anger, or excitement. Practically, point of view involves the actual physical location of this speaker and his or her position to see and record the main actions and ideas. More abstractly and psychologically, point of view may be considered as the centralizing or guiding intelligence in a work—the mind that filters the fictional experience and presents only the most important details to create the maximum possible impact. It may also be considered as a way of seeing, the perspective into which the work of art is cast.

Bear in mind that authors try not only to make their works vital and interesting but also to bring their *presentations* alive. The situation is like that of actors performing a play: The actors are always themselves, but in their roles they *impersonate* the characters they act and temporarily *become* them.

Authors, too, impersonate characters who do the talking, with the difference that authors also create these impersonations, such as Sammy of Updike's "A & P" and the unnamed speaker of Hawthorne's "Young Goodman Brown." Thus Updike creates Sammy as a real person telling readers about an important event in his own life. We read Sammy's words, and we know that Sammy is a distinct though fictional character; but because Updike is the author we know that Updike is the one putting the words in Sammy's mouth. Unlike Sammy, Hawthorne's speaker is telling a story about someone else and is distant from the action and objective about it. Because of this distance the speaker is not easily separated from the author, even though the words we read may be different from those that Hawthorne himself might have chosen to use in his own person. In other words, the speaker is Hawthorne's authorial creation or impersonation for "Young Goodman Brown."

AN EXERCISE IN POINT OF VIEW:
REPORTING AN ACCIDENT

As an exercise to show that point of view is derived from lifelike situations, let us imagine that there has been an accident: Two cars, driven by Lucy and Evan, have collided, and the scene is as we see it in the drawing. How might this accident be reported by a number of people? What would Lucy say? What would Evan say?

Now assume that Michael, who is Evan's best friend, and Whitney, who knows neither Evan nor Lucy, were witnesses. What might Michael say about who was responsible? What might Whitney say? Additionally, assume that you are a reporter for a local newspaper and are sent to report on the accident. You know none of the people involved. How will your report differ from the other reports? Finally, to what degree are all the statements designed to persuade listeners and readers of the correctness of the details and claims made in the respective reports?

The differences in the various accident reports may be explained in terms of point of view. Obviously, because both Lucy and Evan are deeply involved—each of them is a major participant or what may be called a *major mover*—they will arrange their words to make themselves seem blameless. Michael, because he is Evan's best friend, will likely report things in Evan's favor. Whitney will favor neither Lucy nor Evan, but let us assume that she did not look at the colliding cars until she heard the crash; therefore her report will be restricted because she did not *actually see* everything. Most likely, *your* account as an impartial reporter will be the most reliable and objective of all, because your major interest is to learn all the details and report the truth accurately, with no concern about the personal interests of either Lucy or Evan.

Above all, however, each person's report will have the "hidden agenda" of making herself or himself seem honest, objective, intelligent, impartial, and thorough. The ramifications of telling a story are far-reaching, and the consideration of the various interests and situations can become quite subtle. Indeed, of all the aspects of literature, point of view is the most complex because it is so much like life itself. On the one hand, point of view is intertwined with the many interests and wishes of humanity at large; on the other hand, it is linked to the enormous difficulty of uncovering and determining truth.

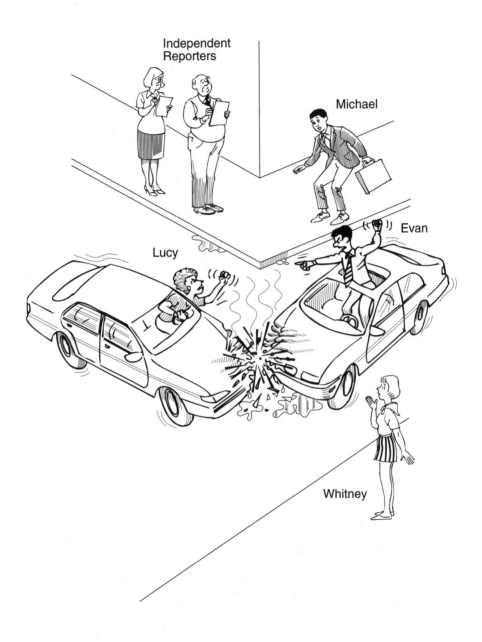

CONDITIONS THAT AFFECT
POINT OF VIEW

Point of view depends on two major factors. First is *the situation of the narrator as an observer*. How much is she or he privileged to know? How accurate and complete is his or her observation? What are the narrator's particular qualifications or limitations to be an observer or commentator? Second is *the narrator's closeness, distance, and involvement in the actions*. From what position, both physical and psychological, does the narrator observe the action? Are the narrator's words colored by any particular interest or direct involvement in the action itself or in the outcome? Does the narrator seem to have any persuasive purpose beyond serving as the recorder or observer?

In stories and many poems, the author develops point of view in light of these considerations. Amy Lowell's speaker in "Patterns" is a woman responding with sorrow and indignation to the news of her lover's death. Mansfield's speaker in "Miss Brill" is not the major character, but is so sympathetic with her that at times the identities of the speaker and major character merge. The speaker of Nye's "Where Children Live" is an objective observer who speaks with love and tenderness about memories of the spontaneous bumptiousness of children.

KINDS OF POINTS OF VIEW

In the various works you read you will encounter a wide variety of points of view. To begin your analysis, first determine the work's grammatical voice. Then, study the ways in which the subject, characterization, dialogue, and form interact with the point of view.

DISTINGUISH POINT OF VIEW FROM OPINION

Be careful to distinguish between *point of view* and *opinions* or *beliefs*. Point of view refers to the dramatic situation occasioning the speaking of a work, including language, audience, and perspective on events and characters (including tense), whereas an opinion is a thought about something. In examining point of view, then, you should draw conclusions about how the speaking situation of the work actually *creates* the work. Philosophical and religious opinions belong to the consideration of ideas but bear on point of view *only if they influence what the narrator says.*

First-Person Point of View

If the voice of the work is an "I," the author is using the **first-person point of view**—the impersonation of a fictional narrator or speaker. In our hypothetical accident, both Lucy and Evan are first-person speakers. In literature, Sammy of Updike's "A & P" and Fortunato of Poe's "The Cask of Amontillado" are also first-person speakers. In Twain's "Luck" there are two separate first-person speakers (the first "I" introduces the second "I").

First-person speakers might report events as though they have acquired their knowledge in a number of ways:

- What they have *done, said, heard,* and *thought* (first-hand experience).
- What they have *observed* others do and say (first-hand witness).
- What *others have told them* (second-hand testimony and hearsay).
- What they are able to *reconstruct* from the information they might have been able to find (*hypothetical* or *imaginative* information).
- What they are able to *imagine* a character or characters might do or think, given the situation.

Of all the points of view, the first person is potentially the most independent of the author, for such a speaker is often given a unique identity, with name, job, and economic and social positions (like Sammy). Just as often, however, the author creates a more anonymous but still independent first-person speaker, as with the unnamed speaker of Arnold's "Dover Beach."

When you encounter a first-person story or poem, determine the narrator's position and ability, prejudices or self-interest, and judgment of their readers or listeners. When first-person speakers describe their own experiences they have great authority and sometimes great power. Whatever their involvement, however, they are to be seen as one of the means by which authors create an authentic, life-like aura around their works.

Second-Person Point of View

The **second-person point of view,** the least common of the points of view, offers the writer two major possibilities. In the first, a narrator tells a present and involved listener what he or she has done and said at a past time. The actions might be a simple retelling of events, as when a parent tells a child about an action of the child during infancy or when a doctor tells a patient with amnesia about events before the causative injury. The actions might also be subject to dispute and interpretation, as when a prosecuting attorney describes a crime for which a defendant is on trial or when a spouse lists grievances against an alienated spouse in a custody or divorce case.

The second possibility is more complex. Some narrators seem to be addressing a "you" but are instead referring mainly to themselves, and to listeners only tangentially, in preference to an "I." In addition, some narrators follow the usage—common in colloquial speech—of the indefinite "you." In this kind of narration, speakers use "you" to refer not to a specific reader or listener but rather to anyone at all—in this way avoiding the more formal use of words like "one," "a person," or "people." (Incidentally, the selection of "you" is non-gender specific, because it eliminates the need for pronouns such as "he," "she," or "he or she.")

Third-Person Point of View

If events in the work are described in the third person (*he, she, it, they*), the author is using the **third-person point of view**. It is not always easy to characterize the voice in this point of view. Sometimes the speaker may use an "I" (as in Hayden's "Those Winter Sundays") and be seemingly identical with the author, but at other times the author may create a distinct **authorial voice,** as in Mansfield's "Miss Brill." There are three variants of the third-person point of view: *dramatic* or *objective, omniscient,* and *limited omniscient.*

DRAMATIC OR OBJECTIVE.   The most direct presentation of action and dialogue is the **dramatic** or **objective point of view** (also called **third-person objective**). It is the basic method of rendering action and speech that all the points of view share. The narrator of the dramatic point of view is an unidentified speaker who reports things in a way that is analogous to a hovering or tracking motion-picture camera or to what some critics have called "a fly on the wall (or tree)." Somehow, the narrator is always on the spot—within rooms, forests, village squares, moving vehicles, or even in outer space—to tell us what is happening and what is being said.

The dramatic presentation is limited only to what is said and what happens. There is no attempt to draw conclusions or make interpretations, because the presupposition underlying the dramatic point of view is that readers, like a jury, can form their own interpretations if they are given the right evidence. Thus Masefield's "Cargoes" objectively describes three different types of ships from three different periods of history. From these descriptions, we the readers are *invited* to draw a number of conclusions about how civilization has changed in the last 3000 years, but because of the dramatic point of view Masefield does not *state* any of these conclusions for us.

OMNISCIENT.   The third-person point of view is **omniscient** (all-knowing) when the speaker not only presents action and dialogue, but also is able to report what goes on in the minds of the characters. The real world does not permit us to *know* absolutely what other people are thinking. However, we are always making assumptions about the mental activities of others, and these assumptions are the basis of the omniscient point of view. Authors use it freely but judiciously to explain responses, thoughts, feelings, and plans—an additional dimension that aids in the development of character. For example, in Maupassant's "The Necklace," the speaker assumes omniscience to explain the responses and thoughts of the major character and, to a lesser degree, of her husband.

LIMITED, OR LIMITED OMNISCIENT.   More common than the omniscient point of view is the *limited third person,* or **limited omniscient third-person point of view,** in which the author confines or *limits* the narration to the actions and thoughts of a major character. In our accident case, Michael, being Evan's friend, would be sympathetic to Evan; thus his report of the collision would likely be third-person limited, with Evan as the center of interest. Depending on whether the narration focuses on action or motivation, the narrative may explore the mentalities of the characters either lightly or in depth. The name given to the central figure on whom the third-person omniscient point of view is focused is the **point-of-view character.** Thus, Miss Brill in "Miss Brill," Peyton Farquhar in "An Occurrence at Owl Creek Bridge," and Goodman Brown in "Young Goodman Brown" are all point-of-view characters. Virtually everything in these stories is there because the point-of-view characters see it, hear it, respond to it, think about it, imagine it entirely, do it or share in it, try to control it, or are controlled by it.

MINGLING POINTS OF VIEW

In some works, an author may shift the point of view in order to sustain interest, create suspense, or put the burden of response entirely upon readers. For example, Mansfield in "Miss Brill" interrupts the limited omniscient focus on Miss Brill's thoughts and reactions immediately after she is insulted. The last paragraphs are objective until the last sentence, when the limited omniscient point of view is resumed. The result is that Miss Brill is made totally alone in her grief, cut off; readers can no longer share her sorrow as they earlier shared her observations about the characters in the park. A similar shift occurs at the end of Hawthorne's "Young Goodman Brown," where the narrator objectively and almost brutally summarizes Brown's morose and loveless life after his nightmare about evil.

GUIDELINES FOR POINTS OF VIEW

The following guidelines summarize and further classify the types of points of view. Use them to distinguish differences and shades of variation in stories and poems.

1. **First person ("I" and "me").** First-person speakers are involved to at least some degree in the actions of the work. Such narrators may have (1) complete understanding, (2) partial or incorrect understanding, or (3) no understanding at all.

   a. *Major participant*
      i. Tells his or her own story and thoughts as a major mover.
      ii. Tells a story about others and also about herself or himself as one of the major movers.
      iii. Tells a story mainly about others, and about himself or herself only tangentially.
   b. *Minor participant,* tells a story about events experienced and witnessed.
   c. *Nonparticipating but identifiable speaker* who learns about events in other ways (e.g., listening to participants, examining documents, hearing news reports). The narrator tells the story as a report, or as a combination report and reconstruction.

POINT OF VIEW AND TENSE

Usually *point of view* refers to the ways narrators and speakers perceive and report actions and speeches. In the broadest sense, however, point of view may be considered as a total way of rendering truth, and for this reason the *tense* chosen by the narrators is important. In most narrations the *past tense* prevails: The actions happened in the past, and they are now over. It is important to note, however, that the inclusion of dialogue, even in a past-tense narrative, is a dramatic means of moving the story into the present. The dialogue concluding "The Necklace" performs such a function in that story. In addition, the narrator may emphasize the narrative's meaning—also a means of transferring tense from past to present. For example, the narrator of "Those Winter Sundays" concludes the poem with his own judgment about his father. In "Luck" the interior narrator makes many comments to accompany the story's past-tense narrative. As noted in Chapter 10, the narrators of *parables* and *fables* perceive past-tense stories as vehicles for teaching lessons in philosophy and religion.

In recent years, a number of writers have increasingly used the present tense as their principal time reference. With the present tense, the narrative aspect of the story or poem is rendered as a virtual drama, being unfolded moment by moment. In "Where Children Live," for instance, Nye employs the present tense to emphasize the constant interrelationship of children and the areas in which they play.

Some writers intermingle the present and past tenses to show how time itself may be merged within the human consciousness, or to show the fusion of past, present, and future within a character's mind. The intermingling of tenses may also demonstrate how that character perceives the social world, including the listeners and/or readers. For example, in Updike's "A & P," Sammy's mixing of tenses shows the vividness of his memory of events in the store (past), and it also shows his friendliness and informality (present).

2. **Second person ("you").** Occurs (a) when the speaker (e.g., parent, psychologist) knows more about a character's actions than the character himself or herself; or (b) when the speaker (e.g., lawyer, spouse, friend, sports umpire) is explaining to another person (the "you") that person's disputable actions and statements. The speaker may also use "you" to mean (c) himself or herself or (d) anyone at all.

3. **Third person ("she," "he," "it," "they").** The speaker is outside the action and is mainly a reporter of actions and speeches. Some speakers may have unique and distinguishing traits even though no separate identity is claimed for them ("the unnamed third-person narrator"). Other third-person speakers who are not separately identifiable may represent the words and views of the authors themselves ("the authorial voice").

   a. *Dramatic or third-person objective.* The narrator reports only what can be seen and heard. The thoughts of characters are included only if they are spoken or written (dialogue, reported or overheard conversation, letters, reports, etc.).

   b. *Omniscient.* The omniscient speaker sees all, reports all, knows all, and explains the inner workings of the minds of any or all characters (when necessary).

   c. *Limited, or limited omniscient.* The focus is on the actions, responses, thoughts, and feelings of a single major character. The narration may involve primarily what the character does, and it may also probe deeply within the consciousness of the character.

WRITING ABOUT POINT OF VIEW

Your goal is to explain how point of view contributes to making the work exactly as it is. In prewriting, therefore, consider language, authority, and opportunity for observation, the involvement or detachment of the speaker, the selection of detail, interpretive commentaries, and narrative development. The following questions will help you get started:

- How is the narration made to seem real and probable? Are the actions and speeches reported authentically, as they might be seen and reported in life? Is the narrator identifiable? What are the narrator's qualifications as an observer? How much of the story seems to result from the imaginative or creative powers of the narrator?

- How does the narrator perceive the time of the actions? If the predominant tense is the past, what relationship, if any, does the speaker establish between the past and the present (e.g., drawing lessons, providing explanations)? If the tense is present, what effect does this tense have on your understanding of the story?

- To what extent does the point of view make the work interesting and effective, or uninteresting and ineffective?

First-Person Point of View

- What situation prompts the speaker to tell the story or explain the situation? What is the speaker's background?

- Is the speaker talking to the reader, a listener, or herself? How does her audience affect what she is saying? Is the level of language appropriate to her and the situation? How much does she tell about herself?

- To what degree is the narrator involved in the action (i.e., as a major participant, minor participant, or nonparticipating observer)? Does he make himself the center of humor or admiration? How? Does he seem aware of changes he undergoes?

- Does the speaker criticize other characters? Why? Does she seem to report fairly and accurately what others have told her?

Second-Person Point of View

- What is the situation that prompts the use of the second person? How does the speaker acquire the authority to explain things to the listener? How directly involved is the listener? If the listeners are indefinite, why does the speaker choose "you" as the basis of the narration?

Third-Person Point of View

- Does the author seem to be speaking in an authorial voice, or has the author adopted a special but unnamed voice for the work?

- What is the speaker's level of language? Are actions, speeches, and explanations made fully or sparsely?

- From what apparent vantage point does the speaker report action and speeches? Does this vantage point make the characters seem distant or close? How much sympathy does the speaker express for the characters?

- To what degree is your interest centered on a particular character? Does the speaker give you thoughts and responses of this character (limited third person)?

- If the work is third-person omniscient, how extensive is this omniscience (e.g., all the characters or just a few)? Generally, what limitations or freedoms can be attributed to this point of view?

- What special kinds of knowledge does the narrator assume that the listeners or readers possess (e.g., art, religion, history, navigation, music)?

Organizing Your Essay About Point of View

INTRODUCTION.   Briefly state the major influence of the point of view on the work. (Examples: "The omniscient point of view permits many insights into the major character"; or "The first-person point of view permits the work to resemble an exposé of back-room political deals.") How does the point of view make the work interesting and effective? How will your analysis support your central idea?

BODY. Your object is to develop your analysis of how the point of view determines such aspects as situation, form, general content, and language. The questions in the preceding section will help you decide how the point of view interacts with these other elements.

An excellent way to strengthen your argument is to explore how some other point of view might affect the work you are considering. Hardy's poem "Channel Firing," for example, uses a first-person speaker—a skeleton long buried in a churchyard cemetery near the ocean. This speaker is awakened by the noise of nearby naval guns, a bizarre situation prompting ironic humor that could not be duplicated with a third-person point of view. The first-person point of view is essential because we learn, first hand, about the narrator's actual feelings. Indeed, the poem is totally dependent on this narrator. Conversely, Mansfield's "Miss Brill" employs the third-person limited point of view, with the speaker presenting an intimate portrait of the major character but also preserving an objective and ironic distance. If Miss Brill herself were the narrator, we would get the intimacy that encourages us to sympathize with her, but we would lose the distance which permits us to see her objectively.

You can see that this approach requires creative imagination, for you must speculate about a point of view that is not present. Considering alternative points of view deeply, however, will greatly enhance your analytical and critical abilities.

CONCLUSION. In your conclusion, evaluate the success of the point of view: Is it consistent, effective, truthful? What does the writer gain or lose (if anything) by the selection of point of view?

Sample Essay

Ambrose Bierce's Control Over Point of View in "An Occurrence at Owl Creek Bridge"°

[1] Ambrose Bierce's control over point of view in "An Occurrence at Owl Creek Bridge" is essential to his success in showing that people may perceive immense amounts of time in no more than an instant.* The story is based on the idea that it is the mind of the individual, not the actual passage of time, that governs perception of time. Ordinarily, time seems steady and unvarying, like the ticking of a clock (see paragraph 5 of the story); but at certain heightened instances of perception—in the story, the moment just before death—a person may fully imagine experiences that take immeasurably longer than the measurable, real time. Bierce brings this idea to life by using narrative told in the dramatic point of view to frame narrative told in the third-person limited omniscient point of view.†

[2] The story is framed, at both the opening and closing, by materials narrated from the dramatic point of view. The opening is an objective account of the story's basic circumstances: During the Civil War, Peyton Farquhar, a Southern loyalist, is about to be hanged by the Union army, apparently for the attempted sabotage of the railroad bridge spanning Owl Creek, a stream in northern Alabama. Bierce changes from the objective point of view in the fourth paragraph, and he then centers on Farquhar through the limited omniscient point of view. The second section of the story, which views Farquhar objectively, explains how Farquhar got to the point of hanging. Almost the entire third section—twenty descriptive paragraphs—focuses exclusively on Farquhar's last moments of life. Beginning with the reality of his drop, he perceives that the rope breaks and that he falls into the water, avoids the rifle and cannon fire of the Union soldiers, swims to shore, walks home, and is greeted by his wife. This dream of happiness is ended in paragraph 37, the last, which is an abrupt and brutal return to the dramatic point of view with which the story opens:

> Peyton Farquhar was dead; his body, with a broken neck, swung gently from side to side beneath the timbers of the Owl Creek bridge.

[3] The best part of the story, the "framed" part, is Bierce's use of a limited third-person narration to render Farquhar's mental perceptions. We first encounter this method in the narrator's ironic statement about Farquhar: "The arrangement [i.e., the apparatus for hanging] commended itself to his judgment as simple and effective" (paragraph 4). Bierce carefully explains how the rest of the story is to be told. First, he states that Farquhar's "thoughts, which have here to be set down in words, were flashed into the doomed man's brain" (paragraph 7). He also states that the hanging man's agony heightens his under-

---

°See pages 278–84 for this story.
*Central idea.
†Thesis sentence.

[3] standing: "something in the awful disturbance of his organic system" exalts and refines his physical senses so that they record things "never before perceived" (paragraph 20, underlining added). On this principle of narration, Bierce's narrator plumbs the depths of Farquhar's dying consciousness—an entire narrative of escape and return home that is flashed through Farquhar's mind during his last moments.

[4] The escape, which forms the narrative of the third section, seems to be happening plausibly and realistically just as both the reader (and Farquhar) want it to happen. The power of the story results from this tension between desire and actuality. Bierce's limited omniscient narrator is careful in the very second sentence of the third section to fuse together the two elements of time and perception so vital to the story's development: "ages later, it seemed to him" (paragraph18). All the details about Farquhar's dreams of escape stem out of the words ages and seemed. Under special circumstances, in other words, human perception can fit a small eternity into no more than a few moments.

[5] It is therefore the dying man's perception of detail that constitutes the major part of the story. At first, the narrator's descriptions indicate that Farquhar's imagination is fresh and sharp enough even to record the eye color of one of the Union soldiers. Farquhar's mind soon gets weaker, however, and his perceptions become more dreamlike and impressionistic. By describing the road bordered by "black bodies" of trees forming "a straight wall on both sides, terminating on the horizon in a point," Bierce's narrator demonstrates Farquhar's dimming consciousness and increasing distortion of reality (paragraph 34). Paragraph 36, which changes the narrative from the past to the present tense, contains Farquhar's vision during the last split second of his life. His final mental image is that his wife "steps down from the verandah to meet him," and "stands waiting" for him (present tenses underlined). It is then that his life is ended forever by the very realistic "blow upon the back of the neck."

[6] Even though the events are told through Farquhar's hopeful vision of escape, however, this realistic blow reminds us that the narrative constantly reveals his physical agony. A number of times we are told that Farquhar is feeling "pain," that he is "suffocating," that he feels a "sharp pain in his wrist" and that "his neck ached horribly; his brain was on fire" (paragraphs 18, 19, 35). We may take as equally real Farquhar's sensation that his "visible world" seems to be wheeling "slowly round" (paragraph 21), for this perception is consistent with the sensations of a hanging, dying man. In other words, just as the narrative concentrates on Farquhar's understanding of reality, it also demonstrates the true reality of his final death pangs.

[7] Without doubt, the merging of Bierce's narrative voice with the consciousness of the dying man makes the story unique. No other method could give the story its credibility and power, which depend on the disclosure of what is happening in the protagonist's mind. For example, the use of the dramatic point of view, with which the story opens and closes, does not permit access to the internal thoughts of a character. In much the same way, the first-person point of view—focusing on an unconscious and dying man—does not permit any recording of what is happening. It is therefore clear that Bierce's limited omniscient point of view is absolutely right. The method permits him to make the events seem both realistic and convincing and also to create sympathy for Farquhar because of his poignant hopes and dreams.

Such masterly control over point of view is a major cause of Bierce's success in "An Occurrence at Owl Creek Bridge." His narrative method is to establish a frame of normal reality and normal time, and then to render contrasting interior perceptions of perceived reality and perceived time. He is so successful

[8] that a casual reader might at first conclude that Farquhar's escape is real. The reality is not in the events, however, but in the perceptions. Without Bierce's mingling of the dramatic and the limited points of view, it would not be possible to claim such success for the story.

COMMENTARY ON THE ESSAY

The strategy of this essay is to explain how Bierce's use of the limited omniscient point of view is fundamental to his success in demonstrating how time may be compressed in heightened moments of awareness. Words of tribute throughout the essay are "success," "control," "dominating," "right," and "masterly."

The introductory paragraph sets out two major areas of investigation for the essay: first, the use of the dramatic point of view as a frame, and, second, the limited omniscient point of view as the center of concentration.

The first part of the essay (paragraph 2) is relatively brief. Only enough is brought out about the dramatic point of view to establish that Bierce uses it as a beginning and ending frame for the deep examination of the narration happening in the protagonist's mind.

The second part of the body (paragraphs 3–7) emphasizes how Bierce delves into the dying protagonist's mind. The goal of paragraphs 3–5 is to show how the narrator's point of view virtually merges with that of Farquhar. Paragraph 6 is designed as a defense of the narrative method because throughout the narration, Bierce always reports the immense pain that Farquhar is feeling. In other words, the story faithfully and truthfully renders the agony along with the imagination. Continuing the thread of the argument, paragraph 7 examines other narrative possibilities for presenting Farquhar's vision and concludes that Bierce's actual choices are the best that could have been made.

The concluding paragraph (8) emphasizes again how Bierce's success is attributable to his use of both the dramatic and the limited omniscient points of view.

WRITING TOPICS FOR POINT OF VIEW

1. Write a short narrative from the point of view of one of these characters:
   a. Mathilde Loisel in "The Necklace": *How I ruined ten years of my life by not telling the truth.*
   b. The baker in "Miss Brill": *My favorite customer.*
   c. Faith in "Young Goodman Brown": *I will never understand what happened to my husband.*
   d. Lengel in "A & P": *What could possibly have gotten into Sammy?*

2. How would the story "Young Goodman Brown" be affected if told by the narrators in "Luck," "A Worn Path," or "The Cask of Amontillado"?

3. Recall a childhood occasion on which you were punished. Write an explanation of the punishment as though you were the adult who was in the position of punishing you. Be sure to consider your childhood self objectively, in the third person. Present things from the viewpoint of the adult and try to determine how the adult would have learned about your action, judged it, and decided on your punishment.

4. Consider the proposition that people never speak without showing their motives, and that therefore we need to judge all things that we are told.

chapter 6

Writing About Setting:

The Background of Place, Objects, and Culture in Literature

Like all human beings, literary characters do not exist in isolation. Just as they become human by interacting with other characters, they gain identity because of their cultural and political allegiances, their possessions, their jobs, and where they live and move and have their being. Plays, stories, and narrative poems must therefore necessarily include descriptions of places, objects, and backgrounds—the **setting**.

WHAT IS SETTING?

Setting is the natural, manufactured, political, cultural, and temporal environment, including everything that characters know and own. Characters may be either helped or hurt by their surroundings, and they may fight about possessions and goals. Further, as characters speak with each other, they reveal the degree to which they share the customs and ideas of their times.

Types of Settings

NATURE AND THE OUTDOORS. The natural world is an obvious location for the action of many narratives and plays. It is therefore important to note natural surroundings (hills, shorelines, valleys, mountains, meadows, fields, trees, lakes, streams), living creatures (birds, dogs, horses, snakes), and also the times, seasons, and conditions in which things happen (morning or night, summer or winter, sunlight or darkness, heat or cold, fog, calm, wind, rain, snow, or storm)—any or all of which may influence character and action.

OBJECTS OF HUMAN MANUFACTURE AND CONSTRUCTION. To reveal or highlight qualities of character, and also to make literature lifelike, authors include many details about objects of human manufacture and construction. Houses, both interiors and exteriors, are common, as are possessions such as walking sticks, fences, park benches, toys, necklaces, hair ribbons, or cash registers. In Maupassant's "The Necklace," the loss of a comfortable home brings out the best in a character by causing her to adjust to her economic reversal. The lugubrious vaults in Poe's "The Cask of Amontillado" reveal the similarly lugubrious and sinister nature of Poe's narrator.

Objects also enter directly into fictional action and character. The wearing of bathing suits is a major cause of conflict in "A & P"; a broken birdcage reveals the pathetic husband–wife relationship in *Trifles*; a fur piece leads to heartbreak in "Miss Brill"; and Welty uses a bottle of medicine to represent the beauty of a character's love as well as the goal of her journey in "A Worn Path."

CULTURAL CONDITIONS AND ASSUMPTIONS. Just as physical setting influences characters, so do historical and cultural conditions and assumptions. In Chekhov's *The Bear*, for example, the action takes place on a relatively isolated nineteenth-century Russian estate, and the characters therefore see life in ways that are vastly different from our own. The broad cultural setting of Layton's poem "Rhine Boat Trip" brings out the contrast between the ugliness of atrocities in World War II and the beauty of German scenery and mythology. Piercy's "A Work of Artifice" builds up the contrast between women's right to freedom and their traditionally subordinate role.

THE LITERARY USES OF SETTING

Just as painters include backgrounds and objects to render ideas, authors use setting to create statement and meaning. For example, in Welty's "A Worn Path" and Hawthorne's "Young Goodman Brown," woodland paths that are difficult to trace and filled with obstacles are a major topographical feature. These are central to the time and circumstances of the stories, but they also convey the idea that life is difficult and uncertain. Similarly, in Glaspell's *Trifles*, the fixtures and utensils in the kitchen of the Wright farm indicate that midwestern homesteads early in the twentieth century were bleak and oppressive.

Important Purposes of Setting

To study the setting in a narrative or play, discover the important details and then try to explain their function. Depending on the author's purpose, the amount of detail may vary. Poe provides many graphic and also impressionistic details in "The Cask of Amontillado," so that we may follow, almost visually, the bizarre action at the story's end. In some works the setting is so intensely present, like the woods in Welty's "A Worn Path," that it is almost literally an additional participant in the action.

SETTING AND CREDIBILITY.   One of the major purposes of literary setting is to establish **realism,** or **verisimilitude.** As the description of location and objects becomes particular and detailed, the events of the work become more believable. Langston Hughes locates the speaker of "Theme for English B" in the area near Columbia University in New York City, and for this reason the speaker's assertions have a close connection with the real world. Even futuristic, symbolic, and fantastic stories, as well as ghost stories, seem more believable if they include places and objects from everyday experience. Hawthorne's "Young Goodman Brown" and Poe's "The Cask of Amontillado" are such stories. Though they make no pretenses at everyday realism, their credibility is enhanced because their settings are so realistic.

SETTING AND CHARACTER.   Setting may intersect with character as a means by which authors underscore the importance of place, circumstance, and time on human growth and change. Glaspell's setting in *Trifles* is the kitchen of the lonely, dreary Wright farm. The kitchen is a place of such hard work, oppression, and unrelieved joylessness that it explains the extinguishing of Minnie's early brightness and promise and also helps us understand her angry act. (A blending of setting and character as seen in Maupassant's "The Necklace" is explored in the two drafts of the sample essay in Chapter 1.)

The way characters respond and adjust to setting can reveal their strength or weakness. Peyton Farquhar's scheme to make an escape from his fate, even when it is almost literally hanging before him, suggests his character strength ("An Occurrence at Owl Creek Bridge"). In contrast, Goodman Brown's Calvinistic religious conviction that human beings are totally depraved, which not reality but his nightmarish encounter confirms, indicates the weakness of his character because it alienates him from family and community ("Young Goodman Brown").

SETTING AND ORGANIZATION.   Authors often use setting to organize the story, as in Maupassant's "The Necklace" where Mathilde and her husband move from a respectable apartment to a cheap attic flat. The story's final scene is believable because Mathilde takes a nostalgic walk on the Champs Elysées, the most fashionable street in Paris. Without this shift of setting, she could not have encountered Jeanne Forrestier again, for their usual ways of life would no longer bring them together.

Another organizational application of place, time, and object is the **framing** or **enclosing setting**, when an author opens with a particular description and then returns to the same setting at the end. An example is Welty's "A Worn Path," which begins with the major character walking toward Natchez and ends with her walking away from it. The use of objects as a frame may be seen in Mansfield's "Miss Brill," which opens and closes with references to the heroine's shabby fur piece. In such ways, framing creates a formal completeness, just as it may underscore the author's ideas about the human condition.

SETTING AND SYMBOL   If the scenes and materials of setting are highlighted or emphasized, they also may be taken as symbols through which the author expresses ideas. The horse Toby in Chekhov's *The Bear* is such a symbol. Mrs. Popov has made caring for the horse, which was her dead husband's favorite, a major part of her memorial obligations. When Mrs. Popov tells the servants not to give oats to the horse, Chekhov is using this ordinary barnyard animal to indicate that new commitments replace old ones. In Updike's "A & P," the reference to the local Congregational church symbolizes the decorum and restraint that the people of the town—including those shopping at the A & P—are expected to exercise.

SETTING AND ATMOSPHERE.   Setting also helps to create **atmosphere** or **mood.** Most actions *require* no more than a functional description of setting. Thus, taking a walk in a forest needs just the statement that there are trees. However, if you find descriptions of shapes, light and shadows, animals, wind, and sounds, you may be sure that the author is creating an atmosphere or mood for the action (as in Hawthorne's "Young Goodman Brown"). There are many ways to develop moods. Descriptions of bright colors (red, orange, yellow) may contribute to a mood of happiness. Darkness and dark colors, like those in Poe's "The Cask of Amontillado," may invoke gloom or augment hysteria. References to smells and sounds further bring the setting to life by asking additional sensory responses from the reader. The setting of a story in a small town or large city, in green or snow-covered fields, or in middle-class or lower-class residences may evoke responses to these places that contribute to the work's atmosphere.

SETTING AND IRONY.   Just as setting may reinforce character and theme, so it may establish expectations that are the opposite of what occurs. The lovely, orderly garden described in Lowell's "Patterns," for example, is an ironic background for the speaker's deep anguish and grief. A bizarre situation is created by Hardy in "Channel Firing" when the noise of large guns at sea wakens the skeletons buried in an English churchyard. The irony is that those engaged in the gunnery practice, if "red war" gets still redder, will soon join the skeletons.

WRITING ABOUT SETTING

In preparing to write about setting, determine the number and importance of locations, artifacts, and customs. Ask questions such as the following:

- How extensive are the visual descriptions? Does the author provide such vivid and carefully arranged detail about surroundings that you could draw a map or plan? Or is the scenery vague and difficult to imagine?

- What connections, if any, are apparent between locations and characters? Do the locations bring characters together, separate them, facilitate their privacy, make intimacy and conversation difficult?

- How fully are objects described? How vital are they to the action? How important are they in the development of the plot or idea? How are they connected to the mental states of the characters?

- How important to plot and character are shapes, colors, times of day, clouds, storms, light and sun, seasons of the year, and conditions of vegetation?

- Are the characters poor, moderately well off, or rich? How does their economic condition affect their actions and attitudes? How does their economic lot determine what happens to them?

- What cultural, religious, and political conditions are assumed in the story? How do the characters accept and adjust to these conditions? How do the conditions affect the characters' judgments and actions?

- What is the state of houses, furniture, and objects (e.g., new and polished, old and worn)? What connections can you find between this condition and the outlook and behavior of the characters?

- How important are sounds or silences? To what degree is music or other sound important in the development of character and action?

- Do characters respect or mistreat the environment? If there is an environmental connection, how central is it to the story?

- What conclusions do you think the author expects you to draw as a result of the neighborhood, culture, and larger world of the story?

Organizing Your Essay About Setting

INTRODUCTION. The introduction should contain a brief description of the setting or scenes of the work, specifying the amount and importance of detail.

BODY. Following are five possible approaches to essays on setting. Choose one that seems most appropriate, bearing in mind that some works invite one approach rather than others. As you develop your essay, however, you may find it necessary to introduce one or more of the other approaches. Whatever approach you use, be sure to consider setting not as an end in itself, but rather as illustration and evidence.

1. *Setting and Action.* Explore the importance of setting in the work. How extensively is the setting described? Are locations essential or incidental to the actions? Does the setting serve as part of the action (e.g., places of flight or concealment; public places where people meet openly, or hidden places where they meet privately; natural or environmental conditions; seasonal conditions such as searing heat or numbing cold; customs and conventions)? Do any objects cause inspiration, difficulty, or conflict (for example, a bridge, a cellar, a fur piece, a walking stick, a necklace, a nickel, a hair ribbon, a toy windmill, a dead bird)? How directly do these objects influence the action?

2. *Setting and Organization.* How is the setting connected to the various parts of the work? Does it undergo any changes as the action develops? Why are some parts of the setting more important than others? Is the setting used as a structural frame or enclosure for the story? How do objects, such as money or property, affect the motivation of the characters? How do descriptions made at the start become important in the action later on?

3. *Setting and Character.* (For examples of this approach, see the two drafts of the sample essay in Chapter 1.) Analyze the degree to which setting influences and interacts with character. Are the characters happy or unhappy where they live? Do they get into discussions or arguments about their home environments? Do they want to stay or leave? Do the economic, philosophical, religious, or ethnic aspects of the setting make the characters undergo changes? What jobs do the characters perform because of their ways of life? What freedoms or restraints do these jobs cause? How does the setting influence their decisions, transportation, speech habits, eating habits, attitudes about love and honor, and general behavior?

4. *Setting and Atmosphere.* To what extent does setting contribute to mood? Does the setting go beyond the minimum needed for action or character? How do descriptive words paint verbal pictures and evoke moods through references to colors, shapes, sounds, smells, or tastes? Does the setting establish a mood, say, of joy or hopelessness, plenty or scarcity? Do events happen in daylight or at night? Do the movements and locations of the characters suggest permanence or impermanence (like the return to a darkened room, the creation of a brick wall, or the purchase of a fragile toy)? Are things warm and pleasant, or cold and harsh? What connection do you find between the atmosphere and the author's thoughts about existence?

5. *Setting and Other Aspects.* Does setting reinforce the story's credibility and meaning? Does it establish irony about the circumstances and ideas in the story? If you choose this approach, consult the earlier sections of this chapter, (the introductory paragraph on "The Literary Uses of Setting," "Setting and Credibility," and "Setting and Irony." If you want to write about the symbolic implications of a setting, consult the discussions of symbolism in Chapter 10.

CONCLUSION.   To conclude, summarize your major points or write about related aspects of setting that you have not considered. Thus, if your essay treats the relationship of setting and action, your conclusion could mention connections of the setting with character or atmosphere. You might also point out whether your central idea about setting also applies to other major aspects of the story.

Sample Essay

Poe's Use of Setting to Create a Mood of Horror and Repulsion in "The Cask of Amontillado"°

---

[1]
In "The Cask of Amontillado," Edgar Allan Poe uses many details of setting to create a mood of horror and repulsion.* The story is a detailed narration of an act of premeditated and ghastly vengeance. Poe's character Montresor is both the narrator and the principal creator of the twisted act of murder. He believes that his vengeance must be known by the victim, Fortunato, and that it must be threatening and irrevocable. At the end he is successful, and the reader is both fascinated and repulsed by the story's mood of ghastliness and heartlessness. The mood is established through Poe's descriptions of underground rooms, space, and sound.†

[2]
The height of Poe's graphic description is the story's evocation of gloomy and threatening vaults. The journey into the hellish "catacombs of the Montresors" (paragraph 25), which are also the area for the storage of Montresor's wine collection, ends with a room "lined with human remains, piled to the vault overhead" (paragraph 68). The walls in the rooms leading to this last, horrible room are dark and damp, and they drip moisture from the river above; they also become increasingly airless and suffocating. The bones on the walls and floors are evidence of generations of death. In addition, Montresor uses the bones first to hide his bricks and mortar and then to disguise the wall within which he entombs Fortunato. The mood is further fixed by the narrator's observations that each of the catacomb rooms is progressively more covered and shrouded by spiderlike white and ghostly films of nitre, which gloomily suggest increasing death and decay.

[3]
The most disturbing of the catacomb rooms is the last one, the "interior recess" that is to be Fortunato's vertical grave. It is an inauspicious area, which Poe indicates was built "for no especial use within itself" (paragraph 68), but its dimensions are ominous. It is no accident that Poe gives us the exact size of the recess. It is four feet deep, three feet wide, and 6 or 7 feet high—exactly the size of a large coffin standing on end. The failure of the faltering torches to illuminate the area suggests the ending of breath and light, and the beginning of death. What could be more appropriately sinister, distressing, and ghostly?

°See pages 297–30 for this story.
*Central idea.
†Thesis sentence.

[4] <u>The rooms not only provoke horror, but they are spatially arranged to complement Montresor's horrible act of vengeance</u>. To reach these increasingly dark areas, the characters must continually walk downward. A circular staircase begins the descent, followed by a first and then a second set of stairs that end in the last deep crypt. The downward direction is like an inevitable journey toward the grave, and it also suggests a journey into a bleak, cold, dark, and damp hell.

[5] <u>Within this interior of death, Poe adds the eeriness of fearsome sound</u>. Fortunato has a terrible rasping cough, to which Poe devotes an entire paragraph (paragraph 32). The jingling of the bells on Fortunatos's carnival cap appears at first ordinary (paragraph 26), then bizarre (paragraph 40), and finally sepulchral (paragraph 89). Fortunato's attempt to get free of the chains results in desperate clanking (paragraph 76). He also moans (paragraph 76), laughs in fear and disbelief (paragraph 78), speaks weakly and sadly (paragraph 78), and at the end is silent (paragraph 89). Perhaps the most grisly sounds described by Poe are those of Fortunato's screams of protest, which Montresor cruelly stifles by screaming even louder and longer (paragraph 77)—an action that was duplicated for the insane man in the film <u>The Silence of the Lambs.</u> These described sounds, having their source in Montresor's diabolical action, create a mood of uneasiness, anxiety, repulsion, and horror.

[6] Thus Poe's setting within the eerie catacombs is both descriptive and evocative. The major action takes place in the last room, in the gravelike recess, leading to the climax of the story's movement into darkness and the very walls of death. <u>In this way, Poe uses his setting to show the horror of a twisted mind prompting a diseased individual to create a cruel and pitiless act of revenge</u>. The events of the story, the sustained mood, and the narrator's compulsion for vengeance are all tied together by Poe's masterly control of setting.

COMMENTARY ON THE ESSAY

Because it treats the relationship of setting to mood or atmosphere, this essay illustrates the fourth approach described on page 93. The essay considers those aspects of setting needed for the story and then stresses how Poe's descriptions create the story's dominant mood of horror and repulsion.

In the body, paragraphs 2 and 3 form a unit describing the physical layout of the deathly catacombs, and they also point out both the exactness and evocativeness of Poe's descriptions. Paragraph 4 concentrates on Poe's description of downward movement, suggesting that this use of space is a visual accompaniment of the story's conclusion in Fortunato's death.

Paragraph 5 treats Poe's use of sound as an accompaniment to the descriptions of the deadly catacombs. The paragraph's topic idea is that the sounds move progressively toward silence, in keeping with Montresor's creation of death. The sounds are therefore one of Poe's major means of achieving an atmosphere complementary to the repulsive and horrible action.

The conclusion summarizes the central idea, stressing once again that

Poe goes beyond simple description to heighten the twisted, macabre mood of his story.

SPECIAL WRITING TOPICS FOR SETTING

1. Compare and contrast how details of setting are used to establish the qualities and traits of the following characters: Mrs. Popov of *The Bear*, Miss Brill of "Miss Brill," the speakers of "Patterns" or "Theme for English B," or Montresor of "The Cask of Amontillado."

2. Write a short narrative for possible inclusion in a longer story (which you may also wish to write for the assignment), using option *a* and/or *b*.

   a. Relate a natural setting or type of day to a mood—for example, a nice day to happiness and satisfaction or a cold, cloudy, rainy day to sadness. Or create irony by relating the nice day to sadness or the terrible day to happiness.

   b. Indicate how an object or circumstance causes the principal conflict and action in a story or play (such as the bathing suits in "A & P," the medicine in "A Worn Path," the lost necklace in "The Necklace," the dead canary in *Trifles*, or the trip through the forest in "Young Goodman Brown."

3. Choose a story in Appendix D and, first, rewrite several pages, taking the characters out of their setting and placing them in the setting of another story or in an entirely new setting. Then, write an essay dealing with these questions: How were your characters affected by their new settings? Did you make them change slowly or rapidly? Why? As a result of your rewriting, what can you conclude about the uses of setting in literature?

chapter 7

Writing About an Idea or Theme:

The Meaning and the Message in Literature

The word **idea** refers to the result or results of general and abstract thinking. Synonymous words are *concept, thought, opinion,* and *principle.* In literary study the consideration of ideas relates to *meaning, interpretation, explanation,* and *significance.* Though ideas are usually extensive and complex, separate ideas may be named by a single word, such as *justice, right, good, love, piety, causation,* and, not unsurprisingly, *idea* itself.

IDEAS AND ASSERTIONS

Although a single word may name an idea, it does not operate as an idea until it is put into a sentence or assertion. In other words, an idea needs a subject and a predicate before we can use it as a basis of understanding. It is important to recognize that an assertion of an idea is not the same as an ordinary sentence, such as "It's a nice day." This observation may be true (depending on the weather), but it cannot be called an *idea*. Rather, an idea should indicate *thought* about the day's quality, such as "A nice day requires blue sky and a warm sun." Because this sentence deals with an assertion about "nice," it lends itself to the consideration of the idea of a nice day.

In studying literature, always phrase ideas as assertions. For example, you might claim that an idea in Chekhov's *The Bear* is "love," but it would be difficult to write anything more unless you make an assertion such as *"The*

Bear demonstrates the idea that love is irresistible and irrational." This assertion would lead you to explain the unlikely love that bursts out in the play.
Similarly, for Eudora Welty's "A Worn Path" you might make the following
assertion: "Phoenix embodies the idea that caring for others gives no reward
but the continuation of the duty itself."

Although we have noted only one idea in these stories, there are usually many separate ideas. When one of the ideas seems to be the major one, it
is called the **theme.** In practice, the words *theme* and *major idea* are the same.

IDEAS AND VALUES

Literature embodies **values** along with ideas. This means that ideas are presented along with the expression or implication that certain conditions and
standards should be—or should not be—highly valued. For example, the *idea
of justice* may be considered abstractly and broadly, as Plato does in his *Repub-
lic* when developing his concept of a just government. In comparison, justice
is also considered by Langston Hughes in "Theme for English B"; Hughes is
not abstract and speculative, like Plato, but rather personal. Hughes's idea is
that human beings are equal regardless of race, and he asserts the need for
equal treatment by showing that his young African-American speaker shares
many traits with other human beings. In short, to talk about Hughes's idea is
also to talk about his values. Another poem dealing with justice is Lowell's
"Patterns," in which the speaker, in despair because of her lover's death in
battle, questions the justice of "the pattern called war." Lowell's values clearly
place individual lives above the politics of state warfare.

THE PLACE OF IDEAS IN LITERATURE

Because writers of poems, plays, and stories are usually not systematic
philosophers, it would be a mistake to go "message hunting" as though their
works contained nothing but ideas. Indeed, there is great benefit and pleasure
to be derived from just savoring a work, from being taken up in the developing pattern of narrative and conflict, from following its implications and suggestions, and from listening to the sounds of its words—to name only a few
of the reasons for which literature is treasured.

Nevertheless, ideas are vital to understanding and appreciating literature: Writers have ideas and want to communicate them. For example, in *The
Bear* Chekhov's purpose is to make his audience laugh at two unlikely people suddenly falling in love. The play is funny, however, not only because it
is preposterous, but also because it is based on the *idea* that love takes prece-
dence over other resolutions that people might make. Eudora Welty in "A
Worn Path" tells the poignant *story* of an aging woman on a hopeless quest,

but the story embodies *ideas* about the strength of human character and the beauty of human kindness.

Distinguishing Between Ideas and Actions

As you analyze works for ideas, it is important to avoid the trap of confusing ideas and actions. Such a trap is contained in the following sentence about Updike's story "A & P": "The major character, Sammy, quits his job to protest the way his boss mistreats the girls." This sentence successfully describes the story's major action, but it does not express an *idea* that connects characters and events, and for this reason it obstructs understanding. Some possible connections might be achieved with sentences like these: "'A & P' illustrates the idea that making a protest also makes life hard," or "'A & P' demonstrates that individual rights are more important than arbitrary regulations." A study based on these connecting formulations could be focused on ideas and would not be sidetracked into doing no more than retelling Updike's story.

Distinguishing Between Ideas and Situations

You should also distinguish between ideas and situations. For example, in Lowell's "Patterns" the narrator describes what is happening to her as a result of her fiancé's death. This is a *situation*, but it is not any of the *ideas* brought out by the situation. For example, one of the poem's major ideas is that future plans may be destroyed by uncontrollable circumstances. In such ways, if you try to distinguish a work's various situations from the writer's major idea or ideas, you will be able to focus on ideas and therefore sharpen your own thinking.

HOW TO FIND IDEAS

Ideas are not as obvious as characters or setting. To determine an idea, you need to consider the meaning of what you read, and then develop explanatory and comprehensive assertions. Your assertions need not be the same as those that others might make. People notice different things, and individual formulations vary. A study of Hughes's "Theme for English B" might produce any of the following ideas: (1) Young people are ambitious, regardless of color. (2) Similarities in taste demonstrate the similarity of persons of all races. (3) Despite many breakdowns of color barriers, whites are still freer than blacks. (4) People become human through common experiences. In discovering ideas, you should follow a similar process—making a number of formulations for an idea and then selecting one for further development.

As you read, be alert to the different ways in which authors present ideas. One author might prefer an indirect way through a character's speeches, and another may prefer direct statements. In practice, authors may employ any or all of the following methods.

Direct Statements by the Authorial Voice

Although authors mainly render action, dialogue, and situation, they sometimes state ideas to guide us and deepen our understanding. In the second paragraph of "The Necklace," for example, Maupassant's authorial voice presents the idea that women have only charm and beauty to get on in the world. Ironically, however, Maupassant uses the story to show that for the major character Mathilde, nothing is effective, for her charm cannot prevent disaster. Another example is Shakespeare's authorial voice in "Let Me Not to the Marriage of True Minds," which states that true love is always constant and supportive.

Direct Statements by the First-Person Speaker

First-person narrators or speakers frequently express ideas along with their depiction of actions and situations. (See also Chapter 5.) Because their ideas are part of a dramatic presentation, they may be right or wrong, well considered or thoughtless, or brilliant or half-baked, depending on the speaker. At the beginning of Poe's "The Cask of Amontillado," for example, the narrator provides ideas about the nature of personal revenge. Relatively unconsidered ideas are expressed by Sammy, the narrator of Updike's "A & P," who seems engulfed in intellectual commonplaces, particularly in his insinuation about the intelligence of women (paragraph 2). In his defense, however, Sammy *acts* upon the worthy idea that people generally have the right to dress any way they please.

Dramatic Statements Made by Characters

In many stories, characters express their own views, which may be right or wrong, admirable or contemptible. When you consider such dramatic speeches, you must do considerable interpreting and evaluating yourself. For example, in Chekhov's *The Bear*, both Smirnov and Mrs. Popov express many silly ideas as they begin speaking to each other, and it is their sudden love that reveals to them how wrong-headed their ideas have been. The men in Glaspell's *Trifles* express conventional masculine ideas about the need for men to control women ("a sheriff's wife is married to the law" [speech 143]).

The play itself, however, demonstrates both the shortcomings and pompousness of their thought.

Figurative Language

Figurative language is one of the major components of poetry. In the poem "Bright Star," for example, Keats symbolizes the idea of constancy with his references to a fixed star, presumably the North Star. Writers of fiction and drama also freely use figurative language. At the opening of "Miss Brill," Mansfield's narrator compares a sunny day to gold and white wine—a lovely comparison conveying the idea that the world is a place of beauty and happiness—an idea that contrasts ironically with the indifference and cruelty that Miss Brill experiences. In Glaspell's *Trifles*, a character compares John Wright, the murdered man, to "a raw wind that gets to the bone" (speech 103). With this figurative language, Glaspell conveys the idea that bluntness, indifference, and cruelty create great personal damage.

Characters Who Stand for Ideas

Characters and their actions may often be equated with certain ideas and values. The power of Mathilde's story in "The Necklace," for example, causes her to stand for the idea that unrealizable dreams may invade and damage the real world. Two diverse or opposed characters may embody contrasting ideas, as with Sammy and Lengel of Updike's "A & P," who stand for opposing views about rights of expression.

In effect, characters who stand for ideas may assume symbolic status, as in Hawthorne's "Young Goodman Brown," where the protagonist symbolizes the alienation accompanying zealousness. The speaker of Frost's "Desert Places" invites identification as a symbol of the frightening qualities of emptiness and unconcern within individual human beings. In such ways, characters may be equated directly with particular ideas, and to talk about them is a shorthand way of talking about the ideas.

The Work Itself as It Represents Ideas

One of the most important ways in which authors express ideas is to interlock them within all parts and aspects of the work. The art of painting is instructive here, for a painting may be taken in with a single view that comprehends all the aspects of color, form, action, and expression, which may also be considered separately. In the same way, when a work is considered in its totality, the various parts collectively may embody a major idea. For example, in "Theme for English B," Hughes makes objective the idea that the urgency of ending racial barriers overrides the socially convenient reasons for which they have been established. The entire third section of Bierce's "An Occurrence at Owl Creek Bridge" is postulated on the idea that under stressful conditions the human mind operates with lightning speed. Most works represent ideas in a similar way. Even "escape literature," which ostensibly enables readers to forget their immediate concerns, contains conflicts between good and evil, love and hate, good spies and bad, earthlings and aliens, and so on. Thereby, such stories *do* embody ideas, even though their avowed intention is not to make readers think but rather to help them forget.

WRITING ABOUT A MAJOR IDEA IN LITERATURE

Most likely you will write about a major idea or theme, but you may also get interested in one of your story's other ideas. As you begin brainstorming and developing your first drafts, consider questions such as the following:

- How do you discover ideas in the work? Through action? Character depiction? Scenes? Particularly effective language? How compelling are the ideas? Could the work be appreciated without reference to any ideas at all?
- Is the idea asserted directly, indirectly, dramatically, ironically? Does any one method predominate? Why?
- Which characters in their own right represent ideas? What ideas are brought out by what these characters do?
- To what do the ideas pertain? Individuals and their emotional and private lives? Social concerns? Social justice? Political justice? Economic justice? The condition of religion?
- Are the ideas limited to members of the groups represented by the characters (age, social group, race, nationality, personal status)? Or are they applicable to general conditions of life? Explain.
- If characters express ideas, how effective are they? How intelligent and well considered do the ideas seem? How germane to the story are the ideas? How germane to more general conditions?
- With children, young adults, or the old, how can their circumstances reveal an idea?
- How pervasive in the story is the idea (throughout for a major idea, intermittently, or just once for a secondary idea)?
- How balanced are the ideas? If a particular idea is strongly presented, what conditions and qualifications are also presented (if any)? What contradictory ideas are presented?
- What value or values are embodied in the idea? Of what importance are the values to the story's meaning?

Organizing Your Essay About Idea or Theme

Remember that in well-written stories, poems, and plays, narrative and dramatic elements have a strong bearing on ideas. In this sense, an idea is like a key in music or like a continuous thread tying together actions, characters, statements, symbols, and dialogue. As readers, we can trace such threads throughout the entire fabric of the work.

As you write about ideas, you may find yourself relying most heavily on the direct statements of the authorial voice or on a combination of these and your interpretation of characters and action, or you might focus exclusively on a first-person speaker and use his or her ideas to develop your analysis. Always make clear the sources of your details and distinguish the sources from your own commentary.

INTRODUCTION.   In your introduction you might state any special circumstances in the work that affect ideas generally or your chosen idea specifically. Your statement of the idea will serve as the central idea for your essay.

BODY.   Your general goal is to define an idea and show its importance in the work. Each separate work will invite its own approach, but you might use any of the following strategies in organizing your essay.

1. *Analyzing the idea as it applies to character.* Example: "Minnie Wright embodies the idea that living with cruelty and insensitivity leads to alienation, unhappiness, despair, and sometimes to violence."

2. *Showing how actions bring out the idea.* Example: "That Mrs. Popov and Smirnov fall in love rather than fight their duel indicates Chekhov's idea that love literally rescues human lives."

3. *Showing how dialogue and separate speeches bring out the idea.* Example: "Mrs. Popov's speeches to Luka, Smirnov, and the entering servants illustrate the idea that the poses people adopt may mask and contradict their true self-interest."

4. *Showing how a work's organization or structure is determined by the idea.* Example: "Twain's idea that luck may be better than brains is the dominant influence in the structure of 'Luck,' which is organized as a set of progressively more important incidents showing how chance and fortune enable the protagonist to succeed despite his stupidity."

5. *Treating variations or differing manifestations of the idea.* Example: "The idea that zealousness leads to destruction is shown in Brown's nightmarish distortion of reality, his rejection of others, and his dying gloom."

6. *Dealing with a combination of these (together with any other significant aspect).* Example: "Chekhov's idea that love is complex and contradictory is shown in Smirnov's initial scorn of Mrs. Popov, his self-declared independence of character, and his concluding embrace." (Here the idea is traced through speech, character, and action.)

CONCLUSION.   Your conclusion might begin with a summary, together with your evaluation of the validity or force of the idea. If you have been convinced by the author's ideas, you might say that the author has expressed the idea forcefully and convincingly, or else you might show the relevance of the idea to current conditions. If you are not persuaded by the idea, you should not only state your disagreement but should also demonstrate the idea's shortcomings or limitations. If you wish to mention a related idea, whether in the work you have studied or in some other work, you might introduce that here, but be sure to stress the connections.

Sample Essay

The Idea of Love's Power in Chekhov's The Bear°

---

[1] In the one-act farce <u>The Bear</u>, Anton Chekhov shows a man and woman who have never met before falling suddenly in love. With such an unlikely main action, ideas may seem unimportant, but the play nevertheless contains a number of ideas. Some of these are that responsibility to life is stronger than to death, that people may justify even the most stupid and contradictory actions, that love makes people do foolish things, and that lifelong commitments may be made with hardly any thought at all. <u>One of the play's major ideas is that love and desire are powerful enough to overcome even the strongest obstacles.</u>* <u>This idea is shown as the force of love conquers commitment to the dead, renunciation of womankind, unfamiliarity, and anger.</u>†

[2] Commitment to her dead husband is Mrs. Popov's obstacle to love. She states that she has made a vow never to see daylight because of her mourning (speech 4), and she wallows in her own self-righteousness. Her devotion is so intense that she claims to be almost dead herself out of sympathy for her husband:

> My life is already ended. <u>He</u> lies in his grave; I have buried myself in these four walls . . . we are both dead. (speech 2)

In her, Chekhov has created a strong obstacle so that he might show the power of all-conquering love. By the play's end, Mrs. Popov's embracing Smirnov is a visual example of the idea (speech 151, S.D.).

[3] Renunciation of women is Smirnov's obstacle. He tells Mrs. Popov that women have made him bitter and that he no longer gives "a good goddamn" about them (speech 69). These words seem to make him an impossible candidate for love; but, in keeping with Chekhov's idea, Smirnov soon confesses his sudden and uncontrollable love at the peak of his anger against Mrs. Popov.

°See pages 332–41 for this play.
*Central idea.
†Thesis sentence.

[3] Within him, the force of love operates so strongly that he would even claim happiness at being shot by Mrs. Popov's "little velvet hands" (speech 140).

[4] As if these personal causes were not enough to stop love, a genuine obstacle is that the two people are strangers. Not only have they never met, but they have never even heard of each other. According to the main idea, however, this unfamiliarity is no major problem. Chekhov is dramatizing the power of love and shows that it is strong enough to overcome even the lack of familiarity or friendship.

Anger and the threat of violence, however, make the greatest obstacle. The two characters get so irritated about Smirnov's demand for payment that, as an improbable climax of their heated words, Smirnov challenges Mrs. Popov, a woman, to a duel! He shouts:

[5] And do you think just because you're one of those romantic creations, that you have the right to insult me with impunity? Yes? I challenge you! (speech 105)

Along with their own personal barriers against loving, it would seem that the threat of shooting each other, even if poor Luka could stop them, would cause lifelong hatred. Yet love knocks down all these obstacles, in line with Chekhov's idea that love's power is as irresistible as a flood.

[6] The idea is not new or unusual. It is the subject of popular songs, stories, other plays, movies, and T.V. shows. What is surprising about Chekhov's use of the idea is that love in The Bear overcomes such unlikely conditions, and wins so suddenly. These conditions bring up an interesting and closely related idea: Chekhov is showing that intensely negative feeling may lead not to hatred but rather to love. The speeches of Smirnov and Mrs. Popov contain disappointment, regret, frustration, annoyance, anger, rage, and potential destructiveness. Yet at the high point of these negative feelings, love takes over. It is as though hostility finally collapses because it is the nature of people to prefer loving to hating. The Bear is an uproarious dramatization of the power of love, and it is made better because it is founded on a truthful judgment of the way people really are.

COMMENTARY ON THE ESSAY

This essay follows the sixth strategy (p. 103) by showing how separate components from the play exhibit the pervasiveness of the idea. Throughout, dialogue, situations, soliloquies, and actions are evidence for the various conclusions. Transitions between paragraphs are effected by phrases such as "these personal causes" (paragraph 4), "greatest obstacle" (paragraph 5), and "the idea" (paragraph 6), all of which emphasize the continuity of the topic.

The introduction notes that the play contains a number of ideas, the major one being that love has the power to surmount great obstacles. The thesis sentence lists the four obstacles to be explored in the body.

As the operative aspects of Chekhov's idea, paragraphs 2 through 5 detail the nature of each of the obstacles. The obstacle of paragraph 2, Mrs. Popov's commitment to her husband's memory, is "strong." The one in paragraph 3, Smirnov's dislike of women, is seemingly "impossible." The one in paragraph 4, their being total strangers, is a "genuinely real" difficulty. In paragraph 5, the obstacle of anger is more likely to produce "hatred" than love.

The last paragraph, beyond providing a brief summary, suggests another related and important idea, namely that people cannot long sustain potentially destructive anger. Obviously this second idea is a broad generalization and could bear extensive treatment in its own right. Even though the topic would require greater development if it came at the beginning, it is effective as a part of the conclusion. The final sentence blends the two ideas, thereby looking both inward into the essay and outward toward the consideration of new ideas.

SPECIAL WRITING TOPICS
FOR IDEA OR THEME

1. On the basis of ideas, write an essay criticizing the ideas or values in a story, poem, or play in Appendix D that you dislike or to which you are indifferent. You might consult Chapter 2 to get ideas about how to proceed. Explain how your responses are conditioned by your own beliefs and values, and be sure that your criticism is based accurately in the work.

2. Consider "The Necklace" as an example of the idea of economic determinism (see also Appendix C, p. 271). That is, to what degree are the circumstances and traits of the characters, particularly Mathilde, controlled and limited primarily by their economic status? According to the idea, how likely is it that the characters can ever rise above their circumstances?

3. Compare two works containing similar ideas (examples: "Dover Beach" and "Channel Firing"; "Bright Star" and "Let Me Not to the Marriage of True Minds"; "Desert Places" and "Young Goodman Brown"; "Those Winter Sundays" and "Where Children Live"; "Rhine Boat Trip" and "The Cask of Amontillado"; "A Work of Artifice" and *Trifles*). For help in developing your essay, consult Chapter 13, on the technique of comparison–contrast.

4. Select an idea that particularly interests you and write a poem or story showing how characters may or may not live up to the idea. If you have difficulty getting started, try one of these possible ideas:

   a. Interest and enthusiasm are hard to maintain for long.
   b. People always want more than they have or need.
   c. The concerns of adults are different from those of children.
   d. It is awkward to confront another person about a grievance.

chapter 8

Writing About Imagery:
The Work's Link to the Senses

In literature, **imagery** refers to words that trigger your imagination to recall and recombine **images**—memories or mental pictures of sights, sounds, tastes, smells, sensations of touch, and motions. The process is active, for when words or descriptions produce images, you are using your own personal experience with life and language to help you understand the works you are reading. In effect, you are re-creating the work *in your own way* through the controlled stimulation produced by the writer's words. Imagery is therefore one of the strongest modes of literary expression because it provides a channel to your active imagination, and along this channel, writers bring their works directly into your consciousness.

For example, reading the word *lake* may bring to your mind your literal memory of a particular lake. Your mental picture—or image—may be a distant view of calm waters reflecting blue sky, a nearby view of gentle waves rippled by the wind, a view of the lake bottom from a boat, or an overhead view of a sandy and sunlit shoreline. Similarly, the words *rose, apple, hot dog, malted milk,* and *pizza* all cause you to recollect these objects and, in addition, may cause you to recall their smells and tastes. Active and graphic words like *row, swim,* and *dive* stimulate you to picture moving images of someone performing these actions.

RESPONSES AND THE WRITER'S USE OF DETAIL

In studying imagery we try to comprehend and explain our imaginative reconstruction of the pictures and impressions evoked by the work's images. We let the words simmer and percolate in our minds. To get our imaginations stirring, we might follow Coleridge in this description from the poem "Kubla Khan" (lines 37–41):

> A damsel with a dulcimer
> In a vision once I saw:
> It was an Abyssinian maid,
> And on her dulcimer she played,
> Singing of Mount Abora.

We do not read about the color of the young woman's clothing or anything else about her appearance except that she is playing a stringed instrument, a dulcimer, and that she is singing a song about a mountain in a foreign, remote land. Coleridge's image is enough. From it we can imagine a vivid, exotic picture of a young woman singing, together with the loveliness of her song (even though we never hear it or understand it). The image lives.

IMAGERY, IDEAS, AND ATTITUDES

Images do more than elicit impressions. By the *authenticating* effects of the vision and perceptions underlying them, they give you new ways of seeing the world or strengthen your old ways of seeing it. The range of objects or activities that writers employ as imagery is both vast and unpredictable. Indeed, an important quality about imagery is its very unpredictability. Langston Hughes, in "Theme for English B," for example, develops the idea that human beings are equal. Rather than stating the idea directly, he uses a number of images of everyday, ordinary activities that his speaker shares in common with most human beings (line 21):

> I like to eat, sleep, drink, and be in love.

These literal action images form an equalizing link that is not only true, but unarguable. Such uses of imagery are one of the strongest means by which literature reinforces ideas.

In addition, as you form mental pictures from a writer's images, you also respond with appropriate attitudes and feelings. Thus the phrase "beside a lake, beneath the trees," from Wordsworth's poem "Daffodils" ("I Wandered Lonely As a Cloud"), prompts both the visualization of a wooded lakeshore and also the related pleasantness of outdoor relaxation and happiness. Piercy, in "A Work of Artifice," creates a contrasting image of a tree by introducing the image of a pruned and stunted bonsai tree, which she applies to the status of women. By such a use of imagery, writers not only create sensory vividness but also influence and control the attitudes of their readers.

CLASSIFICATION OF IMAGERY

SIGHT.   Sight is the most significant of our senses, for it is the key to our remembrance of other impressions. Therefore, the most frequently occurring literary imagery is to things we can visualize either exactly or approximately—**visual images.** In "Cargoes" (the subject of the sample essay, pp. 112–13), Masefield asks us to re-create mental pictures or images of ocean-going merchant vessels from three periods of human history. He refers to a quinquereme from the ancient Near East, associated with the Biblical King Solomon; then he turns to a "stately Spanish galleon" and finally refers to a modern British ship caked with salt, carrying grubby and cheap freight over the English Channel. His images are vivid as they stand. In order to reconstruct them imaginatively, we do not need ever to have seen the ancient Biblical lands or waters, or ever to have seen or handled the cheap commodities on a modern merchant ship. We have seen enough in our lives both in reality and in pictures to *imagine* places and objects like these, and hence Masefield is successful in implanting his visual images into our minds.

SOUND.   **Auditory images** trigger our experiences with sound. In Owen's poem "Anthem for Doomed Youth," which is about death in warfare, the speaker asks what "passing bells" may be tolled for "those who die as cattle." Owen's speaker is referring to the traditional tolling of a parish church bell to announce the burial of a parishioner. Such a ceremony suggests a period of peace and order, when there is time to pay respect to the dead. The poem then points out that the only sound for those who have fallen in battle is the "rapid rattle" of "stuttering" rifles—in other words, not the solemn, dignified sounds of peace, but the horrifying noises of war. Owen's auditory images evoke corresponding sounds in our imaginations and help us experience the poem and hate the uncivilized depravity of war.

SMELL, TASTE, AND TOUCH.   In addition to sight and sound, you will also find images from the other senses. An **olfactory image** refers to smell, a **gustatory image** to taste, and a **tactile image** to touch. A great deal of love poetry, for example, includes *olfactory images* about the fragrances of flowers.

Images derived from and referring to taste—*gustatory images*—are also common, though less frequent than those to sight and sound. In lines 5 and 10 of Masefield's "Cargoes," for example, there are references to "sweet white wine" and "cinnamon." Although the poem refers to these commodities as cargoes, the words themselves also register in our minds as gustatory images because they appeal to our sense of taste.

Tactile images of touch and texture are not as common because touch is difficult to render except in terms of effects. The speaker of Lowell's "Patterns," for example, uses tactile imagery when imagining a never-to-happen embrace with her fiancé who we learn has been killed in war. Her imagery records the effect of the embrace ("bruised"), while her internalized feelings are expressed in metaphors ("aching, melting"):

> And the buttons of his waistcoat bruised my body as he clasped me
> Aching, melting, unafraid. (lines 51–52)

Tactile images are not uncommon in love poetry, where references to touch and feeling are natural.

IMAGES OF MOTION AND ACTIVITY.   References to movement are also images. Images of general motion are *kinetic* (remember that *motion pictures* are also called "cinema"), and the term **kinesthetic** is applied to human or animal movement. Imagery of motion is closely related to visual images, for motion is most often seen. Masefield's British coaster, for example, is a visual image, but when it goes "Butting through the channel," the motion makes it also kinetic. When Hardy's skeletons sit upright at the beginning of "Channel Firing," the image is kinesthetic, as is the action of Amy Lowell's speaker walking in the garden after hearing about her fiancé's death.

The areas from which kinetic and kinesthetic imagery may be derived are almost too varied to describe. Occupations, trades, professions, businesses, recreational activities—all these might furnish images. One writer introduces references from gardening, another from money and banking, another from modern real estate developments, another from life in the jungle. The freshness, newness, and surprise of literature result from the many and varied areas from which writers draw their images.

WRITING ABOUT IMAGERY

In preparing to write you should develop a set of thoughtful notes, dealing with issues such as the following:

- What type or types of images prevail in the work? Visual (shapes, colors)? Auditory (sounds)? Olfactory (smells)? Tactile (touch and texture)? Gustatory (taste)? Kinetic or kinesthetic (motion)? Or is the imagery a combination of these?

- To what degree do the images reflect (a) the writer's actual observation or (b) the writer's reading and knowledge of fields like science or history?

- How well do the images stand out? How vivid are they? How is this vividness achieved?

- Within a group of images, say visual or auditory, do the images pertain to one location or area rather than another (e.g., natural scenes rather than interiors, snowy scenes rather than grassy ones, loud and harsh sounds rather than quiet and civilized ones)?

- What explanation is needed for the images? (Images might be derived from the classics or the Bible, the Revolutionary War or World War II, the behaviors of four-footed creatures or birds, and so on.)

- What effect do the work's circumstances (e.g., conditions of brightness or darkness, warmth or cold) have upon the images and your responses to them? What literary purpose is served by your responses?

- How well are the images integrated within the work's argument or development?

Answering questions like these should provide you with a sizable body of ready-made material that you can convert directly to the body of your essay.

Organizing Your Essay About Imagery

INTRODUCTION.   Connect a brief overview of the work to your plan for the body of your essay, such as that the writer uses images to strengthen ideas about war, character, love, and so on, or that the writer relies predominantly on images of sight, sound, and action.

BODY.   You might choose to deal exclusively with one of the following aspects, or, equally likely, you may combine your approaches, as you wish.

1. *Images Suggesting Ideas and/or Moods.* Such an essay should emphasize the results of the imagery. What ideas or moods are evoked by the images? (The auditory images beginning "Anthem for Doomed Youth," for example, all point toward a condemnation of war's brutal cruelty.) Do the images promote approval or disapproval? Cheerfulness? Melancholy? Are the images drab, exciting, vivid? How? Why? Are they conducive to humor, or surprise? How does the writer achieve these effects? Are the images consistent, or are they ambiguous? (For example, the images in Masefield's "Cargoes" indicate first approval and then disapproval, with no ambiguity.)

2. *The Types of Images.* Here the emphasis is on the categories of images themselves. Is there a predominance of a particular type of image (e.g., visual or auditory), or is there a blending? Is there a bunching of types at particular points in the poem or story? If so, why? Is there any shifting as the work develops (as, for example, in Owen's "Anthem for Doomed Youth," where the auditory images first evoke loudness and harshness but later bring out quietness and sorrow)? Are the images appropriate, granting the nature and apparent intent of the work? Do they assist in making the ideas seem convincing? If there seems to be any inappropriateness, what is its effect?

3. *Systems of Images.* Here the emphasis should be on the areas from

which the images are drawn. This is another way of considering the appropriateness of the imagery. Is there a pattern of similar or consistent images, such as darkness and gloom (Poe's "The Cask of Amontillado") or brightness changing to darkness (Mansfield's "Miss Brill")? Do all the images adhere consistently to a particular frame of reference, such as a sunlit garden (Lowell's "Patterns"), an extensive recreational forest and garden (Coleridge's "Kubla Khan"), a graveyard (Hardy's "Channel Firing"), or a darkened forest (Bierce's "An Occurrence at Owl Creek Bridge")? What is unusual or unique about the set of images? What unexpected or new responses do they produce?

CONCLUSION.   Your conclusion, in addition to recapitulating your major points, is the place for additional insights. It would not be proper to go too far in new directions here, but you might briefly take up one or more of the ideas that you have not developed in the body. In short, what have you learned from your study of imagery in the work?

Sample Essay

The Images of Masefield's "Cargoes"°

---

[1] In the three-stanza poem "Cargoes," John Masefield develops imagery to create a negative impression of modern commercial life.° There is a contrast between the first two stanzas and the third, with the first two idealizing the romantic, distant past and the third demeaning the modern, gritty, grimy present. Masefield's images are thus both positive and lush, on the one hand, and negative and stark, on the other.†

[2] The most evocative and pleasant images in the poem are in the first stanza. The speaker asks that we imagine a "Quinquereme of Nineveh from distant Ophir" (line 1), an ocean-going, many-oared vessel loaded with treasure for the Biblical King Solomon. As Masefield identifies the cargo, the visual images are rich and romantic (lines 3–5):

With a cargo of ivory,
And apes and peacocks,
Sandalwood, cedarwood, and sweet white wine.

Ivory suggests richness, which is augmented by the exotic "apes and peacocks" in all their exciting strangeness. The "sandalwood, cedarwood, and sweet white wine" evoke pungent smells and tastes. The "sunny" light of ancient Palestine (line 2) not only illuminates the imaginative scene (visual), but invites readers to

°See page 326 for this poem.
°Central idea.
†Thesis sentence.

[2] imagine the sun's warming touch (tactile). The references to animals and birds also suggest the sounds that these creatures would make (auditory). Thus, in this lush first stanza, images derived from all the senses are introduced to create impressions of a glorious past.

[3] <u>Almost equally lush are the images of the second stanza, which completes the poem's first part.</u> Here the visual imagery evokes the royal splendor of a tall-masted, full-sailed galleon (line 6) at the height of Spain's commercial power in the sixteenth century. The galleon's cargo suggests great wealth, with sparkling diamonds and amethysts, and Portugese "gold moidores" gleaming in open chests (line 10). With cinnamon in the second stanza's bill of lading (line 10), Masefield includes the image of a pleasant-tasting spice.

[4] <u>The negative imagery of the third stanza is in stark contrast to the first two stanzas.</u> Here the poem draws the visual image of a modern "Dirty British coaster" (line 11) to focus on the griminess and suffocation of modern civilization. This spray-swept ship is loaded with materials that pollute the earth with noise and smoke. The smoke-stack of the coaster (line 11) and the firewood it is carrying suggest choking smog. The Tyne coal (line 13) and road-rails (line 14) suggest the noise and smoke of puffing railroad engines. As if this were not enough, the "pig-lead" (line 14) to be used in various industrial processes indicates not just more unpleasantness but also something more poisonous and deadly. In contrast to the lush and stately imagery of the first two stanzas, the images in the third stanza invite the conclusion that people now, when the "Dirty British coaster" butts through the English Channel, are surrounded and threatened by visual, olfactory, and auditory pollution.

[5] The poem thus establishes a romantic past and ugly present through images of sight, smell, and sound. The images of motion also emphasize this view: In stanzas 1 and 2 the quinquereme is "rowing" and the galleon is "dipping." These kinetic images suggest dignity and lightness. The British coaster, however, is "butting," an image indicating bull-like hostility and stupid force. <u>These, together with all the other images, focus the poem's negative views of modern life.</u> The facts that existence for both the ancient Palestinians and the Renaissance Spaniards included slavery (of those men rowing the quinquereme) and piracy (by those Spanish "explorers" who robbed and killed the natives of the isthmus) should probably not be emphasized as a protest against Masefield's otherwise valid contrasts in images. His final commentary may hence be thought of as the banging of his "cheap tin trays" (line 15), which makes a percussive climax of the oppressive images filling too large a portion of modern lives.

COMMENTARY ON THE ESSAY

The strategy illustrated in this sample essay is the first (p. 111), using images to develop ideas and moods. All the examples—derived directly from the poem—emphasize the qualities of Masefield's images. This method permits the introduction of imagery drawn from all the senses in order to demonstrate Masefield's ideas about the past and the present.

The essay's introductory paragraph presents the central idea that Masefield uses his images climactically to lead to his negative view of modern commercialism. The thesis sentence indicates that the topics to be developed are those of lushness and starkness.

Paragraphs 2 and 3 form a unit stressing the lushness and exoticism of stanza 1 and the wealth and colorfulness of stanza 2. In particular, paragraph 2 uses words such as *lush, evocative, rich, exotic, pungent,* and *romantic* to characterize the pleasing mental pictures the images invoke. Although the paragraph indicates enthusiastic responses to the images, it does not go beyond the limits of the images themselves.

Paragraph 4 stresses the contrast of Masefield's images in stanza 3 with those of stanzas 1 and 2. To this end the paragraph illustrates the imaginative reconstruction needed to develop an understanding of this contrast. The unpleasantness, annoyance, and even the danger of the cargoes mentioned in stanza three are therefore emphasized as the qualities evoked by the images.

The last paragraph demonstrates that the imagery of motion—not much stressed in the poem—is in agreement with the rest of Masefield's imagery. As a demonstration of the need for fair, impartial judgment, the conclusion introduces the possible objection that Masefield's imagistic portraits may be slanted because they include not a full but rather a partial view of their respective historical periods. Thus the concluding paragraph adds balance to the analysis illustrated in paragraphs 2, 3, and 4.

SPECIAL WRITING TOPICS FOR IMAGERY

1. Compare the images of home in "Anthem for Doomed Youth" and "An Occurrence at Owl Creek Bridge." Describe the differing effects of the images. How are the images used? What are the relationships of the images to the dead men and the prisoner about to be hanged? How is your reading of the poems affected by the knowledge that both Owen and Bierce were killed in wars (in Europe and Mexico)?

2. Based on the poems in Appendix D by Coleridge, Frost, Layton, and Nye, write an essay discussing the use of images drawn from nature and the outdoors. What sorts of references do the writers make? What attitudes do they express about the details they select? What judgments about nature and humankind do the poets show by their images?

3. Using the imagery of Hardy's "Channel Firing," write an essay explaining the power of imagery. As you develop your thoughts, be sure to consider the dramatic nature of Hardy's images, and to account for the impressions and ideas that they create.

4. Write a poem or short narrative including one of the following:

    a. Athletes who have just completed an exhausting run.
    b. Children getting out of school for the day.
    c. The antics of your dog, cat, horse, or other pet.

   d. The best concert you ever attended.

   e. Driving to work or school on a rainy or snowy day.

Then write an analysis of your images and explain your choices. What details stand out in your mind? What do you recall best—sight, smell, sound, action? What is the relationship between your images and your ideas?

chapter 9

Writing About Metaphor and Simile:

A Source of Depth and Range in Literature

Figurative language refers to expressions that conform to regularized arrangements of words and thought. These patterns, called **rhetorical figures** or **rhetorical devices**, are the tools that help make literary works effective, persuasive, and forceful. The figures are modes of comparison, and they may be expressed in single words, phrases, clauses, and entire structures. The two most important figures are *metaphor* and *simile*. Indeed, the words *metaphor* and *metaphorical* are often broadly applied to most rhetorical figures, including symbols.

METAPHORS AND SIMILES

A **metaphor** (a "carrying out of a change") describes one thing as though it were something else, thereby enhancing understanding and insight. One of Shakespeare's best-known metaphors is "All the world's a stage, / And all the men and women merely players," in which Shakespeare's character Jacques (from *As You Like It*, II.7) explains human life in terms of stage life. It is important to recognize that the comparison, as a metaphor, does not state that the world is *like* a stage, but that it literally *is* a stage.

While a metaphor merges identities in this way, a **simile** (the "showing of similarity or oneness") utilizes *similarity* to carry out the explanation. A simile is distinguishable from a metaphor because it is introduced by "like" with nouns and "as" (also "as if" and "as though") with clauses. Thus the sentence "Come with . . . eyes as bright / As sunlight on a stream" from Rossetti's poem "Echo," (p. 194), compares the listener's eyes with a natural scene. Because the comparison is introduced by "as," the speaker's emphasis is on the *similarity* of the eyes to sunlight, not on the *identification* or *equality* of the two.

Imagery, Metaphor, and Simile

In Chapter 8 we saw how imagery stimulates the imagination and recalls memories (*images*) of sights, sounds, tastes, smells, sensations of touch, and motions. Metaphors and similes go beyond such literal imagery to introduce perceptions and comparisons that may be unusual, unpredictable, and surprising. They connect the thing or things to be communicated—such as qualities of love or the excitement of unexpected discovery—with a new insight that is made objective through the comparison of a simile or the equation of a metaphor.

For example, to communicate a character's joy and excitement, the sentence "She was happy" is accurate but not interesting or effective. A more vivid way of saying the same thing is to use an image of an action, such as "She jumped for joy." This image gives us a literal picture of an action demonstrating happiness. But an even better way of communicating a happy state is the following simile: "She felt as if she had just inherited fifty million tax-free dollars." Because readers easily understand the excitement, disbelief, exhilaration, and joy that such an event would bring, they also understand—and feel—the character's happiness. It is the *simile* that evokes this perception, for no simple description could help a reader comprehend the same degree of emotion.

As a poetic example, let us refer to Keats's sonnet "On First Looking into Chapman's Homer," which Keats wrote soon after reading the translation of Homer's *Iliad* and *Odyssey* by the Renaissance poet George Chapman. Keats's main idea is that Chapman not only translated Homer's words but also transmitted his greatness:

John Keats (1795–1821)

On First Looking into Chapman's Homer°

1816

Much have I travell'd in the realms of gold,
    And many goodly states and kingdoms seen:
    Round many western islands have I been
Which bards in fealty to Apollo° hold.
Oft of one wide expanse had I been told   5
    That deep-brow'd Homer ruled as his demesne;°
    Yet did I never breathe its pure serene°
Till I heard Chapman speak out loud and bold:
Then felt I like some watcher of the skies
    When a new planet swims into his ken;°   10
Or like stout Cortez° when with eagle eyes
    He star'd at the Pacific—and all his men
Look'd at each other with a wild surmise—
    Silent, upon a peak in Darien.

Chapman's Homer: George Chapman (c. 1560–1634) published his translations of Homer's *Iliad* in 1612 and *Odyssey* in 1614–1615.
bards . . . Apollo: writers who are sworn subjects of Apollo, the Greek god of light, music, poetry, prophecy, and the sun.
demesne: realm, estate.
serene: a clear expanse of air; also grandeur, clarity; rulers were also sometimes called "serene majesty."
ken: range of vision.
Cortez: Hernando Cortez (1485–1547), a Spanish general and the conqueror of Mexico. Keats confuses him with Vasco de Balboa (c. 1475–1519), the first European to see the Pacific Ocean (in 1510) from Darien, an early name for the Isthmus of Panama.

To illustrate the power of metaphorical language, we may first briefly paraphrase the sonnet's content:

I have enjoyed much art and read much European literature and have been told that Homer is the best writer of all. However, because I do not know Greek, I could not really appreciate his works until I discovered them in Chapman's translation. To me, this experience was exciting and awe-inspiring.

If all Keats had written were a paragraph like this one, we would pay no attention to it, for it carries no sense of excitement or stimulation. But the last six lines of the sonnet contain two memorable similes ("like some watcher" and "like stout Cortez"). They stand out and demand a special effort of imagination. When we mull them over, we might suppose that we actually *are* astronomers just discovering a new planet, and that we actually *are* the first explorers to see the Pacific Ocean. As we imagine ourselves in these roles, we can understand the amazement, wonder, excitement, exhilaration, anticipation, joy, and feeling of accomplishment that would accompany such discoveries. If we imagine these feelings, then Keats has unlocked experiences that the relatively unpromising title does not suggest. He has given us something new. He has enlarged us.

Characteristics of Metaphorical Language

It would be difficult to find any piece of good writing that does not use metaphors and similes. Such language is most vital, however, in imaginative writing, particularly poetry, where it compresses thought, promotes understanding, and shapes response.

As we saw in Chapter 8, the images embodied in words and descriptions are largely confined to their literal meaning in nature and experience. Let us consider, for a moment, a description of falling leaves in autumn. If a writer's intention is accuracy and fidelity to Nature, she might write a description that is primarily informative—appropriate perhaps for an article or text on deciduous trees. But if a writer wishes to bring out metaphorical meanings, he would try to bring out the associations of falling leaves in an equative or comparative way, as in the opening lines of Shakespeare's Sonnet 73:

> That time of year thou mayest in me behold,
> When yellow leaves, or none, or few, do hang
> Upon those boughs that shake against the cold, . . .

Shakespeare's speaker is telling us about fears that he is getting old and close to death. We know that the topic of age and death can occasion extensive philosophical reflections, but the poet knows that too great a preoccupation with mortality might become boring and depressing. He therefore creates metaphorical interest by equating the speaker's time of life to the falling of leaves and the complete denuding of the trees, in this way drawing on our own knowledge, associations, and feelings about fall and the year's end: After the green lushness of summer, the autumnal season moves inevitably to shorter days, cold, and the onset of winter. The associations of falling leaves are therefore drabness, the loss of summer's green, and the seasonal shutdown of the earth's fertility. Once we have expanded the metaphor in this way, we have come close to comprehending the speaker's apprehension about life's shortness, and we have done so without wading through extensive statements about age, infirmity, and death.

This development of Shakespeare's metaphor may seem at first like much more than Shakespeare intended; indeed, it uses many more words in prose than he uses in verse. However, it reflects the power of metaphorical language: Once it unlocks our minds, we may then give our thoughts free rein as we consider the full ramifications of metaphors, which equal, and similes, which compare. Similes and metaphors therefore constitute one of the ways in which great literature leads us to see the world originally and freshly.

WRITING ABOUT
METAPHORS AND SIMILES

Begin by determining the use, line by line, of metaphors or similes. Obviously, similes are the easiest figures to recognize, because they introduce comparisons with the words "like" or "as." Metaphors may be recognized because the topics are discussed not as themselves but as other topics. If the poems speak of falling leaves or law courts, for example, but the subjects are memory or increasing age, you are looking at metaphors. Here are some exploratory questions:

- What figures does the work contain? Where do they occur? Under what circumstances? How extensive are they?

- How do you recognize them? Are they signaled by a single word or phrase, such as "desert places" in Frost's "Desert Places," or are they more extensively detailed, as in Shakespeare's Sonnet 30, "When to the Sessions of Sweet Silent Thought" (p. 122)?

- How vivid are the figures? How obvious? How unusual? What kind of effort is needed to understand them in context?

- Structurally, how are the figures developed? How do they rise out of the situation? To what degree are the figures integrated into the work's development of ideas? How do they relate to other aspects of the work?

- Is one type of figure used in a particular section while another predominates in another? Why?

- If you have discovered a number of figures, what relationships can you find among them (such as the judicial and financial connections in Shakespeare's "When to the Sessions")?

- How do they broaden, deepen, or otherwise assist in making the ideas in the work forceful?

- In short, how appropriate and meaningful are the figures in the work? What effect do the figures have on your understanding and appreciation of the work?

ORGANIZING YOUR ESSAY ABOUT METAPHOR
AND SIMILE

INTRODUCTION.   Relate the quality of the figures to the nature of the work. Thus, metaphors and similes of suffering might be appropriate to a religious, redemptive work, while those of sunshine and cheer might be right for a romantic one. If there is a contrast between the metaphorical language and the topic, you might take that contrast for a central idea, for it would clearly indicate the writer's ironic perspective. Suppose that the topic of the poem is love, but the figures put you in mind of darkness and cold: What would the writer be saying about the quality of love? You should also try to justify any claims that you make about the figures. Your introduction is the place to establish ideas and justifications of this sort.

BODY.   The following approaches for discussing rhetorical figures are not mutually exclusive, and you may combine them as you wish. Most likely, your essay will bring in most of the following classifications.

1. *Interpret the meaning and effect of the figures.* Here you explain how the figures enable you to make an interpretation. In lines 17–19 of "Kubla Khan," for example, Coleridge introduces the following simile:

> And from this chasm, with ceaseless turmoil seething,
> As if this earth in fast thick pants were breathing,
> A mighty fountain momently was forced:

Coleridge's simile of "fast thick pants" almost literally animates the earth as a moving, working power, panting as it forces the fountain out of the chasm. The idea is that the phenomena of nature are not dead, but vigorously alive. Such a direct, interpretive approach requires that metaphors, similes, or other figures be expanded and interpreted, including the explanation of necessary references and allusions.

2. *Analyze the frames of reference and their appropriateness to the subject matter.* Here you classify and locate the sources and types of the references and determine the appropriateness of these to the poem's subject matter. Ask questions similar to those you might ask in a study of imagery: Does the writer refer extensively to nature, science, warfare, politics, business, reading (e.g., Shakespeare's metaphor equating personal reverie with courtroom proceedings)? How appropriate is the metaphor? Does it seem right in the poem's development? How?

3. *Focus on the interests and sensibilities of the writer.* In a way this approach is like the second one, but the emphasis here is on what the selectivity of the writer might show about his or her vision and interests. You might begin by listing the figures in the poem and then determining the sources, just as you would do in discussing the sources of images. But then you should raise questions such as the following: Does the writer use figures derived from one

sense rather than another (i.e., sight, hearing, taste, smell, touch)? Does he or she record color, brightness, shadow, shape, depth, height, number, size, slowness, speed, emptiness, fullness, richness, drabness? Has the writer relied on the associations of figures of sense? Do metaphors and similes referring to green plants and trees, to red roses, or to rich fabrics, for example, suggest that life is full and beautiful; or do references to touch suggest amorous warmth? This approach is designed to help you draw whatever conclusions you can about the author's—or the speaker's—taste or sensibility.

4. *Examine the effect of one figure on the other figures and ideas of the poem.* The assumption of this approach is that each literary work is unified and organically whole, so that each part is closely related and inseparable from everything else. Usually it is best to pick a figure that occurs at the beginning of the work and then determine how this figure influences your perception of what follows. Your aim is to consider the relationship of part to parts, and part to whole. The beginning of Frost's "Desert Places," for example, describes "snow falling and night falling." What is the effect of this opening upon the poem's metaphor of human "desert places"? To help you in approaching such a question, you might substitute a totally different detail, such as, here, a rising sun on a beautiful day or playing with a kitten, rather than the onset of cold and night. Such suppositions, which would clearly be out of place and inappropriate, may help you to understand and then explain the writer's metaphorical language.

CONCLUSION. In your conclusion, summarize your main points, describe your general impressions, try to describe the impact of the figurative language, indicate your personal responses, or show what might further be done along the lines you have been developing. If you know other works by the same writer or works by other writers who use comparable or contrasting figures, you might explain the relationship of the other work or works to your present analysis.

Sample Essay

A Study of Shakespeare's Metaphors in Sonnet 30

> When to the sessions of sweet silent thought,
> I summon up remembrance of things past,
> I sigh the lack of many a thing I sought,
> And with old woes new wail my dear time's waste:
> Then can I drown an eye (un-used to flow)   (5)
> For precious friends hid in death's dateless night,
> And weep afresh love's long since canceled woe,
> And moan th' expense of many a vanished sight.

> Then can I grieve at grievances foregone,
> And heavily from woe to woe tell o'er (10)
> The sad account of fore-bemoaned moan,
> Which I new pay, as if not paid before.
> But if the while I think on thee (dear friend)
> All losses are restored, and sorrows end.

[1] In this sonnet Shakespeare's speaker stresses the sadness and regret of remembered experience, but he states that a person with these feelings may be cheered by the thought of a friend. <u>His metaphors, cleverly used, create new and fresh ways of seeing personal life in this perspective.</u>* <u>He presents metaphors drawn from the public and business world of law courts, money, and banking or money-handling.</u>†

[2] <u>The courtroom metaphor of the first four lines shows that memories of past experience are constantly present and influential.</u> Like a judge commanding defendants to appear in court, the speaker "summon[s]" his memory of "things past" to appear on trial before him. This metaphor suggests that people are their own judges and that their ideals and morals are like laws by which they measure themselves. The speaker finds himself guilty of wasting his time in the past. Removing himself, however, from the strict punishment that a real judge might require, he does not condemn himself for his "dear time's waste" but instead laments it (line 4). The metaphor is thus used to indicate that a person's consciousness is made up just as much of self-doubt and reproach as by more positive qualities.

[3] <u>With the closely related reference of money in the next group of four lines, Shakespeare shows that living is a lifelong investment and is valuable for this reason.</u> According to the money metaphor, living requires the spending of emotions and commitment to others. When friends move away and loved ones die, it is as though this expenditure has been lost. Thus, the speaker's dead friends are "precious" because he invested time and love in them, and the "sights" that have "vanished" from his eyes make him "moan" because he went to great "expense" for them (line 8).

[4] <u>Like the money metaphor, the metaphor of banking or money-handling in the next four lines emphasizes that memory is a bank in which life's experiences are deposited.</u> The full emotions surrounding experience are recorded there, and may be withdrawn in moments of "sweet silent thought" just as a depositor may withdraw money. Thus the speaker states that he counts out the sad parts of his experience—his woe—just as a merchant or banker counts money: "And heavily from woe to woe <u>tell</u> o'er" (line 10). Because strong emotions still accompany his memories of past mistakes, the metaphor extends to borrowing and the payment of interest. The speaker thus says that he pays again with "new" woe the accounts that he had already paid with old woe. The metaphor suggests that the past is so much a part of the present that a person never stops feeling pain and regret.

[5] <u>The legal, financial, and money-handling metaphors combine in the last two lines to show how a healthy present life may overcome past regrets.</u> The "dear friend" being addressed in these lines has the resources (financial) to settle all the emotional judgments that the speaker as a self-judge has made against himself (legal). It is as though the friend is a rich patron who rescues him

---

*Central idea.
†Thesis sentence.

[5] from emotional bankruptcy (legal and financial) and the possible doom resulting from the potential sentence of emotional misery and depression (legal).

[6] In these metaphors, therefore, Shakespeare's references are drawn from everyday public and business actions, but his use of them is creative and unusual. In particular, the idea of line 8 ("And moan th' expense of many a vanished sight") stresses that people spend much emotional energy on others. Without such personal commitment, one cannot have precious friends and loved ones. In keeping with this metaphor of money and investment, one could measure life not in months or years, but in the spending of emotion and involvement in personal relationships. Shakespeare, by inviting readers to explore the values brought out by his metaphors, gives new insights into the nature and value of life.

COMMENTARY ON THE ESSAY

This essay treats the three classes of metaphors that Shakespeare introduces in Sonnet 30. It thus illustrates the second approach (p. 121); but the aim of the discussion is not to explore the extent and nature of the comparison between the metaphors and the personal situations described in the sonnet. Instead the goal is to explain how the metaphors develop Shakespeare's meaning. This method therefore also illustrates the first approach (p. 121).

The primary objective of the introductory paragraph is to include a brief general description of the work together with a brief specific description of the essay's topic. Of particular note is that Shakespeare's metaphors are introduced in relation to the issue of their possibly being overly clever and far-fetched, and, as a result, inappropriate. This issue is raised as a concession to be argued against. From it, the assertion is presented that the metaphors, because they lead to new and fresh insights, do just what metaphors are supposed to do, and thus they are appropriate. Once this argument is established, the central idea and thesis sentence follow logically. The introductory paragraph hence brings out all the necessary topics and issues to be considered in the body.

Paragraph 2 deals with the meaning of Shakespeare's courtroom metaphor. His money metaphor is explained in paragraph 3. Paragraph 4 considers the banking, or money-handling, figure. The fifth paragraph shows how Shakespeare's last two lines bring together the three strands of metaphor. The conclusion comments generally on the creativity of Shakespeare's metaphors, and it also amplifies the way in which the money metaphor leads toward an increased understanding of life.

Throughout the essay, transitions are brought about by the linking words in the topic sentences. In paragraph 3, for example, the words "closely related" and "next group" move the reader from paragraph 2 to the new content. In paragraph 4, the words effecting the transition are "like the money metaphor" and "the next four lines." The opening sentence of paragraph 5 refers collectively to the subjects of paragraphs 2, 3, and 4, thereby focusing them on the new topic of paragraph 5.

SPECIAL WRITING TOPICS
FOR METAPHOR AND SIMILE

1. Consider some of the metaphors and similes in the works (poems, stories, plays) included in Appendix D. Write an essay that answers the following questions: How effective are the figures you select? What insights do the figures provide within the contexts of their respective poems? How appropriate are they? Might they be expanded more fully, and if they were, what would be the effect? You might choose any of the following topics:

   - The "darkling plain" simile in Arnold's "Dover Beach"
   - The metaphors of constancy in Shakespeare's "Let Me Not to the Marriage of True Minds," or of autumn in his "That Time of Year Thou Mayest in Me Behold"
   - The metaphorical significance of the knot in Glaspell's *Trifles*
   - Metaphor in Piercy's "A Work of Artifice"
   - The metaphor of the Rhine in Layton's "Rhine Boat Trip"
   - Similes in Owen's "Anthem for Doomed Youth" or Coleridge's "Kubla Khan"
   - The metaphor of "red war" in Hardy's "Channel Firing"
   - Metaphor and simile in Keats's "On First Looking into Chapman's Homer"
   - The metaphor of the path and the journey in Welty's "A Worn Path"
   - The title of Poe's "The Cask of Amontillado" as a metaphor
   - The horse Toby as a metaphor in Chekhov's *The Bear*

2. Write a poem in which you create a governing metaphor or simile. An example might be: My girl/boy friend is like (a) an opening flower, (b) a difficult book, (c) an insoluble mathematical problem, (d) a bill that cannot be paid, (e) a slow-moving chess game. Another example: Teaching a person how to do a particular job is like (a) shoveling heavy snow, (b) climbing a mountain during a landslide, (c) having someone force you underwater when you're gasping for breath. When you finish, describe the relationship between your comparison and the development and structure of your poem.

chapter 10

Writing About Symbolism and Allegory:
Keys to Extended Meaning

Symbolism and *allegory* are modes that expand meaning. Although they are literary devices, they are based on the fact that people associate important qualities of their existence with particular objects, places, or occurrences—either through experience or reading. One person might remember making a vital realization about his moral being during a rowboat ride. Another might associate her belief in freedom with catching a large fish and then letting it go. Still another person might connect a friendly word of advice with a major career decision. The significance of details like these can be meaningful not just at the time they occur, but throughout an entire lifetime. Merely speaking about them or bringing them to mind unlocks all their meanings, implications, and consequences. It is as though the reference alone can be the same as pages upon pages of explanation and analysis.

It is from this principle that both symbolism and allegory are derived. By highlighting details as *symbols*, and stories or parts of stories as *allegories*, writers can expand meaning while keeping their works within reasonable lengths.

SYMBOLISM

The words **symbol** and **symbolism** are derived from the Greek word meaning "to throw together" (*syn*, together, and *ballein*, to throw). A symbol creates a direct meaningful equation between (1) a specific object, scene, character, or action and (2) ideas, values, persons, or ways of life. In effect, a symbol is a *substitute* for the elements being signified, much as the flag stands for the ideals of the nation.

In stories, symbols are verbal descriptions—of persons, objects, places, actions, and situations. Each symbol has its own objective identity and may function at an ordinary level. There is often a close topical relationship between the symbol and its meaning or meanings, but the symbol may also have no apparent connection. What is important is that symbols extend beyond their immediate identity and point toward additional levels of meaning. Something is a symbol when it consistently refers beyond itself to a significant idea, emotion, or quality. There are two types of symbols—*cultural* and *contextual*.

Cultural Symbols

Many symbols are *generally* or *universally* recognized and are therefore **cultural** (also called **universal**). They embody ideas and emotions that writers and readers share as heirs of the same historical and cultural tradition. When using these symbols, a writer assumes that readers already know what the symbols represent. For example, the ancient mythological character Sisyphus is a widely recognized symbol. In the ancient Greek mythological underworld, Sisyphus is forever doomed to roll a large boulder up a high hill. Just as he gets it to the top, it rolls down, and then he is fated to roll it up again—and again—and again—because the rock always rolls back. The plight of Sisyphus is a symbol of the human condition: In spite of constant struggle, a person rarely if ever completes anything. Work must always be done over and over from day to day and from generation to generation, and the same problems confront humanity throughout all time. Because of such fruitless effort, life seems to have little or no meaning. Nevertheless, there is hope. People who confront their tasks, as Sisyphus does, stay involved and active; and even if they are only temporarily successful, their work makes their lives meaningful. A writer referring to Sisyphus would expect us to understand that this ancient mythological figure symbolizes these conditions.

Similarly, ordinary water, because living creatures could not live without it, is recognized as a symbol of life. It has this meaning in the ceremony of baptism, and it can convey this meaning and dimension in a variety of literary contexts. Thus, a spouting fountain may symbolize optimism (as upwelling, bubbling life), and a stagnant pool may symbolize the pollution and diminution of life. Water is also a universal symbol of sexuality, and its condition or state may symbolize various romantic relationships. For instance, stories in which lovers meet near a turbulent stream, a roaring waterfall, a wide river, a stormy sea, a muddy puddle, or a calm lake are symbolically representing love relationships that range from uncertainty to serenity.

Contextual Symbols

Objects and descriptions that are not universal symbols can be symbols *only if they are made so within individual works*. These are **contextual, private,** or **authorial** symbols. Unlike cultural symbols, these gain symbolic meaning within their *context*. For example, the word *pattern* is an ordinary word, but in Amy Lowell's "Patterns," we realize that the word takes on symbolic value. Things conforming to patterns come to symbolize not only confining and stultifying cultural expectations, but also the organized destructiveness of warfare. It is the *context* of the poem that creates this symbolism. Similarly, Arnold uses the ebbing surf in "Dover Beach" to symbolize his speaker's sadness at the loss of religious and philosophical certainty. Like Lowell's patterns, then, Arnold's surf is a major *contextual* symbol. There is no carryover, however. In other works, pounding surf or formal patterns are not symbolic unless the writers deliberately give them symbolic meaning. Further, if they are symbolic in other works, they may represent very different qualities than in the poems by Lowell and Arnold.

Determining What Is Symbolic

In determining whether a particular object, action, or character is a symbol, you need to judge the importance the author gives to it. If the element is prominent and also maintains a constancy of meaning, you may justify interpreting it as a symbol. For example, Miss Brill's fur piece in Mansfield's "Miss Brill" is shabby and moth-eaten. It has no value; but because Mansfield makes it especially important at both the beginning and ending of the story, it contextually symbolizes Miss Brill's poverty and isolation. At the end of Welty's "A Worn Path," Phoenix, the major character, plans to spend all her money for a toy windmill for her sick grandson. Readers will note that the windmill is small and fragile, like her life and that of her grandson, but that Phoenix wants to give the boy a little pleasure despite their poverty and hopelessness. For these reasons the windmill is a contextual or authorial symbol of Phoenix's strong character, generous nature, and pathetic existence.

ALLEGORY

An **allegory** is like a symbol because it transfers and broadens meaning. The term is derived from the Greek word *allegorein*, which means "to speak so as to imply other than what is said." Allegory, however, is more sustained than symbolism. An allegory is to a symbol as a motion picture is to a still picture. In form, an allegory is a complete and self-sufficient narrative, but it also signifies another series of events or conditions. While some stories are allegories from beginning to end, many stories that are not allegories may nevertheless contain brief sections or episodes that are *allegorical*.

The Use of Allegory

Allegories and the allegorical method are more than literary exercises. Without question, readers and listeners learn and memorize stories more easily than moral lessons, and therefore allegory is a favorite method of teaching morality. In addition, thought and expression have not always been free. The threat of censorship and the danger of reprisal have sometimes caused authors to express their views indirectly in the form of allegory rather than to write directly and risk political reprisal or accusations of libel. Hence, the double meaning of many allegories is based in both need and reality.

In studying a story for allegory, determine whether all or part of your work may have an extended, allegorical meaning. The continuing popularity of George Lucas's film *Star Wars* and its sequels, for example, is attributable at least partly to its being an allegory about the conflict between good and evil. Obi Wan Kenobi (intelligence) enlists the aid of Luke Skywalker (heroism, boldness), and instructs him in "the force" (moral or religious faith). Thus armed and guided, Skywalker opposes the powers of Darth Vader (evil) to rescue the Princess Leia (purity and goodness) with the aid of the latest spaceships and weaponry (technology). The story is an exciting adventure film, accompanied by dramatic music and ingenious visual and sound effects. With the obvious allegorical overtones, however, it stands for any person's quest for self-fulfillment.

To apply a part of the allegory more specifically, consider that for a time the evil Vader imprisons Skywalker and that Skywalker must exert all his skill and strength to get free and overcome Vader. In the allegorical application of the episode, this temporary imprisonment signifies those moments of doubt, discouragement, and depression that people experience while trying to better themselves through education, work, self-improvement, friendship, marriage, and so on.

Almost from the beginning of recorded literature, similar heroic deeds have been represented in allegorical forms. From ancient Greece, the allegorical hero Jason sails the *Argo* to distant lands to gain the Golden Fleece (those who take risks are rewarded). From Anglo-Saxon England, the hero Beowulf saves the kingdom by killing Grendel and his monstrous mother (victory comes to those who rely on the forces of good). From seventeenth-century England, Bunyan's *The Pilgrim's Progress* tells how the hero Christian overcomes difficulties and temptations while traveling from this world to the next (belief, perseverance, and resistance to temptation save the faithful). As long as the parallel connections are close and consistent, such as those mentioned here, an allegorical interpretation is valid.

FABLE, PARABLE, AND MYTH

Closely related to symbolism and allegory in the ability to extend and expand meaning are three additional forms—*fable, parable,* and *myth.*

FABLE.   The **fable** (from Latin *fabula,* a story or narration) is an old and popular form. It is usually short and often features animals with human traits (these are called **beast fables**), to which writers and editors attach "morals" or explanations. Aesop (sixth century B.C.) was supposedly a slave who composed fables in ancient Greece. His fable "The Fox and the Grapes," for example, signifies the trait of belittling things we cannot have. More recent contributions to the fable tradition include Walt Disney's Mickey Mouse and Walt Kelly's Pogo. The adjective *fabulous* refers to the collective body of fables of all sorts, even though the word is often used as a vague term of approval.

PARABLE.   A **parable** (from Greek *paraballein,* to set aside) is a short, simple allegory with a moral or religious bent. Parables are most often associated with Jesus, who used them to embody unique religious insights and truths. His parables "The Good Samaritan" and "The Prodigal Son," for example, are interpreted to show God's love, concern, understanding, and forgiveness.

MYTH.   A **myth** (from Greek *muthos,* a story) is either a narrative story or narrative protagonist—such as the myths of Sisyphus, Oedipus, or Atalanta—that is associated with the religion, philosophy, and collective psychology of various societies or cultures. Myths embody and codify the religious, social, and cultural values of the civilization in which they are composed. Unfortunately, the words *myth* and *mythical* are sometimes used to mean "fanciful" or "untrue." Such disparagement reflects a limited understanding, for in fact the truths of mythology are not to be found literally in the stories themselves but rather in their symbolic or allegorical interpretations.

ALLUSION IN SYMBOLISM AND ALLEGORY

Cultural or universal symbols and allegories often allude to other works from our cultural heritage, such as the Bible, ancient history and literature, and works of the British and American traditions. Sometimes understanding a story may require knowledge of politics and current events.

     If the meaning of a symbol is not immediately clear to you, you will need a dictionary or other reference work. The scope of your college dictionary will surprise you. If you cannot find an entry there, however, try one of the major encyclopedias or ask your reference librarian, who can direct you to shelves loaded with helpful books. A few excellent guides are *The Oxford Companion to Classical Literature* (ed. M. C. Howatson), *The Oxford Companion to English Literature* (ed. Margaret Drabble), William Rose Benet's *The Reader's Encyclopedia*, Timothy Gantz's *Early Greek Myth: A Guide to Literary and Artistic Sources*, and Richmond Y. Hathorn's *Greek Mythology*. Useful aids in finding Biblical references are *Cruden's Complete Concordance*, which in various editions has been used since 1737, or *Strong's Exhaustive Concordance*, which is fuller and more up to date. These concordances list all the major words used in the Bible, so you can easily locate the chapter and verse of any and all Biblical passages. If you still have trouble after using sources like these, see your instructor.

WRITING ABOUT SYMBOLISM OR ALLEGORY

To discover possible parallels that determine the presence of symbolism or allegory, consider the following questions:

a. Symbolism

- What cultural or universal symbols can you discover in names, objects, places, situations, or actions in a work (e.g., the character Faith and the walking stick in "Young Goodman Brown," the funeral bells in "Anthem for Doomed Youth," the snow in "Desert Places," or the woods in either "Young Goodman Brown" or "A Worn Path")?
- What contextual symbolism can be found in a work? What makes you think it is symbolic? What is being symbolized? How definite or direct is the symbolism? How systematically is it used? How necessary to the work is it? To what degree does it strengthen the work? How strongly does the work stand on its own without the reading for symbolism?
- Is it possible to make parallel lists to show how qualities of a particular symbol match the qualities of a character or action? Here is such a list for the toy windmill in Welty's "A Worn Path":

Qualities of the Windmill	Comparable Qualities in Phoenix and Her Life
1. Cheap	1. Poor, but she gives all she has for the windmill
2. Breakable	2. Old, and not far from death
3. A gift	3. Generous
4. Not practical	4. Needs relief from reality and practicality
5. Colorful	5. Needs something new and cheerful

b. Allegory

- How clearly does the author point you toward an allegorical reading (i.e., through names and allusions, consistency of narrative, literary context)?
- How consistent is the allegorical application? Does the entire work, or only a part, embody the allegory? On what basis do you draw these conclusions?
- How complete is the allegorical reading? How might the allegory yield to a diagram such as the following, which shows how characters, actions, objects, or ideas correspond to an allegorical meaning?

STAR WARS	Luke Skywalker	Obi Wan Kenobi	Darth Vader	Princess Leia	Capture	Escape, and defeat of Vader
ALLEGORICAL APPLICATION TO MORALITY AND FAITH	Forces of good	Education and faith	Forces of evil	Object to be saved, ideals to be rescued and restored	Doubt, spiritual negligence	Restoration of faith
ALLEGORICAL APPLICATION TO PERSONAL AND GENERAL CONCERNS	Individual in pursuit of goals	The means by which goals may be reached	Obstacles to be overcome	Occupation, happiness, goals	Temporary failure, depression, discouragement, disappointment	Success

c. Other forms

- What enables you to identify the story as a parable or fable? What lesson or moral is either clearly stated or implicit?
- What mythological identification is established in the work? What do you find in the story (names, situations, etc.) that enables you to determine its mythological significance? How is the myth to be understood? What symbolic value does the myth have? What current and timeless application does it have?

Organizing Your Essay About Symbolism and Allegory

Relate the central idea of your essay to the meaning of the major symbols or allegorical thrust of the story. An idea about "Young Goodman Brown," for example, is that fanaticism darkens and limits the human soul. An early incident in the story provides symbolic support for this idea. Specifically, when Goodman Brown enters the woods, he resolves "to stand firm against the devil," and he then looks up "to heaven above." As he looks, a "black mass of cloud" appears to hide the "brightening stars." Within the limits of our central idea, the cloud may be seen as a symbol, just like the widening path or the night walk itself. Look for ways to make solid connections like this in your symbolic ascriptions.

INTRODUCTION. The introduction should establish the grounds for your discussion. There may be a recurring symbol, for example, or a regular symbolic pattern, or actions with allegorical applications. Your discussion should determine the nature of the symbols or allegory, such as Miss Brill's opening and closing of the box for her shabby fur piece, the darkness in "Young Goodman Brown," or the freezing cold in Glaspell's *Trifles*.

BODY. There are a number of strategies for discussing symbolism and allegory. You might use one exclusively, or a combination. If you want to write about symbolism, you might consider the following:

1. *The meaning of a major symbol.* Identify the symbol and what it stands for. Then answer questions such as these: Is the symbol cultural or contextual? How do you decide? How do you derive your interpretation of the symbolic meaning? What is the extent of the meaning? Does the symbol undergo modification or new applications if it reappears? How does the symbol affect your understanding of the work? Does the symbol bring out any ironies? How does the symbol add strength and depth to the work?

2. *The development and relationship of symbols.* For two or more symbols, consider issues such as these: How do the symbols connect with each other (like night and the cloud in "Young Goodman Brown" as symbols of a darkening mind)? What additional meanings do the symbols provide? Are they complementary, contradictory, or ironic? (The windmill and the medicine in "A Worn Path," for example, are ironic because the windmill suggests cheer while the medicine suggests hopelessness.) Do the symbols control the form of the work? How? (For example, in "The Cask of Amontillado" the descent into the catacombs of the Montresors begins at dusk and the time lapse of the story suggests that the conclusion takes place in total darkness. A similar movement may be seen in "Miss Brill," in the movement from the sunlit outdoors to the protagonist's small and dark room.) Might such contrasting times of day be viewed symbolically in relationship to the development of the two stories? Other issues to consider are whether the symbols fit naturally or artificially into the context of the story, or whether and how the writer's symbols create unique qualities or excellences.

If you write about allegory, you might use one of the following approaches:

1. *The application and meaning of the allegory.* What is the subject of the story (allegory, fable, parable, myth)? How may it be more generally applied to ideas or to qualities of human character, not only of its own time but also of our own? What other versions of the story do you know, if any? Does it illustrate, either closely or loosely, particular philosophies or religious views? If so, what are these? How do you know?

2. *The consistency of the allegory.* Is the allegory used consistently throughout the story, or is it used intermittently? Explain and illustrate this use. Would it be correct to call your story *allegorical* rather than an *allegory*? Can you determine how parts of the story are introduced for their allegorical importance? Examples are the natural obstacles in the woods in Welty's "A Worn Path," which are allegorical equivalents of life's difficulties, and the final battle scene in "Luck," which corresponds to the unpredictable and serendipitous nature of fame and fortune.

CONCLUSION.   Here you might summarize main points, describe general impressions, explain the impact of the symbolic or allegorical methods, indicate personal responses, or suggest further lines of thought and application. You might also assess the quality and appropriateness of the symbolism or allegory (such as the opening of "Young Goodman Brown" being in darkness, with the closing in gloom).

Sample Essay

Allegory and Symbolism in Hawthorne's "Young Goodman Brown"°

---

[1]   It is hard to read beyond the third paragraph of Nathaniel Hawthorne's "Young Goodman Brown" without realizing the story's allegory and symbolism. The opening at first seems realistic. Goodman Brown, a young Puritan, leaves his home in colonial Salem to take an overnight trip. His wife's name, "Faith," however, suggests a symbolic reading, and as soon as Brown goes into the forest, his ordinary walk changes into an allegorical trip into evil. The idea that Hawthorne shows by this trip is that rigid belief destroys even the best human qualities.* He develops this thought in the allegory and in many symbols, particularly the sunset, the walking stick, and the path.†

[2]   The allegory is about how people develop destructive ideas. Most of the story is dreamlike and unreal, and the ideas that Brown gains are also unreal. At the weird "witch meeting," he concludes that everyone he knows is sinful, and he then permits mistrust and loathing to distort his previous love for his wife and neighbors. As a result, he becomes harsh and gloomy for the rest of his life. The location of the story in colonial Salem indicates that Hawthorne's allegorical target is the zealous pursuit of religious principles that dwell on sinfulness rather than love. However, modern readers may also apply the allegory to the ways in which people uncritically accept any ideal (most often political loyalties or racial or national prejudices), and thereby reject the integrity and rights of others. If

°See pages 284–93 for this story.
*Central idea.
†Thesis sentence.

[2] people like Brown apply a rigid standard and if they never try to understand those they condemn, they can condemn anyone. In this way, Hawthorne's allegory applies to any narrow-minded acceptance of ideals or systems that exclude the importance of love, understanding, and tolerance.

[3] Hawthorne's attack on such dehumanizing belief is found not just in the allegory but also in his many symbols. For example, the seventh word in the story, "sunset," may be taken as a symbol. In reality, sunset merely indicates the end of day. Coming at the beginning of the story, however, it suggests that Goodman Brown is beginning his long night of hatred, his spiritual death. For him the night will never end because his final days are shrouded in "gloom" (paragraph 72).

The next symbol, the guide's walking stick or staff, suggests the arbitrariness of the standard by which Brown judges his neighbors. Hawthorne's description indicates the symbolic nature of this staff:

[4]
> . . . the only thing about him [the guide] that could be fixed upon as remarkable, was his staff, which bore the likeness of a great black snake, so curiously wrought, that it might almost be seen to twist and wriggle itself like a living serpent. This, of course, must have been an ocular deception, assisted by the uncertain light. (paragraph 13)

The serpent symbolically suggests Satan, who in Genesis (3:1–7) is the originator of all evil, but the phrase "ocular deception" creates an interesting and realistic ambiguity about the symbol. Since the perception of the snake may depend on nothing more than the "uncertain" light, the staff may be less symbolic of evil than of the tendency to find evil where it does not exist (and could the uncertain light symbolize the uncertainty of human understanding?).

[5] In the same vein, the path through the forest is a major symbol of the destructive mental confusion that overcomes Brown. As he walks, the path grows "wilder and drearier, and more faintly traced," and "at length" it vanishes (paragraph 51). This is like the Biblical description of the "broad" way that leads "to Destruction" (Matthew 7:13). As a symbol, the path shows that most human acts are bad, but a small number, like the "narrow" way to life (Matthew 7:14), are good. Goodman Brown's path is at first clear, as though sin is at first unique and unusual. Soon, however, it is so indistinct that he can see only sin wherever he turns. The symbol suggests that when people follow evil, their moral vision becomes blurred and they soon fall prey to "the instinct that guides mortal man to evil" (paragraph 51).

[6] Through Hawthorne's allegory and symbols, "Young Goodman Brown" presents the paradox of how noble beliefs can backfire. Goodman Brown dies in gloom because he believes that his wrong vision is true. This form of evil is the hardest to stop, because wrongdoers who are convinced of their own goodness are beyond reach. In view of such self-righteous evil, whether cloaked in the apparent virtues of Puritanism or of some other blindly rigorous doctrine (political as well as religious), Hawthorne writes that "the fiend in his own shape is less hideous, than when he rages in the breast of man" (paragraph 53). Young Goodman Brown thus is the central symbol of the story. He is one of those who think they walk in light but who really create their own darkness.

COMMENTARY ON THE ESSAY

The introduction justifies the treatment of allegory and symbolism on the grounds that Hawthorne early in the story invites such a reading. The central idea relates Hawthorne's method to the idea that rigid belief destroys the best human qualities.

Paragraph 2 considers the allegory as a criticism of rigid Puritan morality. The major thread running through each of the major parts of the paragraph is the hurtful effect of monomaniacal views like those of Brown. Paragraphs 3, 4, and 5 deal with three major symbols: sunset, the staff, and the path. The aim of this discussion is to show how the symbols apply to Hawthorne's attack on unquestioning belief. Throughout these three paragraphs the central idea—the relationship of rigidity to destructiveness—is stressed. Hawthorne's allusions to both the Old and New Testaments are pointed out in paragraphs 4 and 5. The last paragraph builds to the conclusion that Brown symbolizes the idea that the primary cause of evil is the inability to separate reality from unreality.

If you write exclusively about allegory, use paragraph 2 of the sample essay as a guide either for a single paragraph or, as expanded, for an entire essay. If the allegory of "Young Goodman Brown," for example, were to be expanded, additional topics might be Brown's gullibility, the meaning of faith and the requirements for maintaining it, and the causes for preferring to think evil rather than good of other people. Such points are sufficiently important to sustain an entire essay on the topic of allegory.

SPECIAL WRITING TOPICS
FOR SYMBOLISM AND ALLEGORY

1. Write an essay on the allegorical method of one or more of the allegories included in the Gospel According to St. Luke, such as "The Bridegroom" (5:34–35), "The Garments and the Wineskins" (5:36–39), "The Sower" (8:4–15), "The Good Samaritan" (10:25–37), "The Prodigal Son" (15:11-32), "The Ox in the Well" (14:5–6), "The Watering of Animals on the Sabbath" (13:15–17), "The Rich Fool" (12:16–21), "Lazarus" (16:19–31), "The Widow and the Judge" (18:1–8), and "The Pharisee and the Publican" (18:9–14).

2. Describe and discuss the symbolism in Hughes's "Theme for English B" and Hayden's "Those Winter Sundays." To what degree do the poems rely on contextual symbols? On cultural or universal symbols?

3. Consider the symbolism in "A Work of Artifice," "Miss Brill," "A Worn Path," or *The Bear* first, in terms of male dominance, and, second, as myths about the obstacles to a woman's freedom and independence. Before you begin, you may wish to consult the section on feminist criticism in Appendix C.

4. Write a poem or story using a widely recognized cultural symbol such as the flag (patriotism, love of country, a certain type of politics), water (life, sexuality, regeneration), or the population explosion (the end of life on earth). By arranging actions and dialogue, make clear the issues conveyed by your symbol, and also try to resolve the conflicts that the symbol might raise among your characters.

5. Write a poem or story in which you develop your own *contextual symbol*. You might, for example, demonstrate how holding a job brings out character strengths or how neglecting to care for the inside or outside of a house indicates a character's decline. The principle is to bring out the symbolism in something that is usually considered only normal and ordinary.

chapter 11

Writing About Tone:

The Writer's Control
Over Attitudes and Feelings

Tone refers to the methods by which writers and speakers reveal attitudes or feelings. It is an aspect of all spoken and written statements—from earnest declarations of love, requests to pass a dish at dinner, letters from students asking parents for money, to official government notices threatening penalties if fines are not paid. Because tone is often equated with *attitude*, it is important to realize that tone refers not so much to attitudes themselves but instead to those techniques and modes of presentation that reveal or create attitudes.

As a literary concept, *tone* is adapted from the phrase *tone of voice* in speech. Tone of voice reflects attitudes toward a particular object or situation, and also toward listeners. Let us suppose that Mary has a difficult assignment, which she expects to work on all day. Things go well, and she finishes quickly. She happily tells her friend Anne, "I'm so pleased. I needed only two hours for that." Then she decides to buy tickets for a popular play and must wait through a long and slow line. After getting her tickets, she tells the people at the end of the line, "I'm so pleased. I needed only two hours for that." The sentences are exactly the same, but by changing her emphasis and vocal inflection, Mary indicates her disgust and impatience with her long wait and also shows her sympathy with the people still in line. By controlling the *tone* of her statements, in other words, Mary conveys attitudes of satisfaction at one time, and indignation and also sympathy at another.

As this example indicates, an attitude itself may be summarized with a word or phrase (satisfaction or indignation, love or contempt, deference or command, and so on), but the study of tone examines those aspects of situation, language, action, and background that *bring out* the attitude. In Welty's "A Worn Path," for example, the attendant offers Phoenix "a few pennies," but Phoenix wants more. Being a recipient of charity but also being an independent sort, Phoenix makes the following response:

> "Five pennies is a nickel," said Phoenix stiffly. (paragraph 99)

This request is indirect, but it is nevertheless demanding. Although Phoenix is not a literary master, she is a master of tone in this conversational situation.

TONE AND ATTITUDES

ATTITUDE TOWARD THE MATERIAL. By reading a story carefully, we may deduce the author's attitude or attitudes toward the subject matter. In "Anthem for Doomed Youth," for example, Wilfred Owen shows detestation of war and sympathy for those whose loved ones have been killed. In "A Work of Artifice," Marge Piercy brings out anger against traditional treatment of women. In "Echo" (p. 194), Rossetti's speaker addresses a lover who is long dead, and by this means Rossetti renders attitudes of yearning and sorrow. In a broader perspective, authors may view human beings with amused affection, as in Chekhov's *The Bear*, or with amused resignation, as in Hardy's "Channel Firing."

ATTITUDE TOWARD READERS. Authors recognize that readers participate in the creative act and that all elements of a story—word choice, characterization, allusions, levels of reality—must take readers' responses into account (note the discussion of "Reader Response" criticism in Appendix C). When Hawthorne's woodland guide in "Young Goodman Brown" refers to King Philip's War, for example, Hawthorne assumes that his readers know that this war was inhumanly greedy and cruel. By not explaining this part of history, he indicates respect for the knowledge of his readers, and he also assumes their agreement with his interpretation. Updike in "A & P" assumes that readers understand his use of Sammy's diction to reveal Sammy as a perceptive and independent but insecure young man. Authors always make such considerations about readers by implicitly complimenting them on their knowledge and also by satisfying their curiosity and desire to be interested, stimulated, and pleased.

OTHER DOMINANT ATTITUDES. Beyond general authorial tone, there are many internal and dramatically rendered expressions of attitude. For example, the speaker of Lowell's "Patterns" is a prim and proper upper-class young woman. Yet at the news of her fiancé's death, her sorrowful meditation brings out that she had made a promise to him to make love outside, on a "shady seat" in the garden (lines 86–89). This personal confession reveals the inner warmth that her external appearance does not suggest, and it also makes the poem pathetically poignant.

In addition, as characters interact, their tone dramatically shows their judgments about other characters and situations. The brusque young woman in Mansfield's "Miss Brill" compares Miss Brill's fur muff to a "fried whiting" (paragraph 14). Her speech indicates contempt, indifference, and cruelty. A complicated control of tone occurs in Glaspell's *Trifles* where the two major characters, Mrs. Hale and Mrs. Peters, decide to cover up incriminating evidence about Minnie Wright. When Mrs. Peters agrees to this obstruction of justice, however, she speaks not about illegality, but rather about the possible embarrassment of the action:

> "My!" she began, in a high, false voice, "it's a good thing the men couldn't hear us! Getting all stirred up over a little thing like a—dead canary." She hurried over that. "As if that could have anything to do with—with— My, wouldn't they *laugh*?" (speech 137)

Notice that her words reveal her knowledge that men scoff at feminine concerns, like Minnie's quilting knots, and therefore she openly anticipates the men's amusement.The reader, however, knows that she is joining Mrs. Hale in covering up the evidence about Minnie.

TONE AND HUMOR

A major aspect of tone is the communication of humor. Everyone likes to laugh, and shared laughter is part of good human relationships; but not everyone can explain or convey humor. Laughter resists close analysis; it is unplanned, personal, idiosyncratic, and usually unpredictable. Nonetheless, there are a number of common elements:

1. *An object to laugh at.* There must be something to laugh at—a person, thing, situation, custom, habit of speech or dialect, or arrangement of words.

2. *Incongruity.* People normally know what to expect under given conditions, and anything contrary to these expectations is *incongruous* and may therefore generate laughter. When the temperature is 100°F, for example, you expect people to dress lightly. If you see a person dressed in a heavy overcoat, a warm hat, a muffler, and large gloves, who is waving his arms and stamping his feet to keep warm, this person violates your expectations. Because his garments and behavior are *inappropriate* or *incongruous*, you would probably find him amusing. A student in a language class once wrote about a "*congregation* of verbs" and also about parts of speech as "nouns, verbs, and *proverbs*." The student meant the *conjugation* of verbs, of course, and also (maybe) either *adverbs* or *pronouns*, but somehow his understanding slipped

and he created humorous incongruities. Such inadvertent verbal errors are called **malapropisms**, after Mrs. Malaprop, a character in Sheridan's eighteenth-century play *The Rivals*. In the literary creation of malapropisms, the tone is directed against the speaker, for the amusement of both readers and author alike.

3. *Safety and/or goodwill.* Seeing a person slip on a banana peel and hurtle through the air may cause laughter, but only if we ourselves are not that person, for laughter depends on insulation from danger and pain. In humorous situations that involve physical abuse—falling down stairs or being hit in the face by cream pies—the abuse never harms the participants. The incongruity of such situations causes laughter, and the immunity from pain and injury prevents grave or even horrified responses. Goodwill enters into humor in romantic comedy or in any other work where we are drawn into general sympathy with the major figures, such as Smirnov and Mrs. Popov in Chekhov's *The Bear*. As the author leads the characters toward recognizing their love, our involvement produces happiness, smiles, and even sympathetic laughter.

4. *Unfamiliarity, newness, uniqueness, spontaneity.* Laughter depends on seeing something new or unique or on experiencing something familiar in a new light. Because laughter is prompted by flashes of insight or sudden revelations, it is always spontaneous, even when readers already know what they are laughing at. Indeed, the task of the comic writer is to develop ordinary materials to that point when spontaneity frees readers to laugh. Thus you can read and reread *The Bear* and laugh each time because, even though you know what happens, the play shapes your responses to the growth of love from anger. The love between Mrs. Popov and Smirnov is and always will be comic because it is so illogical, incongruous, and spontaneous.

TONE AND IRONY

The capacity to have more than one attitude toward someone or something is a uniquely human trait. We know that people are not perfect, but we love a number of them anyway. Therefore we speak to them not only with love and praise but also with banter and criticism. On occasion, you may have given mildly insulting greeting cards to your loved ones, not to affront them but to amuse them. As you share smiles and laughs, you also remind them of your affection.

The word **irony** describes such contradictory statements or situations. Irony is natural to human beings, who are aware of life's ambiguities and complexities. It develops from the realization that life does not always measure up to promise, that friends and loved ones are sometimes angry and bitter toward each other, that the universe contains incomprehensible mysteries, that the social and political structure is often oppressive rather than liberating, that doubt exists even in the certainty of knowledge and faith, and that human character is built through chagrin, regret, and pain as much as through emulation and praise. In expressing an idea ironically, writers pay the greatest compliment to their reading audience, for they assume that readers have sufficient intelligence and skill to discover the real meaning of quizzical or ambiguous statements and situations.

VERBAL IRONY. Irony can be *verbal, situational*, or *dramatic*. In **verbal irony** one thing is said and the opposite is meant. In the example at the opening of this chapter, Mary's ironic expression of pleasure after her two-hour wait for tickets really means that she is disgusted. There are important types of verbal irony. In **understatement** the expression does not fully describe the importance of a situation and therefore makes its point by implication. For example, in Bierce's "An Occurrence at Owl Creek Bridge," the condemned man contemplates the apparatus designed by the soldiers to hang him. After considering the method, the man's response is described by the narrator: "The arrangement commended itself to his judgment as simple and effective" (paragraph 4). These words would be appropriate for the appraisal of ordinary machinery, perhaps, but because the apparatus will cause the man's death, the understated observation is ironic.

By contrast, in **overstatement** or **hyperbole**, the words are far in excess of the situation, and readers or listeners therefore understand that the true meaning is considerably less than what is said. In the sonnet "That Time of Year Thou Mayest in Me Behold," for example, Shakespeare is establishing the perspective that life does not last forever. To exemplify this point, the speaker states that his own autumnal leaves are falling, his sun of life is going down, and his youth is no more than ashes. Without denying the seriousness of death, Shakespeare's comparisons make the speaker's death seem imminent, and hence they constitute overstatement.

Often verbal irony is ambiguous, having double meaning or **double entendre**. Midway through "Young Goodman Brown," for example, the woodland guide leaves Brown alone while stating, "when you feel like moving again, there is my staff to help you along" (paragraph 40). The word "staff" is ambiguous, for it refers to the staff that resembles a serpent (paragraph 13). The word therefore suggests that the devilish guide is leaving Brown not only with a real staff but also with the spirit of evil (unlike the divine "staff" of Psalm 23 that gives comfort). Ambiguity of course may be used in relation to any topic. Quite often *double entendre* is used in statements about sexuality, usually for the amusement of listeners or readers.

SITUATIONAL IRONY. **Situational irony,** or **irony of situation,** refers to the chasm between what we hope for or expect and what actually happens. It is often pessimistic because it emphasizes that human beings usually have little or no control over their lives or anything else. The forces of opposition may be psychological, social, cultural, political, or environmental. The situation is not temporary, one might add, but permanent and universal, as in Hardy's "Channel Firing," which deals with the situation that warfare has been and will be constant in past, present, and future times. Although situational irony often involves disaster, it need not always do so. For example, a happier occurrence of situational irony is in Chekhov's *The Bear*, for the two characters shift from anger to love as they fall into the grips of emotions that are "bigger than both of them."

COSMIC IRONY.   A special kind of situational irony that emphasizes the pessimistic and fatalistic side of life is **cosmic irony,** or **irony of fate.** By the standard of cosmic irony, the universe is indifferent to individuals, who are subject to blind chance, accident, uncontrollable emotions, perpetual misfortune, and misery. Even if things temporarily go well, people's lives end badly, and their best efforts do not rescue them or make them happy. A play illustrating cosmic irony is Glaspell's *Trifles*, which develops out of the stultifying conditions of farm life experienced by Minnie Wright. She has no profession, no other hope, no other life except the lonely, dreary farm—nothing. After thirty years of wretchedness, she buys a canary who warbles for her to make life a little pleasant. After a year, her boorish and insensitive husband wrings the bird's neck, and she in turn, with her only meager pleasure destroyed, strangles him at night in his bed. Her situation is cosmically ironic, for the implication of *Trifles* is that human beings are caught in a web of adverse circumstances from which there is no escape.

DRAMATIC IRONY.   Like cosmic irony, **dramatic irony** is a special kind of situational irony. It happens when a character either lacks information about a situation or else misjudges it, but readers (and often some of the other characters) see everything completely and correctly. The model of dramatic irony is found in *Oedipus the King* by the ancient Greek dramatist Sophocles. In this play everyone—other characters and readers alike—knows the truth long before Oedipus knows it. Writers of nondramatic works also make use of dramatic irony. For instance, in "A Worn Path," we observe the strength and determination of Phoenix, but we know that in the long run her efforts to help her grandson will be ineffective.

WRITING ABOUT TONE

Begin with a careful reading, noting those elements of the work that convey attitudes. Consider whether the work genuinely creates the attitudes it is designed to evoke. In "The Cask of Amontillado," for example, do the gloomy catacombs evoke emotions of fear, or do they seem exaggerated? In Masefield's "Cargoes," how adequately does the British coaster convey disapproval of modern industry? Depending on the work, your devising and answering such questions can help you understand the degree of an author's control over tone. Similar questions apply when you study internal qualities such as style and characterization.

- How strongly do you respond to the work? What attitudes can you identify and characterize? What elements in the story elicit your concern, indignation, fearfulness, anguish, amusement, or affirmation?

- What causes you to sympathize or not to sympathize with the characters, situations, or ideas? What makes the circumstances in the work admirable or understandable (or deplorable)?

- In fiction and drama, what does the dialogue suggest about the author's attitudes toward the characters? How does it influence your attitudes? What qualities of diction permit and encourage your responses?

- To what degree, if any, does the work supersede any previous ideas you might have had about the same or similar subject matter? What do you think effected any changes in your attitude?

- What role does the narrator/speaker play in your attitudes toward the dramatic or fictional material? Does the speaker seem intelligent or stupid, friendly or unfriendly, sane or insane, idealistic or pragmatic?

- In an amusing or comic story, what elements of plot, character, and diction are particularly comic? How strongly do you respond to humor-producing situations? Why?

- What ironies do you find in the story (verbal, situational, cosmic)? How is the irony connected to philosophies of marriage, family, society, politics, religion, or morality?

- To what extent are the characters controlled by forces like fate, social or racial discrimination, limitations of intelligence, economic and political inequality, and limited opportunity?

- Do any words seem unusual or noteworthy, such as words in dialect, polysyllabic words, or foreign words or phrases that the author assumes you know? Are there any especially connotative or emotive words? What do these words suggest about the author's apparent assumptions about the readers?

Organizing Your Essay About Tone

INTRODUCTION.   Your introduction should describe the general situation of the work and its dominant moods or impressions, such as that the work leads to cynicism, as in "Channel Firing," or to laughter and delight, as in *The Bear*. Problems connected with describing the work's tone should also be introduced here.

BODY.   Your goal is to show how the author establishes the dominant moods of the work. Some possibilities are the use or misuse of language, the exposé of a pretentious speaker, the use of exact and specific descriptions, the isolation of a major character, the failure of plans, or continued naiveté in a disillusioned world. Some of the things to discuss are these:

1. *Audience, situation, and characters.* Is any person or group directly addressed by the speaker? What attitude is expressed (love, respect, condescension, confidentiality, confidence, etc.)? What is the basic situation in the story? Do you find irony? If so, what kind is it? What does the irony show (optimism or pessimism, for example)? How is the situation controlled to shape your responses? That is, can actions, situations, or characters be seen as expressions of attitude or as embodiments of certain favorable or unfavorable ideas or positions? What is the nature of the speaker or persona? Why does the speaker speak exactly as he or she does? How is the speaker's character manipulated to show apparent authorial attitude and to elicit reader response? Does the story promote respect, admiration, dislike, or other feelings about character or situation? How?

2. *Descriptions, diction.* Your concern here is not to analyze descriptions or diction for themselves alone, but to relate these matters to attitude. *For descriptions:* To what degree do descriptions of natural scenery and conditions (snowstorms, cold, rain, ice, intense sunlight) convey an attitude that complements or opposes the circumstances of the characters? Are there any systematic references to colors, sounds, or noises that collectively reflect an attitude? *For diction:* Do connotative meanings of words control response in any way? To what degree does the diction require readers to have a large or technical vocabulary? Do speech patterns or the use of dialect evoke attitudes about speakers or their condition of life? Is the level of diction normal, slang, standard, or substandard? What is the effect of such a level? Are there unusual or particularly noteworthy expressions? If so, what attitudes do these show? Does the author use verbal irony? To what effect?

3. *Humor.* Is the story funny? How funny, how intense? How is the humor achieved? Does the humor develop out of incongruous situations or language, or both? Is there an underlying basis of attack in the humor, or are the objects of laughter still respected or even loved despite having humor directed against them?

4. *Ideas.* Are any ideas advocated, defended mildly, or attacked? How does the author clarify his or her attitude toward these ideas—directly, by statement, or indirectly, through understatement, overstatement, or a character's speeches? In what ways does the story assume a common ground of assent between author and reader? That is, what common assumptions do you find about religious views, political ideas, moral and behavioral standards, and so on? Is it easy to give assent (temporary or permanent) to these ideas, or is any concession needed by the reader to approach the story? (For example, a major subject of "Dover Beach" is that absolute faith in the truth of religion has been lost. This subject may not be important to everyone, but even an irreligious reader or a follower of another faith may find common ground in the poem's psychological situation or in the desire to learn as much as possible about so important a subject.)

5. *Unique characteristics of the story.* Each story has unique properties that

contribute to the tone. Rossetti's "Echo" (p. 194), for example, considers the speaker's memory of her dead lover and presents details suggesting her poignancy and despair. Hardy's "Channel Firing" develops from the comic idea that the firing of guns at sea is so loud it could awaken the dead. In other works there might be some recurring word or phrase that seems special. For example, Mark Twain in "Luck" develops a passage centering on the word *blunder* and thereby makes his attitude clear about the boob hero, Scoresby (paragraph 12).

CONCLUSION.   In the conclusion, first summarize your main points and then go on to redefinitions, explanations, or afterthoughts, together with ideas reinforcing earlier points. You might also mention some other major aspect of the story's tone that you did not develop in the body.

Sample Essay

The Tone of Confidence in "Theme for English B"
by Langston Hughes°

[1] "Theme for English B" grows from the situational irony of racial differences as seen by the speaker, an African-American college student. This situation might easily produce bitterness, anger, outrage, or vengefulness. However, the poem contains none of these. It is not angry or indignant; it is not an appeal for revenge or revolution. It is rather a declaration of personal independence and individuality. The tone is one of objectivity, daring, occasional playfulness, but above all, confidence.° These attitudes are made plain in the speaker's situation, the ideas, the poetic form, the diction, and the expressions.†

[2] Hughes's poetic treatment is objective, factual, and personal, not emotional or political. The poem contains a number of clearly expressed factual details: The speaker is black in an otherwise all-white college English class. He has come from North Carolina and is now living alone at the Harlem YMCA, away from family and roots. He is also, at 22, an older student. All this is evidence of disadvantage, yet the speaker does no more than present the facts objectively, without comment.

[3] Hughes's thoughts about equality—the idea underlying the poem—are presented in the same objective, cool manner. The speaker writes to his instructor as an equal, not as an inferior. His idea is that all people are the same, regardless of race or background. In defining himself, therefore, he does not deal in abstractions, but emphasizes that he, like everyone else, has ordinary likes and needs, and that his abilities and activities are like those of everyone else. By causing the speaker to avoid emotionalism and controversy, Hughes makes counterargument difficult if not impossible.

°See page 320 for this poem.
°Central idea.
†Thesis sentence.

[4] The argument for equality is carried out even in Hughes's actual use of the poetic form. The title here is the key, for it does not promise the most exciting of topics. Normally, in fact, one would expect nothing much more than a short prose essay in response to an English assignment, but a poem is unexpected and therefore daring and original, particularly one like this that touches on the topic of equality and identity. The wit, originality, and skill of the speaker's use of the form itself demonstrate the self-confidence and self-sufficiency that underlie the theoretical claim for equality.

[5] Hughes's diction is also in keeping with the poem's confidence and daring. Almost all the words are short and simple—of no more than one or two syllables—showing the speaker's confidence in the truth and power of his ideas. This high proportion of short words reflects a conscious attempt to keep the diction clear and direct. A result is that Hughes avoids any possible ambiguities, as the following words show:

> Well, I like to eat, sleep, drink, and be in love.
> I like to work, read, learn, and understand life.
> I like a pipe for a Christmas present,
> or records—Bessie, bop, or Bach. (lines 21–24)

With the exception of what it means to "understand life," these descriptive words are free of emotional overtones. They reflect the speaker's confident belief that equality should replace inequality and prejudice.

A number of the speaker's phrases and expressions also show this same confidence. Although most of the language is simple and descriptive, it is also playful and ironic. In lines 18–20 there seems to be a deliberate use of confusing language to bring about a verbal merging of the identities of the speaker, the instructor, Harlem, and the greater New York area:

> Harlem, I hear you:
> hear you, hear me—we two—you, me talk on this page.
> (I hear New York, too.) Me—who?

[6] One may also find a certain whimsicality in the way in which the speaker treats the irony of the black-white situation:

> So will my page be colored that I write? (line 27)

Underlying this last expression is an awareness that, despite the claim that people are equal and are tied to each other by common humanity, there are also strong differences among individuals. The speaker is confidently asserting grounds for independence as well as equality.

[7] Thus, an examination of "Theme for English B" reveals vitality and confidence. The poem is a statement of trust and an almost open challenge on the personal level to the unachieved ideal of equality. Hughes makes this point through the deliberate simplicity of the speaker's words and descriptions. Yet the poem is not without irony, particularly at the end, where the speaker mentions that the instructor is "somewhat more free" than he is. "Theme for English B" is complex and engaging. It shows the speaker's confidence through objectivity, daring, and playfulness.

COMMENTARY ON THE ESSAY

Because this essay embodies a number of approaches by which tone may be studied in any work (situation, common ground, diction, special characteristics), it is typical of many essays that use a combined, eclectic approach. The central idea is that the dominant attitude in "Theme for English B" is the speaker's confidence and that this confidence is shown in the similar but separable attitudes of objectivity, daring, and playfulness.

Paragraph 2 deals with situational irony in relation to the social and political circumstance of racial discrimination (see approach 1, p. 145). Paragraph 3 considers the objectivity with which Hughes considers the idea of equality (approach 4).

Paragraph 4 shows how a topic that might ordinarily be taken for granted—in this case the basic form or genre of expression—can be seen as a unique feature of tone (approach 5). The paragraph contrasts the *expected* student response (no more than a brief prose essay) with the *actual* response (the poem itself, with its interesting twists and turns). Since the primary tone of the poem is that of self-confidence, which is the unspoken basis for the speaker's assertion of independence and equality, the paragraph stresses that the form itself embodies this attitude.

Paragraphs 5 and 6 consider how Hughes's word choices exhibit his attempts at clarity, objectivity, playfulness, and confidence (approach 2). The attention given in these paragraphs to Hughes's simple, direct diction is justified by its importance in the poem's tone.

The concluding paragraph stresses again the attitude of confidence in the poem and also notes additional attitudes of trust, challenge, irony, daring, and playfulness.

SPECIAL WRITING TOPICS FOR TONE

1. Write an essay comparing and contrasting attitudes toward the following female characters: Phoenix in "A Worn Path," Mathilde in "The Necklace," and Miss Brill in "Miss Brill." How does the presentation shape your attitudes toward them? What particular details of tone would become important in a feminist approach to these works (see Appendix C)?

2. Consider a short story or poem in which the speaker is the central character (for example: "A & P," "The Cask of Amontillado," "Patterns," "Dover Beach," "Channel Firing"). Write an essay showing how the language of the narrator affects your attitudes toward him or her (that is, your sympathy for the narrator, your interest in the narrative, your feelings toward the other characters and what they do). Be sure to emphasize the relationship between their language and your responses.

3. Describe the tone in *Trifles* about personal marital abuse. On the basis of the

details and outcome of the play, how does Glaspell cause you to approve (or disapprove) of the women's decision not to report their thoughts to the men?

4. Assume that you are writing a story or play involving, for example, a student, a supervisor, or a politician. Write a fragment treating your character with dramatic irony; that is, your character thinks he or she knows all the details about a situation but really does not (e.g., a woman declares her interest in a man without realizing that he is engaged to another woman, or the supervisor expresses distrust in a person who is one of the best workers in the firm). Explain the action, words, and situations that you choose to make your irony clear.

chapter 12

Writing About a Problem:
Challenges to Overcome
in Reading

A **problem** is any question that you cannot answer easily and correctly about a body of material that you know. The question, "Who is the major character in Shakespeare's *Hamlet*?" is not a problem, because the obvious answer is Hamlet.

Let us, however, ask another question: "Why is it *correct* to say that Hamlet is the major character?" This question is not as easy as the first, and for this reason it is a problem. It requires that we think about our answer, even though we do not need to search very far. Hamlet is the title character. He is involved in most of the actions of the play. He is so much the center of our liking and concern that his death causes sadness and regret. To "solve" this problem has required a set of responses, all of which provide answers to the question "why?"

More complex, however, and more typical of most problems, are questions such as "Why does Hamlet talk of suicide in his first soliloquy?" "Why does he treat Ophelia so coarsely in the 'nunnery' scene?" "Why does he delay in avenging his father's death?" Essays on a problem are normally concerned with such questions because they require a good deal of thought, together with a number of interpretations knitted together into a whole essay. More broadly, dealing with problems is one of the major tasks of the intellectual, scientific, social, and political disciplines. Being able to advance and then explain solutions is therefore one of the most important techniques that you can acquire.

STRATEGIES FOR DEVELOPING AN ESSAY ABOUT A PROBLEM

Your first purpose is to convince your reader that your solution is a good one. This you do by making sound conclusions from supporting evidence. In non-scientific subjects like literature you rarely find absolute proofs, so your conclusions will not be *proved* in the way you prove triangles congruent in geometry. But your organization, your use of facts from the text, your interpretations, and your application of general or specific knowledge should all make your conclusions convincing. Thus your basic strategy is *persuasion*.

STRATEGY 1: DEMONSTRATE THAT CONDITIONS FOR A SOLUTION ARE FULFILLED. This type of development is the most basic in writing—namely, illustration. You first explain that certain conditions need to exist for your solution to be plausible. Your central idea—really a brief answer to the question—is that the conditions do indeed exist. Your development is to show how the conditions may be found in the work.

Suppose that you are writing on the problem of why Hamlet delays revenge against Claudius, his uncle and also the murderer of his father. Suppose also that you make the point that Hamlet delays because he is never sure that Claudius is guilty. This is your "solution" to the problem. In your essay you support your answer by challenging the credibility of the information Hamlet receives about the crime (i.e., the two visits from the Ghost and Claudius's distress at the play within the play). Once you have "attacked" these sources of data on the grounds that they are unreliable, you have succeeded because your solution is consistent with the details of the play.

STRATEGY 2: ANALYZE WORDS IN THE PHRASING OF THE PROBLEM. Your object in this approach is to clarify important words in the statement of the problem and then to decide how applicable they are. This kind of attention to words, in fact, might give you enough material for all or part of your essay. Thus, an essay on the problem of Hamlet's delay might focus in part on a treatment of the word *delay*: What, really, does *delay* mean? For Hamlet, is there a difference between delay that is reasonable and delay that is unreasonable? Does Hamlet delay unreasonably? Is his delay the result of a psychological fault? Would speedy revenge be more or less reasonable than the delay? By the time you have answered such pointed questions, you will also have sufficient material for your full essay.

STRATEGY 3: REFER TO LITERARY CONVENTIONS OR EXPECTATIONS. With this strategy, the argument is to establish that the problem can be solved by reference to the literary mode or conventions of a work, or to the work's own self-limitations. In other words, what appears to be a problem is really no more than a normal characteristic. For example, a question might be raised about why Mathilde in "The Necklace" does not tell her friend Jeanne about the loss of the necklace. A plausible answer is that, all motivation aside, the story builds up to a surprise, which could be spoiled by an early disclosure. To solve the problem, in other words, one has recourse to the structure of the story—to the literary convention that Maupassant observes in "The Necklace."

Other problems that might be dealt with in this way might concern levels of reality. A problem about the uncertainty of what happens in Hawthorne's "Young Goodman Brown," for example, can be answered by the assertion that the story is fanciful and dreamlike (or nightmarish). In everyday life, things could not happen as they do in the story. A question about the sudden love of Mrs. Popov and Smirnov in Chekhov's *The Bear* can be answered by reference to the play's being a farce. Because in farces unlikely events occur without apparent logic, such a quick infatuation is not unusual at all. The principal strategy in dealing with problems like these is to establish a context in which the problems vanish. Problems, in other words, may be seen as resulting from no more than normal occurrences, granted the generic qualities or levels of reality of particular works.

STRATEGY 4: ARGUE AGAINST POSSIBLE OBJECTIONS.   With this strategy, you raise your own objections and then argue against them. Called *procatalepsis* or *anticipation*, this approach helps you sharpen your arguments because *anticipating* and dealing with objections force you to make analyses and use facts that you might otherwise overlook. Although procatalepsis may be used point by point throughout your essay, you may find it most useful at the end.

The situation to imagine is that someone is raising objections to your solution to the problem. It is then your task to show that the objections (a) are not accurate or valid, (b) are not strong or convincing, or (c) are based on unusual rather than usual conditions (on an exception and not the rule). Here are some examples of these approaches. The objections raised are italicized, so you can easily distinguish them from the answers.

a. The objection is not accurate or valid. Here you refute the objection by showing that either the interpretation or the conclusions are wrong and also by emphasizing that the evidence supports your solution.

> Although Hamlet's delay is reasonable, *the claim might be made that his duty is to kill Claudius in revenge immediately after the Ghost's accusations.* This claim is not persuasive because it assumes that Hamlet knows everything the audience knows. The audience accepts the Ghost's word that Claudius is guilty, but Hamlet has no certain reasons to believe the Ghost. Would it not seem insane for Hamlet to kill Claudius, who reigns legally, and then to claim he did it because of the Ghost's words? The argument for speedy revenge is not good because it is based on an incorrect view of Hamlet's situation.

b. The objection is not strong or convincing. Here you *concede* that the objection has some truth or validity, but you then try to show that it is weak and that your own solution is stronger.

One might claim that Claudius's distress at the play within the play is evidence for his guilt and that therefore Hamlet should carry out his revenge right away. This argument has merit, and Hamlet's speech after Claudius has fled the scene ("I'll take the Ghost's word for a thousand pound") shows that the "conscience of the king" has been caught. But the king's guilty behavior is not a strong cause for killing him. Hamlet could justifiably ask for an investigation of his father's death on these grounds, but he could not justify a revenge killing. Claudius could not be convicted in any court on the testimony that he was disturbed at seeing the stage murder of Gonzago. Even after the play within the play, the reasons for delay are stronger than for action.

c. The objection is based on unusual rather than usual conditions. Here you reject the objection on the grounds that it could be valid only if normal conditions were suspended. The objection depends on an exception, not a rule.

The case for quick action is simple: *Hamlet should kill Claudius right after seeing the Ghost (I.3), or else after seeing the King's reaction to the stage murder of Gonzago (III.2), or else after seeing the Ghost again (III.4).* Redress under these circumstances, goes the argument, must be both personal and extra-legal. This argument wrongly assumes that due process does not exist in the Denmark of Hamlet and Claudius. Nothing in the play indicates that the Danes, even though they carouse a bit, do not value legality and the rules of evidence. Thus Hamlet cannot rush out to kill Claudius, because he knows that the King has not had anything close to due process. The argument for quick action is poor because it rests on an exception being made from civilized law.

WRITING ABOUT A PROBLEM

Writing an essay on a problem requires you to argue a position: Either there is a solution or there is not. To develop your position requires that you show the steps to your conclusion. Your general thematic form is thus (1) to describe the conditions that need to be met for the solution you propose, and then (2) to demonstrate that these conditions exist. If you assert that there is no solution, then your form would be the same for the first part, but your second part—the development—would show that these conditions have *not* been met.

Organizing Your Essay About a Problem

INTRODUCTION.   Begin with a statement of the problem and refer to the conditions that must be established for a solution. Your central idea is your answer to the question, and your thesis sentence indicates the main heads of your development.

BODY.   In developing your essay, use one or more of the strategies described in this chapter. These are, again: (1) to demonstrate that conditions for a solution are fulfilled; (2) to analyze the words in the phrasing of the problem; (3) to refer to literary expectations or limitations; and (4) to argue against possible objections. You might combine these. Thus, if we assume that your argument is that Hamlet's delay is reasonable, you might first consider the word *delay* (strategy 2); then you might use strategy 1 to explain the reasons for Hamlet's delay. Finally, to answer objections to your argument, you might show that he acts promptly when he believes he is justified (strategy 4). Whatever your topic, the important thing is to use the method or methods that best help you make a good argument for your solution.

CONCLUSION.   In your conclusion, try to affirm the validity of your solution in view of the supporting evidence. You might do this by reemphasizing your strongest points by simply presenting a brief summary, or by thinking of your argument as still continuing and thus using the strategy of procatalepsis to raise and answer possible objections to your solution, as is done in the last paragraph of the following sample essay.

Sample Essay

The Problem of Frost's Use of the Term "Desert Places" in the Poem "Desert Places"°

[1]   In the last line of "Desert Places," the meaning suggested by the title undergoes a sudden shift. At the beginning it clearly refers to the snowy setting described in the first stanza, but in the last line it refers to a negative state of soul. The problem is this: Does the change happen too late to be effective? That is, does the new meaning come out of nowhere, or does it really work as a closing thought? To answer these questions, one must grant that the change cannot be effective if there is no preparation for it before the last line of the poem. If there is preparation—that is, if Frost does provide hints that the speaker feels an emptiness like that of the bleak, snowy natural world—then the shift is both understandable and effective even though it comes at the very end. It is clear that Frost makes the preparation and therefore that the change is effective.* The preparation may be traced in Frost's references, word choices, and concluding sentences.†

[2]   In the first two stanzas, Frost includes the speaker in his reference to living things being overcome. His opening scene is one of snow that covers "weeds and stubble" (line 4) and that almost literally smothers hibernating animals "in their lairs" (line 6). The speaker then focuses on his own mental state, saying that he is "too absent-spirited to count," and that the "loneliness" of the scene "includes" him "unawares" (lines 7 and 8). This movement—from vegetable, to

°See page 317 for this poem.
*Central idea.
†Thesis sentence.

[2] animal, to human—shows that everything alive is changed by the snow. Obviously the speaker will not die like the grass or hibernate like the animals, but he indicates that the "loneliness" overcomes him. These first eight lines thus connect the natural bleakness with the speaker.

[3] In addition, a number of words in the third stanza are preparatory because they may be applied to human beings. The words "lonely" and "loneliness" (line 9), "more lonely" (line 10), "blanker" and "benighted" (line 11), and "no expression, nothing to express" (line 12) may all refer equally to human or to natural conditions. The word "benighted" is most important, because it suggests not only the darkness of night but also intellectual or moral ignorance. Since these words invite the reader to think of negative mental and emotional states, they provide a context in which the final shift of meaning is both logical and natural.

[4] The climax of Frost's preparation for the last two words is in the sentences of the fourth stanza. All along, the speaker claims to feel an inner void that is similar to the bleakness of the cold, snowy field. This idea emerges as the major focus in the last stanza, where in two sentences the speaker talks about his feelings of emptiness or insensitivity:

> They cannot scare me with their empty spaces
> Between stars—on stars where no human race is.
> I have it in me so much nearer home
> To scare myself with my own desert places.

[5] In the context of the poem, therefore, the shift in these last two words is not sudden or illogical. They rather pull together the two parts of the comparison that Frost has been building from the first line. Just as "desert places" refers to the snowy field, it also suggests human coldness, blankness, unconcern, insensitivity, and cruelty. The phrase does not spring out of nowhere but is the strong climax of the poem.

[6] Although Frost's conclusion is effective, a critic might still claim that it is weak because Frost does not develop the thought about the negative soul. He simply mentions "desert places" and stops; the poem is not a long psychological study. To ask for more than Frost gives would be to expect more than sixteen lines can provide. A better claim against the effectiveness of the concluding shift of meaning is that the phrase "desert places" is both vague and perhaps boastfully humble. If the phrase were taken away from the poem, this criticism might be acceptable. The fact is that the phrase is in the poem, and thus it must be judged only in the poem. There, it takes on the connotations of the previous fifteen lines and does so with freshness and surprise. Thus the shift of meaning is a major reason for Frost's success in "Desert Places."

COMMENTARY ON THE ESSAY

The general development of this essay illustrates strategy 1 described in this chapter (p. 151). The attention to the word *effective* in paragraph 1 briefly illustrates the second strategy (p. 151). The concluding paragraph shows two approaches to the fourth strategy (p. 152), using the arguments that the objections are not good because they (4a) are not accurate or valid (here the inaccuracy is related to strategy 3), and (4c) are based on the need for an exception, namely that the phrase in question be removed from the context in the poem.

After introducing the problem, the first paragraph emphasizes that a solution is available only if the poem prepares the reader for the problematic shift of meaning. The central idea is that the poem satisfies this requirement and that the shift is effective. The thesis sentence indicates three subjects for development.

Paragraph 2 asserts that there is preparation even early in the poem. (A discussion of paragraph 3 follows.) Paragraph 4 asserts that the concluding sentences build toward a climax of Frost's pattern or development.

The argument of paragraph 3, like that of paragraph 2, is that the texture of the poem, right from the start, demonstrates the central idea (stated in the introductory paragraph) that the conditions for a solution to the problem are met. The method in this paragraph is to show how particular words and expressions, because they are applicable to both nature and human beings, connect the bleak opening scene with the speaker's professed spiritual numbness. The word "benighted" (line 11) is the most illustrative, because it particularly refers to cultural and intellectual bleakness. The paragraph hence demonstrates how the careful selection and analysis of key words can be part of a total argument.

Paragraphs 5 and 6 form a two-part conclusion to the essay. The fifth paragraph summarizes the arguments and offers an interpretation of the phrase. The last paragraph raises and answers two objections. The essay thus shows that a careful reading of the poem eliminates the grounds for claiming that there is any problem about the last line.

SPECIAL WRITING TOPICS FOR PROBLEMS

1. In "Dover Beach," the lines "Ah, love, let us be true / To one another!" has been read to refer not so much to the need for love as for the need for fidelity in all relationships. Which choice seems more correct? Explain.

2. Coleridge was planning a much longer poem when he began writing "Kubla Khan," but he was interrupted and could write no more. Some critics, however, are satisfied that the poem is complete as it stands. Defend the judgment that the poem may be considered finished.

3. The principal narrator in Twain's "Luck" states that the protagonist, Scoresby, is a fool. What reason might be proposed for doubting his claim?

4. Why might a person conclude that Sammy's decision to quit, in "A & P," is too abrupt? How successfully do the earlier parts of the story prepare readers for this decision?

5. To what degree would more details opposing war make "Anthem for Doomed Youth" a more or less effective poem?

6. Some readers claim that the speaker's reactions to her fiancé's death in "Patterns" are too reserved, not sufficiently angry or passionate. What is your response to this view of the poem?

chapter 13

Writing for Comparison and Contrast:

Learning by Seeing Literary Works Together

A comparison–contrast essay is used to compare and contrast different authors; two or more works by the same author; different drafts of the same work; or characters, incidents, techniques, and ideas in the same work or in different works. The virtue of comparison–contrast is that it enables the study of works in perspective. No matter what works you consider together, the method helps you isolate and highlight individual characteristics, for the quickest way to get at the essence of one thing is to compare it with another. Similarities are brought out by comparison; differences, by contrast. In other words, you can enhance your understanding of what a thing *is* by using comparison–contrast to determine what it *is not*.

For example, our understanding of Shakespeare's Sonnet 30, "When to the Sessions of Sweet Silent Thought" (p. 122), may be enhanced if we compare it with Christina Rossetti's poem "Echo" (p. 194). Both poems treat personal recollections of past experiences, told by a speaker to a listener who is not intended to be the reader. Both also refer to persons, now dead, with whom the speakers were closely involved.

In addition to these similarities, there are important differences. Shakespeare's speaker numbers the dead persons as friends whom he laments generally, but Rossetti refers specifically to one person with whom the speaker was in love. Rossetti's topic is the sorrow of dead love, the irrevocability of the past, and the present loneliness of the speaker. Shakespeare includes the references to dead friends as a way of accounting for present sorrows, but then his speaker turns to the present and asserts that thinking about the "dear friend" being addressed enables him to restore past "losses" and end all "sorrows." In Rossetti's poem, there is no reconciliation of past and present; instead the speaker focuses entirely upon the sadness of the present moment. Though both poems are retrospective, Shakespeare's poem looks toward the present, and Rossetti's looks to the past.

GUIDELINES FOR THE COMPARISON–CONTRAST METHOD

This example, although brief, shows how the comparison–contrast method makes it possible to identify leading similarities and distinguishing differences in both works. Frequently you can overcome difficulty with one work by comparing and contrasting it with another work on a comparable subject. A few guidelines will help direct your efforts in writing comparison–contrast essays.

Clarify Your Intention

When planning a comparison–contrast essay, first decide on your goal, for you may use the method in a number of ways. One objective may be *the equal and mutual illumination of two (or more) works*. For example, an essay comparing Welty's "A Worn Path" with Hawthorne's "Young Goodman Brown" might be designed to (1) compare ideas, characters, or methods in these stories equally, without stressing or favoring either. You might also (2) emphasize "Young Goodman Brown," and therefore you would use "A Worn Path" as material for highlighting Hawthorne's story. You could also (3) show your liking of one story at the expense of another or (4) emphasize a method or idea that you think is especially noteworthy or appropriate.

A first task is therefore to decide what to emphasize. The sample essay (p. 163) gives "equal time" to both works being considered, without claiming the superiority of either. Unless you have a different rhetorical goal, this essay is a suitable model for most comparisons.

Find Common Grounds for Comparison

The second stage in prewriting for this essay is to select a common ground for discussion. It is pointless to compare dissimilar things, for the resulting conclusions will not have much value. Instead, find a common ground. Compare like with like: idea with idea, characterization with characterization, imagery with imagery, point of view with point of view, tone with tone, problem with problem. For example, nothing much can be learned from a comparison of Welty's view of courage and Chekhov's view of love, but a comparison of the relationship of love to stability and courage in Chekhov and Welty suggests common ground, with the promise of important ideas to be developed through the examination of similarities and differences.

In seeking common ground, you will need to be inventive and creative. For instance, if you compare Maupassant's "The Necklace" and Chekhov's *The Bear*, these two works at first seem dissimilar. Yet common grounds can be found, such as the treatment of self-deceit, the effects of chance on human affairs, or the view of women. Although other works may seem even more dissimilar than these, it is usually possible to find a common ground for comparison and contrast. Much of your success with this essay depends on your finding a workable basis—a common denominator—for comparison.

Integrate the Bases of Comparison

Let us assume that you have decided on your rhetorical purpose and on the basis or bases of your comparison. You have done your reading, taken notes, and have a rough idea of what to say. The remaining problem is the treatment of your material. Following are two ways:

A common way (method 1) is to make your points first about one work and then about the other. Unfortunately, this method makes your paper seem like two separate lumps. ("Work 1" takes up one half of your paper, and "work 2" takes up the other half.) Also, the method involves repetition because you must repeat many points when you treat the second subject.

A better method (method 2), therefore, is to treat the major aspects of your main idea and to refer to the two (or more) works as they support your arguments. Thus you refer constantly to *both* works, sometimes within the same sentence, and remind your reader of the point of your discussion. There are reasons for the superiority of this method: (1) You do not repeat your points needlessly; you develop them as you raise them. (2) By constantly referring to the two works, you make your points without requiring a reader with a poor memory to reread previous sections.

As a model, here is a paragraph on "Natural References as a Basis of Comparison in Frost's 'Desert Places' and Shakespeare's Sonnet 73, 'That Time of Year Thou Mayest in Me Behold.'" The virtue of the paragraph is that it uses material from both poems simultaneously (as nearly as the time sequence of sentences allows) as the substance for the development of the ideas:

[1] Both writers link their ideas to events occurring in the natural world. [2] Night as a parallel with death is common to both poems, with Frost speaking about it in his first line, and Shakespeare introducing it in his seventh. [3] Along with night, Frost emphasizes the onset of winter and snow as a time

of death and desolation. [4] With this natural description, Frost also symbolically refers to empty, secret, dead places in the inner spirit—crannies of the soul where bleak winter snowfalls correspond to selfishness and indifference to others. [5] By contrast, Shakespeare uses the fall season, with the yellowing and dropping of leaves and also the flying away of birds, to stress the closeness of real death and therefore also the need to love fully during the time remaining. [6] Both poems therefore share a sense of gloom, because both present death as inevitable and final, just like the oncoming season of barrenness and waste. [7] Because Shakespeare's sonnet is addressed to a listener who is also a loved one, however, it is more outgoing than the more introspective poem of Frost. [8] Frost turns the snow, the night, and the emptiness of the universe inwardly in order to show the speaker's inner bleakness, and by extension, the bleakness of many human spirits. [9] Shakespeare instead uses the bleakness of seasons, night, and dying fires to state the need for loving "well." [10] The poems thus use common and similar references for different purposes and effects.

The paragraph links Shakespeare's references to nature with those of Frost. Five sentences speak of both authors together. Three speak of Frost alone and two of Shakespeare alone, but all the sentences are unified topically. This interweaving of references indicates that the writer has learned both poems well enough to think of them at the same time, and it also enables the writing to be more pointed and succinct than if the works were separately treated.

You can learn from this example: If you develop your essay by putting your two subjects constantly together, you will write economically and pointedly (not only for essays, but also for tests). Beyond that, if you digest the material as successfully as this method indicates, you demonstrate that you are fulfilling a major educational goal—the assimilation and *use* of material. Too often, because you learn things separately (in separate works and courses, at separate times), you tend also to compartmentalize them. Instead, you should always try to relate them, to *synthesize* them. Comparison and contrast help in this process of putting together, of seeing things not as fragments but as parts of wholes.

Avoid the "Tennis-Ball" Method

As you make your comparison, do not confuse an interlocking method with a "tennis-ball" method in which you bounce your subject back and forth constantly and repetitively, almost as though you were hitting observations back and forth over a net. The tennis-ball method is shown in the following example from a comparison of the characters Mathilde (Maupassant's "The Necklace") and Miss Brill (Mansfield's "Miss Brill"):

Mathilde is a young married woman, but Miss Brill is single and getting older. Mathilde has at least some kind of social life, even though she doesn't have more than one friend; Miss Brill leads a life of solitude. Mathilde's daydreams are responsible for her misfortune, but the shattering of Miss Brill's is done by someone from the outside. Therefore, Mathilde is made unhappy because of her own shortcomings, but Miss Brill is a helpless victim. In Mathilde's case the focus is on adversity not only causing trouble but also strengthening character. In Miss Brill's case the focus is on the weak getting hurt and becoming weaker.

Imagine the effect of an entire essay written in this boring "1,2—1,2—1,2" order. Aside from the repetition and unvaried patterning of subjects, the tennis-ball method does not permit much illustrative development. You should not feel so constrained that you cannot take two or more sentences to develop a point about one writer or subject before you include comparative references to another. If you remember to interlock the two subjects of comparison, however, as in the paragraph about Frost and Shakespeare, your method will give you the freedom to develop your topics fully.

WRITING A COMPARISON–CONTRAST ESSAY

First, narrow and simplify your subject so that you can handle it conveniently. Should your subject be a comparison of Amy Lowell and Wilfred Owen (as in the sample essay), pick out one or two of each poet's poems on the same or a similar topic and write your essay about these.

Once you have found an organizing principle along with the relevant works, begin to refine and focus the direction of your essay. As you study each work, note common or contrasting elements and use these to form your central idea. At the same time, you can select the most illustrative works and classify them according to your topic, such as war, love, work, faithfulness, or self-analysis.

Organizing Your Comparison–Contrast Essay

INTRODUCTION. In your introduction, state the works, authors, characters, or ideas that you are considering. Then show how you have narrowed the topic. Your central idea should briefly highlight the principal grounds of comparison and contrast, such as that both works treat a common topic, exhibit a similar idea, use a similar form, or develop an identical attitude, and also show that major or minor differences help make the works unique. You may also assert that one work is superior to the other, if you wish to make this judgment and defend it.

BODY. The body of your essay is governed by the works and your basis of comparison (ideas and themes, depictions of character, uses of setting, qualities of style, uses of point of view, and so on). For a comparison–contrast treatment on such a basis, your goal should be to shed light on both of the works you are treating. For example, you might examine a number of stories written in the first-person point of view (see Chapter 5). An essay on this topic might compare the ways each author uses the point of view to achieve similar or distinct effects. You might compare a group of poems that employ similar images, symbols, or ironic methods. Sometimes, the process can be as simple as identifying female or male protagonists and comparing the ways in which their characters are developed. Another approach is to compare the *subjects*, as opposed to the *theme*. You might identify works dealing with general subjects like love, death, youth, race, or war. Such groupings provide a basis of excellent comparisons and contrasts.

As you develop the body, remember to keep comparison–contrast foremost. That is, your discussions of point of view, metaphorical language, or whatever you choose should not so much explain these topics as topics, but rather explore similarities and differences about the works you are comparing. If your topic is an idea, for example, you need to explain the idea, but only enough to establish points of similarity or difference. As you develop such an essay, you might illustrate your arguments by referring to related uses of elements such as setting, characterization, rhythm or rhyme, symbolism, point of view, or metaphor. When you introduce these new subjects, you will be on target as long as you treat them comparatively.

CONCLUSION.   The conclusion may reflect on other ideas or techniques in the works you have compared, make observations about similar qualities, or summarize briefly the grounds of your comparison. If there is a point that you have considered especially important, you might stress that point again in your conclusion. Also, your comparison might have led you to conclude that one work is superior to the other. Stressing that point again would make an effective conclusion.

Sample Essay

The Treatment of Responses to War in Lowell's "Patterns" and Owen's "Anthem for Doomed Youth"°

---

[1]
"Patterns" and "Anthem for Doomed Youth" are both powerful and unique condemnations of war.* Wilfred Owen's short poem speaks broadly and generally about the ugliness of war and also about large groups of sorrowful people, while Amy Lowell's longer poem focuses upon the personal grief of just one person. In a sense, Lowell's poem begins where Owen's ends, a fact that accounts

---

°See pages 323 and 328 for these poems.
*Central idea.

[1]   for both the similarities and differences between the two works. The anti-war themes may be compared on the basis of their subjects, their lengths, their concreteness, and their use of a common metaphor.†

[2]   "Anthem for Doomed Youth" attacks war more directly than "Patterns." Owen's opening line, "What passing bells for those who die as cattle," suggests that in war human beings are depersonalized before they are slaughtered, like so much meat; and his observations about the "monstrous" guns and the "shrill, demented" shells unambiguously condemn the horrors of war. By contrast, in "Patterns" warfare is far away, on another continent, intruding only when the messenger delivers the letter stating that the speaker's fiancé has been killed (lines 63–64). Similar news governs the last six lines of Owen's poem, quietly describing how those at home respond to the news that their loved ones have died in war. Thus the anti-war focus in "Patterns" is the contrast between the calm, peaceful life of the speaker's garden and the anguish of her responses; in "Anthem for Doomed Youth" the stress is more on the external horrors of war that bring about the need for ceremonies honoring the dead.

[3]   Another difference is that Owen's poem is less than one-seventh as long as Lowell's. "Patterns" is an interior monologue or meditation of 107 lines, but it could not be shorter and still be convincing. In the poem the speaker thinks of the past and contemplates her future loneliness. Her final outburst, "Christ, what are patterns for?", could make no sense if she does not explain her situation as extensively as she does. On the other hand, "Anthem for Doomed Youth" is brief—a 14-line sonnet—because it is more general and less personal than "Patterns." Although Owen's speaker shows great sympathy, he or she views the sorrows of others distantly, unlike Lowell, who goes right into the mind and spirit of the grieving woman. Owen's use, in his last six lines, of phrases like "tenderness of patient minds" and "drawing down of blinds" is a powerful representation of deep grief. He gives no further detail even though thousands of individual stories might be told. In contrast, Lowell tells one of these stories as she focuses on her solitary speaker's lost hopes and dreams. The contrasting lengths of the poems are thus governed by each poet's treatment of the topic.

[4]   Despite these differences of approach and length, both poems are similarly concrete and real. Owen moves from the real scenes and sounds of far-off battlefields to the homes of the many soldiers who have been killed in battle, and Lowell's scene is a single place—the garden of her speaker's estate. The speaker walks on real gravel along garden paths that contain daffodils, squills, a fountain, and a lime tree. She thinks of her clothing and her ribboned shoes and also of her fiancé's boots, sword hilts, and buttons. The images in Owen's poem are equally real, but are not associated with individuals as in "Patterns." Thus Owen's images are those of cattle, bells, rifle shots, shells, bugles, candles, and window blinds. While both poems thus reflect reality, Owen's details are more general and public, whereas Lowell's are more personal and intimate.

[5]   Along with this concreteness, the poems share a major metaphor: that cultural patterns both control and frustrate human wishes and hopes. In "Patterns" this metaphor is shown in warfare itself (line 106), which is the supremely destructive political structure, or pattern. Further examples of the metaphor are found in details about clothing (particularly the speaker's stiff, confining gown in lines 5, 18, 21, 73, and 101, but also the lover's military boots in lines 46 and 49); the orderly, formal garden paths in which the speaker is walking (lines 1,

†Thesis sentence.

93); her restraint at hearing about her lover's death; and her courtesy, despite her grief, in ordering refreshment for the messenger (line 69). Within such rigid patterns, her hopes for happiness have vanished, along with the sensuous spontaneity symbolized by her lover's plans to make love with her on a "shady seat" in the garden (lines 85–89). The metaphor of the constricting pattern may also be seen in "Anthem for Doomed Youth," except that in this poem the pattern is the funeral, not love or marriage. Owen's speaker contrasts the calm, peaceful tolling of "passing-bells" (line 1) with the frightening sounds of war represented by the "monstrous anger of the guns," "the rifles' rapid rattle," and "the demented choirs of wailing shells" (lines 2–8). Thus, Lowell uses the metaphor to reveal the irony of hope and desire being destroyed by war, and Owen uses it to reveal the irony of war's negation of peaceful ceremonies.

[5]

<u>Though the poems in these ways share topics and some aspects of treatment, they are distinct and individual</u>. "Patterns" is visual and kinesthetic, whereas "Anthem for Doomed Youth" is auditory. Both poems conclude on powerfully emotional although different notes. Owen's poem dwells on the pathos and sadness that war brings to many unnamed people, and Lowell's expresses the most intimate thoughts of a solitary woman in the first agony of sorrow. Although neither poem attacks the usual platitudes and justifications for war (the needs to mobilize, to sacrifice, to achieve peace through fighting, and so on), the attack is there by implication, for both poems make their appeal by stressing how war destroys the relationships that make life worth living. For this reason, despite their differences, both "Patterns" and "Anthem for Doomed Youth" are parallel anti-war poems, and both are strong expressions of feeling.

[6]

COMMENTARY ON THE ESSAY

This example shows how an essay may devote approximately equal attention to the two works being studied. Words stressing the similarity of elements in the two poems are "common," "share," "equally," "parallel," "both" "similar," and "also." Contrasting elements are stressed by words such as "while," "whereas," "different," "dissimilar," "contrast," "although," and "except." Transitions from paragraph to paragraph are not different in this type of essay from those in other essays. Thus, "despite," "along with this . . . " and "in these ways," which are used here, could be used anywhere for the same transitional purpose.

The central idea—that the poems mutually condemn war—is brought out in the introductory paragraph, together with the supporting idea that the poems blend into each other because both show responses to news of battle casualties.

Paragraph 2, the first in the body, discusses how each poem brings out its attack on warfare. Paragraph 3 explains the differing lengths of the poems as a function of differences in perspective. Because Owen's sonnet views war and its effects at a distance, it is brief; but Lowell's interior monologue views death intimately, so it needs more detail and a greater length.

Paragraph 4, on the topic of concreteness and reality, shows that the two works may receive equal attention without the bouncing of the tennis-ball method. Three of the sentences in this paragraph (3, 4, and 6) are devoted exclusively to details in one or the other poem, while sentences 1, 2, 5, and 7 refer to both works, stressing points of broad or specific comparison. The scheme demonstrates that the two works are, in effect, interlocked within the paragraph.

Paragraph 5, the last in the body, considers the similar and dissimilar ways in which the poems treat the common metaphor of cultural patterns.

The final paragraph summarizes the central idea, and it also stresses the ways in which both poems, while similar, are distinct and unique.

SPECIAL WRITING TOPICS
FOR COMPARISON–CONTRAST

1. The use of the speaker in Hughes's "Theme for English B" and Hayden's "Those Winter Sundays"

2. The description of fidelity to love in Keats's "Bright Star" and Shakespeare's "Let Me Not to the Marriage of True Minds"

3. The view of women in Mansfield's "Miss Brill" and Welty's "A Worn Path," or in Glaspell's *Trifles* and Piercy's "A Work of Artifice"

4. The use of descriptive scenery in Wordsworth's "Daffodils" and Lowell's "Patterns," or in Poe's "The Cask of Amontillado" and Bierce's "An Occurrence at Owl Creek Bridge"

5. Symbols of disapproval in Hardy's "Channel Firing" and Twain's "Luck"

chapter 14

Writing About Prosody:
Rhythm and Sound
in Poetry

Prosody (*the pronunciation of a song or poem*) is the general word describing the study of poetic sounds and rhythms. Common alternative words are **metrics, versification, mechanics of verse**, and the **music of poetry**. Most readers, when reading poetry aloud, interpret the lines and develop an appropriate speed and expressiveness of delivery—a proper *rhythm*. Indeed, some people think that rhythm and sound are the *music* of poetry because they are like musical rhythms and tempos. Like music, poetry often requires a regular beat. The tempo and loudness may vary freely, however, and a reader may stop at any time to repeat the sounds and to think about the words and ideas.

It is important to recognize that poets, being especially attuned to language, blend words and ideas together so that "the sound" becomes "an echo to the sense" (Pope). Readers may therefore accept as a rule that *prosodic technique cannot be separated from a poem's content*. For this reason, the study of prosody aims at determining how poets have controlled their words so that the sound of a poem complements its expression of emotions and ideas.

IMPORTANT DEFINITIONS
FOR STUDYING PROSODY

To study prosody you need a few basic linguistic facts. Individual sounds in combination make up syllables and words, and separate words in combination make up lines of poetry. Syllables and words are made up of

segments, or individually meaningful sounds (*segmental phonemes*). In the word *top* there are three segments: *t*, *o*, and *p*. When you hear these three sounds in order, you recognize the word "top." It takes three alphabetical letters—*t*, *o*, and *p*—to spell (*graph*) "top," because each letter is identical with a segment. Sometimes, however, it takes more than one letter to spell a segment. For example, in the word *enough* there are four segments (*e, n, u, f*), although six letters are required for the correct spelling: *e, n, ou*, and *gh*. The last two segments (*u* and *f*) require two letters each (two letters forming one segment are called a *digraph*). In the word *through* there are three segments but *seven* letters. To be correctly spelled in this word, the o͞o segment must have four letters (*ough*). Note, however, that in the word *flute* the o͞o segment requires only one letter, *u*. When we study the effects of various segments in relationship to the poetic rhythm, we deal with **sound**; usually our concern is with prosodic devices such as **alliteration, assonance,** and **rhyme.**

When segments are meaningfully combined, they make up syllables and words. A **syllable**, in both prose and poetry, consists of a single meaningful strand of sound such as the article *a* in "*a* table," *lin* in "*linen*," and *flounce* in "the little girls *flounce* into the room." (The article *a*, which is both a syllable and a word, has only one segment; *lin*, the first syllable of a two-syllable word [*lin* never occurs alone; it is always used in combinations such as *lingerie* and *linoleum*], contains three segments; *flounce* is a word of one syllable consisting of six segments: *f, l, ow, n, t*, and *s*.) The understanding of what constitutes syllables is important because the rhythm of most poetry is determined by the measured relationship of heavily stressed to less heavily stressed syllables.

SOUND AND SPELLING

It is important—vital—to distinguish between spelling (**graphics**) and pronunciation (**phonetics**). Not all English sounds are spelled and pronounced in the same way, as with *top*. For example, the letter *s* has three very different sounds in the words *sweet, sugar,* and *flows: s, sh* (as in "sharp"), and *z*. On the other hand, the words *shape, ocean, nation, sure, fissure, Eschscholtzia,* and *machine* use different letters or combinations of letters to spell the same *sh* sound.

Vowel sounds may also be spelled in different ways. The *e* sound, for example, can be spelled *i* in *machine, ee* in *speed, ea* in *eat, e* in *even,* and *y* in *funny;* yet the vowel sounds in *eat, break,* and *bear* are not the same even though they are spelled the same. Remember this: With both consonants and vowel sounds, *do not confuse spellings with sounds.*

VOWEL AND CONSONANT SOUNDS

Studying the nature of vocal production can take, and has taken, entire careers. A brief reference to the production of sound, however, is still in order, for without introductory knowledge you will have difficulty determining segments and their effects.

Vowel sounds result from vibrations resonating in the space between the tongue and the top of the mouth. As our tongues go up or down, or forward or backward, or as they curl or flatten out, and as our lips move synchronously with our tongues, we form our vowel sounds. Some vowel sounds are "long," such as ē (flee), ā (stay), ō (open), and o͞o (food). Others are "short," such as ĭ (fit), ŭ (fun) and ĕ (set). Some vowels are called "front" (e.g., see, play) and some are called "back" (knowing, moon). Some are rounded (hōpe, ho͞op), and more are unrounded (green, swim).

Many of our English vowel sounds are pronounced as a *schwa*, or minimal sound, despite their spellings (e.g., the *e* in "the boy"). Thus, "about," "stages," "rapid," "nation," and "circus" contain the vowels *a, e, i, o,* and *u,* but all the italicized letters make the same *schwa* sounds, which in pronunciation receive a light stress.

There are three **diphthongs**—that is, sounds that begin with one vowel sound and move to another vowel sound, namely ī (fly), *ou* (house), and *oi* (foil).

Consonant sounds are classified into three major groups.

(1) *Stop sounds,* also called *plosives,* are percussive and abrupt. They are made by the momentary stoppage and release of breath either when the lips touch each other or when the tongue touches the teeth or palate. The stops are *p, b, t, d, k,* and *g.*

(2) *Continuant sounds* are flowing and continuous. They are produced by the steady release of the breath in conjunction with various positions of the tongue in relation to the lips, teeth, and palate, as in *n, ng, l, r, th* (thorn), *th* (the); *f, v, s, z, sh* (sharp), and *zh* (pleasure); or with the touching of the lower lip and upper teeth for the sounds *f* and *v;* or with the touching of both lips for the sound *m.* Two special sounds called *affricates* begin with the stops *t* and *d* and then become the continuants *sh* and *zh* (as in *chew* and *judge*).

(3) *Semivowel sounds* are midway between vowels and consonants but are more like consonants than vowels. These have in common that they move from an originating sound and then move to another vowel sound. They are *w* (wagon, win, weather); *y* (yes, young, union); and *h* (hope, heap).

Consonant sounds are either *voiced,* that is, produced with the vibration of the vocal chords (e.g., *b, d, g, v, z, zh*), or *voiceless,* produced by the breath alone, as a whisper (e.g., *p, t, k, f, s, sh*). Among the semivowels, *w* and *y* are voiced, but *h* is unvoiced.

RHYTHM

Rhythm in speech is a combination of vocal speeds, rises and falls, starts and stops, vigor and slackness, and relaxation and tension. In ordinary speech and in prose, rhythm is not as important as the flow of ideas. In poetry, rhythm is significant because poetry is so emotionally charged, compact, and intense. Poets invite us to change speeds while reading—to slow down and linger over some words and sounds and to pass rapidly over others. They also invite us to give more-than-ordinary vocal stress or emphasis to certain syllables and less stress to others. The more intense syllables are called **heavy stress** (or simply **stressed**) syllables, and it is the heavy stresses that determine the **accent** or **beat** of a poetic line. The less intense syllables receive **light stress** (and are often called **unstressed**). In traditional verse, poets select patterns called **feet,** which consist of a regularized relationship of heavy stresses to light stresses.

Rhythm and Scansion

To study the patterns of versification in any poem, you **scan** the poem. The act of scanning—**scansion**—enables you to discover how the poem establishes a prevailing metrical pattern, and also how and why there are variations in the pattern.

RECORDING STRESSES OR BEATS.   In scansion, it is important to use a commonly recognized notational system to record stresses or accents. A *heavy* or *primary* stress (also called an **accented syllable**) is commonly indicated by a prime mark or acute accent (´). A *light* stress is indicated by a bowl-like half circle called a **breve** (˘) or sometimes by a raised circle or degree sign (°). To separate one foot from another, a **virgule** or slash (/) is used. Thus, the following line, from Coleridge's "The Rime of the Ancient Mariner," is schematized formally in this way:

```
 ´   ˘   ´   ˘   ´   ˘   ´
Wa - ter, / wa - ter, / ev - ery where,
```

Here the virgules show that the line contains two two-syllable feet followed by a three-syllable foot.

RECORDING THE METER OR MEASURE.   Another important part of scansion is the determination of a poem's **meter,** or the number of feet in its lines. Lines containing five feet are **pentameter,** four are **tetrameter,** three are **trimeter,** two are **dimeter**, and one is **monometer.** (To these may be added the less common line lengths **hexameter,** a six-foot line; **heptameter** or **the septenary,** seven feet; and **octameter,** eight feet.) In terms of accent or beat, a trimeter line has three beats (heavy stresses), a pentameter line five beats, and so on.

Metrical Feet

Equipped with this knowledge, you are ready to scan poems and determine the rhythmical patterns of feet. The most important ones, the specific names of which are derived from Greek poetry, are the two-syllable foot, the three-syllable foot, and the one-syllable (or imperfect) foot.

THE TWO-SYLLABLE FOOT

(a) **The Iamb.** The most important two-syllable foot in English is the **iamb**, which contains a light stress followed by a heavy stress:

˘ ́
the winds

The iamb is the most common foot in English poetry because it most nearly duplicates natural speech while also elevating speech to poetry. It is the most versatile of English poetic feet, and it is capable of great variation. Even within the same line, iambic feet may vary in intensity, so they may support or undergird the shades of meaning designed by the poet. For example, in this line of iambic pentameter from Wordsworth ("The World is Too Much with Us"), each foot is unique:

˘ ́ ˘ ́ ˘ ́ ˘ ́ ˘ ́
The winds / that will / be howl- / ing at / all hours.

Even though *will* and *at* receive the heavy stress in their individual iambic feet, they are not as strongly emphasized as *winds, howl-,* and *hours* (indeed, they are also less strong than *all*, which is in the light-stress position in the concluding iamb). Such variability, approximating the stresses and rhythms of actual speech, makes the iamb suitable for both serious or light verse, and it therefore helps poets focus attention on ideas and emotions. If they use it with skill it never becomes monotonous, for it does not distract readers by drawing attention to its own rhythm.

(b) **The Trochee.** The trochee consists of a heavy accent followed by a light:

́ ˘
flow - er

Rhythmically, most English words are trochaic, as may be seen in the words *water, snowfall, author, willow, morning, early, follow, singing, window,* and *something.* A major exception is seen in two-syllable words beginning with prefixes, such as *sublime, because,* and *impel.* Another exception is found in two-syllable words that are borrowed from another language but are still pronounced as in the original language, as with *machine, technique, garage,* and *chemise,* all of which are French importations. To see the strength of the trochaic tendency in English, French words borrowed six hundred or more years ago have lost their original iambic rhythm and have become trochaic, as with *language, very, nation,* and *castle.*

Because trochaic rhythm has often been called *falling, dying, light,* or *anti-climactic,* while iambic rhythm is *rising, elevating, serious,* and *climactic,* poets have preferred the iambic foot. They therefore have arranged various placements of two-syllable words, using single-syllable words and a variety of other means, so that the heavy-stress syllable is at the end of the foot, as in Shakespeare's line:

    ˘ ´   ˘ ´   ˘ ´   ˘   ´
his bend - / ing sick - / le's com - / pass come /,

in which three successive trochaic words are arranged to match the iambic meter.

(c) The Spondee. The **spondee**—also called a **hovering accent**—consists of two successive, equally heavy accents, as in *men's eyes* in Shakespeare's line:

When, in / dis -grace / with for - / tune and / men's eyes.

The spondee is mainly a substitute foot in English verse because successive spondees usually become iambs or trochees. An entire poem written in spondees would be quite unlikely. As a substitute, however, the spondee creates emphasis. The usual way to indicate the spondaic foot is to link the two syllables together with chevronlike marks ( ), like this:

men's eyes

(d) The Pyrrhic. The **pyrrhic** consists of two unstressed syllables (even though one of them may be in a normally stressed position), as in *on their* in Pope's line:

  ˘ ´   ˘ ´   ˘ ˘   ˘ ´
Now sleep - / ing flocks / on their / soft fleec - / es lie.

The pyrrhic is made up of weakly accented words such as prepositions (e.g., *on, to*) and articles (*the, a*). Like the spondee, it is usually substituted for an iamb or trochee, and therefore a complete poem cannot be in pyrrhics. As a substitute foot, however, the pyrrhic acts as a rhythmic catapult to move the reader swiftly to the next heavy-stress syllable, and therefore it undergirds the ideas conveyed by more important words.

SPECIAL METERS

In many poems you may find meters other than those described in the text. Poets such as Browning, Tennyson, Poe, and Swinburne introduce special or unusual meters. Other poets manipulate pauses or **caesurae** (discussed later) to create the effects of unusual meters. For these reasons, you should know about metrical feet such as the following:

1. **Amphibrach.** A light, heavy, and light:

   ˘ / ˘   ˘ / ˘   ˘ / ˘

   Ah feed me / and fill me / with pleas - sure (Swinburne).

2. **Amphimacer or cretic.** A heavy, light, and heavy:

   / ˘ /

   Love is best (Browning).

3. **Bacchius or bacchic.** A light stress followed by two heavy stresses:

   ˘ / /   / ˘

   Some late lark / [sing - ing] (Henley).

4. **Dipodic or syzygy.** Dipodic measure (literally, "two feet" combining to make one) develops in longer lines when a poet submerges two regular feet under a stronger beat so that a "galloping" or "rollicking" rhythm results. The following line from Masefield's "Cargoes," for example, may be scanned as trochaic hexameter, with the concluding foot being an iamb:

   / ˘   / ˘   / ˘   / ˘   / ˘   ˘ /

   Quin-que / reme of / Nin-e- / veh from / dis-tant / O-phir.

In reading, however, a stronger beat is superimposed, which makes one foot out of two—dipodic measure or syzygy:

   /   /   /   /

   Quinquereme of / Nineveh from / distant Ophir.

THE THREE-SYLLABLE FOOT

(a) The Anapaest.   The anapaest consists of two light accents followed by a heavy accent:

ᵕ ᵕ ´   ᵕ ᵕ ´
by the dawn's / ear - ly light. (Key)

(b) The Dactyl.   A heavy stress followed by two lights:

´ ᵕ ᵕ ´ ᵕᵕ   ´ ᵕ ᵕ   ´ ᵕᵕ
green as our / hope in it, / white as our / faith in it. (Swinburne)

THE IMPERFECT FOOT.   The imperfect foot consists of a single syllable (´) by itself, or (ᵛ) by itself. This foot is a variant or substitute occurring in a poem in which one of the major feet forms the metrical pattern. The second line of Key's "The Star-Spangled Banner," for example, is anapaestic, but it contains an imperfect foot at the end:

ᵕ ᵕ ´   ᵕᵕ   ´ ᵕ ᵕ ´ ᵕ   ᵕ   ´ ᵕ
What so proud -/ ly we hailed/ at the twi-/ light's last gleam-/ing.

Other Rhythmic Devices

ACCENTUAL, STRONG-STRESS, AND "SPRUNG" RHYTHMS.   Accentual or strong-stress lines are historically derived from the poetry of Old English. At that time, each line was divided in two, with two major stresses, also alliterated, occurring in each half. In the nineteenth century, Gerard Manley Hopkins (1844–1889) developed what he called "sprung" rhythm, a rhythm in which the major stresses would be released or "sprung" from the line. The method is complex, but one characteristic is the juxtaposing of one-syllable stressed words, as in this line from "Pied Beauty":

ᵕ ´   ´   ´   ´   ᵕ´ ᵕ ´
With swift, slow; sweet, sour; adazzle, dim;

Here a number of elements combine to create six major stresses. Many of Hopkins's lines combine alliteration and strong stresses in this way to create the same effect of heavy emphasis.

THE CAESURA, OR PAUSE.   Whenever we speak, we run our words together rapidly, without pause. We do, however, stop briefly and almost unnoticeably between significant units or phrases. These significant units, both grammatically and rhythmically, are **cadence groups.** In poetry that emphasizes a regular meter, the cadence groups operate just as they do in prose to make the ideas intelligible. Although we are following the poetic rhythm, we also pause briefly at the ends of phrases and make longer pauses at the ends of sentences. In scansion, the name of these pauses—which linguists call *junctures*—is **caesura** (plural **caesurae**). When scanning a line, we note a caesura with two diagonal lines or virgules (//), so that the caesura may be distinguished from the single virgule separating feet. Sometimes the caesura coincides with the end of a foot, as at the end of the second iamb in this line by William Blake ("To Mrs. Anna Flaxman"):

$$\smile \, / \quad \smile \, / \quad \smile \, / \quad \smile \, / \quad \smile \, /$$
With hands / di - vine // he mov'd / the gen - / tle Sod. /

The caesura, however, may fall within a foot, and there may be more than one in a line, as within the second and third iambs in this line by Ben Jonson:

$$\smile \, / \quad \smile \, / \quad \smile \quad / \, \smile \, / \quad \smile \, /$$
Thou art / not, //Pens - / hurst, // built / to en - / vious show./

When a caesura ends a line, usually marked by a comma, semicolon, or period, that line is **end-stopped,** as in the opening line of Keats's "Endymion":

$$\smile \, / \quad \smile \, / \quad \smile \quad / \, \smile \, / \quad \smile \, / \, \smile$$
A thing / of beau - / ty // is / a joy / for - ev -er. //

If a line has no punctuation at the end and runs over to the next line, it is called **run-on.** Another term used for run-on lines is **enjambement.** The following passage, a continuation of the line from Keats, contains three run-on lines:

> Its loveliness increases; // it will never
> Pass into nothingness; // but still will keep
> A bower quiet for us, // and a sleep
> Full of sweet dreams, // . . .

FORMAL SUBSTITUTION. Most regular poems follow a formal pattern that may be analyzed according to the feet we have been describing here. For interest and emphasis, however (and also perhaps because of the natural rhythms of English speech), poets may **substitute** other feet for the regular feet of the poem. For example, the following line is from the January eclogue of Edmund Spenser's *Shepherd's Calendar*. Although the pattern of the poem is iambic pentameter (i.e., five iambs per line), Spenser includes two substitute feet in the line:

$$/ \, \smile \quad \smile \, / \quad \wedge\!\!\wedge \quad \smile \, / \quad \smile \, /$$
All in / a sun - / shine day, / as did / be - fall./

In the first foot, *All in* is a trochee, and *shine day* is a spondee. These are *formal substitutions*; that is, Spenser uses separate, formally structured feet in place of the normal iambic feet. The effect is to move rapidly from "All" to "sunshine day" in order to allow the reader to delight in the sound of the words and also to savor the idea of unexpectedly nice weather during the middle of winter.

RHETORICAL SUBSTITUTION.   By manipulating the caesura, poets may achieve the effects that are provided by formal substitution. If the pauses are placed within feet, they may cause us actually to *hear* trochees, amphibrachs, and other variant feet even though the line may scan regularly in the established meter. This type of *de facto* variation is **rhetorical substitution.** A noteworthy example in an iambic pentameter line is this one from Pope's *Essay on Man:*

His ac-/tions',//pas-/sions',//be-/ing's,//use/and end.

The theory of this type of line is that there should be a caesura after the fourth syllable, but in this one Pope has made three, each producing a strong pause. The line is regularly iambic, but the effect is different in actual reading or speaking. Because of the caesurae after the third, fifth, and seventh syllables, the rhythm produces an amphibrach, a trochee, another trochee, and an amphimacer, thus:

His ac-tions',//pas-sions',//be-ing's,//use and end.
AMPHIBRACH   TROCHEE   TROCHEE   AMPHIMACER

The spoken substitutions produced by the caesurae in this regular line produce the effect of substitution and therefore tension and interest.

When studying rhythm, your main concern in noting substitutions is to determine the formal metrical pattern and then to analyze the formal and rhetorical variations on this pattern and their principal techniques and effects. Always try to show how these variations have enabled the poet to get points across and to achieve emphasis.

SEGMENTAL POETIC DEVICES

Once you have completed your analysis of rhythms, you may go on to consider the segmental poetic devices in the poem. Usually these devices are used to create emphasis, but sometimes in context they may echo or imitate actions and objects. The segmental devices most common in poetry are *assonance, alliteration, onomatopoeia,* and *euphony* and *cacophony.*

Assonance

Assonance is the repetition of identical *vowel* sounds in different words—for example, the short *i* in "swift Camilla skims." It is a strong means of emphasis, as in the following line, where the *ŭ* sound connects the two words *lull* and *slumber,* and the short *ĭ* connects *him, in,* and *his:*

And more, to lull him in his slumber soft. (Spenser)

In some cases, poets may use assonance elaborately, as in the first line of Pope's *An Essay on Criticism:*

'Tis hard to say, if greater want of skill.

Here the line is framed and balanced with the short *ĭ* in *'Tis, if,* and *skill.* The *ä* in *hard* and *want* forms another, internal frame, and the *ā* in *say* and *greater* creates still another frame. Such a balanced use of vowels is unusual, however, for most lines assonance occurs simply as a means of highlighting important words, without such elaborate patterning.

Alliteration

Like assonance, **alliteration** is a means of highlighting ideas by words containing the same *consonant* sound—for example, the repeated *m* in Spenser's "Mixed with a *m*ur*m*uring wind," or the *s* sound in Waller's praise of Cromwell, "Your never-failing *s*word made war to *c*ease," which emphasizes the connection between the words "sword" and "cease."

There are two kinds of alliteration. Most commonly, alliteration is regarded as the repetition of identical consonant sounds that begin syllables in close patterns—for example, in Pope's lines "La*b*orious, heavy, *b*usy, *b*old, and *b*lind," and "While *p*ensive *p*oets *p*ainful vigils keep." Used judiciously, alliteration gives strength to ideas by emphasizing key words but too much can *c*ause *c*omic and *c*razy *c*onsequences. The second form of alliteration occurs when a poet repeats identical or similar consonant sounds that do not begin syllables but nevertheless create a pattern—for example, the *z* segment in the line "In these places freezing breezes easily cause sneezes," or the *b, m,* and *p* segments (all of which are made *bilabially,* that is, with both lips) in "The *m*iserably *m*umbling and *m*o*m*entously *m*ur*m*uring *b*eggar *p*ropels *p*egs and *p*ebbles in the *b*u*b*bling *p*ool." Such clearly designed patterns are hard to overlook.

Onomatopoeia

Onomatopoeia is a blend of consonant and vowel sounds designed to *imitate* or *suggest* a situation or action. It is made possible in poetry because many English words are **echoic** in origin; that is, they are verbal echoes of the actions they describe, such as *buzz, bump,* or *slap.* Coleridge imitates the sound of bounding and rushing water in the following lines from "Kubla Khan":

And from this chasm, with ceaseless turmoil seething,
As if this earth in fast, thick pants were breathing,
A mighty fountain momently was forced:
Amid whose swift half-intermitted burst,
Huge fragments vaulted like rebounding hail,
Or chaffy grain beneath the thresher's flail.

(lines 17–22)

One might speak extensively of the various excellences of this passage, in which rhythm, alliteration, and assonance all come together to create in sound what the lines describe in words.

Euphony and Cacophony

Words describing smooth or jarring sounds, particularly those resulting from consonants, are **euphony** and **cacophony**. Euphony ("good sound") refers to words containing consonants that permit an easy and smooth flow of spoken sound. Although there is no rule that some consonants are inherently more pleasant than others, students of poetry often cite sounds like *m, n, ng, l, v,* and *z,* together with *w* and *y,* as being especially easy on the ears. The opposite of euphony is cacophony ("bad sound"), in which percussive and choppy sounds make for vigorous and noisy pronunciation, as in tongue-twisters like "black bug's blood" and "shuffling shellfish fashioned by a selfish sushi chef." Obviously, unintentional cacophony is a mark of imperfect control. When a poet deliberately creates it for effect, however, as in Tennyson's line "The bare black cliff clang'd round him," or Pope's "The hoarse, rough verse should like the torrent roar," cacophony is a mark of poetic skill. Although poets generally aim at easily flowing, euphonious lines, cacophony does have a place, always depending on the poet's intention and subject matter.

WRITING ABOUT PROSODY

Because studying prosody requires a good deal of specific detail and description, it is best to limit your study to a short poem or to a short passage from a long poem. A sonnet, a stanza of a lyric poem, or a fragment from a long poem will usually be sufficient. If you choose a fragment, it should be self-contained, such as an entire speech or short episode or scene (as in the example from Tennyson chosen for the sample essay on pp. 182–87).

The analysis of even a short poem, however, can grow long because of the need to describe word positions and stresses, and also to determine the various effects. For this reason you do not have to exhaust your topic. Try to make your discussion representative of the prosody of your poem or passage.

Your first reading in preparation for your essay should be for comprehension. On second and third readings, make notes of sounds, accents, and rhymes by reading the poem aloud. To perceive sounds, one student helped herself by reading aloud in an exaggerated way in front of a mirror. If you have privacy or are not self-conscious, you might do the same. Let yourself go a bit. As you dramatize your reading (maybe even in front of fellow students), you will find that heightened levels of reading also accompany the poet's expression of important ideas. Mark these spots for later analysis so that you will be able to make strong connections between sense and sound.

In planning, it is vital to prepare study sheets so that your observations will be correct, for if your factual analysis is wrong, your writing will also be wrong. Experience has shown that it is best to make three triple-spaced copies of the poem or passage (with photocopy or, if necessary, carbon paper), for the separate analysis of rhythm, assonance, and alliteration. If you have been assigned just one of these, of course, only one copy will be necessary. Leave spaces between syllables and words for marking out the various feet of the poem. Ultimately, this duplication of the passage, with your markings, should be included as a first page, as in the sample essay.

Carry out your study of the passage in the following way:

- Number each line of the passage, regardless of length, beginning with 1, so that you may use these numbers as location references in your essay.
- Determine the formal pattern of feet, using the short acute accent or stress mark for heavily stressed syllables (´), and the breve for unaccented or lightly stressed syllables (˘). Use chevrons to mark spondees (⋀).
- Indicate the separate feet by a diagonal slash or virgule (/). Indicate caesurae and end-of-line pauses by double virgules (//).
- Use colored pencils to underline, circle, make boxes, or otherwise mark the formal and rhetorical substitutions that you discover. Because such substitutions may occur throughout the poem, develop a numbering system for each type (e.g., 1 = spondee, 7 = trochee, as in the sample work sheet). Provide a key to your numbers at the bottom of the page.
- Do the same for alliteration, assonance, and onomatopoeia. It has proved particularly effective to draw lines to connect the repeating sounds, for these effects will be close together in the poem, and your connections will dramatize this closeness. The use of a separate color for each separate effect is helpful, for different colors make prosodic distinctions stand out clearly.
- Use your work sheets as a reference for your reader's benefit. In writing your essay, however, make your examples specific by including brief illustrative quotations, as in the examples (i.e., words, phrases, and entire lines, with proper marks and accents). Do not rely on line numbers alone.

Once you have analyzed the various effects of the poem, and you have recorded these on your work sheets and in your notes, you will be ready to formulate a central idea and organization. The focus of your essay should reflect the most significant features of prosody in relationship to some other element of the poem, such as speaker, tone, or ideas. For example, in an essay about Masefield's "Cargoes," you might argue that the dipodic rhythms undergird the poem's alternating notes of admiration and irony. An essay about Coleridge's "Kubla Khan" might state that the segmental effects, through onomatopoeia, graphically complement the poem's descriptions. An essay about Hardy's "Channel Firing" may state that the four-stress lines perfectly complement Hardy's acidic view of the increasing capacity for destruction represented by the guns at sea.

Organizing Your Essay About Prosody

Depending on your assignment, you might wish to discuss all aspects of rhythm or sound, or perhaps just one, such as the poet's use of regular meter, a particular substitution, alliteration, or assonance. It would be possible, for example, to devote an entire essay to (1) regular meter, (2) one particular variation in meter, such as the anapest or spondee, (3) the caesura, (4) assonance, (5) alliteration, or (6) onomatopoeia. For brevity, we here treat rhythm and segments together in one essay.

INTRODUCTION. After a brief description of the poem (such as that it is a sonnet, a two-stanza lyric, or a tetrameter burlesque poem), establish the scope of your essay. Your central idea will outline the thought you wish to carry out through your prosodic analysis, such as that regularity of meter is consistent with a happy, firm vision of love or life, or that frequent spondees emphasize the solidity of the speaker's wish to love, or that particular sounds echo some of the poem's actions.

BODY.   1. *Rhythm.* Establish the formal metrical pattern. What is the dominant metrical foot and line length? Are some lines shorter than the pattern? What relationship do the variable lengths have with the subject matter? If the poem is a lyric or a sonnet, are important words and syllables successfully placed in stressed positions in order to achieve emphasis? Try to relate line lengths to exposition, development of ideas, and rising or falling emotions. It is also important to look for either repeating or varying metrical patterns as the subject matter reaches peaks or climaxes. Generally, deal with the relationship between the formal rhythmical pattern and the poem's ideas and attitudes.

When noting substitutions, analyze the formal variations and the principal effects of these. If you concentrate on only one substitution, describe any apparent pattern in its use; that is, its locations, recurrences, and effects on meaning.

For caesurae, treat the effectiveness of the poet's control. Can you see any pattern of use? Are the pauses regular or random? Describe noticeable principles of placement, such as (1) the creation of rhythmical similarities in various parts of the poem, (2) the development of particular rhetorical effects, or (3) the creation of interest through rhythmical variety. Do the caesurae bring out important ideas and attitudes? Are the lines all end-stopped, or do you discover enjambement? How do these rhythmical characteristics aid in descriptions and in the expressions of ideas?

2. *Segmental Effects.* Here you might be discussing, collectively or separately, the use and effects of assonance, alliteration, onomatopoeia, and cacophony and euphony. Be sure to establish that the instances you choose occur systematically enough within the poem to form a pattern. You might make separate paragraphs on alliteration, assonance, and any other seemingly important pattern. Also, because space is always at a premium, you might concentrate on only one noteworthy effect, such as a certain pattern of assonance, rather than on everything. Throughout your discussion, always keep foremost the relationship between content and sound.

CONCLUSION. In your conclusion, try to develop a short evaluation of the poet's prosodic performance. If we accept the premise that poetry is designed not only to stimulate emotions but also to provide information and transfer attitudes, to what degree do the prosodic techniques of your poem contribute to these goals? Without going into excessive detail (and writing another essay), what more can you say here? What has been the value of your study to your understanding and appreciating the poem? If you think your analysis has helped you to develop new awareness of the poet's craft, it would be appropriate to state what you have learned.

Note: To make illustrations clear, underline all sounds to which you are calling attention. If you use an entire word to illustrate a sound, underline only the sound and not the entire word, but put the word within quotation marks (for example, The poet uses a t ["tip," "top," and "terrific"]). When you refer to entire words containing particular segments, however, underline these words (for example, "The poet uses a t in tip, top, and terrific").

Sample Essay

A Study of Tennyson's Rhythm and Segments in "The Passing of Arthur," Lines 349–360

> Note: For illustration, this essay analyzes a passage from Tennyson's "The Passing of Arthur," which is part of *Idylls of the King*. Containing 469 lines, "The Passing of Arthur" describes the last battle and death of Arthur, legendary king of early Britain. After the fight, in which Arthur has been mortally wounded by the traitor Mordred, only Arthur and his follower Sir Bedivere remain alive. Arthur commands Bedivere to throw the royal sword *Excalibur* into the lake from which Arthur had originally received it. After great hesitation and false claims, Bedivere does throw the sword into the lake, and a hand rises out of the water to catch it. Bedivere then carries Arthur to the lake shore, where the dying king is taken aboard a mysterious funeral barge. In the passage selected for analysis (lines 349–360), Tennyson describes Bedivere carrying Arthur down the hills and cliffs from the battlefield to the lake below.

1. *RHYTHMICAL ANALYSIS*

But the o- / ther swift- /ly strode // from ridge / to ridge, //   1

Clothed with / his breath, // and look- / ing, // as / he walk'd, //   2

Lar-ger / than hu- / man // on / the fro- / zen hills. //   3

He heard / the deep / be-hind/ him, // and / a cry   4

Be-fore. // His own / thought drove / him // like / a goad. //   5

Dry clash'd / his har- / ness // in / the i /cy caves   6

And bar-ren / chasms, // and all / to left / and right   7

The bare / black cliff / clang'd round / him, // as / he based   8

His feet / on juts / of slip- / pe-ry crag // that rang   9

Sharp-_smit-_ / ten// with / the / dint / of ar- / med heels— //   10

And on / a sud- / den, // lo! // the lev- / el lake, //   11

And the / long glor- / ies // of / the win- / ter moon. //   12

¹ = Anapaest, or effect of anapaest.	⁴ = Effect of imperfect foot.
² = Amphibrach, or the effect of amphibrach.	⁵ = Pyrrhic.
	⁶ = Trochee, or the effect of trochee.
³ = Spondee.	

2. ALLITERATION

But the other Ⓢ wiftly Ⓢ trode from ridge to ridge,   1

Clothed with his breath, and looking, as Ⓗ e walked,   2

Larger than Ⓗ uman on the frozen Ⓗ ills.   3

Ⓗ e Ⓗ eard the deep be Ⓗ ind Ⓗ im, and a cry   4

Before. Ⓗ is own thought drove him like a goad.   5

Dry Ⓒ lashed Ⓗ is Ⓗ arness in the icy Ⓒ aves   6

And Ⓑ arren Ⓒⓗ asms, and all to left and right   7

The Ⓑ are Ⓑ Ⓛ ack Ⓒ Ⓛ iff Ⓒ Ⓛ anged round him, as he Ⓑ ased   8

His feet on juts of s Ⓛ ippery Ⓒ rag that rang   9

Sharp-smitten with the dint of armed heels—   10

And on a sudden, Ⓛ o! the Ⓛ evel Ⓛ ake,   11

And the Ⓛ ong g Ⓛ ories of the winter moon.   12

mmmmmmm = s   ——————— = b

----------- = h   wwwwwwwww = l as second consonant
                                                            sound in words

· · · · · · · · · · · = k   -—·—·—- = l

3. ASSONANCE

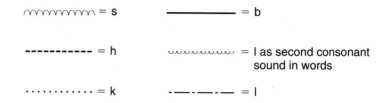

But the other sw ⓘ ftly str ⓞ de from r ⓘ dge to r ⓘ dge,   1

Cl ⓞ thed w ⓘ th h ⓘ s breath, and looking, as he walked,   2

Larger than human on the fr ⓞ zen hills.   3

He heard the deep beh ⓘ nd him, and a cr ⓨ   4

Before. His ⓞⓦ n thought dr ⓞ ve him l ⓘ ke a g ⓞⓐ d.   5

Dr ⓨ clashed his harness in the ⓘ cy caves   6

And barren ch ⓐ sms, and all to left and r ⓘ ght   7

The bare bl ⓐ ck cliff cl ⓐ nged round him, as he based   8

H ⓘ s feet on juts of sl ⓘ ppery cr ⓐ g that r ⓐ ng   9

Sh ⓐⓡ p-sm ⓘ tten w ⓘ th the d ⓘ nt of ⓐⓡ med heels—   10

And on a sudden, lo, the level lake,   11

And the long glories of the winter moon!   12

———————— = ō*   -—·—·—- = ä

----------- = ī   mmmmmm = ĭ

· · · · · · · · · · · = a

* Pronunciation symbols as in *Webster's New World Dictionary*, 2nd ed.

[1] In these twelve lines, Tennyson describes the ordeal of Sir Bedivere as he carries the dying King Arthur down from the mountainous heights, where Arthur was wounded, to the lake, where the king will be sent to his final rest. Tennyson emphasizes the bleakness and hostility of this ghostly and deserted landscape. The metrical pattern he uses is unrhymed iambic pentameter—blank verse— which is suitable for descriptions of actions and scenes. Appropriately, the verse augments the natural descriptions and echoes first Bedivere's tenseness and then his relaxation.* Tennyson's control enables a true blending of sound and sense, as may be seen in his use of rhythm and in his manipulation of segmental devices, including onomatopoeia.†

[2] Tennyson controls his meter to emphasize exertions and moods. In line 1 the meter is regular, except for an anapaest in the first foot. This regularity may be interpreted as emphasizing the swiftness and surefootedness of Bedivere. Bedivere is about to undergo a severe test, however, and the rhythm quickly becomes irregular, as though to strain the pentameter verse in illustration of his exertions. Tennyson therefore uses variations to highlight key words. For example, he uses the effect of anapaests in a number of lines. In line 2 he emphasizes the chill air and Bedivere's vitality in the following way:

/ ⌣ ⌣ /
Clothed with / his breath.//

The image is one of being surrounded by one's own breath, which vaporizes on hitting the cold air; and the rhythmical variation—a trochaic substitution in the first foot—enables the voice to build up to the word breath, a most effective internal climax.

[3] Tennyson uses the same kind of rhythmical effect in line 3. He emphasizes the frozen hills by creating a caesura in the middle of the third foot. The heavy stress of the third foot falls on the preposition on, which with the creates the effect of an anapaest consisting of two unstressed syllables leading up to the first, stressed, syllable of frozen. The effect is that the voice builds up to the word and thus emphasizes the extreme conditions in which Bedivere is walking:

/ ⌣ / ⌣ /
// on / the fro - / zen hills.//

Tennyson uses this rhythmical effect twelve times in the passage. It is one of his major means of rhetorical emphasis.

[4] Tennyson's most effective metrical variation is the spondee, which appears in lines 5, 6, 8 (twice), 10, and 12. These substitutions, occurring mainly in the section describing how Bedivere forces his way down the frozen hills, permits the descriptive lines to ring out, as in:

⌣ /
The bare / black cliff / clanged round /

and

---

* Central idea.
† Thesis sentence.

[4]
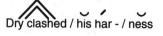
Dry clashed / his har - / ness

These substitutions are so strong that they are almost literally like the actual sounds of Bedivere's exertions. In addition to this use of the spondee as a sound effect, a remarkable use of the spondee for psychological effect occurs in line 5. Here, the stresses internalize Bedivere's distress, reaching a climax on the word <u>drove</u>:

His own / thought drove / him //

There is other substitution, too, both formal and rhetorical, and the tension these variations create keeps the responsive reader aware of Bedivere's tasks. One type of variation is the appearance of amphibrachic rhythm, which is produced in lines 2, 3, 4, 6, 7, and 11. The effect is achieved by a pattern that complements the rhetorical anapaests. A caesura in the middle of a foot leaves the [5] three preceding syllables as a light, heavy, and light, the rhythmical form of the amphibrach. In line 2, for example, it appears thus:

// and look - / ing //

In line 6 it takes this form:

/ his har - / ness //

Still another related variation is that of the apparently imperfect feet in lines 5, 8, 11, and 12. These imperfect feet are produced by a caesura, which isolates the syllable, as <u>him</u> is in line 8:

[6]
The bare / black cliff / clang'd round / him. //

In line 11 the syllable (on the word <u>lo!</u>) is surrounded by two caesurae and is therefore thrust into a position of great stress:

And on / a sud - / den // lo! // the lev - / el lake

Other, less significant substitutions are the trochees in lines 3 and 7, and the pyrrhic in line 12. All the described variations suggest the energy that Bedivere expends during his heroic action.
Many of the variations are produced by Tennyson's sentence structure, which results in a free placement of the caesurae and in a free use of end-stopping and enjambement. Four of the first five lines are end-stopped (two by commas, two by periods). Bedivere is exerting himself during these lines, and he is [7] making short tests to gather strength. His dangerous descent is described during the next four lines, and none of these lines is end-stopped. Bedivere is disturbed (being goaded by "his own thought"), but he must keep going; and the free sentence structure and free metrical variation underscore his physical and

[7] mental difficulties. In the last two lines, however, when he has reached the lake, the lines "relax" with falling caesurae exactly at the fifth syllable. In other words, the sentence structure of the last two lines is regular, an effect suggesting the return to order and beauty after the previous, rugged chaos.

[8] This rhythmical virtuosity is accompanied by a similarly brilliant control over segmental devices. Alliteration is the most obvious, permitting Tennyson to tie key words and their signifying actions together, as in the s's in swiftly strode in line 1, or the b's in barren, bare, black, and based in lines 7 and 8. Other notable examples are the aspirated h's in lines 2–6 (he, human, hills, heard, behind, him, his, harness); the k's in lines 6–9 (clashed, caves, chasms, cliff, clanged, crag); and the l's in lines 11 and 12 (lo, level, lake, long, glories). One might compare these l's with the l's in the more anguished context of lines 8 and 9, where the sounds appear as the second segment in the heavy, ringing words there (black, cliff, clanged, slippery). The sounds are the same, and the emphasis is similar, but the effects are different.

[9] Assonance is also present throughout the passage. In the first five lines, for example, the ō appears in six words. The first three ō's are in descriptive or metaphoric words (strōde, clōthed, frōzen), and the last three are in words describing Bedivere's pain and anguish (ōwn, drōve, gōad). The ō therefore ties the physical to the psychological. Other patterns of assonance are the ă in lines 7, 8, and 9 (chăsms, clăng'd, blăck, crăg, răng), the ă of line 10 (shărp, ărmed), the ī of lines 4–7 (behīnd, crȳ, līke, drȳ, īcy, rīght), and the short ĭ of lines 1 and 2, and 9 and 10 (swĭftly, rĭdge, wĭth, hĭs, slĭppery, smĭtten, wĭth, dĭnt). One might remark also that in the last two lines, which describe the level lake and the moon, Tennyson introduces a number of relaxed o and oo and similar vowel sounds:

> And on a sudden, lo! the level lake,
> And the long glories of the winter moon.

[10] The last two lines are, in fact, onomatopoeic, since the liquid l sounds suggest the gentle lapping of waves on a lake shore. There are other examples of onomatopoeia, too. In line 2 Tennyson describes Bedivere in the cold air as being "Clothed with his breath," and in the following five lines Tennyson employs many words with the aspirate h (e.g., his harness). In the context, these sounds enable readers to see and hear sights and sounds just like those of Bedivere as he carries his royal burden. Similarly, the explosive stops b and k, and d, and t in lines 6–10 imitate the sounds of Sir Bedivere's feet on the "juts of slippery crag."

[11] This short passage is filled with many examples of poetic excellence. Tennyson's sounds and rhythms actually speak along with the meaning. They emphasize the grandeur of Arthur and his faithful follower, and for one brief moment they bear out the magic that Tennyson associated with the fading past.

COMMENTARY ON THE ESSAY

This essay presents a full treatment of the prosody of the passage from Tennyson. Paragraphs 2 through 7 deal with the relationship of the rhythm to the content. Note that prosody is not discussed in isolation, but as it augments Tennyson's descriptions of action and scenes. Thus, paragraph 4 refers to the use of the spondee as a substitute foot to reinforce ideas. Also in this paragraph, there is a short comparison of alternative ways of saying what Tennyson says so well. While such a speculative comparison should not be attempted often, it is effective here in bringing out the quality of Tennyson's use of the spondee as a means of emphasis.

Paragraphs 8 and 9 present a discussion of the alliteration and assonance of the passage, and paragraph 10 considers onomatopoeia.

Of greatest importance for the clarity of the essay, there are many supporting examples, spaced, indented, accurately marked, and numbered by line. In any essay about prosody, readers are likely to be unsure of the validity of the writer's observation unless such examples are provided and located within the poem.

SPECIAL WRITING TOPICS FOR PROSODY

1. Shakespeare's use of spondees in "That Time of Year"
2. Coleridge's varying line lengths in "Kubla Khan"
3. Arnold's use of end-stopped lines and enjambement in "Dover Beach"
4. Hardy's rhythms for the speakers in "Channel Firing"
5. Layton's use of assonance in "Rhine Boat Trip"
6. Hayden's use of alliteration in "Those Winter Sundays"
7. Hughes's conversational lines in "Theme for English B"

chapter 15

Writing About Rhyme:
Line-Ending Sounds
That Clinch Ideas

Rhyme refers to words containing identical final syllables. One type of rhyme involves words with identical concluding vowel sounds, or assonance, as in *day, weigh, grey, bouquet, fiancé,* and *matinée.* A second type of rhyme is created by assonance combined with identical consonant sounds, as in *ache, bake, break,* and *opaque;* or *turn, yearn, fern, spurn,* and *adjourn;* or *apple* and *dapple;* or *slippery* and *frippery.* Rhymes like these, because their rhyming sounds are identical, are called **exact rhymes**. It is important to note that rhymes result from *sound* rather than spelling: Words do not have to be spelled the same way or look alike to rhyme. All the words rhyming with *day*, for example, are spelled differently, but because they all contain the same *ā* sound, they rhyme.

THE NATURE AND FUNCTION OF RHYME

Rhyme, above all, gives delight. It also strengthens a poem's psychological impact. Through its network of similar sounds that echo and resonate in our minds, it promotes memory by clinching feelings and ideas and has been an important aspect of poetry for hundreds of years. Although many poets have not used it, and other poets have shunned it because they find it restrictive and artificial, it is closely connected with how well given poems move us or leave us flat.

Most often, rhymes are placed at the ends of lines. Two successive lines may rhyme, for example, and rhymes may appear in alternating lines. It is also possible to introduce rhyming words at intervals of four, five, or more lines. A problem, however, is that if rhyming sounds are too far away from each other, they lose their immediacy and therefore their effectiveness.

Poets who are skillful and original rhymers are able to create fresh, unusual, and surprising turns of thought. We may therefore judge poets on their use of rhyme. Often poets become quite creative rhymers, putting together words like "bent 'em" and "Tarentum" or "masterly" and "dastardly." Some rhymers (called a "rakehelly route of ragged rhymers" by a sixteenth-century critic) are satisfied with easy rhymes, or **cliché rhymes**, like *trees* and *breeze* (a rhyme that Alexander Pope criticized in 1711). But good rhymes and good poets go together, in creative cooperation. The seventeenth-century poet John Dryden, who wrote volumes of rhyming couplets, acknowledged that the need to find rhyming words inspired ideas that he had not anticipated. In this sense, rhyme has been—and still is—a vital element of poetic creativity.

There are few restrictions on English rhymes. Poets may rhyme nouns with other nouns, with verbs and adjectives, or with any other rhyming word, regardless of part of speech. Of course, exact rhymes are to be preferred, but the shortage of exact rhymes in English has enabled poets to be creative, rhyming words that almost rhyme but don't exactly (*slant rhyme*) or words that look alike but sound different (*eye rhyme*). Some poets use the same words to complete a rhyming pattern (*identical rhyme*), although this repetition eliminates some of the surprise and interest that good rhymes should produce.

RHYME AND METER

HEAVY-STRESS RHYME.   The effects of rhyme are closely connected with those of rhythm and meter. Rhymes that are produced with one-syllable words—like *moon, June, tune,* and *soon*—or with multisyllabic words in which the accent falls on the last syllable—like *combine, decline, supine,* and *refine*—are called **heavy-stress rhyme, accented rhyme,** or **rising rhyme.** In general, rising rhyme lends itself to serious effects. The accenting of heavy-stress rhyme appears in the concluding lines of Owen's "Anthem for Doomed Youth":

> Their flowers the tenderness of patient minds,
> And each slow dusk a drawing-down of blinds.

Here, the rhyming sounds are produced by one-syllable words—*minds* and *blinds*—that occur in the final heavy-stress positions of the lines.

TROCHAIC AND DACTYLIC RHYME.   Rhymes using words of two or more syllables in which the heavy stress falls on any syllable other than the last are called *trochaic* or *double rhyme* for rhymes of two syllables, and *dactylic* or *triple rhyme* for rhymes of three syllables. Less technically, these types of rhymes are also called **falling** or **dying rhymes**, probably because the intensity of pronunciation decreases on the light accent or accents following the heavy accent.

In general, **trochaic** or **double rhymes** are appropriate to light, amusing, and satiric poetry, as may be seen in lines 2 and 4 of the first stanza of "Miniver Cheevy" by Edwin Arlington Robinson:

> Miniver Cheevy, child of scorn
>   Grew lean while he assailed the *seasons;*
> He wept that he was ever born,
>   And he had *reasons.*

In this poem the effect of the double rhyme is humorous, thus helping to make Miniver Cheevy seem ridiculous and pathetic.

Double rhymes can also be a means of emphasizing or underscoring irony or anticlimax in serious poems, as in *a-flying* and *dying* in the first stanza of Herrick's "To the Virgins, to Make Much of Time":

> Gather ye rosebuds while ye may,
>   Old time is still a-flying;
> And this same flower that smiles today
>   Tomorrow will be dying.

Herrick uses falling rhymes in the second and fourth lines of every stanza of this poem. The result is a poignant contrast between pleasures of everyday life and the eternal truths of mortality.

Dactylic or **triple rhyme** is often light or humorous because it tends to divert attention from the subject to the words, as in these lines from Browning's "The Pied Piper of Hamelin" (italics added):

> Small feet were *pattering*, wooden shoes *clattering*,
> Little hands clapping and little tongues *chattering*.
> And, like fowls in a farm-yard where barley is *scattering*,

Here, the ending words *clattering, chattering,* and *scattering* are all instances of triple rhyme. The poem indeed does make a serious point (about the failure to keep a pledge); but in this stanza, which deals with the children following the Pied Piper, the triple rhyme is appropriate to the sounds of running children.

Variations in Rhyme

INTERNAL RHYME.   As the stanza from Browning shows, the fourth word in the first line, *pattering*, rhymes with the line-ending rhymes. This is an example of **internal rhyme**—the presence of a rhyming word within a line of verse. It is not a common variation, but you should be alert for it and make note of it when it occurs.

INEXACT RHYME.   Writers of English poetry have often felt limited in selecting rhymes because our language is short in exactly rhyming words. (Italian, by contrast, in which most words end in vowel sounds, offers virtually endless rhyming possibilities.) A tradition has therefore grown in English that words may be rhymed even though they are not exact.

Rhymes may often be created out of words with similar but not identical sounds. In most of these instances, either the vowel segments are different while the consonants are the same, or vice versa. This type of rhyme is variously called **slant rhyme**, **near rhyme**, **half rhyme**, **off rhyme**, **analyzed rhyme**, or **suspended rhyme**. In employing slant rhyme, a poet can pair *bleak* with *broke* or *could* with *solitude*. Amy Lowell creates an interesting slant rhyme in "Patterns." She uses the rhyme of *blossom* and *bosom* twice. A poet who uses slant rhyme extensively is Emily Dickinson. She takes great freedom with inexact rhymes by pairing words like *bird* and *crowd*, *port* and *chart*, *listens* and *distance*, and *surplice* and *church*.

Another common variation is **eye rhyme** or **sight rhyme**. In eye rhyme, the sounds to be eye-rhymed are *identical in spelling* but *different in pronunciation*. Entire words may be eye-rhymed; for example, *wind* (verb) may be joined to *wind* (noun), and *cóntest* (noun) may be used with *contést* (verb). In most eye rhymes, however, it is only the relevant parts of words that must be spelled identically. Thus *stove* may pair with *prove* and *above*; and *bough* may match *cough*, *dough*, *enough*, and *through*, despite all the differing pronunciations. The following lines are eye-rhymed:

> Although his claim was not to praise but *bury*,
> His speech for Caesar roused the crowd to *fury*.

The different pronunciations of *bury* and *fury* make clear the contrast between exact rhyme and eye rhyme. In exact rhyme identical sound is crucial; spelling is usually the same but may be different as long as the sounds remain identical. In eye rhyme, the eye-rhyming patterns must be spelled identically, but the sounds must be different.

ADDITIONAL VARIATIONS.   Poets sometimes may use **identical rhyme** (noted earlier); that is, the same words in rhyming positions, such as *veil* and *veil*, or *stone* and *stone*. **Vowel rhyme** is the use of any vowels in rhyming positions, as in *day* and *sky*, or *key* and *play*.

Rhyme Schemes

A **rhyme scheme** refers to a poem's pattern of rhyming sounds, which are indicated by alphabetical letters. The first rhyming sounds, such as *love* and *dove*, receive an *a*; the next rhyming sounds, such as *swell* and *fell*, receive a *b*; and the next sounds, such as *first* and *burst*, receive a *c*, and so on. Thus, a pattern of lines ending with the words *love, moon, thicket; dove, June, picket*; and *above, croon,* and *wicket* may be schematized as *a b c; a b c; a b c*.

To formulate a rhyme scheme or pattern, you include the meter and the number of feet in each line as well as the letters indicating rhymes. Here is such a formulation:

Iambic pentameter: *a b a b, c d c d, e f e f*

This scheme shows that all the lines in the poem are iambic, with five feet in each. Commas separating the units indicate a stanzaic pattern of three 4-line units, or **quatrains,** with the rhymes falling on the first and third lines of each quatrain, and then on the second and fourth.

Should the number of feet in the lines of a poem or **stanza** vary, you show this fact by using a number in front of each letter:

Iambic: *4a 3b 4a 3b 5a 5a 4b*

This formulation shows an intricate pattern of rhymes and line-lengths in a stanza of seven lines. The first, third, fifth, and sixth lines rhyme and vary from four to five feet. The second, fourth, and seventh lines also rhyme and vary from three to four feet.

The absence of a rhyme sound is indicated by an *x*. Thus, you formulate the rhyme scheme of **ballad measure** like this:

Iambic: *4x 3a 4x 3a*

The formulation shows that the quatrain alternates iambic tetrameter with trimeter. In this ballad quatrain, only lines 2 and 4 rhyme; there is no end rhyme in lines 1 and 3.

WRITING ABOUT RHYME

For your analysis, select either a short, representative passage from a long poem or an entire shorter poem such as a sonnet or three-stanza song. At the beginning, as for the essay on prosody, include a work sheet. This should be a double-spaced copy of the poem or passage, with each line numbered beginning with 1. At the right margin, list the numbers of feet in each line and letter each rhyme (5a, 4b, 3c, 4d, etc.). Underline or otherwise draw attention to any particularly notable or outstanding aspect of the rhyme.

Organizing Your Essay About Rhyme

INTRODUCTION.   Make any general remarks you wish about the poem, but concentrate on the relationship of the rhyme to the content. That is, does the rhyme seem like no more than a decorative adjunct, or is it integrated in some way? What is the way? Try to define and describe this relationship.

BODY. Try to discuss any or all of the following aspects of rhyme:

- *The Major Features of the Poem's Rhymes.* What is the dominant rhyme scheme? What variations do you find? What are the lengths and features of the rhyming words? Are there any unusual rhyming words? Are there any noteworthy segmental characteristics about the rhymes?
- *The Grammatical Features of the Rhymes.* As a general principle, the forms of rhyming words should not be the same but should vary. In your poem, what kinds of words are used for rhymes (i.e., verbs, nouns, etc.)? Are they all the same? Does one form predominate? Is there variety? Can you determine the grammatical positions of the rhyming words? How may these characteristics be related to the idea or theme of the poem?
- *The Qualities of the Rhyming Words.* Are the words specific? Concrete? Abstract? Are there any striking rhymes? Any surprises? Any rhymes that are especially clever and witty? Do any rhymes give unique comparisons or contrasts? How?
- *Any Particularly Striking or Unique Effects in the Rhymes.* Without becoming overly subtle or farfetched, you can make valid and interesting conclusions. Do any sounds in the rhyming words appear in patterns of assonance or alliteration elsewhere in the poem? Do the rhymes enter into any onomatopoeic effects? Broadly, what aspects of rhyme are uniquely effective because they blend so fully with the poem's thought and mood?

CONCLUSION. In your conclusion, try to develop a short evaluation of the poem's rhymes. You might also include any additional observations about the rhymes as well as any comparisons between the rhymes in your poem and in other poems by the same poet or other poets. A short summary of your main ideas is here, as always, appropriate.

Sample Essay

The Rhymes in Christina Rossetti's "Echo"

1	Come to me in the silence of the night; (n)		5a
2	Come in the speaking silence of a dream; (n)		5b
3	Come with soft rounded cheeks and eyes as bright (adj)		5a
4	As sunlight on a stream; (n)		3b
5	Come back in tears, (n)		2c
6	O memory, hope, love of finished years. (n)		5c

		adj	
7	O dream how sweet, too sweet, too bitter sweet,		5d
		n	
8	Whose wakening should have been in Paradise,		5e
		v	
9	Where souls brimful of love abide and meet;		5d
		n	
10	Where thirsty longing eyes		3e
		n	
11	Watch the slow door		2f
		adv	
12	That opening, letting in, lets out no more.		5f
		v	
13	Yet come to me in dreams, that I may live		5g
		n	
14	My very life again though cold in death:		5h
		v	
15	Come back to me in dreams, that I may give		5g
		n	
16	Pulse for pulse, breath for breath:		3h
		adj	
17	Speak low, lean low,		2i
		adj	
18	As long ago, my love, how long ago!		5i

Repeated words:
∿∿∿ dream, dreams   n = noun
─── sweet   v = verb
─·─·─ breath   adj = adjective
·········· low   adv = adverb
------ long ago
∿∿∿ come

[1] In the three-stanza lyric poem "Echo," Christina Rossetti uses rhyme as a way of saying that one might regain in dreams a love that is lost in reality.* As the real love is to the dream of love, so is an original sound to an echo. This connection underlies the poem's title and also Rossetti's unique use of rhyme. Aspects of her rhyme are the lyric pattern, the forms and qualities of the rhyming words, and the special use of repetition.†

The rhyme pattern is simple, and, like rhyme generally, it may be thought of as a pattern of echoes. Each stanza contains four lines of alternating rhymes concluded by a couplet, as follows:

[2]   Iambic: 5a, 5b, 5a, 3b, 2c, 5c.

There are nine separate rhymes throughout the poem, three in each stanza. Only two words are used for each rhyme, and no rhyme is used twice. Of the

* Central idea.
† Thesis sentence.

eighteen rhyming words, sixteen are one syllable long—almost all the rhymes.

[2]   The remaining two words consist of two and three syllables. With such a great number of single-syllable words, the rhymes are all rising ones, on the accented halves of iambic feet, and the end-of-line emphasis is on simple words.

The grammatical forms and positions of the rhyming words lend support to the introspective subject matter. Although there is variety, more than half the rhyming words are nouns. There are ten in all, and eight are placed as the objects of prepositions (e.g., of a dream, on a stream, of finished years). The nouns that are not the objects of prepositions are the subject and object of the same subordinate clause (lines 10 and 11). It seems clear that much of the poem's verbal energy occurs in the first parts of the lines, leaving the rhymes to

[3]   occur in modifying elements, as in these lines:

Come to me in the silence of the night (1)

Yet come to me in dreams, that I may live (13)

My very life again though cold in death; (14)

Most of the other rhymes are also in such internalized positions. This careful arrangement is consistent with the speaker's emphasis on her yearning to relive her love within dreams.

The qualities of the words are also consistent with the poem's emphasis on the speaker's internal life. Most of the rhyming words are impressionistic. Even the specific words—stream, tears, eyes, door, and breath—reflect the speaker's mental condition. In this regard, the rhyming words of lines 1 and 3 are effective. These are night and bright, which contrast the bleakness of the

[4]   speaker's solitary condition with the vitality of her inner life. Another effective contrast is in lines 14 and 16, where death and breath are rhymed. This rhyme underscores the sad fact that even though the speaker's love has vanished, it lives in present memory just as an echo continues after the original sound is gone.

It is in emphasizing how memory echoes experience that Rossetti creates her special use of rhyming words. She creates an ingenious repetition of a number of words; these are the poem's echoes. The major echoing word is the verb come, which appears six times at the beginnings of lines in stanzas 1 and 3. But some of the rhyming words are also repeated. The most notable is dream, the rhyming word in line 2. Rossetti repeats the word in line 7 and uses the plural,

[5]   dreams, in lines 13 and 15. In line 7 the rhyming word sweet is the third use of that word, a climax of "how sweet, too sweet, too bitter sweet." Concluding the poem, Rossetti repeats breath (line 16), low (line 17), and the phrase long ago (line 18). These repeating words justify the title "Echo," and they also stress the major idea that it is only in memory that experience has reality, even if dreams are no more than echoes.

Thus rhyme is not just ornamental in "Echo," but integral. Rossetti exerts the same rhyming skill in her half-serious, half-mocking poem "Eve," even though the two poems are different. In "Eve," Rossetti uses plain rhyming words together with comically intended double rhymes. In "Echo," the ease of her

[6]   rhymes, like the poem's diction generally, keeps the focus on regret and yearning rather than self-indulgence. As in all rhyming poems, Rossetti's rhymes emphasize the line-endings. The rhymes go beyond this effect, however,

[6] because of the internal repetition—echoes—of the rhyming words. <u>"Echo" is a poem in which rhyme is inseparable from meaning</u>.

COMMENTARY ON THE ESSAY

Throughout, illustrative words are underlined, and numbers are used to indicate the lines from which the illustrations are drawn. The introductory paragraph asserts that rhyme is vital in Rossetti's poem. It also attempts to explain the title "Echo." The thesis statement indicates the four topics to be developed in the body.

Paragraph 2 deals with the mechanical, mathematical aspects of the poem's rhymes. The high number of monosyllabic rhyming words is used to explain the rising, heavy-stress rhyme.

Paragraph 3 treats the grammar of the rhymes. For example, an analysis and count reveal that there are ten rhyming nouns and three rhyming verbs. The verb of command "come" is mentioned to show that most of the rhyming words exist within groups modifying this word. The grammatical analysis is thus related to the internalized nature of the poem's subject.

Paragraph 4 emphasizes the impressionistic nature of the rhyming words and also points out two instances in which rhymes stress the contrast between real life and the speaker's introspective life. Paragraph 5 deals with how Rossetti repeats five of the poem's rhyming words. This repetition creates a pattern of echoes, in keeping with the poem's title.

In the concluding paragraph, the rhymes in "Echo" are compared briefly with those in "Eve," another Rossetti poem. The conclusion is that Rossetti is a skilled rhymer because she uses rhyme appropriately in both poems.

SPECIAL WRITING TOPICS FOR RHYME

1. Analyze the rhymes in the Shakespeare sonnets included in Appendix D, or else the rhymes in Coleridge's "Kubla Khan" or Arnold's "Dover Beach" (or in another poem of your choice). What is interesting or unique about the various rhyming words? What relationships can you discover between the rhymes and the topics of the poems?

2. Compare one of the rhyming poems with one of the non-rhyming poems in Appendix D. What differences in reading and sound can you discover as a result of the use or non-use of rhyme? What benefits does rhyme give to the poem? What benefits does non-rhyme give?

3. Analyze Hardy's use of rhymes in "Channel Firing." What effects does he create by making rhymes with words such as *hatters* and *matters*, and *saner be* and

century? What is the relationship of such "falling" or "dying" rhymes to the heavy-stress rhymes that he uses in the poem?

4. Write a short poem of your own using double or triple rhymes, with words such as *computer, emetic, scholastic, remarkable, inedible, moron, anxiously, along with me, emotion, fishing,* and so on. If you have trouble with exact rhymes, see what you can do with slant rhymes and eye rhymes. The idea is to use your ingenuity. Have fun.

chapter 16

Writing an Essay Based on the Close Reading of a Poem or Short Prose Passage

An essay on a close reading is a detailed study of an entire short work or else a passage of prose or verse that is part of a longer work. This type of essay is specific because it focuses on the selected passage. It is also general because you do not consider only a single topic (such as *character, setting*, or *theme*), but rather deal with *all* the elements to be found in the passage. If the passage describes a person, for example, you must discuss character, but your emphasis should be on what the passage itself brings out about the character. You would also stress action, setting, and ideas, or even make comparisons, if you find that these matters are important. In other words, the content of a close-reading essay is variable; your passage dictates your content.

THE PURPOSE AND REQUIREMENTS OF A CLOSE-READING ESSAY

The general purpose of a close-reading essay is clear: If you can read a paragraph in a book, you can read the entire book; if you can read a speech, you can read the entire play or story; if you can read one poem by a poet, you can read other poems by the same poet or other poets. This is not to say that writing a close-reading essay automatically means you can immediately understand every work by the same author. Few people would insist that reading a passage from Joyce's *Dubliners* makes it possible to understand *Finnegans*

Wake. What a close-reading essay gives you is a skill upon which you can build, an approach to any other text you will encounter.

The essay is designed as an explanation of what is in the assigned passage. General content is the objective, together with anything else that is noteworthy. To write the essay, you do not need to undertake a detailed analysis of diction, grammar, or style. Instead, you should get at what you consider the most important aspects of the passage. Although you are free to discuss special words and phrases, and should do so if you find them important, your aim is primarily to get at the content of your passage.

THE LOCATION OF THE PASSAGE
IN THE WORK

Close-reading essays about portions of a work should demonstrate how the passage is connected to the rest of the work. The principle is that all parts are equally important and essential. Analyzing an individual part, therefore, should bring out not only the meaning of the part but also the function of the part within the larger structure of the work.

FOR AN EARLY PASSAGE.   If your passage occurs early in the play, poem, or story, you may conclude that the author is setting things in motion (exposition, complication). Thus, you should determine how themes, characterizations, and arguments in the passage are related to later developments. Always assume that everything is there for a purpose, and then find and explain that purpose.

FOR A LATER, MIDPOINT PASSAGE.   In a passage at the work's midpoint, the story or idea usually takes a particular turn—either expected or unexpected. If the change is unexpected, you should explain how the passage focuses the various themes or ideas and then propels them toward the forthcoming crisis or climax (the turning point or high point). It may be that the work features surprises, and the passage thus acquires a different meaning on second reading. It may be that the speaker has one set of assumptions while the readers have others, and that the passage marks the speaker's increasing self-awareness. In short, your task is to determine the extent to which the passage (a) builds on what has happened previously and (b) prepares the way for the outcome.

FOR A CONCLUDING PASSAGE.   A passage at or near the work's end is designed to solve problems or be a focal point or climax for all the cumulative situations and ideas. You will thus need to show how the passage brings together all details, ideas, and themes. What is happening? Is any action described in the passage a major action or a step leading to the major action? Has everything in the passage been prepared for earlier, or are there any surprises?

WRITING ABOUT THE GENERAL CONTENT OF A PASSAGE

Focus on the general meaning and impact of the passage or poem. What is the situation? Who is the speaker? Who is being addressed? What does the speaker want? What ideas are contained in the work? Once you answer such questions, write notes that you can use in your essay. Try to reach specific and focused conclusions: Does the passage (1) describe a scene, (2) develop a character, (3) present an action, (4) reveal a character's thoughts, (5) advance an argument, or (6) introduce an idea? What is the thematic content? How does the passage relate to earlier and later parts of the whole text? (To deal with this question, you may assume that your reader is familiar with the entire work.)

Organizing Your Essay About a Close Reading

INTRODUCTION.   Because the close-reading essay is concerned with details, you might have a problem developing a thematic structure. You can overcome this difficulty if you begin to work with either a generalization about the passage or a thesis based on the relationship of the passage to the work. Suppose, for example, that the passage is factually descriptive or that it introduces a major character or raises a major idea. Any one of these observations may serve as a thesis.

BODY.   Develop the body of the essay according to what you find in the passage. For a passage of character description, analyze what is disclosed about the character together with your analysis of what bearing this information has on the story or play as a whole. For a passage presenting an idea or ideas, analyze the idea and also demonstrate how the idea is important for the rest of the work. In short, your aim in this kind of essay is double: First, discuss the passage itself, and, second, show how the passage functions within the entire play.

CONCLUSION.   To conclude, stress the important details of your analysis. In addition, you may want to deal with secondary issues that arise in the passage but do not merit full consideration. The passage may contain specific phrases or underlying assumptions that you have not considered in the body

---

NUMBERS FOR EASY REFERENCE

In preparing your essay, prepare a copy of the entire passage just as it appears in the text. Include the copy at the beginning, as in the sample essay. For your reader's convenience, number lines in poetry and sentences in prose.

of your essay. The conclusion is the place to mention these matters, without developing them fully.

Sample Essay

A Study of Paragraph 31 of Updike's "A & P"°

> [1] Lengel sighs and begins to look very patient and old and gray. [2] He's been a friend of my parents for years. [3] "Sammy, you don't want to do this to your Mom and Dad," he tells me. [4] It's true, I don't. [5] But it seems to me that once you begin a gesture it's fatal not to go through with it. [6] I fold the apron, "Sammy" stitched in red on the pocket, and put it on the counter, and drop the bow tie on top of it. [7] The bow tie is theirs, if you've ever wondered. [8] "You'll feel this for the rest of your life," Lengel says, and I know that's true, too, but remembering how he made that pretty girl blush makes me so scrunchy inside I punch the No Sale tab and the machine whirs "pee-pul" and the drawer splats out. [9] One advantage to this scene taking place in summer, I can follow this up with a clean exit, there's no fumbling around getting your coat and galoshes, I just saunter into the electric eye in my white shirt that my mother ironed the night before, and the door heaves itself open, and outside the sunshine is skating around on the asphalt.

[1]   This paragraph, one of the last in John Updike's "A & P," describes Sammy's gesture supporting the right of the three girls to wear bathing suits in the store. The action is simple: Sammy takes off his apron and tie and walks outside. But the issues in the paragraph are not simple. Even though Sammy's decision is abrupt, a number of reasons are evident, such as that Sammy supports the girls' rights, that he feels sympathy for their embarrassment, that he objects to Lengel's grayness of spirit as well as of hair, and that he perceives (if dimly) the contrast between restrictiveness and freedom. <u>In all these reasons there is a common denominator of Sammy's growth brought about by his sudden decision and action.</u>* <u>This quality is shown in his diction and self-awareness and also in the greater issue of independence.</u>†

[2]   <u>A major aspect of Sammy's diction indicates the limited world that he is growing away from.</u> He uses the present tense rather than the past, for example (see verbs like "sighs," "begins," "fold," and so on), a characteristic of his place in the ordinary life of his home town, where this use of present-for-past tense is probably common. His use of the slang words "scrunchy" and "splats"

°See pages 304–309 for this story.
*Central idea.
†Thesis sentence.

[2] (sentence 8) also reflects this background and demonstrates his lack of sophistication and polish.

[3] The diction also suggests an aspect in which Sammy is limited. He is aware of the meaning of his gesture, but he does not—or cannot—express its significance. He is a young man of nineteen, with two alternatives ahead of him for his future. One is the routine represented by the store and by the various respectable zombies who walk through it. The other is the freedom, independence, and unconventionality represented by the girls in bathing suits. But he goes no further in considering his situation except to note his embarrassment at the way in which Lengel admonishes the "pretty girl" (sentence 8). His limited explanation hence shows that his feelings and perceptions are far ahead of his ability for expression.

[4] Though the language in the paragraph reveals Sammy's shortcomings, there are also words of perceptiveness and skill that show his growth. His memory of Lengel's checkout-counter advice suggests objectivity and accuracy. Also, his observations about Lengel show greater understanding than his abrupt decision to resign would indicate (sentences 1, 3, 6). Some of the paragraph is devoted to description, and Sammy's words here are economical and to the point, ably appropriate for the subject matter. Sammy's most skillful and imaginative language is contained in the last sentence, in which he observes that the sun is "skating around on the asphalt" (sentence 9).

[5] Also demonstrative of Sammy's strength is his strong sense of self-awareness. His self-awareness is so great, in fact, that the paragraph resembles a scene which he himself stages and directs. His sauntering out to make his "clean exit" at the end suggests that he is adopting an outward appearance of defiance to correspond with his gesture. Interestingly, he theorizes not about the implications of his actions but rather about the proper pose to go along with his new independence. His idea is that he recognizes his obligations to his parents and his future, but that he has a larger duty to be consistent with himself. In this context, his surprising observation that "it is fatal not to go through with" a gesture once it has begun is mildly comic (sentence 5). Thus the paragraph brings out Sammy's bravery and daring, even if he expends these virtues on nothing more than suddenly quitting his job.

[6] Because of this daring and insouciance, the paragraph also suggests the major idea that turmoil and sacrifice go along with growth and independence. Even though the circumstances are minor, Sammy's need for independence, like the need of all young people, is great. The paragraph of course is not argumentative but rather narrative, and the difficulties of making choices are therefore made no more prominent than Lengel's statement that Sammy will "feel this for the rest of . . . [his] life" (sentence 8). Lengel means that Sammy will likely suffer because of the action, and therefore regret it, but Sammy probably means that he will be proud for having asserted himself. His going through with his gesture thus points toward the final words of the story, about how hard life will be for him "hereafter" (paragraph 32). In cutting himself free from his tradition-bound town, Sammy leaves a great deal behind, and in recognizing his future difficulties, he accepts the burden of growth.

[7] The paragraph is therefore a major one. As an action, it moves Sammy out of the store in completion of his gesture, and in this respect it climaxes the comedy of a nineteen-year-old losing his job in protest against a prudish boss. As a symbol, it brings out the movement from restrictiveness to freedom, thereby touching on the difficulty and turmoil that go along with growth and independence. There are other potential issues in the paragraph as well, such as those of young against old or of sexual admiration and appreciation against conven-

tional respectability. Although these issues are major in the story, they are not as prominent in the paragraph. <u>This close study shows the paragraph to be a</u>
[7]   <u>packed one, vital in the narrative itself, and also touching on the important issues underlying Sammy's chivalric protest against the store's dress code.</u> In all these respects, it is a rough sketch of Sammy's subsequent life while it also moves the story quickly toward its end.

COMMENTARY ON THE ESSAY

This sample essay shows that a close study depends on the substance of the text paragraph. Because the topic is Sammy's leaving the store, together with the words immediately preceding this action, the essay is devoted to the effect of this action on the process of Sammy's growth (the central idea). If a text paragraph had been selected from earlier in the story, the close reading could deal with the growth only incidentally because the earlier passage would be part of the exposition of the story and would not yet be treating the effects of Sammy's decision.

In paragraph 1, the introduction, the central idea is presented as the link connecting possible topics that might be considered in the text paragraph.

The body contains three major sections. The first consists of three separate paragraphs and is concerned with what the diction shows about the narrator, Sammy. Paragraphs 3 and 4 emphasize the limitations of Sammy's background and analytical ability. Paragraph 5 takes a new direction, emphasizing that the diction also demonstrates Sammy's power and perceptiveness. Cumulatively, therefore, the three paragraphs bring out the central idea that the text paragraph concentrates on Sammy's capacities for growth.

Paragraph 5—concerned with a more abstract topic, that of self-awareness and self-control—continues the emphasis on Sammy's growth. Paragraph 6 demonstrates how important it is to anchor all discussions in both text and central idea and therefore shows how the discussion of a general issue may be approached in a close reading. In addition, the paragraph emphasizes the structural connection of the issue to the story's conclusion. The topic—that Sammy's growth produces disturbance and turmoil for him—is a major one in the story, but the broader applications are not developed because the subject is specifically confined to "A & P."

The concluding paragraph, 7, contains a summary in the form of a contrast between the paragraph as action and symbol. Because an important goal of a close reading essay is to stress the function of the text paragraph within the story, the final note is that the text paragraph points both toward the story's end and also toward the general condition of young people moving out on their own.

SPECIAL WRITING TOPICS
FOR CLOSE READING

For an Entire Poem

- Nye's "Where Children Live" or Hayden's "Those Winter Sundays." Try to establish how the poems bring out the speaker's affection.
- Keats's "On First Looking into Chapman's Homer." How does Keats convey his sense of intellectual excitement and discovery?

For a Paragraph From a Story (You Choose)

- Bierce's "An Occurrence at Owl Creek Bridge." Try to show how the passage connects the main character's imagination with his real death agony.
- Welty's "A Worn Path." Emphasize the connections between the details and the character of Phoenix.

For a Speech From a Play (You Choose)

- Glaspell's *Trifles*. Demonstrate how the speeches show the relationship between men and women.
- Chekhov's *The Bear*. How does the speech create character as it also conveys the play's humor?

chapter 17

Writing About Film:

Drama on the Silver and Color Screens

Film is the word most often used for motion pictures, although other common words are "picture" and (more likely) "movie." It is a specialized type of drama, utilizing, like drama, the techniques of dialogue, monologue, and action. Also like drama, it employs movement and spectacle. For these reasons, film may be studied for aspects such as character, structure, tone, theme, and symbolism. Unlike drama, however, film embodies techniques from photography, film chemistry, sound, and editing. These techniques are so specialized that they require special consideration.

A THUMBNAIL HISTORY OF FILM

Film arose out of technologies developed in the late nineteenth century. The first of these was the creation of a flexible substance—celluloid—that could accept the silver iodide emulsions that in the early years of photography were applied to glass. The other significant inventions were the motion picture camera and projector. Once these were in place, and once producers and directors decided to use the medium for full-length dramas, movies as we know them came into existence.

Although the earliest filmmakers thought of motion pictures as private entertainment, it soon became apparent that the development of large filmmaking studios, national distribution, and a system of local movie theaters could become extremely lucrative. The history of film is hence just as much a history of the film *business* as of the art and development of film dramas and film acting. With the production in 1915 of D. W. Griffith's *Birth of a Nation*, which realized an enormous profit on a small investment, filmmaking became a major industry.

The first motion pictures were black and white and were silent. Producers realized that large profits required easily recognized actors with "big names," and hence the "star system" made national figures out of actors such as Mary Pickford, Charlie Chaplin, and Rudolph Valentino. In 1928 the first talking picture, *Lights of New York*, was made. In 1932, with the first technicolor film, *La Cucaracha*, most of the current basic filmmaking tools were in existence.

For a time after the end of World War II, the growth of television inhibited the power of the large studios. Soon, however, many films were developed specifically for television viewing, and popular pictures were released for television use. In the last decade, with the advent of videotape and laser technology, home viewing has become a normal feature of American life. Today, film rental outlets may be found in shopping districts everywhere, with the result that virtually the entire corpus of movies, from the origins to the present, are within the reach of everyone with a VCR and a television set.[1] Early dramatists dreamed of filling their theaters for a number of consecutive performances, thus reaching perhaps several thousand persons. Film writers today, however, reach millions in the first-run movie houses, and many millions more on television reruns and videocassettes.

STAGE PLAYS AND FILM

While movies are a form of drama, there are a number of important differences between a movie and the stage production of a play. A play may be produced many times, in many different places, with many different people. In bringing a play to life, the producer and director not only employ actors, but also use artists, scene designers, carpenters, painters, lighting technicians, costume-makers, choreographers, and music directors and musicians. Each production is therefore different from every other, because both the actors and the appurtenances of the staging are unique.

---

[1]In addition, the technology of CD-ROM (Compact Disk—Read Only Memory) has recently been introduced. The film *A Hard Day's Night*, starring the Beatles, has been set up as a pilot example of how films may be adapted for CD-ROM on a personal computer. The offering includes the film itself (which may be stopped, moved forward, or moved backward at any point), together with explanations, commentary, the original script, notes on the songs, and other materials. This technology is only in the initial stages for film, but if it is widely adapted and distributed, the implications for film study are overwhelming, particularly if CD-ROM disks can be made available for inexpensive rental, as has happened with videocassettes.

A film, however, because of high production costs, and also because it reaches a mass audience, usually exists in only one version ("remakes" being excepted). Thus Shakespeare's play *Hamlet* has been staged innumerable times since Shakespeare's actors first produced it at the beginning of the seventeenth century. Orson Welles's *Citizen Kane* (1941) is in only one form, however; and, although it was restored and reedited in 1991, it cannot undergo any substantial changes.

As might be expected, then, stage and movie productions are radically different. In a play, actors enter, speak to each other, and remain in front of the audience until they exit. The stage itself limits what can be done. However, the makers of a film have few such limitations, and the absence of restrictions permits the inclusion of any detail whatever, from a car chase to a scene in the Napoleonic wars. If there is to be a scene on a desert island, the filmmaker goes to such an island and presents it in all its reality, complete with beach, palm trees, huts, and authentic natives-turned-actors. Nothing is left to your imagination. If the scene is a distant planet, obviously the filmmaker cannot go on location but instead creates a working location in the studio, with lighting, props, costumes, and special effects. In addition, modern computerized special effects create scenes that were unimaginable in the past. Film, in short, enables a dramatic production to approach almost complete freedom.

THE AESTHETICS OF FILM

To the degree that film is confined to a screen, it may be compared visually to the art of the painter and the still photographer. It uses the language of visual art. One object in a painting may take on special relationships to others as the artist directs the eyes of the observer. A color used in one part may be balanced with the same color, or its complement, in another part. Painters and photographers may introduce certain colors and details as symbols and may suggest allegorical interpretations through the inclusion of mythical figures or universally recognized objects. Particular effects may be achieved with the use of the textures of the paint and control over shutter speed, focus, and various techniques of development. The techniques and effects are extensive.

The filmmaker is able to utilize most of the resources of the still photographer and many of those of the painter, and may augment these with special effects. Artistically, the most confining aspect of film is the rectangular screen, but aside from that, film is unrestricted. Based in a dramatic text called a "film script" or "shooting script," it uses words and their effects, but it also employs the language of visual art, especially the particular vividness and power of moving pictures. When considering film, then, you should realize that film communicates not only with words but also by various techniques. The visual presentation is inseparable from the medium of film itself.

TECHNIQUES OF FILM

There are many techniques of film, and a full description and documentation of them can be—and has become—extensive.[2] In evaluating film, however, you need to familiarize yourself only with those aspects of technique that have an immediate bearing on your responses and interpretations.

Editing or Montage

A finished film is not a continuous work, filmed from start to end, but is instead a composite. The putting together of the film is the process of *editing*, or **montage** (assemblage, mounting, construction), which is a cutting and gluing procedure. Depending on the flexibility of the film script, the various scenes of the film are planned before shooting begins, but the major task of montage is done in a studio by special film editors.

If we again compare film with a stage play, we may note that a theatrical production moves continuously, with pauses only for intermissions and scene changes. Your perception of the action is caused by your distance from the stage (perhaps aided by opera glasses or binoculars). Also, even as you move your eyes from one character to another, you still perceive the entire stage. In a film, however, the directors and editors *create* these continuous perceptions for you by piecing together different parts. The editors begin with many "takes" (separately filmed scenes, including many versions of the same scenes). What they select, or mount, is the film, and we never see the discarded scenes. Thus, it is editing that puts everything together.

MONTAGE AND NARRATIVE CONTINUITY. The first use of montage, already suggested, is narrative continuity. For example, a climb up a steep cliff may be shown at the bottom, middle, and top (with backward slips and falls to show the danger of the climb and to make viewers catch their breath). All such narrative sequences result from the assembling of individual pieces, each one representing phases of the activity. A classic example of a large number of separate parts forming a narrative unit is the well-known shower murder in Alfred Hitchcock's *Psycho* (1959), where a forty-five second sequence is made up of seventy-eight different shots (e.g., the woman in the shower, the murderer behind the curtain, the attack, the slumping figure, the running water, the dead woman's eye, the bathtub drain).

---

[2] See, for example, Louis D. Giannetti, *Understanding Movies*, 7th ed. (Englewood Cliffs: Prentice Hall, 1995); Ephraim Katz, *The Film Encyclopedia* (New York: Crowell, 1979; Katz died in 1993, and a new edition has been completed by other editors); James Monaco et al., *The Encyclopedia of Film* (New York: Perigee, 1991); James Monaco, *How to Read a Film*, rev. ed. (New York: Oxford University Press, 1981); Daniel Talbot, ed., *Film: An Anthology* (Berkeley: University of California Press, 1969); and John Wyver, *The Moving Image* (Oxford: Basil Blackwell, 1989).

EXPLANATION OF CHARACTER AND MOTIVATION.   Montage is used in "flashbacks" to explain present, ongoing actions or characteristics, or in illustration of a character's thoughts and memories, or in brief examples from the unremembered past of a character suffering from amnesia. It also supplies direct visual explanation of character. A famous example occurs in Welles's *Citizen Kane* (the subject of the sample essay in this chapter). The concluding scene shows overhead views of Kane's vast collection of statues and mementos. At the very end, the camera focuses on a raging incinerator into which workmen have thrown his boyhood sled, which bears the brand name "Rosebud" (we have fleetingly seen him playing with this sled as a boy). Because "Rosebud" is Kane's last word—the meaning of which everyone in the film is trying to figure out—this final scene shows that Kane's dying thoughts are about his lost boyhood, before he was taken away from his parents, and that his unhappy life has resulted from his early rejection and personal pain.

DIRECTORIAL COMMENTARY.   In addition, montage is used symbolically as commentary, as in an early sequence in Charlie Chaplin's *Modern Times* (1936), which shows a large group of workers rushing to their factory jobs. Immediately following this scene is a view of a large, milling herd of sheep. By this symbolic montage, Chaplin suggests that the men are being herded and dehumanized by modern industry. Thus, montage and editorial statement go hand in hand.

OTHER USES.   Montage may also produce other characteristics through camera work, development, and special effects. For example, filmmakers can reverse an action to emphasize its illogicality or ridiculousness. Editing can also speed up action (which makes even the most serious things funny), or slow things down. It can also blend one scene with another or juxtapose two or more actions in quick succession to show what people may be doing while they are separated. The possibilities for creativity and uniqueness are extensive.

Visual Techniques

THE CAMERA.   While editing or montage is a finishing technique, the work of film begins with the camera, which permits great freedom in the presentation of characters and actions. In a film, the visual viewpoint can shift. Thus, a film may begin with a distant shot of the actors—a "long shot"—much like the view of actors on stage. The camera can then zoom in to give a closeup or zoom out to present a wide and complete panorama. Usually a speaking actor will be the subject of a closeup, but the camera may also show closeups of other actors who are reacting. You must decide on the effects of closeups and long shots yourself, but it should be plain that the frequent use of either—or of middle-distance photographs—is a means by which film directors control perceptions of their characters and situations.

The camera may also move from character to character or from character to an object. In this way a film may show a series of reactions to an event. It may also concentrate your attention on a character's attitude, or it may be a visual commentary on his or her actions. If a man and woman are in love, for example, the camera may shift, either directly or through montage, from the couple to flowers and trees, thus associating their love visually with objects of beauty and growth. Should the flowers be wilted and the trees leafless, however, the visual commentary might be that their love is doomed and hopeless.

The camera may also create unique effects, such as slow motion, which can focus on a certain aspect of a person's mood or character. The slow-motion filming of a child running happily in a meadow (as in *The Color Purple* [1985] by Steven Spielberg) suggests the joy inherent in such movement. Surprisingly, speed is sometimes indicated by slow motion, which emphasizes strong muscular effort (as in the running scenes in Hugh Hudson's *Chariots of Fire* [1981]).

Many other camera techniques bear on action and character. The focus may be sharp at one point, indistinct at another. Moving a speaking character out of focus may suggest that listeners are bored. Sharp or blurred focus may also show that a character has seen things exactly or inexactly. In action sequences, the camera may be mounted in a moving vehicle to "track" or follow running human beings or horses, speeding bicycles and cars (as in Woody Allen's *Annie Hall*), or moving sailboats, canoes, speedboats, or rowboats. A camera operator on foot may also be the tracker, or the camera may track ground movement from an aircraft. Movement may also be captured by a rotating camera that follows a moving object or character. Then, too, the camera may be fixed while the moving object goes from one side to the other.

LIGHT, SHADOW, AND COLOR. As in the theater, the filmmaker uses light, shadow, and color to reinforce ideas and to create realistic and symbolic effects. A scene in sunshine, which brings out colors, and the same scene in rain and clouds or in twilight, all of which mute colors, create different moods. Characters in bright light are presumably open and frank, whereas characters in shadow may be hiding something, particularly in black and white films. Flashing or strobe lights might show a changeable or sinister character or situation.

Colors, of course, have much the same meaning that they have in any other artistic medium. Blue sky and clear light suggest happiness, and greenish light may indicate something ghoulish. A memorable control of color occurs midway through David O. Selznick's *Gone With the Wind* (1939), when Scarlet O'Hara reflects upon the devastation of her plantation home, Tara. She resolves never to be hungry again, and as she speaks she is silhouetted against a flaming orange sky—a background that suggests how totally the way of life she knew as a young woman has been destroyed. As in this example, you may expect colors to complement the story of the film. Thus, lovers may wear clothing with the same or complementary colors, but incompatible people may wear clashing colors.

Action Techniques

The strength of film is direct action. Actions of all sorts—running, swimming, driving a car, fighting, embracing and kissing, or even just sitting; chases, trick effects, ambushes—all these and more create a sense of immediate reality, and all are tied (or should be) to narrative development. Scenes of action may run on for several minutes, with little or no accompanying dialogue, to carry on the story or to convey ideas about the interests and abilities of the characters.

Closely related to the portrayal of action is the way in which film shows the human body (and animal bodies), together with bodily motion and gesture (or body language). The view or perspective that the filmmaker presents is particularly important. A torso shot of a character may stress no more than the content alone of that character's speech. A closeup shot, however, with the character's head filling the screen, may emphasize motives as well as content. The camera may also distort ordinary reality. With wide-angle lenses and closeups, for example, human subjects may be made bizarre or grotesque, as the faces in the crowd are made to seem in Woody Allen's *Stardust Memories* (1980). Sometimes the camera creates other bodily distortions, enlarging certain limbs—for example, as happens with the forest dweller in Ingmar Bergman's *Virgin Spring* (1959)—or throwing into unnatural prominence a scolding mouth or a suspicious eye. If distortion is used, it invites interpretation: The filmmaker may be asserting that certain human beings, even supposedly normal ones, are odd, sinister, intimidating, or psychotic.

Sound Techniques

DIALOGUE AND MUSIC.   The first business of the sound track is the spoken dialogue, which is "mixed" in editing to be synchronized with the action. There are also many other elements in the sound track. Music, the most important, creates and augment moods. A melody in a major or minor key or in a slow or fast tempo may affect our perception of actions. If a character is thinking deeply, muted strings may create a complementary sound; but if the character is going insane, the music may become discordant and percussive.

Sometimes, music gives a film a special identity. In Hudson's *Chariots of Fire*, for example, Vangelis Papathanassiou wrote music that has become separately popular, but which is always identified with the film. In addition, musical accompaniments may directly render dramatic statement, without dialogue. An example occurs in Welles's *Citizen Kane*. Beginning that portion of the narrative derived from the autobiography of a character who is now dead (the scene first focuses on the character's statue), the musical sound track by Bernard Herrmann quotes the "Dies Irae" theme from the traditional "Mass for the Dead." The instrumentation, however, makes the music funny, and we do not grieve but rather smile. Herrmann, incidentally, varies this theme elsewhere in the film, usually for comic effect.

SPECIAL SOUND EFFECTS. Special sound effects may also augment a film's action. The sound of a blow, for example, may be enhanced electronically to cause an impact similar to the force of the blow itself (as in the boxing scenes from the many *Rocky* films). At times some sounds, such as the noises of wailing people, squeaking or slamming doors, marching feet, or moving vehicles, may be filtered through an electronic apparatus to create weird or ghostly effects. Often a character's words may echo rapidly and sickeningly to show dismay or anguish. In a word, sound is a vital part of film.

WRITING ABOUT A FILM

Obviously the first requirement is to see the film, either in a theater or on videocassette. Watch it at least twice through, making notes, because your discussion takes on value the more thoroughly you know the material. Write down the names of the script writer, director, composer, special effects editor, chief photographer, and major actresses and actors. If particular speeches are worth quoting, remember the general circumstances of the quotation, and also, if possible, key words. Take notes on costume and color, or (if the film is in black and white) light and shade. You will need to rely on memory, but if you have the film on videotape you may easily check important details. A good method is to concentrate on technique in only a few scenes. If you analyze the effects of montage, for example, you may use your VCR's stop-action control to go over the scene a number of times.

Organizing Your Essay on Film

INTRODUCTION. State your central idea and thesis sentence. You should include the background necessary to support points you make in the body of the essay and should also name the major creative and performing persons of the film.

BODY. If you have no other instructions, you might decide on topics discussed earlier in this book, such as plot, structure, character, ideas, or setting. Remember, however, to consider not only dialogue and action but also film techniques. For example, if you choose to discuss a character, or the plot development, you need to develop your argument using the evidence of camera techniques, montage, sound effect, and the like. In planning the body of your essay, consider questions such as the following:

Action

- How important is action? Is there much repetition of action, say, in slow motion, or from different angles? Are actors (and animals) viewed closely or distantly? Why?
- What actions are stressed (chases, concealment, gun battles, lovemaking)? What does the type of action contribute to the film?
- What do closeups show about character and motivation (smiles and laughter, frowns, leers, anxious looks)?
- What actions indicate seasonal conditions (cold by a character's stamping of feet, warmth by the character's removing a coat or shirt)? What connection do these actions have to the film's general ideas?
- Does the action show any changing of mood (from sadness to happiness, from indecision to decision)?

Cinematographic Techniques

- What notable techniques are used (colors, lighting, etc.)? What is their relationship to the film's characterizations and themes?
- What characterizes the use of the camera (tracking, closeups, distant shots, camera angles, etc.)? How do the camera perspectives reinforce or detract from the film's theme and plot?
- How does the editing (the sequencing of scenes) reinforce or detract from the story and theme?
- What scene or scenes best exemplify how the cinematographic techniques interact with the theme, plot, characters, setting, and so on? Why?

Acting

- How well do the actors adapt to the medium of film? How convincing are their performances?
- How well do the actors control their facial expressions and body movement? Are they graceful? Awkward?
- What does their appearance lend to your understanding of their characters?
- Does it seem that the actors are genuinely creating their roles, or just reading through the parts?

CONCLUSION. In your conclusion, you might evaluate the effectiveness of the cinematic form to story and idea. Are all the devices of film used in the best possible way? Is anything overdone? Is anything underplayed? Is the film good, bad, or indifferent up to a point, and then does it change? How? Why?

Sample Essay

Orson Welles's Citizen Kane: *Whittling a Giant Down to Size*°

[1] *Citizen Kane* (1941) is a superbly crafted film in black and white. The script is by Herman Mankiewicz and Orson Welles, with photography by Gregg Toland, music by Bernard Herrmann, direction and production by Welles, and the leading role by Welles. It is the story of a wealthy and powerful man, Charles Foster Kane, who exemplifies the American Dream of economic self-sufficiency, self-determination, and self, period. The film does not explore the "greatness" of the hero, however, but rather exposes him as a misguided, unhappy person who tries to buy love and remake reality.* All aspects of the picture—characterization, structure, and technique—are directed to this goal.†

[2] At the film's heart is the deterioration of Kane, the newly deceased newspaper magnate and millionaire. He is not all bad: He begins well and then goes downward, in a tragic sequence. For example, the view we see of him as a child being taken away from home invites sympathy. When we next see him as a young man, he idealistically takes over a daily newspaper, the Inquirer. This idealism makes him admirable but also makes his deterioration tragic. As he says to Thatcher in a moment of insight, he could have been a great person if he had not been wealthy. His corruption begins when he tries to alter the world to suit himself, such as his demented attempt to make an opera star out of his second wife, Susan, and his related attempt to shape critical praise for her despite her terrible singing. Even though he builds an opera house for her and also sponsors many performances, he cannot change reality. This tampering with truth indicates how completely he loses his youthful integrity.

[3] The structure is progressively arranged to bring out such weaknesses. The film flows out of the opening obituary newsreel, from which we learn that Kane's dying word was the name "Rosebud" (the brand name of his boyhood sled, spoken at the beginning by a person [Kane] whose mouth is shown in closeup). The newsreel director, wanting to get the inside story, assigns a reporter named Thompson to learn about "Rosebud." Thompson's search unifies the rest of the film; he goes from place to place and person to person to collect materials and conduct interviews, which disclose Kane's increasing strangeness and alienation. At the end, although the camera departs from Thompson to focus on the burning sled, Thompson has been successful in uncovering the story of Kane's deterioration (even though Thompson himself never learns what "Rosebud" means). Both the sled and the reporter therefore tie together the many aspects of the film.

°The fiftieth anniversary reedited version (1991) of *Citizen Kane* is available from Turner Home Entertainment (© 1941 RKO Radio Pictures, Inc. Renewed © 1961 RKO General, Inc. All Rights Reserved. Package Design © 1991 Turner Entertainment Co.).
* Central idea.
† Thesis sentence.

[4]

It is through Thompson's searches that the film presents the flashback accounts of Kane's deterioration. The separate persons being interviewed (including Thatcher's handwritten account) each contribute something different to the narrative because their experiences with Kane have all been unique. As a result of these individual points of view, the story is quite intricate. We learn in the Bernstein section, for example, that Jedediah proudly saves a copy of Kane's declaration about truth in reporting. We do not learn in Jedediah's interview, however, that he, Jedediah, sends the copy back to Kane as an indictment of Kane's betrayal of principle. Rather, it is in *Susan's* account that we learn about the return, even though she herself understands nothing about it. This subtlety, so typical of the film, marks the ways in which the biography of Kane is perceptively revealed.

[5]

Thus, the major importance of these narrating characters is to reveal and reflect Kane's disintegration. Jedediah (Joseph Cotten) is a person of principle who works closely with Kane, but after the lost election he rebels when he understands the falseness of Kane's personal life. He is totally alienated after Kane completes the unfinished attack on Susan's performance. Jedediah's change, or perhaps his assertion of principle, thus reveals Kane's increasing corruption. Susan, Kane's second wife (Dorothy Comingore), is naive, sincere, and warm; but her drinking, her attempted suicide, and her final separation show the harm of Kane's warped visions. Bernstein (Everett Sloane), the first person Thompson interviews, is a solitary figure who is uncritical of Kane, but it is he who first touches the theme about the mystery of Kane's motivations. Bernstein also takes on life when he speaks poignantly of his forty-five year memory of the girl in white. Even though this revelation is brief, it suggests layers of feeling and longing.

[6]

In addition to these perceptive structural characterizations, *Citizen Kane* is a masterpiece of film technique. The camera images are sharp, with clear depths of field. In keeping with Kane's disintegration and mysteriousness, the screen is rarely bright. Instead, the film makes strong use of darkness and contrasts, almost to the point at times of blurring distinctions between people. Unique in Gregg Toland's camera work are the many shots taken from waist high or below; these distort the bodies of the characters by distancing their heads, suggesting that the characters are preoccupied with their own concerns and oblivious to normal perspectives. Nowhere is this distortion better exemplified than in the scene between Kane and Jedediah in the empty rooms after the lost election, when Jedediah asks permission to leave for Chicago.

[7]

As might be expected in a film so dominated by its central figure, the many symbols create strong statements about character. The most obvious is the sled, "Rosebud," the dominating symbol of the need for love and acceptance in childhood. Another notable symbol is glass and, in one scene, ice. In the party scene, two ice statues are in the foreground of the employees of the *Inquirer*. In another scene, a bottle looms large in front of Jedediah, who is drunk. In another, a pill bottle and drinking glass are in front of Susan, who has just used them in her suicide attempt. The suggestion of these carefully photographed symbols is that life is brittle and temporary. Particularly symbolic is the bizarre entertainment in the party scene. Because Kane joins the dancing and singing, the action suggests that he is doing no more than taking a role in life, never being himself or knowing himself. Symbols that frame the film are the wire fence and the "No Trespassing" sign at both beginning and end. These symbols suggest that even if we understand a little about Kane, or anyone, there are boundaries we cannot pass, depths we can never reach.

[8] There are also amusing symbols, which suggest not only the diminution of Kane, but also of the other characters. An example is Bernstein's high-backed chair, which makes him look like a small child. Similarly, the gigantic fireplace at Xanadu makes both Kane and Susan seem like pigmies—a symbol that great wealth dwarfs and dehumanizes people. Especially comic is Kane's picnic at Xanadu. In going into the country, Kane and his friends do not walk, but ride in a long line of cars—more like a funeral procession than a picnic—and they stay overnight in a massive tent. Quite funny is the increasing distance between Kane and Emily, his first wife, in the rapid-fire shots that portray their developing separation. Even more comic is the vast distance at Xanadu between Kane and Susan when they discuss their life together. They are so far apart that they must shout to be heard. Amusing as these symbols of diminution and alienation are, however, they are also pathetic, because at first Kane finds closeness with both his wives.

[9] In all respects, *Citizen Kane* is a masterly film. This is not to say that the characters are likable or that the amusing parts make it a comedy. Instead, the film pursues truth, suggesting that greatness and wealth cannot give happiness. It is relentless in whittling away at its major figure. Kane is likable at times, and he is enormously generous (as shown when he sends Jedediah $25,000 in severance pay). But these high moments show the contrasting depths to which Kane falls, with the general point being that people who are powerful and great may deteriorate even at their height. The goal of the newsreel director at the beginning is to get at the "real story" behind the public man. There is more to any person than a two-hour film can reveal, but within its limits, *Citizen Kane* gets at the real story, and the real story is both sad and disturbing.

COMMENTARY ON THE ESSAY

The major point is that the film diminishes the major figure, Kane. In this respect the essay illustrates the analysis of *character* (Chapter 4), and it therefore emphasizes how film may be considered as a form of literature. Also shown in the essay are other methods of literary analysis: *structure* (Chapter 3) and *symbolism* (Chapter 10). Of these topics, only the use of symbols, because they are visually presented in the film, is unique to the medium of film as opposed to the medium of words.

Any one of the topics might be developed as a separate essay. There is more than enough about the character of Susan, for example, to sustain a complete essay, and the film's structure could be extensively explored. *Citizen Kane* itself as a repository of film techniques is rich enough for an exhaustive, book-length account.

Because the essay is about a film, the unique aspect of paragraph 1 is the opening brief description (stressing the medium of black and white), and the credits to the script writers, principal photographer, composer, and director.

Unlike works written by a single author, film is a collaborative medium, and therefore it is appropriate to recognize the separate efforts of the principal contributors.

Paragraph 2 begins the body and carries out a brief analysis of the major character. Paragraphs 3–5 discuss various aspects of the film's structure (the second topic announced in the thesis sentence) as they bear on Kane. In paragraph 3 the unifying importance of the sled and the reporter, Thompson, is explained. Paragraph 4 focuses on the film's use of flashback as a structural technique, and paragraph 5 discusses three of the flashback characters as they either intentionally or unintentionally reveal Kane's flaws.

In paragraphs 6–8 the topic is film technique, the third and last topic of the thesis sentence. Paragraph 6 focuses on light, camera angles, and distortion; paragraph 7 treats visual symbols; paragraph 8 continues the topic of symbols but extends it to amusing ones.

The final paragraph restates the central idea and also relates the theme of deterioration to the larger issue of how great wealth and power affect character. Thus, as a conclusion, this paragraph not only presents a summary but also notes the film's general ideas.

SPECIAL WRITING TOPICS FOR FILM

1. Select a single film technique, such as the use of color, the control of light, or the photographing of action, and write an essay describing how it is used in a film. For best results, use a videocassette for your study. As much as possible, try to explain how the technique is used throughout the film. Determine constant and contrasting features, the relationship of the technique to the development of story and character, and so on.

2. Write an essay explaining how all the film techniques of a particular scene are employed (camera angles, closeups or long shots, tracking, on-camera and off-camera speeches, lighting, depth of field, etc.). For your study, you will have to rerun your scene a number of times, trying to notice elements for the first time and also reinforcing your first observations.

3. Pick out a news story and write a dramatic scene about it. Next consider how to do it for a film, providing directions for actors and camera people (e.g., "As Character A speaks, his face shows that he is lying; the camera zooms slowly in on his face, with a loss of focus"; or, "As Character A speaks, the camera focuses on Character B exchanging looks with Character C"). When you are done, write an explanation of how you designed your directions to bring out details about your story and characters.

chapter 18

Writing the Research Essay:
Using Extra Resources
for Understanding

Broadly, **research** is the act of systematic investigation, examination, and experimentation. It is the basic tool of intellectual inquiry for anyone engaged in any discipline—physics, chemistry, biology, psychology, anthropology, history, and literature, to name just a few. With research, our understanding and our civilization grow; without it, they die.

While research is the animating spark of all disciplines, our topic here is **literary research**—the systematic use of primary and secondary sources in studying a literary problem. In doing literary research, you consult not only individual works themselves (*primary sources*), but also many other works that shed light on them and interpret them (*secondary sources*). Typical research tasks are to learn important facts about a work and about the period in which it was written; to learn about the lives, careers, and other works of authors; to discover some of the comments and judgments of modern or earlier critics; to learn details that help explain the meaning of works; and to learn about critical and artistic taste.

A certain amount of research is always necessary in any literary essay or assignment. Using a dictionary, for example, is a minimal form of research. More involved research uses an array of resources: encyclopedias, biographies, introductions, critical studies, bibliographies, and histories.

SELECTING A TOPIC

In most instances, your instructor assigns a research essay on a specific topic. Sometimes, however, the choice of a topic is left entirely up to you. In such cases, it is helpful to know the types of research essays you might find most congenial. Here are some possibilities:

1. *A Particular Work.* You might treat character (for example, "The Character of Smirnov in *The Bear*" or "The Question of Whether Young Goodman Brown Is a Hero or a Dupe"), or tone, point of view, setting, structure, and the like. A research paper on a single work is similar to an essay on the same work, except that the research paper takes into account more views and facts than those you are likely to have without the research. Please see the sample research essay, on Katherine Mansfield's "Miss Brill," to see how materials may be handled for such an assignment.

2. *A Particular Author.* This essay is about an idea or some facet of style, imagery, setting, or tone of the author, tracing the origins and development of the topic through a number of different stories, poems, or plays. An example might be "The Idea of Sin and Guilt as Developed by Hawthorne." This type of essay is suitable for a number of shorter works, though it is also applicable for a single major work, such as a longer story, novel, or play.

3. *Comparison and Contrast* (see Chapter 13). There are two types:

   a. *An Idea or Quality Common to Two or More Authors.* Your intention might be to show points of similarity or contrast or else to show that one author's work may be read as a criticism of another's. Typical subjects would be "The Use of the Third-Person Limited Point of View by Hawthorne and Mansfield" or "The Theme of Love and Sexuality in Shakespeare, Chekhov, and Lowell."

   b. *Different Critical Views of a Particular Work or Body of Works.* Sometimes much is to be gained from an examination of differing critical opinions on topics such as "The Meaning of Poe's 'The Cask of Amontillado,'" "Opposing Views of Hawthorne's 'Young Goodman Brown,'" or "The Question of Chekhov's Attitude Toward Women as seen in *The Bear*." Such a study would attempt to determine the critical opinion and taste to which a work does or does not appeal, and it might also aim at conclusions about whether the work was or is in the advance or rear guard of its time.

4. *The Influence of an Idea, Author, Philosophy, Political Situation, or Artistic Movement on Specific Works of an Author or Authors.* A paper on influences can be fairly direct, as in "Details of Black American Life as Reflected in Hughes's 'Theme for English B,'" or else more abstract and critical, as in "The Influence of Racial Oppression and the Goal of Racial Equality on the Speaker of 'Theme for English B.'"

5. *The Origin of a Particular Work or Type of Work.* One avenue of research for such an essay might be to examine an author's biography to discover the germination and development of a work—for example, "'Kubla Khan' as an Outgrowth

of Coleridge's Reading." Another way of discovering origins might be to relate a work to a particular type or tradition: "'Theme for English B' and the Harlem Renaissance," or "'Patterns' and Its Relationship to the Anti-War Literature of World War I."

If you consider these types of research essays, an idea of what to write may come to you. Perhaps you have particularly liked one author, or several authors. If so, you might start to think along the lines of types 1, 2, and 3. If you are interested in influences or in origins, then type 4 or 5 may suit you better.

If you still cannot decide on a topic after rereading the works you have liked, then you should carry your search for a topic into your school library. Look up your author or authors in the card or computer catalogue. Your first goal should be to find a relatively recent book-length critical study published by a university press. Look for a title indicating that the book is a general one dealing with the author's major works rather than just one work. Study those chapters relevant to the work or works you have chosen. Most writers of critical studies describe their purpose and plan in their introductions or first chapters, so begin with the first part of the book. If there is no separate chapter on the primary text, use the index and go to the relevant pages. Reading in this way will give you enough knowledge about the issues and ideas raised by the work to enable you to select a promising topic. Once you make your decision, you are ready to go ahead and develop a working bibliography.

SETTING UP A BIBLIOGRAPHY

The best way to develop a working bibliography of books and articles is to begin with major critical studies of the writer or writers. Again, go to the catalogue and pick out books that have been published by university presses. These books usually contain comprehensive bibliographies. Be careful to read the chapters on your primary work or works and to look for the footnotes or endnotes, for often you can save time if you record the names of books and articles listed in these notes. Then refer to the bibliographies at the ends of the books and select likely looking titles. Now, look at the dates of publication of the critical books. Let us suppose that you have been looking at three, published in 1963, 1987, and 1993. The chances are that the bibliography in a book published in 1993 will be complete up through about 1991, for the writer will usually have completed the manuscript about two years before the book was published. What you should do then is to gather a bibliography of works published since 1991; you may safely assume that writers of critical works will have done the selecting for you of works published before that time.

Bibliographical Guides

Fortunately for students doing literary research, the Modern Language Association (MLA) of America has been providing a complete bibliography of literary studies for years, not only in English and American literatures but also in the literatures of many foreign languages. The MLA started achieving completeness in the late 1950s and by 1969 had reached such an advanced state that it divided the bibliography into four parts, which are bound together in library editions. University and college libraries have a set of these bibliographies on open shelves or tables. Recently, the bibliographies have become available on CD-ROM.

There are many other bibliographies useful for students doing literary

---

ONLINE COMPUTERIZED LIBRARY SERVICES

Localized and nationwide online reference services are available through most libraries and library systems. You therefore have the possibility of access to the collections of large research libraries. If your own library does not have a book that you discover through the online reference service, you can use the interlibrary loan service to acquire the copy you need. Also, many associated libraries, such as state colleges and urban public libraries, have pooled their resources in online systems. If you use the services of a network of county libraries, for example, you may locate works that are not available in your college or local library. Usually, with time, the libraries will accommodate as many of your needs as they can. Librarians are immensely helpful and cooperative people.

You may use a personal computer yourself to gain access to the online service of a large library, provided that you have a modem, a telecommunications program, the correct telephone number and other entry information, the ability to follow the program codes, and patience and persistence. Once you gain access, you may ask for books by specific authors or for books about specific topics. If your topic is *Shakespeare*, for example, you may ask for specific titles of his works or for books about him. A recent request for general critical works about Shakespeare from a large urban university library produced a list of 396 items, including all the pertinent bibliographical information. The same library listed 113 works containing specific material about *Hamlet*. Once you have such materials on your screen, you may select and list only the most likely looking titles—the ones you think will be most useful. Such a list comprises a fairly comprehensive search bibliography, which you may use once you physically enter the library to begin collecting and using materials.

If you gain access to online services, be careful to determine the year when the computerization began. Many libraries have a recent commencement date—1973, for example, or 1978. For completeness, therefore, you would need to use the entire catalogue for items published before these years.

research, such as the *Essay and General Literature Index,* the *International Index,* and various specific indexes. For most purposes, however, the *MLA International Bibliography* is more than adequate. Remember that as you progress in your reading, the notes and bibliographies in the works you consult also will constitute an unfolding bibliography. For the sample research essay in this chapter, for example, a number of entries were discovered not from the bibliographies but from the reference lists in critical works.

The *MLA International Bibliography* is conveniently organized by period and author. If your author is Katherine Mansfield, for example, look her up under "English Literature X. Twentieth Century," the relevant listing for all twentieth-century English writers. If your author is Hawthorne, refer to "American Literature III. Nineteenth Century, 1800–1870." You will find most books and articles listed under the author's last name. For special help for students and researchers, the MLA provides an exhaustive topics list that is keyed to the bibliographical entries. Using these topics, you may locate important works that you might miss with only the authors list. In the MLA bibliographies, journal references are abbreviated, but a lengthy list explaining abbreviations appears at the beginning of the volume. Using the MLA bibliographies, begin with the most recent one and then go backward to your stopping point. Be sure to get the complete information, especially volume numbers and years of publication, for each article and book. You are now ready to find your sources and to take notes.

TAKING NOTES AND PARAPHRASING MATERIAL

There are many ways of taking notes, but the consensus is that the best method is to use notecards. If you have never used cards before, you might profit from consulting any one of a number of handbooks and special workbooks on research. A lucid and methodical explanation of using cards and taking notes can be found in Glenn Leggett et al., *Prentice-Hall Handbook for Writers,* 10th ed. (Englewood Cliffs: Prentice Hall, 1988). The principal advantage of cards is that they can be classified, numbered, renumbered, shuffled, tried out in one place, rejected, and then used in another place (or thrown away) and arranged in order when you start to write.

Taking Notes

WRITE THE SOURCE ON EACH CARD. As you take notes, write the source of your information on each card. This may seem like a bother, but it is easier than going back to the library to locate the correct source after you have begun your essay. You can save time if you take the complete data on one card—a "master card" for that source—and then make up an abbreviation for your notes. Here is an example, which also includes the location where the reference was originally found (e.g., card catalogue, computer search, bibliography in a book, the *MLA International Bibliography*). Observe that the author's last name goes first.

Donovan, Josephine, ed. <u>Feminist</u> <u>Literary Criticism: Explorations</u> <u>in Theory</u>. Lexington: The University Press of Kentucky, 1975. DONOVAN Card Catalogue, "Women"	PN 98 .W64 F4

If you take many notes from this book, the name "Donovan" will serve as identification. Be sure not to lose your complete master cards because you will need them when you prepare your list of works cited. If possible, record the complete bibliographical data in a computer file.

RECORD THE PAGE NUMBER FOR EACH NOTE.   It would be hard to guess how much exasperation has been caused by the failure to record page numbers in notes. Be sure to get the page number down first, *before* you begin to take your note, and, to be doubly sure, write the page number again at the end of your note. If the detail goes from one page to the next in your source, record the exact spot where the page changes, as in this example:

Heilbrun and Stimson, in DONOVAN, pp. 63-64
 	
 [63] After the raising of the feminist consciousness
     it is necessary to develop/ [64] "the growth of
     moral perception" through anger and the correction
     of social inequity.

The reason for such care is that you may wish to use only a part of a note you have taken, and when there are two pages you will need to be accurate in locating what goes where.

RECORD ONLY ONE FACT OR OPINION PER CARD.   Record only one major element on each card—one quotation, one paraphrase, one observation—*never two or more*. You might be tempted to fill up the entire card with many separate but unrelated details, but such a try at economy often gets you in trouble because you might want to use some of the details in other places. If you have only one entry per card, you will avoid such hassles and also retain the freedom you need.

USE QUOTATION MARKS FOR ALL QUOTED MATERIAL. In taking notes it is extremely important to distinguish copied material from your own words. *Always put quotation marks around every direct quotation you copy verbatim from a source.* Make the quotation marks immediately, before you forget, so that you will always know that the words of your notes within quotation marks are the words of another writer.

Often, as you take a note, you may use some of your own words and some of the words from your source. In cases like this you should be even more cautious. Put quotation marks around *every word* that you take directly from the source, even if your note looks like a picket fence. Later, when you begin writing your paper, your memory of what is yours and not yours will be dim, and if you use another's words in your own essay without proper acknowledgment, you are risking the charge of plagiarism. Most apparent plagiarism is caused not by deliberate deception but rather by sloppy note taking.

Paraphrasing

When you take notes, it is best to paraphrase the sources. A paraphrase is a restatement in your own words, and because of this it is actually a first step in writing. A big problem in paraphrasing is to capture the idea in the source without duplicating the words. The best way to do this is to read and reread the passage you are noting. Turn over the book or journal and write out the idea *in your own words* as accurately as you can. Once you have this note, compare it with the original and make corrections to improve your thought and emphasis. Add a short quotation if you believe it is needed, but be sure to use quotation marks. If your paraphrase is too close to the original, throw out the note and try again. All this is worth the effort because often you can use part or all of your note directly at an appropriate place in your essay.

To see the problems of paraphrase, let us look at a paragraph of criticism and then see how a student doing research might take notes on it. The paragraph is by Richard F. Peterson, from an essay entitled "The Circle of Truth: The Stories of Katherine Mansfield and Mary Lavin," published in *Modern Fiction Studies* 24 (1978): 383–394. In the passage to be quoted, Peterson is considering the structures of two Mansfield stories, "Bliss" and "Miss Brill":

> "Bliss" and "Miss Brill" are flawed stories, but not because the truth they reveal about their protagonists is too brutal or painful for the tastes of the common

reader. In each story, the climax of the narrative suggests an arranged reality that leaves a lasting impression, not of life, but of the author's cleverness. This strategy of arrangement for dramatic effect or revelation, unfortunately, is common in Katherine Mansfield's fiction. Too often in her stories a dropped remark at the right or wrong moment, a chance meeting or discovery, an intrusive figure in the shape of a fat man at a ball or in the Café de Madrid, a convenient death of a hired man or a stranger dying aboard a ship, or a *deus ex machina* in the form of two doves, a dill pickle, or a fly plays too much of a role in / [386] creating a character's dilemma or deciding the outcome of the narrative. 385–386

Because taking notes necessarily forces a shortening of this or any criticism, it also requires you to discriminate, judge, interpret, and select; good note taking is no easy task. There are some things to guide you, however, when you go through the many sources you uncover.

THINK OF THE PURPOSE OF YOUR RESEARCH. You may not know exactly what you are "fishing for" when you start to take notes, for you cannot prejudge what your essay will contain. Research is a form of discovery. But soon you will notice subjects and issues that your sources constantly explore. If you can accept one of these as your major topic or focus of interest, you may use that as your guide in all further note taking.

For example, suppose you start to take notes on criticism about Katherine Mansfield's "Miss Brill," and after a certain amount of reading you decide to focus on the story's structure. This decision guides your further research and note taking. Thus, for example, Richard Peterson criticizes Mansfield's technique of arranging climaxes in her stories. With your topic being structure, it would therefore be appropriate to take a note on Peterson's judgment. The following note is adequate as a brief reminder of the content in the passage:

Peterson 385   structure: negative

Peterson claims that Mansfield creates climaxes that are too artificial, too unlifelike, giving the impression not of reality but of Mansfield's own "cleverness."   385

Let us now suppose that you want a fuller note, in the expectation that you need not just Peterson's general idea but also some of his supporting detail. Such a note might look like this:

Peterson 385   structure: negative

Peterson thinks that "Bliss" and "Miss Brill" are "flawed" because they have contrived endings that give the impression "not of life but of" Mansfield's "cleverness." She arranges things artificially, according to Peterson, to cause the endings in many other stories. Some of these things are chance remarks, discoveries, or meetings, together with other unexpected or chance incidents and objects. These contrivances make their stories imperfect. 385

In an actual research essay, any part of this note would be useful. The words are almost all the note taker's own, and the few quotations are within quotation marks. Note that Peterson, the critic, is properly recognized as the source of the criticism, so you could adapt the note easily when you are doing your writing. The key here is that your note taking should be guided by your developing plan for your essay.

Note taking is part of your thinking and composing process. You may not always know whether you will be able to use each note that you take, and you will always exclude many notes when you write your essay. You will always find, however, that taking notes is easier once you have determined your purpose.

TITLE YOUR NOTES. To help plan and develop the various parts of your essay, write a title for each of your notes, as in the examples in this chapter. This practice is a form of outlining. Let us continue discussing the structure of Mansfield's "Miss Brill," the actual subject of the sample research essay (pp. 237–43). As you do your research, you discover that there is a divergence of critical thought about how the ending of the story should be understood. Here is a note about one of the diverging interpretations:

Daly 90   Last sentence

Miss Brill's "complete" "identification" with the shabby fur piece at the very end may cause readers to conclude that she is the one in tears but bravely does not recognize this fact, and also to conclude that she may never use the fur in public again because of her complete defeat. Everything may be for "perhaps the very last time."

Notice that the title classifies the topic of the note. If you use such classifications, a number of like-titled cards could underlie a section in your essay about how to understand the concluding sentence of "Miss Brill." In addition, once you decide to explore the last sentence, the topic itself will guide you in further study and note taking. (See the sample essay, in which paragraphs 19–24 concern this topic.)

RECORD YOUR OWN THOUGHTS.   As you take your notes, you will be developing your own responses and thoughts. Do not let these go on the chance of remembering them later but write them down immediately. Often you may notice a detail that your source does not mention, or you may get a hint for an idea that the critic does not develop. Often, too, you may get thoughts that can serve as "bridges" between details in your notes or as introductions or concluding observations. Be sure to title your comment and also to mark it as your own thought. Here is such a note, which is on the emphasis on character as opposed to action in "Miss Brill":

My Own   Last Sentence

    Mansfield's letter of Jan. 17, 1921, indicates that action as such was less significant in her scheme for the story than the sympathetic evocation of Miss Brill's observations, impressions, and moods. She wanted to reveal character.

Please observe that in paragraph 5 of the sample research essay, the substance of this note (also a good deal of the language) is used to introduce new material once the passage from the Mansfield letter has been quoted.

SORT YOUR CARDS INTO GROUPS.   If you have taken your notes well, your essay will have been forming in your mind already. The titles of your cards will suggest areas to be developed as you do your planning and initial drafting. Once you have assembled a stack of notecards derived from a reasonable number of sources (your instructor may have assigned a minimum number), you can sort them into groups according to the topics and titles. For the sample essay, after some shuffling and retitling, the cards were assembled in the following groups:

1. Writing and publication
2. The title: amusement and seriousness
3. General structure
4. Specific structures: season, time of day, levels of cruelty, Miss Brill's own "hierarchies" of unreality
5. The concluding paragraphs, especially the last sentence
6. Concluding remarks

If you look at the major sections of the sample essay, you will see that the topics are closely adapted from these groups of cards. In other words, the arrangement of the cards is an effective means of outlining and organizing a research essay.

ARRANGE THE CARDS IN EACH GROUP. There is still much to do with each group of cards. You cannot use the details as they happen to fall randomly in your stack. You need to decide which notes are relevant. You might also need to retitle some cards and use them elsewhere. Those that remain will have to be arranged in a logical order to be used in the essay.

Once you have your cards in order, you can write whatever comments or transitions are needed to move from detail to detail. Write this material directly on the cards and be sure to use a different color ink so that you can distinguish later between the original note and what you add. Here is an example of such a "developed" notecard:

Magalaner 39   Structure, general

    Speaking of Mansfield's sense of form, and referring to "Miss Brill" as an example, Magalaner states that Mansfield has power to put together stories from "a myriad of threads into a rigidly patterned whole." 39

Some of these "threads" are the fall season, the time of day, examples of unkindness, the park bench sitters from the cupboards, and Miss Brill's stages of unreality (see Thorpe 661). Each of these is separate, but all work together to unify the story.

By adding such commentary to your notecards, you are also simplifying the writing of your first draft. In many instances, the note and the comment may be moved directly into the paper with minor adjustments (some of the content of this note appears in paragraph 6 of the sample essay, and almost all the topics introduced here are developed in paragraphs 9–14).

BE CREATIVE AND ORIGINAL. This is not to say you can always transfer your notes directly into your essay. The major trap to avoid in a research paper is that your use of sources can become an end in itself and therefore a shortcut for your own thinking and writing. Often, students make the mistake of introducing details the way a master of ceremonies introduces performers in a variety show. This is unfortunate because it is the *student* whose essay will be judged, even though the sources, like the performers, do all the work. Thus, it is important to be creative and original in a research essay and to do your own thinking and writing, even though you are relying heavily on your sources. Here are four ways in which research essays may be original:

    1. *Selection.* In each major section of your essay you will include many details from your sources. To be creative you should select different but

related details and avoid overlapping or repetition. The essay will be judged on the basis of the thoroughness with which you make your point with different details (this in turn will represent the completeness of your research). Even though you are relying on published materials and cannot be original on that score, your selection can be original because you bring *these* materials together for the first time and because you emphasize some details and minimize others. Inevitably, your assemblage of details from your sources will be unique and therefore original.

2. *Development.* Your arrangement of your various points is an obvious area of originality: One detail seems naturally to precede another, and certain conclusions stem from certain details. As you present the details, conclusions, and arguments from your sources, you may also add your own original stamp by using supporting details that are different from those in your sources. You may also add your own emphasis to particular points—an emphasis that you do not find in your sources.

Naturally, the words that you use will be original. Your topic sentences, for example, will all be your own. As you introduce details and conclusions, you will need to write "bridges" to get yourself from point to point. These may be introductory remarks or transitions. In other words, as you write, you are not just stringing things out but are actively tying thoughts together in a variety of creative ways. Your success in these efforts will constitute your greatest originality.

3. *Explanation of controversial views.* Closely related to your selection is that in your research you may have found conflicting or differing views on a topic. If you make a point to describe and distinguish these views, and explain the reasons for the differences, you are presenting material originally. To see how differing views may be handled, see paragraphs 19 through 21 of the sample essay.

4. *Creation of your own insights and positions.* There are three possibilities here, all related to how well you have learned the primary texts on which your research in secondary sources is based:

a. *Your own interpretations and ideas.* An important part of taking notes is to make your own points precisely when they occur to you. Often you can expand these as truly original parts of your essay. Your originality does not need to be extensive; it may consist of no more than a single insight. Here is such a card, written during the research on the structure of "Miss Brill":

My Own   Miss Brill's unreality

     It is ironic that the boy and girl sit down on the bench next to Miss Brill just when she is at the height of her fancies. By allowing her to overhear their insults, they introduce objective reality to her. The result is that she is plunged instantly from the height of rapture to the depth of pain.

The originality here is built around the contrast between Miss Brill's exhilaration and her rapid and cruel deflation. The observation is not unusual or startling, but it nevertheless represents an attempt at original thought. When modified and adapted, the material of the note supplies much of paragraph 18 of the sample essay. You can see that here the development of a "my own" notecard is an important part of the prewriting stage for a research essay.

b. *Gaps in the sources.* As you read your secondary sources, you may realize that an obvious conclusion is not being made or that an important detail is not being stressed. Here is an area you can develop on your own. Your conclusions may involve a particular interpretation or major point of comparison, or they may rest on a particularly important but understressed word or fact. For example, paragraphs 21–24 in the sample essay form an argument based on observations that critics have overlooked, or neglected to mention, about the conclusion of "Miss Brill." In your research, whenever you find such a critical "vacuum" (assuming that you cannot read all the articles about some of your topics, where your discovery may already have been made a number of times), it is right to move in with whatever is necessary to fill it.

c. *Disputes with the sources.* Your sources may present arguments that you wish to dispute. As you develop your disagreement you will be arguing originally, for you will be using details in a different way from that of the critic or critics whom you are disputing, and your conclusions will be your own. This area of originality is similar to the laying out of controversial critical views, except that you furnish one of the opposing views yourself. The approach is limited because it is difficult to find many substantive points of interpretation on which there are not already clearly delineated opposing views. Paragraph 13 of the sample research essay shows how a disagreement can lead to a different, if not original, interpretation.

DOCUMENTATION SYSTEMS

It is essential to acknowledge—to *document*—all sources from which you have *quoted or paraphrased* factual and interpretive information. If you do not grant recognition, you run the risk of being challenged for presenting other people's work as your own. This is plagiarism. There are many documentation systems, some using parenthetical references within the text, and others using footnotes or endnotes. Whatever system is used, documentation almost always includes a carefully prepared *bibliography* or a list of *works cited*.

We will first discuss the list of works cited and then review the two major reference systems used in research papers: (1) parenthetical references, preferred by the Modern Language Association (MLA) since 1984, and described in Joseph Gibaldi and Walter S. Achtert, *MLA Handbook for Writers of Research Papers*, 3rd ed. (1988); and (2) footnotes or endnotes, recommended by the MLA before 1984, and still widely required today.

List of Works Cited (Bibliography)

The key to any reference system is a carefully prepared list of *Works Cited* that is included at the end of the essay. *Works Cited* means exactly that; the list should contain just those books and articles you have actually used within your essay. If, on the other hand, your instructor requires that you use foot-notes or endnotes, you may extend your bibliography to include not only works cited but also works consulted but not actually used. *Always, always, always,* check your instructor's preferences.

For the *Works Cited* list, you should include the following information in each entry:

For a Book

1. The author's name (last name first), period.
2. Title (underlined or italicized), period.
3. City of publication (not state), colon; publisher (easily recognized abbreviations or key words may be used unless they seem awkward or strange; see the *MLA Handbook*, 213–16), comma; date, period.

For an Article

1. The author's name (last name first), period.
2. Title of article in quotation marks, period.
3. Name of journal or periodical (underlined or italicized), followed by volume number in arabic numbers (*not* roman) with no punctuation, followed by the year of publication within parentheses, colon. For a daily paper or weekly magazine, omit the parentheses and cite the date in the British style (day, month, year; e.g., 29 Feb. 1988), followed by a colon. Inclusive page numbers, period (without any preceding "p." or "pp.").

The list of works cited should be arranged alphabetically by author, with unsigned articles listed by title. Citation of each work begins at the left margin, with subsequent lines indented, so that the key locating word—usually the author's last name—may be easily seen. The many unpredictable and complex combinations, including ways to describe works of art, musical or other performances, and films, are detailed extensively in the *MLA Handbook* (86–154). Here are two model entries:

Book: Alpers, Antony. Katherine Mansfield, A Biography. New York: Knopf, 1953.

Article: Hankin, Cheryl. "Fantasy and the Sense of an Ending in the Work of Katherine Mansfield." Modern Fiction Studies 24 (1978): 465–74.

Parenthetical References to the List of Works Cited

Within the text of the essay, you may refer parenthetically to the list of works cited. The parenthetical reference system recommended in the *MLA Handbook* (155–77) involves citing the author's last name and the relevant page number or numbers in the body of the essay. If the author's name is mentioned in the discussion, only the page number or numbers are given in parentheses. Here are two examples:

> Pope believed in the idea that the universe is a whole, a totally unified body, which provides a "viable benevolent system for the salvation of everyone who does good" (Kallich 24).

> Martin Kallich draws attention to Pope's belief in the idea that the universe is a whole, a totally unified body, which provides a "viable benevolent system for the salvation of everyone who does good" (24).

For a fuller discussion of the types of in-text references and the format to use, see the *MLA Handbook*, 155–61.

Footnotes and Endnotes

The most formal system of documentation still widely used is that of *footnotes* (references listed at the bottom of each page) or *endnotes* (references listed at the end of the essay). If your instructor wants you to use one of these formats, do the following: The first time you quote or refer to the source, make a note with the details in this order:

For a Book

1. The author's name (first name or initials first), comma.
2. The title (underlined or italicized), no punctuation. If you are referring to a work (article, story, poem) in a collection, use quotation marks for that work, but underline or italicize the title of the book. (Use a comma after the title if an editor, translator, or edition follows.)
3. The name of the editor or translator, if relevant. Abbreviate "editor" or "edited by" as "ed.", "editors" as "eds." Use "trans." for "translator" or "translated by."
4. The edition (if indicated) is abbreviated thus: 2nd ed., 3rd ed., and so on.
5. The publication facts should be given in parentheses, without any preceding or following punctuation, in the following order:
   a. city (but not the state) of publication, colon.
   b. publisher (recognizable short forms are acceptable), comma.
   c. year of publication, comma.

6. The page number(s)—for example, 65, 6–10, 15–19, 201–208, 295–307, 338–46. If you are referring to longer works, such as novels or longer stories that may have division or chapter numbers, include these numbers for readers who may be using an edition different from yours.

For an Article

1. The author (first name or initials first), comma.
2. The title of the article, in quotation marks, comma.
3. The name of the journal (underlined or italicized), no punctuation.
4. The volume number (in arabic numerals), no punctuation.
5. The year of publication (in parentheses), colon. For newspaper and journal articles, omit the parentheses, and include day, month, and year (in the British style), colon.
6. The page number(s); for example, 65, 6–10, 34–36, 98–102, 302–308, 345–47.

For later notes to the same work, use the last name of the author as the reference unless you are referring to two or more works by the same author. Thus, if you refer to only one poem by, say, Shakespeare, the name "Shakespeare" will be enough for all later references. Should you be referring to one or more other poems by Shakespeare, however, you will also need a short reference to the specific poems to distinguish them, such as "Shakespeare, 'That Time of Year,'" and "Shakespeare, 'Let Me Not to the Marriage.'"

Footnotes are placed at the bottom of the page, endnotes in separate pages at the end of the essay. The first line of a footnote and endnote should be paragraph-indented, and continuing lines should be flush with the left margin. Both endnote and footnote numbers are positioned slightly above the line (as superior numbers) like this: (^{12}). Generally, you may single-space footnotes and endnotes, leaving a space between them, but be sure to ask your instructor about what is acceptable. For more detailed coverage of footnoting practices, see the *MLA Handbook*, 185–200.

SAMPLE FOOTNOTES.   In the following examples, book titles and periodicals, which are usually *italicized* in print, are shown underlined, as they would be in your typewritten or carefully handwritten essay (that is, unless you are using a word processor that enables you to create *italics*).

[1] Marvin Magalaner, The Fiction of Katherine Mansfield (Carbondale: Southern Illinois UP, 1971), 134.

[2] Susan Gubar, "The Birth of the Artist as Heroine: (Re)production, the Kunstler-roman Tradition, and the Fiction of Katherine Mansfield," in The Representation of Women in Fiction, ed. Carolyn G. Heilbrun and Margaret R. Higonnet, Selected Papers from the English Institute, 1981 (Baltimore: Johns Hopkins UP, 1982) 25.

[3] Ann L. McLaughlin, "The Same Job: The Shared Writing Aims of Katherine Mansfield and Virginia Woolf," <u>Modern Fiction Studies</u> 24 (1978): 375.
[4] Gubar 29.
[5] Magalaner 55.
[6] McLaughlin 381.

As a principle, you do not need to repeat in a note any material you have already mentioned in the body of your own essay. For example, if you name the author and title of a source, then the note should give merely the publication data. Here is an example:

> In <u>The Fiction of Katherine Mansfield</u>, Marvin Magalaner points out that Mansfield was as skillful in the development of epiphanies (that is, the use of highly significant though perhaps unobtrusive actions or statements to reveal the depths of a particular character) as Joyce himself, the "inventor" of the technique.[9]

---

[9](Carbondale: Southern Illinois UP, 1971), 130.

Other Reference Systems

Some instructors in other disciplines prefer to use the reference systems and style manuals that have been developed for these disciplines, such as mathematics, medicine, and psychology. Generally, however, you may use the systems described here for most of your courses, unless your instructor in these courses tells you otherwise. If you are required to use the documentation methods of other fields, use the *MLA Handbook*, 201–202, for guidance about what style manual to select. As a principle, always consult your instructor.

Some Final Advice

Whatever method of reference you follow, *you must always acknowledge your sources*. If all you want from a reference is the page number of a quotation or a paraphrase, the parenthetical system described briefly here—and detailed fully in the *MLA Handbook*—is the most suitable and convenient. It saves your reader the trouble of searching the bottom of the page or of thumbing through pages of references at the end. However, you may wish to use footnotes or endnotes if you need to add more details or refer your readers to materials you consulted but did not use.

When writing your essay, you may find that you have forgotten a number of details about documentation, and you will certainly discover that you have many questions. Be sure then to ask your instructor, who is your final authority.

WRITING A RESEARCH ESSAY

INTRODUCTION.   For a research essay, the introduction may be longer than for an ordinary essay because you need to relate your research to your topic. You may bring in relevant historical or biographical information (see, for example, the introduction of the sample essay). You might also summarize critical opinion or describe any relevant problems. The idea is to lead your reader into your topic by providing interesting and significant materials that you have found during your research. Obviously, you should include your usual guides—your central idea and your thesis sentence.

Because of the length of research essays, some instructors require a topic outline, which is in effect a brief table of contents. This pattern is observed in the sample essay. Because an outline is a matter of choice with various instructors, be sure that you understand whether your instructor requires it.

BODY AND CONCLUSION.   Your development both for the body and the conclusion will be governed by your choice of subject. Consult the relevant chapters in this book about what to include for whatever approach or approaches you select (e.g., setting, point of view, character, or tone).

A research essay may be from five to fifteen or more pages. Clearly, an essay on only one work may be shorter than one on two or more. If you narrow your topic as suggested in the approaches described above, you can keep your paper within the assigned length. The sample research essay, for example, illustrates the first approach by being limited to the structural aspects of one story. Were you to write on characteristic structures in a number of other stories by Mansfield or any other writer (the second approach), you could limit your total number of pages by stressing comparative treatments and by avoiding excessive detail about problems pertaining to each and every story. In short, you will decide to include or exclude materials by compromising between the importance of the materials and the limits of your assignment.

Although you limit your topic in consultation with your instructor, you will be dealing not with one source alone but with many. Naturally these sources will provide you with details and also with many of your ideas. The problem is to handle the many strands without piling on too many details, and also without digressing. It is therefore important to keep your central idea foremost, for constantly stressing the central idea will help you in selecting relevant materials.

It must be emphasized and reemphasized that you need to distinguish between *your own work* and the *sources* you are using. Your readers will assume that everything you write is your own unless you indicate otherwise. Therefore, when blending your words with the ideas from sources, be clear about proper acknowledgments. Most commonly, if you are simply presenting details and facts, you can write straightforwardly and let parenthetical references suffice as your authority, as in the following sentence from the sample essay:

While Cheryl Hankin suggests that the structuring is perhaps more "instinctive" than deliberate (474), Marvin Magalaner, using "Miss Brill" as an example, speaks of Mansfield's power to weave "a myriad of threads into a rigidly patterned whole" (39).

Here there can be no question about plagiarism, for the names of the authorities are acknowledged in full, the page numbers are specific, and the quotation marks clearly show the important word and phrase that are taken from the sources. If you grant recognition as recommended here, no confusion can result about the authority underlying your essay. Although the words belong to the writer of the essay, the parenthetical references clearly indicate that the sentence is derived from the two sources.

If you are using an interpretation that is unique to a particular writer, or if you are relying on a significant quotation from your source, you should make your acknowledgment as an essential part of your discussion, as in this sentence:

Saralyn Daly, referring to Miss Brill as one of Mansfield's "isolatoes"—that is, solitary persons cut off from normal human contacts (88)—fears that the couple's callous insults have caused Miss Brill to face the outside world with her fur piece "perhaps for the very last time" (90).

Here the idea of the critic is singled out for special acknowledgment. If you indicate your sources in this way, no confusion can possibly arise about how you have used your sources.

Sample Research Essay

The Structure of Mansfield's "Miss Brill"

I. INTRODUCTION
   A. THE WRITING OF "MISS BRILL"
   B. THE CHOICE OF THE NAME "BRILL"
   C. THE STORY'S STRUCTURE
II. SEASON AND TIME AS STRUCTURE
III. INSENSITIVE OR CRUEL ACTIONS AS STRUCTURE
IV. MISS BRILL'S "HIERARCHY OF UNREALITIES" AS STRUCTURE
V. THE STORY'S CONCLUSION
VI. CONCLUSION

I. Introduction

A. The Writing of "Miss Brill"

[1]

Because Katherine Mansfield's "Miss Brill"—one of the eighty-eight short stories and fragments she wrote in her brief life (Magalaner 5)—succeeds so well as a portrait of the protagonist's inner life, it has become well known and has been frequently anthologized (Gargano). She apparently wrote it on the evening of November 11, 1920, when she was staying at Isola Bella, an island retreat in northern Italy where she had gone in her desperate search to overcome tuberculosis. In her own words, she describes the night of composition:

> Last night I walked about and saw the new moon with the old moon in her arms and the lights in the water and the hollow pools filled with stars—and lamented there was no God. But I came in and wrote Mill Brill instead; which is my insect Magnificat now and always. (Letters 594)

Her husband, J. Middleton Murry, who had remained in London, published the story in the November 26, 1920 issue of the journal Athenaeum, which he was then editing. In 1922, Mansfield included "Miss Brill" in her collection entitled The Garden Party and Other Stories (Daly 134).

[2]

She was particularly productive at the time of "Miss Brill" despite her illness, for she wrote a number of superb stories then. The others, as reported by her biographer Antony Alpers, were "The Lady's Maid," "The Young Girl," "The Daughters of the Late Colonel," and "The Life of Ma Parker" (304–305). All these stories share the common bond of "love and pity" rather than the "harshness or satire" that typifies many of her earlier stories (Alpers 305).

B. The Choice of the Name "Brill"

[3]

"Miss Brill," however, does contain at least a minor element of humor. James W. Gargano notes that the title character, Miss Brill, is named after a lowly flatfish, the brill. This fish, with notoriously poor vision, is related to the turbot and the whiting (it is the whiting that the rude girl compares to Miss Brill's fur piece). The Oxford English Dictionary records that the brill is "inferior in flavour" to the turbot. One may conclude that Mansfield, in choosing the name, wanted to minimize her heroine.

[4]

While Mansfield's use of the name suggests a small trick on poor Miss Brill, the story is not amusing but is rather poignant and powerful. Miss Brill is portrayed as one who has been excluded from "public history" (Gubar 31) because she lives exclusively in the "feminine world" (Maurois 337). Her main concerns, in other words, are not power and greatness but the privacy of personal moments, which may be upset by no more than a contemptuous giggle (Gubar 38). The poignancy of the story stems from Miss Brill's eagerness to be "part of a scene that ruthlessly excludes her" and thus makes her "the loneliest of all . . . [characters in] Katherine Mansfield's stories about lonely women" (Fullbrook 103). The story's power results from the feeling with which Mansfield renders the "inarticulate longings and the tumultuous feelings that lie beneath the surface of daily life" (McLaughlin 381). A mark of her skill is the way in which she enters the soul of the heroine and turns it "outward, for her reader to see and understand" (Magill 710), so much so that Claire Tomalin declares that the story is "conceived virtually as [a] dramatic" monologue (213). Mansfield's own description in writing "Miss Brill" bears out these claims, for it shows how deeply she tried to create the pathetic inner life of her character:

[4]
In <u>Miss Brill</u> I choose not only the length of every sentence, but even the sound of every sentence. I choose the rise and fall of every paragraph to fit her, and to fit her on that day at that very moment. After I'd written it I read it aloud—numbers of times—just as one would <u>play over</u> a musical composition—trying to get it nearer to the expression of Miss Brill—until it fitted her. (Letter to Richard Murry of January 17, 1921, qtd. in Sewell, 5–6)

C. The Story's Structure

[5]
<u>Mansfield's description strongly indicates that action in the story was less significant in her scheme than the sympathetic evocation of Miss Brill's mood and impressions—in other words, the depths of her character.</u> Such a design might lead readers to conclude that the story is not so much formed as forming, a free rather than planned development. In reference to Mansfield's talent generally, Edward Wagenknecht reflects that the stories, including "Miss Brill," are "hardly even episodes or anecdotes. They offer reflections [instead] of some aspect of experience or express a mood" (163). In many ways, Wagenknecht's observation is true of "Miss Brill." The story seems to be built up from within the character, and it leaves the impression of an individual who experiences a "crisis in miniature," a "deep cut into time" in which life changes and all hopes and expectations are reversed (Hankin 465).

[6]
It follows that Mansfield's achievement in "Miss Brill" is to fashion a credible character in an especially pathetic and shattering moment. <u>The story therefore embodies an intricate set of structures that simultaneously complement the movement downward.</u>° Whatever the source of Mansfield's control over form, critics agree that her power was great. Marvin Magalaner, using "Miss Brill" as an example, speaks of Mansfield's weaving of "a myriad of threads into a rigidly patterned whole" (39). Noting the same control over form, Cheryl Hankin suggests that her structuring is perhaps more "instinctive" than deliberate (474). <u>These complementary threads, stages, or "levels" of "unequal length"</u> (Harmat uses the terms "niveaux" and "longueur inégale," 49, 51) <u>are the fall season, the time of day, insensitive or cruel actions, Miss Brill's own unreal perceptions, and the final section or dénouement.</u>†

II. Season and Time as Structure

[7]
<u>A significant aspect of structure is Mansfield's use of season and times of day.</u> The autumnal season is integral to the deteriorating circumstances of the heroine. In the first paragraph, for example, we learn that there is a "faint chill" in the air (is the word "chill" chosen to rhyme with "Brill"?), and this phrase is repeated in paragraph 10. Thus the author establishes autumn and the approaching end of the year as the beginning of the movement toward dashed hopes. This seasonal reference is also carried out when we read that "yellow leaves" are "down drooping" in the local <u>Jardins Publiques</u> (paragraph 6) and that leaves are drifting "now and again" from almost "nowhere, from the sky" (paragraph 1). It is the autumn cold that has caused Miss Brill to take out her bedraggled fur piece at which the young girl later is so amused. Thus the chill, together with the fur, forms a structural setting integrated both with the action

°Central idea.
† Thesis sentence.

and mood of the story. The story both begins and ends with the fur (Sewell 25),
[7]   which is the direct cause of Miss Brill's deep hurt at the end.

Like this seasonal structuring, the times of day parallel Miss Brill's dark-ening existence. At the beginning, the day is "brilliantly fine—the blue sky pow-dered with gold," and the light is "like white wine." This metaphorical language suggests the brightness and crispness of full sunlight. In paragraph 6, where we
[8]   also learn of the yellow leaves, "the blue sky with gold-veined clouds" indicates that time has been passing as clouds accumulate during late afternoon. By the story's end, Miss Brill has returned to her "little dark room" (paragraph 18). In other words, the time moves from day to evening, from light to darkness, as an accompaniment to Miss Brill's psychological pain.

III. Insensitive or Cruel Actions as Structure

Mansfield's most significant structural device, which is not emphasized by critics, is the introduction of insensitive or cruel actions. It is as though the hurt felt by Miss Brill on the bright Sunday afternoon is also being felt by many oth-
[9]   ers. Because she is the spectator who is closely related to Mansfield's narrative voice, Miss Brill is the filter through whom these negative examples reach the reader. Considering the patterns that emerge, one may conclude that Mansfield intends the beauty of the day and the joyousness of the band as an ironic con-trast to the pettiness and insensitivity of the people in the park.

The first characters are a silent couple on Miss Brill's bench (paragraph 3) and the incompatible couple of the week before (paragraph 4). Because these seem no more than ordinary, they do not seem at first to be part of the story's
[10]   pattern of cruelty and rejection; but their incompatibility, suggested by their silence and one-way complaining, establishes a structural parallel with the young and insensitive couple who insult Miss Brill. Thus the first two couples prepare the way for the third, and all show behavior of increasing insen-sitivity.

Almost unnoticed as a second level of negation is the vast group of "odd, silent, nearly all old" people filling "the benches and green chairs" (paragraph 5). They seem to be no more than a normal part of the Sunday afternoon landscape. But these people are significant structurally because the "dark little rooms—or
[11]   even cupboards" that Miss Brill associates with them describe her own circum-stances at the story's end (paragraphs 5,18). The reader may conclude from Miss Brill's quiet eavesdropping that she herself is one of these nameless and faceless ones, all of whom lead similar drab lives.

Once Mansfield has set these levels for her heroine, she introduces exam-ples of more active rejection and cruelty. The beautiful woman who throws down the bunch of violets is the first of these (paragraph 8). The causes of her scorn
[12]   are not made clear, and Miss Brill does not know what to make of the incident; but the woman's actions indicate that she has been involved in a relationship that has ended bitterly.

The major figure involved in rejection, who is important enough to be con-sidered a structural double of Miss Brill, is the woman wearing the ermine toque (paragraph 8). She tries to please the "gentleman in grey," but this man insults her by blowing smoke in her face. It could be, as Peter Thorpe observes, that the woman is "obviously a prostitute" (661). More likely, from the conversation overheard by Miss Brill, the "ermine toque" has had a broken relationship with
[13]   the gentleman. Being familiar with his Sunday habits, she deliberately comes to the park to meet him, as though by accident, to attempt a reconciliation. After

[13] her rejection, her hurrying off to meet someone "much nicer" (there is no such person, for Mansfield uses the phrase "as though" to introduce the ermine toque's departure) is her way of masking her hurt. Regardless of the exact situation, however, Mansfield makes it plain that the encounter demonstrates vulnerability, unkindness, and pathos.

[14] Once Mansfield establishes this major incident, she introduces two additional examples of insensitivity. At the end of paragraph 8, the hobbling old man "with long whiskers" is nearly knocked over by the troupe of four girls, who show arrogance if not contempt. The final examples involve Miss Brill herself. These are the apparent indifference of her students and that of the old invalid "who habitually sleeps" when she reads to him.

[15] Although "Miss Brill" is a brief story, Mansfield creates a large number of structural parallels to the sudden climax brought about by the insulting young couple. The boy and girl do not appear until the very end, in other words (paragraphs 11–14), but actions like theirs have been anticipated structurally in all previous parts of the story. Mansfield's speaker does not take us to the homes of the other victims as we follow Miss Brill into her poor lodgings, but the narrative invites us to conclude that the silent couple, the complaining wife and long-suffering husband, the unseen man rejected by the young woman, the ermine toque, and the funny gentleman, not to mention the many silent and withdrawn people sitting like statues in the park, all return to similar loneliness and personal pain.

IV. Miss Brill's "Hierarchy of Unrealities" as Structure

[16] The intricacy of the structure of "Miss Brill" does not end here. Of great importance is the structural development of the protagonist herself. Peter Thorpe notes a "hierarchy of unrealities" governing the reader's increasing awareness of her plight (661). By this measure, the story's actions progressively bring out Miss Brill's failures of perception and understanding—failures that in this respect make her like her namesake fish, the brill (Gargano).

[17] These unrealities begin with Miss Brill's fanciful but harmless imaginings about her shabby fur piece. This beginning sets up the pattern of her pathetic inner life. When she imagines that the park band is a "single, responsive, and very sensitive creature" (Thorpe 661), we are to realize that she is simply making too much out of a band of ordinary musicians. Although she cannot interpret the actions of the beautiful young woman with the violets, she does see the encounter between the ermine toque and the gentleman in grey as an instance of rejection. Her response is correct, but then her belief that the band's drumbeats are sounding out "The Brute! The Brute!" indicates her vivid overdramatization of the incident. The "top of the hierarchy of unrealities" (Thorpe 661) is her fancy that she is an actor with a vital part in a gigantic drama played by all the people in the park. The most poignant aspect of this daydream is her imagining that someone would miss her if she were absent, for this fancy shows how far she is from reality.

[18] In light of this structure, or hierarchy, of unrealities, it is ironic that the boy and girl sit down next to her just when she is at the height of her fancy about her own importance. When she hears the girl's insults, the couple introduces objective reality to her with a vengeance, and she is plunged from rapture to pain. The following, and concluding, two paragraphs hence form a rapid dénouement to reflect her loneliness and despair.

V. The Story's Conclusion

[19] Of unique importance in the structure of "Miss Brill" are the final two paragraphs—the conclusion or dénouement—in which Miss Brill returns to her miserable little room. This conclusion might easily be understood as a total, final defeat. For example, Saralyn Daly, referring to Miss Brill as one of Mansfield's "isolatoes"—that is, solitary persons cut off from normal human contacts (88)—fears that the couple's callous insults have caused Miss Brill to face the outside world with her fur piece "perhaps for the very last time" (90). Eudora Welty points out that Miss Brill is "defenseless and on the losing side" and that her defeat may be for "always" (87). Miss Brill's experience demonstrates a pattern described by Zinman as common in Mansfield's stories, in which the old are destroyed "by loneliness and sickness, by fear of death, by the thoughtless energy of the younger world around them" (457). With this disaster for the major character, the story may be fitted to the structuring of Mansfield stories observed by André Maurois: "moments of beauty suddenly broken by contact with ugliness, cruelty, or death" (342–43).

[20] Because some critics have stated that Miss Brill's downfall is illogically sudden, they have criticized the conclusion. Peterson, for example, complains that the ending is artificial and contrived because of the improbability that the young couple would appear at just that moment to make their insults (385). On much the same ground, Berkman declares that the ending is excessive, mechanical, and obvious (162, 175).

[21] Cheryl Hankin, however, hints at another way in which the conclusion may be taken, a way that makes the story seem both ironic and grimly humorous. In describing patterns to be found in Mansfield's stories, Hankin notes the following situation, which may account for the story's ending:

> [A]n impending disillusionment or change in expectations may be deflected by the central character's transmutation of the experience into something positive. (466)

There is no question that the ending indicates that Miss Brill has been totally shattered. Her deflation is shown by her quietness and dejection on returning to her small "cupboard" room.

[22] Mansfield's very last sentence, however, may be read as a way of indicating that Miss Brill is going back to her earlier habit of making reality over to fit her own needs, in this respect indicating the "something positive" described by Hankin:

> But when she put the lid on she thought she heard something crying. (paragraph 18)

It is hard to read this last sentence without finding irony and pathos in it. By hearing "something crying" Miss Brill may likely be imagining that the fur piece, and not she, has been hurt. One might remember that the thoughtless young girl has laughed at the fur because it resembles a "fried whiting" (paragraph 14). The irony here is that Miss Brill, like the Boss in another Mansfield story "The Fly," is forgetting about the pain of remembrance and slipping back into customary defensive behavior.

[23] This pattern of evasion is totally in keeping with Miss Brill's character. Despite her poverty and loneliness, she has been holding a job (as a teacher of English, presumably to French pupils), and has also been regularly performing

her voluntary task of reading to the infirm old man. She has not had a life filled with pleasure, but her Sunday afternoons of eavesdropping have enabled her, through "the power of her imagination," to share the lives of many others (Han-

[23] son and Gurr 81). Mansfield establishes this vicarious sociability as Miss Brill's major strength, which Hanson and Gurr call "the saving grace of her life" (81). Her method makes her both strange and pathetic, but nevertheless she has been functioning. Within such a framework, the deflating insults of paragraphs 13 and 14 may be seen as another incentive for her to adjust by strengthening her fancy, not abandoning it.

This is not to interpret the story's conclusion as an indication that Miss Brill has shaken off the couple's insults. She is first and foremost a "victim" (Zinman 457), if not of others, then of her own reality-modifying imagination; but she is presented as a character who has positive qualities. Indeed, Mansfield herself

[24] expressed her own personal liking of Miss Brill (despite the name "brill"). Her husband, J. Middleton Murry, shortly after receiving the story from her for publication, sent her a letter in which he expressed his fondness for the protagonist. In a return letter to him of November 21, 1920, Mansfield wrote that she shared this fondness. She went on in the same letter to say:

> One writes (<u>one</u> reason why is) because one does care so passionately that one <u>must show</u> it—one must declare one's love. (qtd. in Magalaner 17)

Surely the author could love her creation out of pity alone, but if she had added an element of strength, such as the brave but sad ability to adjust to "impossible and intolerable conditions" (Zinman 457), then her love would have an additional cause. <u>Therefore it is plausible that the last sentence of "Miss Brill" shows the resumption of the heroine's way of surviving</u>.

VI. Conclusion

<u>"Miss Brill" is a compact story intricately built up from a number of coexisting structures</u>. It is alive, so much so that it justifies the tribute of Antony Alpers that it is a "minor masterpiece" (305). The structural contrast between the pro-

[25] tagonist and the world around her is derived from a deeply felt dichotomy about life attributed to Mansfield herself, a sense that the human soul is beautiful, on the one hand, but that people are often vile, on the other (Moore 245). It is the vileness that Miss Brill seems to be avoiding at the end.

The greater structure of "Miss Brill" is therefore a hard, disillusioned view of life itself, in which those who are lonely, closed out, and hurt are wounded even more. This pattern of exclusion not only affects the restricted lives of the lonely, but it also reaches directly into their minds and souls. Miss Brill's

[26] response is to retreat further and further into an inner world of unreality but also to continue life, even at an almost totally subdued level, within these confines. <u>It is Mansfield's "almost uncanny psychological insight"</u> (Hankin 467) <u>into the operation of this characteristic response that gives "Miss Brill" its structure and also accounts for its excellence</u>.

Works Cited

Alpers, Antony. <u>Katherine Mansfield, A Biography</u>. New York: Knopf, 1953.

Berkman, Sylvia. <u>Katherine Mansfield, A Critical Study</u>. New Haven: Yale UP (for Wellesley College), 1951.

"Brill." Oxford English Dictionary. 1933 ed.

Daly, Saralyn R. Katherine Mansfield. New York: Twayne, 1965.

Fullbrook, Kate. Katherine Mansfield. Bloomington and Indianapolis: Indiana UP, 1986.

Gargano, James W. "Mansfield's Miss Brill." Explicator 19. 2 (1960): item 10 (one page, unpaginated).

Gubar, Susan. "The Birth of the Artist as Heroine: (Re)production, the Kunstler-roman Tradition, and the Fiction of Katherine Mansfield." The Representation of Women in Fiction. Ed. Carolyn Heilbrun and Margaret R. Higonnet. Selected Papers from the English Institute, 1981. Baltimore: Johns Hopkins UP, 1983, 19–58.

Hankin, Cheryl. "Fantasy and the Sense of an Ending in the Work of Katherine Mansfield." Modern Fiction Studies 24 (1978): 465–74.

Hanson, Clare, and Andrew Gurr. Katherine Mansfield. New York: St. Martin's, 1981.

Harmat, Andrée-Marie. "Essai D'Analyse Structurale D'Une Nouvelle Lyrique Anglaise: 'Miss Brill' de Katherine Mansfield." Les Cahiers de la Nouvelle 1 (1983): 49–74.

Heiney, Donald W. Essentials of Contemporary Literature. Great Neck: Barron's, 1954.

McLaughlin, Ann L. "The Same Job: The Shared Writing Aims of Katherine Mansfield and Virginia Woolf." Modern Fiction Studies 24 (1978): 369–82.

Magalaner, Marvin. The Fiction of Katherine Mansfield. Carbondale: Southern Illinois UP, 1971.

Magill, Frank N., ed. English Literature: Romanticism to 1945. Pasadena: Salem Softbacks, 1981.

Mansfield, Katherine. Katherine Mansfield's Letters to John Middleton Murry, 1913–1922. Ed. John Middleton Murry. New York: Knopf, 1951. Cited as "Letters."

———. The Short Stories of Katherine Mansfield. New York: Knopf, 1967.

Maurois, André. Points of View from Kipling to Graham Greene. 1935. New York: Ungar, 1968.

Moore, Virginia. Distinguished Women Writers. 1934. Port Washington: Kennikat, 1962.

Peterson, Richard F. "The Circle of Truth: The Stories of Katherine Mansfield and Mary Lavin." Modern Fiction Studies 24 (1978): 383–94.

Sewell, Arthur. Katherine Mansfield: A Critical Essay. Auckland: Unicorn, 1936.

Thorpe, Peter. "Teaching 'Miss Brill.'" College English 23 (1962): 661–63.

Tomalin, Claire. Katherine Mansfield, A Secret Life. New York: Knopf, 1988.

Wagenknecht, Edward. A Preface to Literature. New York: Holt, 1954.

Welty, Eudora. The Eye of the Story: Selected Essays and Reviews. New York: Random House, 1977.

Zinman, Toby Silverman. "The Snail Under the Leaf: Katherine Mansfield's Imagery." Modern Fiction Studies 24 (1978): 457–64.

COMMENTARY ON THE ESSAY

This essay fulfills an assignment of 2500 to 3000 words, with 15 to 25 sources. The bibliography was developed from a college library card catalogue; references in books of criticism (Magalaner, Daly, Berkman); the *MLA International Bibliography*; and the *Essay and General Literature Index*. The sources were found in a college library with selective, not exhaustive, holdings, and in a local public library. There is only one rare source, an article (Harmat) obtained in Xerox copy form through interlibrary loan from one of only two United States libraries holding the journal in which it appears. The location was made through the national OCLS online service. For most semester-long or quarter-long courses, you will likely not have time to add to your sources by this method; but the article in question refers specifically to "Miss Brill," and it was therefore desirable to examine it.

The sources consist of books, articles, and chapters or portions of books. One article (Sewell) has been published as a separate short monograph. Also, one of the sources is the story "Miss Brill" itself (with locations made by paragraph number) together with editions of Mansfield's letters and a collection of her stories. The sources are used for facts, interpretations, reinforcement of conclusions, and general guidance and authority. The essay also contains passages taking issue with certain conclusions in a few of the sources. All necessary thematic devices, including overall organization and transitions, are unique to the sample essay. Additional particulars about the handling of sources and developing a research essay are included in the discussion of note taking and related matters in this chapter.

The introduction to the sample essay contains essential details about the writing of the story and the title as well as a pointed summary of critical appraisals of the story itself. The idea explored here is that the story dramatizes Miss Brill's emotional responses first to exhilaration and then to pain. The central idea (paragraph 6) is built out of this idea, explaining that the movement of emotions in the story is accompanied by an intricate and complementary set of structures.

Sections II–V examine various elements of the story for their structural relationship to Miss Brill's emotions. Section II details the structural uses of the settings of autumn and times of day, pointing out how they parallel her experiences. The longest part, section III (paragraphs 9–15), is based on an idea not found in the sources—that a number of characters are experiencing difficulties and cruelties such as those that befall Miss Brill. Paragraph 10 cites the three couples of the story, paragraph 11 the silent old people, and paragraph 12 the woman with violets. Paragraph 13 is developed in disagreement with one of the sources, showing how a research essay may be original even though the sources form the basis for argument. Paragraph 14 contains brief descriptions of additional examples of insensitivity, two of them involving Miss Brill herself. Paragraph 15 both concludes and summarizes the story's instances of insensitivity and cruelty, emphasizing again parallels to Miss Brill's situation.

Section IV (paragraphs 16–18) is based on ideas about the story's structure found in one of the sources (Thorpe). It is hence more derivative than the previous section. Section V (paragraphs 19–24) is devoted to the dénouement of the story. Paragraphs 19 and 20 consider critical interpretations of the ending. In paragraph 21, however, a hint found in a source (Hankin) is used to interpret the story's final sentence. An argument in support of this original interpretation is developed in paragraphs 22–24, which conclude with a reference to Mansfield's own personal approval of the main character.

Section VI (paragraphs 25 and 26), the conclusion, relates the central idea to further biographical information and also to Mansfield's achievement in the story. Of the three sources used here, two are used earlier in the essay, and one (Moore) is new.

The list of works cited is the basis of all references in the essay, in accord with the *MLA Handbook for Writers of Research Papers*, 3rd ed. By locating these references, a reader might readily examine, verify, and study any of the ideas and details drawn from the sources and developed in the essay.

SPECIAL WRITING TOPICS FOR RESEARCH

In undertaking any of the following topics, follow the steps in research described in this chapter.

1. Common themes in a number of stories by Hawthorne, Poe, Welty, or Updike
2. Various critical views of Chekhov's *The Bear*
3. Glaspell's use of the narrative material in *Trifles*
4. Hawthorne's use of religious and moral topic material
5. Wordsworth's use of nature as the original cause of moral and ethical values
6. Views about women in Mansfield, Welty, Keats, Piercy, and Glaspell
7. Poe's view of the short story as represented in "The Cask of Amontillado" and a number of other stories

appendix a

Taking Examinations on Literature

Succeeding in literature examinations is largely a matter of preparation. Preparing means (1) studying the material assigned in conjunction with the comments made in class by your instructor and by fellow students in discussion, (2) developing and reinforcing your own thoughts, (3) anticipating the questions by creating and answering your own practice questions, and (4) understanding the precise function of the test in your education.

First, realize that the test is not designed either to trap you or to hold down your grade. The grade you receive is a reflection of your achievement in the course. If your grades are low, you can improve them by studying coherently and systematically. Those students who can easily do satisfactory work might do superior work if they improve their method of preparation. From whatever level you begin, you can increase your achievement by improving your method of study.

Your instructor has three major concerns in evaluating your tests (assuming literate English): (1) to assess the extent of your command over the subject material of the course ("How good is your retention?"); (2) to assess how well you are able to think about the material ("How well are you educating yourself?"); and (3) to assess how well you respond to a question or deal with an issue.

Many elements go into writing good answers on tests, but this last point, about responsiveness, is the most important. A major cause of low exam grades is that students really do not *answer* the questions asked. Does that seem surprising? The problem is that some students do no more than retell a story or restate an argument, never confronting the issues in the question. This common problem has been treated throughout this book. Therefore, if you are asked, "Why does …," be sure to emphasize the *why*, and use the *does* only to exemplify the *why*. If the question is about organization, focus on that. If a problem has been raised, deal with the problem. In short, always *respond directly* to the question or instruction. Compare the following two answers to the same question:

Question: How does the setting of Bierce's "An Occurrence at Owl Creek Bridge" figure in the development of the story?

A

The setting of Bierce's "An Occurrence at Owl Creek Bridge" is a major element in the development of the story. The first scene is on a railroad bridge in northern Alabama, and the action is that a man, Peyton Farquhar, is about to be hanged. He is a Southerner who has been surrounded and captured by Union soldiers. They are ready to string him up and they have the guns and power, so he cannot escape. He is so scared that the sound of his own watch sounds loudly and slowly like a cannon. He also thinks about how he might free himself, once he is hanged, by freeing his hands and throwing off the noose that will be choking and killing him. The scene shifts to the week before, at Farquhar's plantation. A Union spy deceives Farquhar and thereby tempts him to try to sabotage the Union efforts to keep the railroad open. Because the spy tells Farquhar about the punishment, the reader assumes that Farquhar had tried the sabotage, was caught, and now is going to be hanged. The third scene is also at the bridge, but it is about what Farquhar sees and thinks in his own mind: He imagines that he has been hanged and then escapes. He thinks he falls into the creek, frees himself from the ropes, and makes it to shore, from

B

The setting of Bierce's "An Occurrence at Owl Creek Bridge" is a major element in the development of the story. The railroad bridge in northern Alabama, from which the doomed Peyton Farquhar will be hanged, is a frame for the story. The bridge, which begins as the real-life bridge in the first scene, becomes the bridge that the dying man imagines in the third. In between there is a brief scene at Farquhar's home, which took place a week before. The setting thus marks the progression of Farquhar's dying vision. He begins to distort and slow down reality—at the real bridge— when he realizes that there is no escape. The first indication of this distortion is that his watch seems to be ticking as slowly as a blacksmith's hammer. Once he is dropped from the bridge to be hanged, his perceptions slow down time so much that he imagines his complete escape before his death: falling into the water, freeing himself, being shot at, getting to shore, walking through a darkening forest, and returning home in beautiful morning sunshine. The final sentence brutally restores the real setting of the railroad bridge and makes clear that Farquhar is actually dead despite his imaginings. In all respects, therefore, which he makes the long walk home. His final thoughts are of his wife coming out of the house to meet him, with everything looking beautiful in the morning sunshine. Then we find out that all this was just in his mind, because we are back on the bridge, from which Farquhar is swinging, hanged, dead, with a broken neck.

the setting is essential to the story's development.

While column *A* begins well and introduces important details of the story's setting, it does not address the question because it does not show how the details figure into the story's development. On the other hand, column *B* focuses directly on the connection between the locations and the changes in the protagonist's perceptions. Because of this emphasis, *B* is shorter than *A*; with the focus directly on the issue, there is no need for irrelevant narrative details. Thus, *A* is unresponsive and unnecessarily long, while *B* is responsive and includes details only if they exemplify the major points.

PREPARATION

Your challenge is how best to prepare yourself to have a knowledgeable and ready mind at examination time. If you simply cram facts into your head for the examination in hopes that you can adjust to the questions, you will likely flounder. You need a systematic approach.

Read and Reread

Above all, keep in mind that your preparation should begin as soon as the course begins, not on the night before the exam. Complete each assignment by the date due, for you will understand the classroom discussion only if you know the material (see also the guide for study in Chapter 1, pp. 12–13). Then, about a week before the exam, review each assignment, preferably rereading everything completely. With this preparation, your study on the night before the exam will be fruitful and might be viewed as a climax of preparation, not the entire preparation itself.

Construct Your Own Questions: Go on the Attack

To give yourself the masterly preparation you want for an exam, read *actively*, not passively. Read with a goal, go on the attack by anticipating test conditions—composing and answering your own practice questions. Do not waste time trying to guess the questions you think your instructor might ask. That might happen (and wouldn't you be happy if it did?), but do not turn your study into a game of chance. Instead, arrange the subject matter by asking yourself questions that help you get things straight.

How can you construct your own questions? It is not as hard as you might think. Your instructor may have announced certain topics or ideas to be tested on the exam, and you might develop questions from these, or you might apply general questions to the specifics of your assignments, as in the following examples:

1. *About a character and the interactions of characters* (see also Chapter 4). What is *A* like? How does *A* grow or change in the work? What does *A* learn or not learn that brings about the conclusion? To what degree does *A* represent a type, or an idea? How does *B* influence *A*? Does a change in *C* bring about any corresponding change in *A*?

2. *About technical and structural questions.* These may be broad, covering everything from *point of view* (Chapter 6) to *prosody* and *rhyme* (Chapters 14 and 15). The best guide here is to study those technical aspects that have been discussed in class, for it is unlikely that you will be asked to go beyond the levels expected in classroom discussion.

3. *About events or situations.* What relationship does episode *A* have to situation *B*? Does *C*'s thinking about situation *D* have any influence on the outcome of event *E*?

4. *About a problem* (see also Chapter 12). Why is character *A* or situation *X* this way and not that way? Is the conclusion justified by the ideas and events leading up to it?

Convert Your Notes to Questions

One of the best ways to construct questions is to adapt your classroom notes because notes are the fullest record you have about your instructor's views. As you work with your notes, refer to passages from the text that were studied by the class or stressed by your instructor. If there is time, memorize as many important phrases or lines as you can; plan to incorporate these into your answers as evidence to support the points you make. Remember that it is useful to work not only with main ideas from your notes but also with matters such as style, imagery, and organization.

Obviously, you cannot make questions from all your notes, and you will therefore need to select from those that seem most important. As an example, here is a short note from a classroom discussion of *Hamlet*: "In a major respect, a study in how private problems get public, how a court conspiracy may produce disastrous consequences." Notice how you can devise practice questions from this note:

1. In what ways is *Hamlet* not only about private problems but also about public ones?

2. Why should the consequences of Claudius's murder of Hamlet's father be considered disastrous?

The principle shown here is that exam questions should never be asked just about *what* but should rather get into the issues of *why*. Observe that the first question therefore adapts the words *in what ways* to the phrasing of the note. For the second, the word *why* has been adapted. Either question would force pointed study, and neither would ask you merely to describe events. Question 1 would require you to consider the wider political effects of Hamlet's hostility toward Claudius, including his murder of Polonius and the subsequent madness of Ophelia. Question 2, with its emphasis on disaster, would lead you to consider not only the ruination of the hopes and lives of those in the play, but also the importance of young Fortinbras and the eventual establishment of Norwegian control over Denmark after Claudius and Hamlet are gone. If you spent fifteen or twenty minutes writing practice answers to these questions, you could be confident in taking an examination on the material, for it is likely that you could adapt your answers to any exam question about the personal and political implications of Claudius's murder of his brother.

Work with Questions Even When Time Is Short

Whatever your subject, spend as much study time as possible making and answering your own questions. Remember also to work with your own remarks and ideas that you develop in the journal entries you make when doing your regular assignments (see Chapter 1, pp. 13–15). Many of these will give you additional ideas for your own questions, which you may practice along with the questions you develop from your notes.

Obviously, with the limited time before your examination, you will not be able to create your own questions and answers indefinitely. Even so, do not give up on the question method. If time is too short for full practice answers, write out the main heads, or topics, of an answer. When the press of time (or the need for sleep) no longer permits you to make even such a brief outline answer, keep thinking of questions and their answers on the way to the exam. *Try never to read passively or unresponsively, but always with a creative, question-and-answer goal.* Think of studying as a prewriting experience.

The time you spend in this way will be valuable, for as you practice, you will develop control and therefore confidence. Often those who have difficulty with tests, or claim a phobia about them, engage in *passive* rather than *active* preparation. Test questions compel thought, arrangement, and responsiveness; but a passively prepared student is not ready for this challenge and therefore writes answers that are unresponsive and filled with summary. The grade for such a performance is low, and the student's fear of tests is reinforced. The best way to break such long-standing patterns of fear or uncertainty is active, creative study.

Study with a Classmate

Often the thoughts of another person can help you understand the material to be tested. Find a fellow student with whom you can work comfortably but also productively, for both of you together can help each other individually. In view of the need for steady preparation throughout a course, regular discussions about the material are a good idea. You might also make your joint study systematic by setting aside a specific evening or afternoon for work sessions. Make the effort; working with someone else can be stimulating and rewarding.

TWO BASIC TYPES OF QUESTIONS ABOUT LITERATURE

Generally, you will find two types of questions on literature exams. Keep them in mind as you prepare. The first type is *factual*, or *mainly objective*, and the second is *general, comprehensive, broad*, or *mainly subjective*. Except for multiple-choice questions, in a literature course very few questions are purely objective.

Factual Questions

MULTIPLE-CHOICE QUESTIONS.   These are mainly factual. In a literature course, your instructor will most likely use them for short quizzes, usually on days when an assignment is due, to make sure that you are keeping up with the reading. Multiple-choice items test your knowledge of facts and your ingenuity in perceiving subtleties of phrasing. On a literature exam, however, this type of question is rare.

IDENTIFICATION QUESTIONS.   These questions are more interesting and challenging because they require you both to know details and also to develop thoughts about them. This type of question will frequently be used as a check on the depth and scope of your reading. In fact, an entire exam could be composed of only identification questions, each demanding perhaps five minutes to write. Typical examples of what you might be asked to identify are:

1. *A character.* To identify a character, it is necessary to describe briefly the character's position, main activity, and significance. Let us assume that Montresor is

the character to be identified. Your answer should state that he is the narrator of "The Cask of Amontillado" (position) who invites Fortunato into his wine vaults on the pretext of testing the quality of some new Amontillado wine (main activity). He is therefore the major cause of the action, and he embodies one of the story's themes, that revenge makes human beings diabolically cruel (significance). Under the category of "significance," of course, you might develop as many ideas as you have time for, but the short example here is a general model for most examinations.

2. *Incidents or situations.* For example: "A woman mourns the death of her husband." To identify this situation, first give the location (Mrs. Popov in Chekhov's play *The Bear*), then try to demonstrate its significance in the work. That is, in *The Bear* Mrs. Popov is mourning the death of her husband, and in the course of the play Chekhov uses her feelings to show amusingly that life with real emotion is stronger than duty to the dead.

3. *Things, places, and dates.* Your instructor may ask you to identify the work in which a cavalry charge takes place (Twain's "Luck") or name the dates of Mansfield's "Miss Brill" (1920) or Amy Lowell's "Patterns" (1916). For dates, you may be given a leeway of five or ten years. What is important about a date is not so much exactness as historical and intellectual perspective. The date of "Patterns," for example, was the third year of World War I, and the poem consequently reflects a reaction against the protracted and senseless loss of life in that war. To claim "World War I" as the date of the poem would likely be acceptable as an answer if it happens that you cannot remember the exact date.

4. *Quotations.* You should remember enough of the text to identify a passage taken from it, or at least to make an informed guess. Generally, you should (1) locate the quotation, if you remember it, or else describe the probable location; (2) show the ways in which the quotation is typical of the content and style of the work you have read; and (3) describe the importance of the passage. If you suffer a momentary lapse of memory, write a reasoned and careful explanation of your guess. Even if your guess is wrong, the knowledge and cogency of your explanation should give you points.

TECHNICAL AND ANALYTICAL QUESTIONS AND PROBLEMS. In a scale of ascending importance, the third and most difficult type of factual question relates to those matters with which this book has been concerned: technique, analysis, and problems. You might be asked to discuss the *setting, images, point of view*, or *important idea* of a work; you might be asked about a *specific problem*; or you might be asked to analyze a poem that may or may not be duplicated for your benefit (if it is not duplicated, woe to students who have not studied their assignments). Questions like these assume that you have technical knowledge, and they also ask you to examine the text within the limitations imposed by the terms.

Obviously, technical questions occur more frequently in advanced courses than in elementary ones, and the questions become more subtle as the courses become more advanced. Instructors of elementary courses may use main-idea or special-problem questions but will probably not use many of the others unless they state their intentions to do so in advance, or unless technical terms have been studied in class.

Questions of this type are fairly long, perhaps allowing from fifteen to twenty-five minutes for each. If you have two or more of these questions, try to space your time sensibly; do not devote eighty percent of your time to one question and leave only twenty percent for the rest.

Basis of Judging Factual Questions

IDENTIFICATION QUESTIONS. In all factual questions, your instructor is testing (1) your factual command, and (2) your quickness in relating a part to the whole. Thus, suppose you are identifying the incident "a man kills a canary." It is correct to say that Susan Glaspell's play *Trifles* is the location of the incident, that the murdered farmer John Wright was the killer, and that the canary belonged to his wife. Knowledge of these details clearly establishes that you know the facts. But a strong answer must go further. Even in the brief time you have for short answers, you should always connect the facts to (1) major causation in the work, (2) an important idea or ideas, (3) the development of the work, and (4) for a quotation, the style. Time is short and you must be selective, but if you can make your answer move from facts to significance, you will always fashion superior responses. Along these lines, let us look at an answer identifying the action from *Trifles*:

> The action is from Glaspell's *Trifles*. The man who kills the bird is John Wright, and the owner is Mrs. Wright. The killing is important because it is shown as the final indignity in Mrs. Wright's desperate life, and it prompts her to strangle Wright in his sleep. It is thus the cause not only of the murder but also of the investigation bringing the officers and their wives on stage. In fact, the wringing of the bird's neck makes the play possible because it is the wives who discover the dead bird, and this discovery is the means by which Glaspell highlights them as the major characters in the play. Because the husband's brutal act shows how bleak the life of Mrs. Wright actually was, it dramatizes the lonely plight of women in a male-dominated way of life like that on the Wright farm. The discovery also raises the issues of legality and morality, because the two wives decide to conceal the evidence, therefore protecting Mrs. Wright from conviction and punishment.

Any of the points in this answer could be developed as a separate essay, but the paragraph is successful as a short answer because it goes beyond fact to deal with significance. Clearly, such answers are possible at the time of an exam only if you have devoted considerable thought to the various exam works beforehand. The more thinking and practicing you do before an exam, the better your answers will be. Remember this advice as an axiom: *You cannot write really superior answers if you do not think extensively before the exam.* By studying well beforehand, you will be able to reduce surprise to an absolute minimum.

LONGER FACTUAL QUESTIONS.   More extended factual questions also require more thoroughly developed organization. Remember that for these questions your knowledge of essay writing is important, for the quality of your composition will determine a major share of your instructor's evaluation of your answers. It is therefore best to take several minutes to gather your thoughts together before you begin to write, because *a ten-minute planned answer is preferable to a twenty-five minute unplanned answer*. You do not need to write every possible fact on each particular question. Of greater importance is the use to which you put the facts you know and the organization of your answer. Use a sheet of scratch paper to jot down the facts you remember and your ideas about them in relation to the question. Then put them together, phrase a thesis sentence, and use your facts to exemplify and support your thesis.

It is always necessary to begin your answer pointedly, using key words or phrases from the question or direction if possible, so that your answer will have thematic shape. You should never begin an answer with "Because" and then go on from there without referring again to the question. To be most responsive during the short time available for an exam, you should use the question as your guide for your answer. Let us suppose that you have the following question on your test: "How does Glaspell use details in *Trifles* to reveal the character of Mrs. Wright?" The most common way to go astray on such a question—and the easiest thing to do also—is to concentrate on Mrs. Wright's character rather than on how Glaspell uses detail to bring out her character. The word *how* makes a vast difference in the nature of the final answer, and hence a good method on the exam is to duplicate key phrases in the question to ensure that you make your major points clear. Here is an opening sentence that uses the key words and phrases (underlined here) from the question to direct thought and provide focus:

> Glaspell <u>uses details</u> of setting, marital relationships, and personal habits <u>to</u> <u>reveal the character of Mrs. Wright</u> as a person of great but unfulfilled potential whom anger has finally overcome.

Because this sentence repeats the key phrases from the question and also because it promises to show *how* the details are to be focused on the character, it suggests that the answer to follow will be responsive.

General or Comprehensive Questions

General or comprehensive questions are particularly important on final examinations, when your instructor is testing your total comprehension of the course material. Considerable time is usually allowed for answering this type of question, which may be phrased in a number of ways:

1. A *direct question* asking about philosophy, underlying attitudes, main ideas, characteristics of style, backgrounds, and so on. Here are some possible questions in this category:

   "What use do _____, _____, and _____ make of the topic of _____?"
   "Define and characterize the short story as a genre of literature."
   "Explain the use of dialogue by Hawthorne, Welty, and Maupassant."
   "Contrast the technique of point of view as used by _____, _____, and _____."

2. A *"comment" question*, often based on an extensive quotation, borrowed from a critic or written by your instructor for the occasion, asking about a broad class of writers, a literary movement, or the like. Your instructor may ask you to treat this question broadly (taking in many writers) or else to apply the quotation to a specific writer.

3. A *"suppose" question*, such as "What advice might Mrs. Wright of *Trifles* give the speakers of Lowell's 'Patterns' and Keats's 'Bright Star'?" or "What might the speaker of Rossetti's poem 'Echo' say if she learned that her dead lover was Goodman Brown of Hawthorne's 'Young Goodman Brown'?" Although suppose questions might seem whimsical at first sight, they have a serious design and should prompt original and radical thinking. The first question, for example, should cause a test writer to bring out, from Mrs. Wright's perspective, that the love of both speakers was or is potential, not actual. She would likely sympathize with the speaker's loss in "Patterns" but might also say the lost married life might not have been as totally happy as the speaker assumes. For the speaker of "Bright Star," a male, Mrs. Wright might say that the steadfast love sought by him should also be linked to kindness and toleration as well as passion.

Although "suppose" questions (and answers) are speculative, the need to respond to them requires a detailed consideration of the works involved, and in this respect the suppose question is a salutary means of learning. It is of course difficult to prepare for a suppose question, which you may therefore regard as a test not only of your knowledge but also of your inventiveness and ingenuity.

Basis of Judging General Questions

When answering broad, general questions, you are dealing with an unstructured situation; and you must not only supply an *answer* but—equally important—you must also create a *structure* within which your answer can have meaning. You might say that you make up your own specific question out of the original general question. If you were asked to "Consider the role of women as seen in Lowell, Mansfield, and Glaspell," for example, you would do well to structure the question by focusing a number of clearly defined topics. A possible way to begin answering such a question might be this:

Lowell, Mansfield, and Glaspell present a view of female resilience by demonstrating inner control, power of adaptation, and endurance.

With this sort of focus you would be able to proceed point by point, introducing supporting data as you form your answer.

As a general rule, the best method for answering a comprehensive question is comparison–contrast (see also Chapter 13). The reason is that in dealing with, say, a general question on Rossetti, Chekhov, and Keats, it is too easy to write *three* separate essays rather than *one*. Thus, you should try to create a topic such as "The treatment of real or idealized love" or "The difficulties in male–female relationships," and then develop your answer point by point rather than writer by writer. By creating your answer in this way, you can bring in references to each or all of the writers as they become relevant to your main idea. If you were to treat each writer separately, your comprehensive answer would lose focus and effectiveness, and it would be needlessly repetitive.

Remember that in judging your response to a general question, your instructor is interested in seeing: (1) how effectively you perceive and explain the significant issues in the question; (2) how intelligently and clearly you organize your answer; and (3) how persuasively you use materials from the work as supporting evidence.

Bear in mind that in answering comprehensive questions, you don't have complete freedom. What you have is the freedom to create your own structure. The underlying idea of the comprehensive, general question is that you possess special knowledge and insights that cannot be discovered by more factual questions. You must therefore formulate your own responses to the material and introduce evidence that reflects your own insights and command of information.

Two final words: Good luck.

appendix b

The Integration of Quotations and Other Important Details, and the Use of Tenses in Writing About Literature

In establishing evidence for the points you make in your essays and essay examinations, you will constantly need to refer to various parts of stories, plays, and poems. You will also need to include shorter and longer quotations and to keep time sequences straight within works. In addition, you may need to refer to biographical and historical details that have a bearing on the work or works you are studying. So that your own writing will flow as accurately and naturally as possible, it is most important for you to be able to integrate these references and time distinctions clearly and easily.

DISTINGUISH YOUR THOUGHTS FROM THOSE OF YOUR AUTHOR. Ideally, your essays should reflect your own thought as it is prompted and illustrated by an author's work. Sometimes a problem arises, however, because it is hard for your reader to know when *your* ideas have stopped and your *author's* have begun. You must therefore arrange things to make the distinction clear, but you must also blend your materials so that your reader may follow you easily. You will be moving from paraphrase, to general interpretation, to observation, to independent application of everything you choose to discuss. It is not always easy to keep these various elements integrated. Let us see an example in which the writer moves from reference to an author's ideas—really paraphrase—to an independent application of the idea:

[1] In the "Preface to the Lyrical Ballads," Wordsworth states that the language of poetry should be the same as that of prose. [2] That is, poetic diction should not be artificial or contrived in any sense but should consist of the words normally used by people in their everyday lives (lines 791–793). [3] If one follows this principle in poetry, then it would be improper to refer to the sun as anything but *the sun*. [4] To call it a *heavenly orb* or the *source of golden gleams* would be inadmissible because these phrases are not used in common speech.

Here the first two sentences paraphrase Wordsworth's ideas about poetic diction, the second going so far as to locate a passage where Wordsworth develops the idea. The third and fourth sentences apply Wordsworth's idea to examples chosen by the writer. Here the blending is provided by the transitional clause, "If one follows this principle," and the reader is thus not confused about who is saying what.

INTEGRATE MATERIAL BY USING QUOTATION MARKS.   Sometimes you will use short quotations from your author to illustrate your ideas and interpretations. Here the problem of distinguishing your thoughts from the author's is solved by quotation marks. In such an internal quotation you may treat prose and poetry in the same way. If a poetic quotation extends from the end of one line to the beginning of another, however, indicate the line break with a virgule (/) and use a capital letter to begin the next line, as in the following:

> Wordsworth states that in his boyhood all of nature seemed like his own personal property. Rocks, mountains, and woods were almost like food to him, and he claimed that "the sounding cataract / Haunted . . . [him] like a passion" (lines 76–80).

BLEND QUOTATIONS INTO YOUR OWN SENTENCES.   Making internal quotations still creates the problem of blending materials, however, for quotations should never be brought in unless you prepare your reader for them in some way. *Do not*, for example, bring in quotations in the following manner:

> Alexander Pope's pastoral sky is darkened by thick clouds, bringing a feeling of gloom that is associated with the same feeling that can be sensed at a funeral. "See gloomy clouds obscure the cheerful day."

This abrupt quotation throws the reader off-balance because it is not blended into the previous sentence. It is better to prepare the reader to move from the discourse to the quotation, as in the following revision:

> Alexander Pope's pastoral scene is marked by sorrow and depression, as though the spectator, who is asked to "see gloomy clouds obscure the cheerful day," is present at a funeral.

Here the quotation is made an actual part of the sentence. This sort of blending is satisfactory, provided that the quotation is brief.

INDENT AND BLOCK LONG QUOTATIONS.   The standard for how to place quotations should be not to quote within a sentence any passage longer than twenty or twenty-five words (but consult your instructor, for the exact number of words allowable may vary [*MLA Handbook*, 56–58]). Quotations of greater length demand so much separate attention that they interfere with your own sentence. It is possible but not desirable to have one of your sentences conclude with a quotation, but you should never make an extensive quotation in the *middle* of a sentence. By the time you finish such an unwieldy sentence, your reader will have lost sight of how it began. When your quotation is long, you should make a point of introducing it and setting it off separately as a block.

The physical layout of block quotations should be as follows: Leave three blank lines between your own discourse and the quotation. Double-space the quotation (like the rest of your essay) and indent it five spaces from your left margin to distinguish it from your own writing. You might use fewer spaces for longer lines of poetry, but the standard should always be to create a balanced, neat page. After the quotation leave a three-line space again and resume your own discourse. Here is a specimen from an essay about Marge Piercy's "A Work of Artifice":

> To demonstrate the traditional suppression of women, Piercy uses the image of a bonsai tree. While the tree is capable of growing as high as eighty feet, a great height, through pruning and stunting it is kept more than a hundred times smaller, small enough to be kept on a shelf. The metaphorical application of the idea to women's lives is that through a variety of ways, women have been prevented from growing, while at the same time they have been reminded that they should feel fortunate because they have a place to call home (the "pot to grow in") and create their own "small and cozy" niche in the world. Piercy concludes her poem ironically by asserting the uglier aspects of this suppression:
>
> > With living creatures
> > one must begin very early
> > to dwarf their growth:
> > the bound feet,
> > the crippled brain,
> > the hair in curlers,
> > the hands you
> > love to touch.
> >   (lines 17–24)
>
> These images are comprehensive, ranging from traditional Chinese footbinding to the worldwide denial of education to most women. In addition, the beauty aids for hair and silky skin are seen here not as enhancements of life, but suppressions of it.

When quoting lines of poetry, always remember to quote them *as lines*. Do not run them together. When you create such block quotations, as in the example above, you do *not* need quotation marks.

USE THREE SPACED PERIODS (AN *ELLIPSIS*) TO SHOW OMISSIONS. Whether your quotation is long or short, you will often need to change some of the material in it to conform to your own sentence requirements. You might wish to omit something from the quotation that is not essential to your point. Indicate such omissions with three spaced periods (. . .), as follows:

> Under the immediate threat of death, Farquhar's perceptions are sharpened and heightened. In actuality there is "swirling water . . . racing madly beneath his feet," but his mind is racing swiftly, and he accordingly perceives that a "piece of dancing driftwood . . . down the current" moves so slowly that he believes the stream is "sluggish."

If your quotation is very brief, however, do not use spaced periods, as they might be more of a hindrance than a help. Do not, for example, use the three spaced periods in a quotation like this:

> Keats asserts that ". . . a thing of beauty . . ." always gives joy.

Instead, make your quotation without the ellipsis:

> Keats asserts that "a thing of beauty" always gives joy.

USE SQUARE BRACKETS FOR YOUR OWN WORDS WITHIN QUOTATIONS. If you add words of your own to integrate the quotation into your own train of discourse or to explain words that may seem obscure, put square brackets around these words, as in the following passage:

> In the "Tinturn Abbey Lines," Wordsworth refers to a trance-like state, in which the "affections gently lead . . . [him] on." He is unquestionably describing a state of extreme relaxation, for he mentions that the "motion of . . . human blood [was] / Almost suspended [i.e., his pulse slowed]" and that in these states he considered himself to be "a living soul" (lines 42–49).

DO NOT CHANGE YOUR SOURCE.   Always reproduce your source exactly. Although most anthologies modernize the spelling of older writers, the works of British authors may include words like *tyre* and *labour*. Also, you may encounter "old-spelling" editions in which all words are spelled exactly as they were centuries ago. Your principle should be *to duplicate everything exactly as you find it*, even if this means spelling words like *achieve* as *atchieve* or *joke* as *joak*. A student once took the liberty of amending the word *an* to "and" in the construction "an I were" in an Elizabethan text. The result was inaccurate, because in introductory clauses, *an* really meant *if* (or *and if*) and not *and*. Difficulties like this one are rare, but you will avoid them if you reproduce the text as you find it. Should you think that something is either misspelled or confusing as it stands, you may do one of two things:

1. Clarify or correct the confusing word or phrase within brackets, as in the following:

   In 1714, fencing was considered a "Gentlemany [i.e., gentlemanly] subject."

2. Use the word *sic* (Latin for *thus*, meaning "It is this way in the text") immediately after the problematic word or obvious mistake:

   He was just "finning [sic] his way back to health" when the next disaster struck.

DO NOT OVERQUOTE.   A word of caution: *Do not use too many quotations.* You will be judged on your own thought and on the continuity and development of your own essay. It is tempting to include many quotations on the theory that you need to use examples from the text to illustrate and support your ideas. Naturally, it is important to introduce examples, but realize that too many quotations can disturb the flow of *your own* thought. If your essay consists of many illustrations linked together by no more than your introductory sentences, how much thinking have you actually shown? Try, therefore, to create your own discussion, using examples appropriately to connect your thought to the text or texts you are analyzing.

USE THE PRESENT TENSE OF VERBS WHEN REFERRING TO ACTIONS AND IDEAS IN A WORK.   Literary works spring into life with each and every reading. You may thus assume that everything happening takes place in the present, and when writing about literature you should use the *present tense of verbs*. It is correct to say "Mathilde and her husband *work* and *economize* (not *"worked* and *economized"*) for ten years to pay off the 18,000-franc debt that they *undertake* (not *"undertook"*) to pay for the lost necklace."

On the principle that the words of an author are just as alive and current today (and tomorrow) as they were at the moment of writing, when you consider an author's ideas the present tense is also proper—even if this same author has been dead for hundreds or even thousands of years.

Because it is incorrect to shift tenses inappropriately, you may encounter a problem when you want to refer to actions that have occurred prior to the time of the main action. An instance occurs in Bierce's "An Occurrence at Owl Creek Bridge," where the narrator explains an event that occurred shortly before the time of the action. In such a situation it is important to keep details in order, and thus you may use the past tense as long as you keep the relationship clear between past and present, as in this example: "Farquhar *had clearly planned* to blow up the bridge after the Union spy *spoke* to him, and hence he *is therefore now living* his last moments on earth." This use of the past influencing the present is acceptable because it corresponds to the cause-and-effect relationship brought out in the story.

A problem also arises when you introduce historical or biographical details about a work or author. It is appropriate to use the *past tense* for such details as long as they actually do belong to the past. Thus it is correct to state that "Shakespeare **lived** from 1564 to 1616" or that "Shakespeare **wrote** *Hamlet* in about 1599–1600." It is also permissible to mix past and present tenses when you are treating historical facts about a literary work and are also considering it as a living text. Of prime importance is to keep things straight. Here is a paragraph example showing how past and present tenses may be used when appropriate:

> Because *Hamlet* **was** first **performed** in about 1600, Shakespeare most probably **wrote** it shortly before this time. In the play, a tragedy, Shakespeare **treats** an act of vengeance, but more importantly he **demonstrates** the difficulty of ever learning the exact truth. The hero, Prince Hamlet, **is** the focus of this difficulty, for the task of revenge **is assigned** to him by the Ghost of his father. Though the Ghost **claims** that his brother, Claudius, **is** his murderer, Hamlet **is** not able to verify this claim.

Here, the historical details are presented in the past tense; but all details about the play *Hamlet*, including Shakespeare as the creating author whose ideas and words are still alive, are considered in the present.

As a general principle, you will be right most of the time if you use the present tense exclusively for literary details and the past tense for historical details. *When in doubt, however, consult your instructor.*

appendix c

Critical Approaches Important to the Study of Literature

A number of critical theories or approaches for understanding and interpreting literature are available to critics and students alike. Many of these have been developed during the twentieth century to create a discipline of literary studies comparable with disciplines in the natural and social sciences. Literary critics have often borrowed liberally from other disciplines (e.g., history, psychology, anthropology) but have primarily aimed at developing literature as a course of study in its own right.

At the heart of the various critical approaches have been many fundamental questions: What is literature? What does it do? Is its concern only to tell stories, or is it to express emotions? Is it private? Public? How does it get its ideas across? What more does it do than express ideas? How valuable was literature in the past and how valuable is it now? What can it contribute to intellectual, artistic, and social history? To what degree is literature an art, as opposed to an instrument for imparting knowledge? How is literature used, and how and why is it misused? What theoretical and technical expertise may be invoked to enhance literary studies?

Questions such as these indicate that criticism is concerned not only with reading and interpreting stories, poems, and plays, but also with establishing theoretical understanding. Because of such extensive aims, you will understand that a full explanation and illustration of the approaches would fill the pages of a long book. The following descriptions are therefore intended as no more than brief introductions. Bear in mind that in the hands of skilled critics, the approaches are so subtle, sophisticated, and complex that they are not only critical stances but also philosophies.

Although the various approaches provide widely divergent ways to study literature and literary problems, they reflect major tendencies rather than absolute straitjacketing. Not every approach is appropriate for every work, nor are the approaches always mutually exclusive. Even the most devoted practitioners of the methods do not pursue them rigidly. In addition, some of the approaches are more "user-friendly" for certain types of discovery than others. To a degree at least, most critics therefore utilize methods that technically belong to one or more of the other approaches. A critic stressing the topical/historical approach, for example, might introduce the close study of a work that is associated with the method of the New Criticism. Similarly, a psychoanalytical critic might include details about archetypes. In short, a great deal of criticism is *pragmatic* or *eclectic* rather than rigid.

The approaches to be considered here are these: *moral/intellectual; topical/historical; New Critical/formalist; structuralist; feminist; economic determinist/Marxist; psychological/psychoanalytic; archetypal/symbolic/mythic; Deconstructionist;* and *Reader-Response.*

Following each description is a brief paragraph showing how Hawthorne's story "Young Goodman Brown" might be considered in the light of the particular approach. The paragraph following the discussion of structuralism, for example, shows how the structuralist approach can be applied to Goodman Brown and his story.

MORAL/INTELLECTUAL

The moral/intellectual approach is concerned with content and values (see Chapter 7). The approach is as old as literature itself, for literature is a traditional mode of imparting morality, philosophy, and religion. The concern in moral/intellectual criticism is not only to discover meaning but also to determine whether works of literature are both *true* and *significant.*

To study literature from the moral/intellectual perspective is therefore to determine whether an individual work conveys a lesson or a message, and whether it can help readers lead better lives and improve their understanding of the world: What ideas does the work contain? How strongly does the work bring forth its ideas? What application do the ideas have to the work's characters and situations? How may they be evaluated intellectually? Morally? A discussion based on such questions does not necessarily require a position of command or exhortation. Ideally, moral/intellectual criticism should differ from sermonizing to the degree that readers should always be left with their own decisions about whether they wish to assimilate the content of a work and about whether this content is personally or morally acceptable.

Sophisticated critics have sometimes demeaned the moral/intellectual approach on the grounds that "message hunting" reduces a work's artistic value by treating it like a sermon or political speech; but the approach will be valuable as long as readers expect literature to be applicable to their own lives.

Example

"Young Goodman Brown" raises the issue of how an institution designed for human elevation, such as the religious system of colonial Salem, can be so ruinous. Does the failure result from the system itself or from the people who misunderstand it? Is what is true of religion as practiced by Brown also true of social and political institutions? Should any religious or political philosophy be given greater credence than goodwill and mutual trust? One of the major virtues of "Young Goodman Brown" is that it provokes questions like these but at the same time provides a number of satisfying answers. A particularly important one is that religious and moral beliefs should not be used to justify the condemnation of others. Another important answer is that attacks made from the refuge of a religion or group, such as Brown's puritanical judgment, is dangerous because it enables the judge to condemn without thought and without personal responsibility.

TOPICAL/HISTORICAL

This traditional approach stresses the relationship of literature to its historical period, and for this reason it has had a long life. Although much literature may be applicable to many places and times, much of it also directly reflects the intellectual and social worlds of the authors. When was the work written? What were the circumstances that produced it? What major issues does it deal with? How does it fit into the author's career? Keats's poem "On First Looking into Chapman's Homer," for example, is his excited response to his reading of one of the major literary works of Western civilization. Hardy's "Channel Firing" is an acerbic response to continued armament and preparation for war during the twentieth century.

The topical/historical approach investigates relationships of this sort, including the elucidation of words and concepts that today's readers may not immediately understand. Obviously, the approach requires the assistance of footnotes, dictionaries, histories, and handbooks.

A common criticism of the topical/historical approach is that in the extreme it deals with background knowledge rather than with literature itself. It is possible, for example, for a topical/historical critic to describe a writer's life, the period of the writer's work, and the social and intellectual ideas of the time—all without ever considering the meaning, importance, and value of the work itself.

Example

"Young Goodman Brown" is an allegorical story by Nathaniel Hawthorne (1804–1864), the New England writer who probed deeply into the relationships between religion and guilt. His ancestors had been involved in religious persecutions, including the Salem witch trials, and he, living 150 years afterward, wanted to probe the weaknesses and uncertainties of the sin-dominated religion of the earlier period. Not surprisingly, therefore, "Young Goodman Brown" takes place in Puritan, colonial Salem. Although the immediate concerns of the story belong to a vanished age, Hawthorne's treatment is still valuable because it is still timely.

NEW CRITICAL/FORMALIST

The New Criticism began in the 1930s and 1940s and has since been a dominant force in twentieth-century literary studies. To the degree that New Criticism focuses upon literary texts as formal works of art, it departs from the topical/historical approach. The objection raised by the New Critics is that as topical/historical critics consider literary history, they avoid close contact with actual texts.

The inspiration for the formalist or New Critical approach was the French practice of *explication de texte*, a method that emphasizes detailed examination and explanation. The New Criticism is therefore at its most brilliant in the analysis of smaller units such as entire poems and short passages. The New Criticism also utilizes a number of techniques for the analysis of larger structures, many of which form the basis for the chapters in this book. Discussions of "point of view," "tone," "plot," "character," and "structure," for example, are ways of looking at literature derived from the New Criticism.

The aim of the formalist study of literature is to provide readers not only with the means of explaining the content of works ("What, specifically, does this say?"), but also with the critical tools needed for evaluating the artistic quality of individual works and writers ("How well is it said?"). A major aspect of New Critical thought is that content and form—including all ideas, ambiguities, subtleties, and even apparent contradictions—were originally within the conscious or subconscious control of the author. There are no accidents. It does not necessarily follow, however, that today's critic is able to define the author's intentions exactly, for such intentions require knowledge of biographical details that are irretrievably lost. Each literary work therefore takes on its own existence and identity, and the critic's work is to discover a reading or readings that explain the facts of the text. Note that the New Critic does not claim infallible interpretations and does not exclude the validity of multiple readings of identical works.

Dissenters from the New Criticism have noted a tendency by New Critics to ignore relevant knowledge that history and biography may bring to literary studies. In addition, the approach has been subject to the charge that stressing the examination of texts alone fails to deal with the value and appreciation of literature.

Example

A major aspect of Hawthorne's "Young Goodman Brown" is that the details are so vague and dreamlike that many readers are uncertain about what is happening. The action is a nighttime walk by the protagonist, Young Goodman Brown, into a deep forest where he encounters a mysterious Satanic ritual that leaves him bitter and misanthropic. This much seems clear, but the precise nature of Brown's experience is not clear, nor is the identity of the stranger (father, village elder, devil) who accompanies Brown as he begins his walk. At the story's end Hawthorne's narrator states that the whole episode may have been no more than a dream or nightmare. Yet when morning comes, Brown walks back into town as though returning from an overnight trip, and he recoils in horror from his fellow villagers, including his wife Faith (paragraph 70). Could his attitude result from nothing more than a nightmare?

Even at the story's end these uncertainties remain. For this reason one may conclude that Hawthorne deliberately creates the uncertainties to reveal how persons like Brown build defensive walls of judgment around themselves. The story thus implies that the real source of Brown's anger is as vague as his nocturnal walk, but he doesn't understand it in this way. Because Brown's vision and judgment are absolute, he rejects everyone around him, even if the cost is a life of bitter suspicion and spiritual isolation.

STRUCTURALIST

The principle of *structuralism* stems from the attempt to find relationships and connections among elements that appear to be separate and discrete. Just as physical science reveals unifying universal principles of matter such as gravity and the forces of electromagnetism (and is constantly searching for a "unified field theory"), structuralism attempts to discover the forms unifying all literatures. Thus a structural description of Maupassant's "The Necklace" would stress that the main character, Mathilde, is an *active* protagonist who undergoes a *test* (or series of tests) and emerges with a victory, though not the kind she had originally hoped for. The same might be said of Phoenix in Welty's "A Worn Path." If this same kind of structural view is applied to Bierce's "An Occurrence at Owl Creek Bridge," the protagonist would emerge in defeat. Generally, the structural approach applies such patterns to other works of literature to determine that some protagonists are active or submissive, that they pass or fail their tests, or that they succeed or fail at other encounters. The key is that many apparently unrelated works reveal many common patterns or contain similar structures with important variations.

The structural approach has become important because it enables critics to discuss works from widely separate cultures and historical periods. In this respect, critics have followed the leads of modern anthropologists, most notably Claude Lévi-Strauss (b. 1908). Along such lines, critics have undertaken the serious examination of folk tales and fairy tales. Some of the groundbreaking structuralist criticism, for example, was devoted to the structural principles underlying Russian folk tales. The method also bridges popular and serious literature, making little distinction between the two insofar as the description of the structures is concerned. Indeed, structuralism furnishes an ideal approach for comparative literature, and the method also enables critics to consolidate genres such as modern romances, detective tales, soap operas, and films.

Like the New Criticism, structuralism aims at comprehensiveness of description, and many critics would insist that the two are complementary and not separate. A distinction is that the New Criticism is at its best in dealing with smaller units of literature, whereas structuralism is best in the analysis of narratives and therefore larger units such as novels, myths, and stories. Because structuralism shows how fiction is organized into various typical situations, the approach merges with the *archetypal* approach, and at times it is difficult to find any distinctions between structuralism and archetypalism.

Structuralism, however, deals not just with narrative structures, but also with structures of any type, wherever they occur. For example, structuralism makes great use of linguistics. Modern linguistic scholars have determined that there is a difference between "deep structures" and "surface structures" in language. A structuralist analysis of style, therefore, would stress the ways in which writers utilize such structures. The structuralist interpretation of language also perceives distinguishing types or "grammars" of language that are recurrent in various types of literature. Suppose, for example, that you encounter opening passages like the following:

> Once upon a time a young prince fell in love with a young princess. He decided to tell her of his love, and early one morning he left his castle on his white charger, riding toward her castle home high in the mountains.

> Early that morning, Alan had found himself thinking about Anne. He had believed her when she said she loved him, but his feelings about her were not certain, and his thinking had left him still unsure.

The words of these two passages create different and distinct frames of reference. One is a fairy tale, the other the internalized reflection of feeling. The passages therefore demonstrate how language itself fits into predetermined patterns or structures. Similar uses of language structures can be associated with other types of literature.

Example

Young Goodman Brown is a hero who is passive, not active. Essentially, he is a witness, a receiver rather than a doer. His only action—taking his trip in the forest—occurs at the story's beginning. After that point, he no longer acts but instead is acted upon, and what he sees puts his life's beliefs to a test. Of course, many protagonists undergo similar testing (such as rescuing victims and slaying particularly terrible dragons), and they emerge triumphant. Not so with Goodman Brown. He is a responder who allows himself to be victimized by his own perceptions—or misperceptions. Despite all his previous experiences with his wife and with the good people of his village, he generalizes too hastily. He lets the single disillusioning experience of his nightmare govern his entire outlook on others, and thus he fails his test and turns his entire life into failure.

FEMINIST

The feminist approach holds that most of our literature presents a masculine–patriarchal view in which the role of women is negated or at best minimized. As an adjunct of the feminist movement in politics, the feminist critique of literature seeks to raise consciousness about the importance and unique nature of women in literature.

Specifically, the feminist view attempts (1) to show that writers of traditional literature have ignored women and have also transmitted misguided and prejudiced views of them, (2) to stimulate the creation of a critical milieu that reflects a balanced view of the nature and value of women, (3) to recover the works of women writers of past times and to encourage the publication of present women writers so that the literary canon may be expanded to recognize women as thinkers and artists, and (4) to urge transformations in the language to eliminate inequities and inequalities that result from linguistic distortions.

In form, the feminist perspective seeks to evaluate various literary works from the standpoint of the presentation of women. For works such as "The Necklace" (story), "A Work of Artifice" (poem), and The Bear (play), a feminist critique would focus on how such works treat women and also on either the shortcomings or enlightenment of the author as a result of this treatment: How important are the female characters, how individual in their own right? Are they credited with their own existence and their own character? In their relationships with men, how are they treated? Are they given equal status? Ignored? Patronized? Demeaned? Pedestalized? How much concern do the male characters exhibit about women's concerns?

Example

At the beginning of "Young Goodman Brown," Brown's wife, Faith, is only peripheral. In the traditional patriarchal spirit of wife-as-adjunct, she asks her husband to stay at home and take his journey at another time. Hawthorne does not give her the intelligence or dignity, however, to let her explain her concern (or might he not have been interested in what she had to say?), and she therefore remains in the background with her pink hair ribbon as her distinguishing characteristic. During the mid-forest Satanic ritual she appears again and is given power, but only the power to cause her husband to go astray. Once she is led in as a novice in the practice of demonism, her husband falls right in step. Unfortunately, by following her, Brown may conveniently excuse himself from guilt by claiming that "she" had made him do it, just as Eve "made" Adam eat the apple. Hawthorne's attention to the male hero, in other words, permits him to distort the female's role.

ECONOMIC DETERMINIST/MARXIST

The concept of cultural and economic determinism is one of the major political ideas of the last century. Karl Marx (1818–1883) emphasized that the primary influence on life was economic, and he saw society as an opposition between the capitalist and working classes. The literature that emerged from this kind of analysis features individuals in the grips of the class struggle. Often called "proletarian literature," it emphasizes persons of the lower class—the poor and oppressed who spend their lives in endless drudgery and misery, and whose attempts to rise above their disadvantages usually result in renewed suppression.

Marx's political ideas were never widely accepted in the United States and have faded still more after the political breakup of the Soviet Union, but the idea of economic determinism (and the related term "Social Darwinism") is still credible. As a result, much literature can be judged from an economic perspective: What is the economic status of the characters? What happens to them as a result of this status? How do they fare against economic and political odds? What other conditions stemming from their class does the writer emphasize (e.g., poor education, poor nutrition, poor health care, inadequate opportunity)? To what extent does the work fail by overlooking the economic, social, and political implications of its material? In what other ways does economic determinism affect the work? How should readers consider the story in today's developed or underdeveloped world? Seemingly, the specimen work "Young Goodman Brown" has no economic implications, but an economically oriented discussion might take the following turns:

Example

"Young Goodman Brown" is a fine story just as it is. It deals with the false values instilled by the skewed acceptance of sin-dominated religion, but it overlooks the economic implications of this situation. One suspects that the real story in the little world of Goodman Brown's Salem should be about survival and the disruption that an alienated member of society can produce. After Brown's condemnation and distrust of others force him into his own shell of sick imagination, Hawthorne does not consider how such a disaffected character would injure the economic and public life of the town. Consider this, just for a moment: Why would the people from whom Brown recoils in disgust want to deal with him in business or personal matters? Would they want to follow his opinion in town meetings on crucial issues of public concern and investment? Would his preoccupation with sin and damnation make him anything more than a horror in his domestic life? Would his wife, Faith, be able to discuss household management with him, or how to take care of the children? All these questions of course are pointed toward another story—a story that Hawthorne did not write. They also indicate the shortcomings of Hawthorne's approach, because it is clear the major result of Young Goodman Brown's selfish preoccupation with evil would be a serious disruption of the economic and political affairs of his small community.

PSYCHOLOGICAL/PSYCHOANALYTIC[1]

The scientific study of the mind is a product of psychodynamic theory as established by Sigmund Freud (1856–1939) and of the psychoanalytic method practiced by his followers. Psychoanalysis provided a new key to the understanding of character by claiming that behavior was caused by hidden and unconscious motives and drives. It was greeted as a virtual revelation, and not surprisingly it had a profound effect on twentieth-century literature.

In addition, its popularity produced a psychological/psychoanalytic approach to criticism. Some critics use the approach to explain fictional characters, as in the landmark interpretation by Freud and Ernest Jones that Shakespeare's Hamlet suffers from the "Oedipus Complex." Still other critics use it as a way of analyzing authors and the artistic process. For example, John Livingston Lowes's *The Road to Xanadu* presents a detailed examination of the mind, reading, and neuroses of Coleridge, the author of "Kubla Khan."

Critics using the psychoanalytic approach treat literature somewhat like information about patients in therapy. In the work itself, what are the obvious and hidden motives that cause a character's behavior and speech? How much background (childhood trauma, adolescent memories, etc.) does the author reveal about a character? How purposeful is this information with regard to the character's psychological condition? How much is important in analyzing and understanding the character?

In the consideration of authors, critics utilizing the psychoanalytic mode consider questions like these: What particular life experiences explain characteristic subjects or preoccupations? Was the author's life happy? miserable? upsetting? solitary? social? Can the death of someone in the author's family be associated with melancholy situations in that author's work? (All

[1]See also Chapter 4, "Writing About Character: The People in Literature."

eleven of the brothers and sisters of the English poet Thomas Gray, for example, died before reaching adulthood. Gray was the only one to survive. In his poetry, Gray often deals with death, and he is therefore considered as one of the "Graveyard School" of eighteenth-century poets. A psychoanalytical critic might make much of this connection.)

Example

At the end of "Young Goodman Brown," Hawthorne's major character is no longer capable of normal existence. His nightmare should be read as a symbol of what in reality would have been lifelong mental subjection to the type of puritanical religion that emphasizes sin and guilt. Such preoccupation with sin is no hindrance to psychological health if the preoccupied people are convinced that God forgives them and grants them mercy. In their dealings with others, they remain healthy as long as they believe that other people have the same sincere trust in divine forgiveness. If their own faith is short and uncertain, however, and they cannot believe in forgiveness, then they are likely to project their own guilt—really a form of personal terror—into others. They remain conscious of their own sins, but they find it easy to claim that others are sinful—even those who are spiritually spotless, and even their own family, who should be dearest to them. When this process of projection occurs, such people have created the rationale of condemning others because of their own guilt. The cost they pay is a life of gloom, a fate that Hawthorne makes for Goodman Brown after the nightmare about demons in human form.

ARCHETYPAL/SYMBOLIC/MYTHIC[2]

The archetypal approach, derived from the work of the Swiss psychoanalyst Carl Jung (1875–1961), presupposes that human life is built up out of patterns, or *archetypes* ("first molds" or "first patterns"), that are similar throughout various cultures and historical times. The approach is similar to the structuralist analysis of literature, for both approaches stress the connections that may be discovered in literature written in different times and in vastly different locations in the world.

In literary evaluation, the archetypal approach is used to support the claim that the very best literature is grounded in archetypal patterns. The archetypal critic therefore looks for archetypes such as God's creation of human beings, the sacrifice of a hero, or the search for paradise. How does an individual story, poem, or play fit into any of the archetypal patterns? What truths does this correlation provide (particularly truths that cross historical, national, and cultural lines)? How closely does the work fit the archetype? What variations may be seen? What meaning or meanings do the connections have?

---

[2] Symbolism and myths are also considered in Chapter 10.

The most tenuous aspect of archetypal criticism is Jung's assertion that the recurring patterns provide evidence for a "universal human conscious-ness" that all of us, by virtue of our humanity, still retain in our minds and in our very blood.

Not all critics accept the hypothesis of a universal human conscious-ness, but they nevertheless consider the approach important for comparisons and contrasts (see Chapter 13). Many human situations, such as adolescence, dawning love, the search for success, the reconciliation with one's mother and father, and the encroachment of age and death, are similar in structure and may be analyzed as archetypes. For example, the following situations may be seen as a pattern or archetype of initiation: A young man discovers the power of literature and understanding ("On First Looking into Chapman's Homer"); a man determines the importance of truth and fidelity amidst uncertainty ("Dover Beach"); a man and woman fall in love despite their wishes to remain independent (*The Bear*); a woman gains strength and integrity because of pre-viously unrealized inner resources ("The Necklace"). The archetypal approach encourages the analysis of variations on the same theme, as in Glaspell's *Trifles*, when the two women develop their impromptu cover-up of the crime (one sort of initiation) and also begin to assert their freedom of thought and action independent of their husbands (another sort).

Example

In the sense that Brown undergoes a change from psychological normality to rigidity, the story is a reverse archetype of the initiation ritual. According to the archetype of successful initiation, initiates seek to demonstrate their wor-thiness to become full-fledged members of society. Telemachus in Homer's *Odyssey*, for example, is a young man who in the course of the epic goes through the initiation rituals of travel, discussion, and battle. But in "Young Good-man Brown" we see initiation in reverse, for just as there is an archetype of suc-cessful initiation, Brown's initiation leads him into failure. In the private areas of life on which happiness depends he falls short. He sees evil in his fellow vil-lagers, condemns his own minister, and shrinks even from his own wife. His life is one of despair and gloom. His suspicions are those of a Puritan of long ago, but the timeliness of Hawthorne's story is that the archetype of misunder-standing and condemnation has not changed. Today's headlines of misery and war are produced by the same kind of intolerance that is exhibited by Goodman Brown.

DECONSTRUCTIONIST

The *Deconstructionist* approach—which Deconstructionists explain not as an approach but rather as a performance—was developed by the French critic Jacques Derrida (b. 1930). In the 1970s and 1980s it became a major but also

controversial mode of criticism. As a literary theory, Deconstructionism produces a type of analysis that stresses ambiguity and contradiction.

A major principle of Deconstructionism is that Western thought has
been *logocentric*; that is, Western philosophers have assumed that central truth
is knowable and entire. The Deconstructionist view is that there is no central
truth because circumstances and time, which are changeable and sometimes
arbitrary, govern the world of the intellect. This analysis leads to the declaration "All interpretation is misinterpretation." That is, literary works cannot
be encapsulated as organically unified entireties, and therefore there is not *one*
correct interpretation but only *interpretations*, each one possessing its own
validity.

In "deconstructing" a work, therefore, the Deconstructionist critic raises
questions about what other critics have claimed about the work: Is a poem
accepted as a model of classicism? Then it also exhibits qualities of romanticism. Is a story about a young Native American's flight from school commonly taken as a criticism of modern urban life? Then it may also be taken as
a story of the failure of youth. In carrying out such criticism, Deconstructionist critics place heavy emphasis on the ideas contained in words such as
ambivalence, discrepancy, enigma, uncertainty, delusion, indecision, and *lack of res-*
olution, among others.

The Deconstructionist attack on "correct," "privileged," or "accepted"
readings is also related to the principle that language, and therefore literature,
is unstable. "Linguistic instability" means that the full understanding of
words is never exact because there is a never-ending *play* between the words
in a text and their many shades of meaning, including possible future meanings. That is, the words do not remain constant and produce a definite
meaning, but instead call forth the possibility of "infinite substitutions" of
meaning. Each work of literature is therefore ambiguous and uncertain
because its full meaning is constantly being *deferred*. This infinite play or
semantic tension renders language unstable and makes correct or accepted
readings impossible.

It is fair to state that Deconstructionism, among all the literary theories,
has received intense criticism that has sometimes bordered on discrediting
the theory entirely. A number of critics find that the position is elusive and
vague. They grant that literary works are often ambiguous, uncertain, and
apparently contradictory, but explain that the cause of these conditions is not
linguistic instability but rather authorial intention. They also point out that
the Deconstructionist linguistic analysis is derivative and misunderstood,
and that it does not support Deconstructionist assertions about linguistic
instability. Critics also draw attention to the contradiction that Deconstructionism cannot follow its major premise about there being no "privileged
readings" because it must recognize the privileged readings in order to inval-
idate or "subvert" them.

Example

There are many uncertainties in the details of "Young Goodman Brown." If one starts with the stranger on the path, one might conclude that he could be Brown's father, because he recognizes Brown immediately and speaks to him jovially. On the other hand, the stranger could be the devil (he is recognized as such by Goody Cloyse) because of his wriggling walking stick. After disappearing, the stranger also takes on the characteristics of an omniscient cult leader, because at the Satanic celebration he knows all the secret sins committed by Brown's neighbors and the community of greater New England. Additionally, he might represent a perverted conscience whose aim is to mislead and befuddle people by steering them into the holier-than-thou judgmentalism that Brown adopts. This method would be truly diabolical—to use religion in order to bring people to their own damnation. That the stranger is an evil force is therefore clear, but the pathways of his evil are not as clear. He seems to work his mission of damnation by reaching souls like that of Goodman Brown through means ordinarily attributed to conscience. If the stranger represents a Satanic conscience, what are we to suppose that Hawthorne is asserting about what is considered real conscience?

READER-RESPONSE[3]

The theory of Reader-Response is rooted in *phenomenology*, a branch of philosophy that deals with "the understanding of how things appear." The phenomenological idea of knowledge is that reality is to be found not in the external world itself but rather in the mental *perception* of externals. That is, all that we human beings can know—actual *knowledge*—is our collective and personal understanding of the world and our conclusions about it.

As a consequence of the phenomenological concept, Reader-Response theory holds that the reader is a necessary third party in the author–text–reader relationship that constitutes the literary work. The work, in other words, is not fully created until readers make a *transaction* with it by assimilating it and *actualizing* it in the light of their own knowledge and experience. The representative questions of the theory are these: What does this work mean to me, in my present intellectual and moral makeup? What particular aspects of my life may help me understand and appreciate the work? How can the work improve my understanding and widen my insights? How can my increasing understanding help me understand the work more deeply? The theory is that the free interchange or transaction that such questions bring about leads toward interest and growth so that readers may assimilate literary works and accept them as part of their lives.

As an initial way of reading, the Reader-Response method may be personal and anecdotal. In addition, by stressing response rather than interpre-

[3] See "Special Writing Topics for Likes and Dislikes" in Chapter 2, p. 48.

tation, one of the leading exponents of the method (Stanley Fish) has raised the extreme question about whether texts, by themselves, have objective identity. These aspects have been cited as both a shortcoming and an inconsequentiality of the method.

It is therefore important to stress that the Reader-Response theory is *open*. It permits beginning readers to bring their own personal reactions to literature, but it also aims at increasing the discipline and skills of readers. The more that readers bring to literature through lifelong interests and disciplined studies, the more "competent" and comprehensive their responses will be. With cumulative experience, the disciplined reader will habitually adjust to new works and respond to them with increasing skill. If the works require special knowledge in fields such as art, politics, science, philosophy, religion, or morality, then competent readers will possess such knowledge or seek it out, and utilize it in improving their responses. Also, because students experience many similar intellectual and cultural disciplines, it is logical to conclude that responses will tend not to diverge but rather to coalesce; agreements result not from personal but from cultural similarities. The Reader-Response theory, then, can and should be an avenue toward informed and detailed understanding of literature, but the initial emphasis is the transaction between readers and literary works.

Example

"Young Goodman Brown" is a worrisome story because it shows so disturbingly that good intentions may cause harmful results. I think that a person with too high a set of expectations is ripe for disillusionment, just as Goodman Brown is. When people don't measure up to this person's standard of perfection, they can be thrown aside as though they are worthless. They may be good, but their past mistakes make it impossible for the person with high expectations to endure them. I have seen this situation occur among some of my friends and acquaintances, particularly in romantic relationships. Goodman Brown makes the same kind of misjudgment, expecting perfection and turning sour when he learns about flaws. It is not that he is not a good man, because he is shown at the start as a person of belief and stability. He uncritically accepts his nightmare revelation that everyone else is evil (including his parents), however, and he finally distrusts everyone because of this enduring suspicion. He cannot look at his neighbors without avoiding them like an "anathema," and he turns away from his own wife "without a greeting" (paragraph 70). Brown's problem is that he equates being human with being unworthy. By such a distorted standard of judgment, all of us fail, and that is what makes the story so disturbing.

appendix d

Works Used for Sample Themes and References

STORIES

Ambrose Bierce (1842–1914?)

An Occurrence at Owl Creek Bridge   1891

A man stood upon a railroad bridge in northern Alabama, looking down into the swift water twenty feet below. The man's hands were behind his back, the wrists bound with a cord. A rope closely encircled his neck. It was attached to a stout cross-timber above his head and the slack fell to the level of his knees. Some loose boards laid upon the sleepers supporting the metals of the railway supplied a footing for him and his executioners—two private soldiers of the Federal army, directed by a sergeant who in civil life may have been a deputy sheriff. At a short remove upon the same temporary platform was an officer in the uniform of his rank, armed. He was a captain. A sentinel at each end of the bridge stood with his rifle in the position known as "support," that is to say, vertical in front of the left shoulder, the hammer resting on the forearm thrown straight across the chest—a formal and unnatural position, enforcing an erect carriage of the body. It did not appear to be the duty of these two men to know what was occurring at the center of the bridge; they merely blockaded the two ends of the foot planking that traversed it.

Beyond one of the sentinels nobody was in sight; the railroad ran straight away into a forest for a hundred yards, then, curving, was lost to view. Doubtless there was an outpost farther along. The other bank of the stream was open ground—a gentle acclivity topped with a stockade of vertical tree trunks, loopholed for rifles, with a single embrasure through which protruded the muzzle of a brass cannon commanding the bridge. Midway of the slope between the bridge and fort were the spectators—a single company of infantry in line, at "parade rest," the butts of the rifles on the ground, the barrels inclining slightly backward against the right shoulder, the hands crossed upon the stock. A lieutenant stood at the right of the line, the point of his sword upon the ground, his left hand resting upon his right. Excepting the group of four at the center of the bridge, not a man moved. The company faced the bridge, staring stonily, motionless. The sentinels, facing the banks of the stream, might have been statues to adorn the bridge. The captain stood with folded arms, silent, observing the work of his subordinates, but making no sign. Death is a dignitary who when he comes announced is to be received with formal manifestations of respect, even by those most familiar with him. In the code of military etiquette silence and fixity are forms of deference.

The man who was engaged in being hanged was apparently about thirty-five years of age. He was a civilian, if one might judge from his habit, which was that of a planter. His features were good—a straight nose, firm mouth, broad forehead, from which his long, dark hair was combed straight back, falling behind his ears to the collar of his well-fitting frock coat. He wore a mustache and pointed beard, but no whiskers; his eyes were large and dark gray, and had a kindly expression which one would hardly have expected in one whose neck was in the hemp. Evidently this was no vulgar assassin. The liberal military code makes provision for hanging many kinds of persons, and gentlemen are not excluded.

The preparations being complete, the two private soldiers stepped aside and each drew away the plank upon which he had been standing. The sergeant turned to the captain, saluted and placed himself immediately behind that officer, who in turn moved apart one pace. These movements left the condemned man and the sergeant standing on the two ends of the same plank, which spanned three of the cross-ties of the bridge. The end upon which the civilian stood almost, but not quite, reached a fourth. This plank had been held in place by the weight of the captain; it was now held by that of the sergeant. At a signal from the former the latter would step aside, the plank would tilt and the condemned man go down between two ties. The arrangement commended itself to his judgment as simple and effective. His face had not been covered nor his eyes bandaged. He looked a moment at his "unsteadfast footing," then let his gaze wander to the swirling water of the stream racing madly beneath his feet. A piece of dancing driftwood caught his attention and his eyes followed it down the current. How slowly it appeared to move! What a sluggish stream!

He closed his eyes in order to fix his last thoughts upon his wife and children. The water, touched to gold by the early sun, the brooding mists under the banks at some distance down the stream, the fort, the soldiers, the piece of driftwood—all had distracted him. And now he became conscious of a new disturbance. Striking through the thought of his dear ones was a sound which he could neither ignore nor understand, a sharp, distinct, metallic percussion like the stroke of a blacksmith's hammer upon the anvil; it had the same ringing quality. He wondered what it was, and whether immeasurably distant or near by—it seemed both. Its recurrence was regular, but as slow as the tolling of a death knell. He awaited each stroke with impatience and—he knew not why—apprehension. The intervals of silence grew progressively longer; the delays became maddening. With their greater infrequency the sounds increased in strength and sharpness. They hurt his ear like the thrust of a knife; he feared he would shriek. What he heard was the ticking of his watch.

He unclosed his eyes and saw again the water below him. "If I could free my hands," he thought, "I might throw off the noose and spring into the stream. By diving I could evade the bullets and, swimming vigorously, reach the bank, take to the woods and get away home. My home, thank God, is as yet outside their lines; my wife and little ones are still beyond the invader's farthest advance."

As these thoughts, which have here to be set down in words, were flashed into the doomed man's brain rather than evolved from it the captain nodded to the sergeant. The sergeant stepped aside.

II

Peyton Farquhar was a well-to-do planter of an old and highly respected Alabama family. Being a slave owner and like other slave owners a politician he was naturally an original secessionist and ardently devoted to the Southern cause. Circumstances of an imperious nature, which it is unnecessary to relate here, had prevented him from taking service with the gallant army that had fought the disastrous campaigns ending with the fall of Corinth, and he chafed under the inglorious restraint, longing for the release of his energies, the larger life of the soldier, the opportunity for distinction. That opportunity, he felt, would come, as it comes to all in war time. Meanwhile he did what he could. No service was too humble for him to perform in aid of the South, no adventure too perilous for him to undertake if consistent with the character of a civilian who was at heart a soldier, and who in good faith and without too much qualification assented to at least a part of the frankly villainous dictum that all is fair in love and war.

One evening while Farquhar and his wife were sitting on a rustic bench near the entrance to his grounds, a gray-clad soldier rode up to the gate and asked for a drink of water. Mrs. Farquhar was only too happy to serve him with her own white hands. While she was fetching the water her husband approached the dusty horseman and inquired eagerly for news from the front.

10   "The Yanks are repairing the railroads," said the man, "and are getting ready for another advance. They have reached the Owl Creek bridge, put it in order and built a stockade on the north bank. The commandant has issued an order, which is posted everywhere, declaring that any civilian caught interfering with the railroad, its bridges, tunnels or trains will be summarily hanged. I saw the order."

"How far is it to the Owl Creek bridge?" Farquhar asked.

"About thirty miles."

"Is there no force on this side the creek?"

"Only a picket post half a mile out, on the railroad, and a single sentinel at this end of the bridge."

15   "Suppose a man—a civilian and student of hanging—should elude the picket post and perhaps get the better of the sentinel," said Farquhar, smiling, "what could he accomplish?"

The soldier reflected. "I was there a month ago," he replied. "I observed that the flood of last winter had lodged a great quantity of driftwood against the wooden pier at this end of the bridge. It is now dry and would burn like tow."

The lady had now brought the water, which the soldier drank. He thanked her ceremoniously, bowed to her husband and rode away. An hour later, after nightfall, he repassed the plantation, going northward in the direction from which he had come. He was a Federal scout.

III

As Peyton Farquhar fell straight downward through the bridge he lost consciousness and was as one already dead. From this state he was awakened—ages later, it seemed to him—by the pain of a sharp pressure upon his throat, followed by a sense of suffocation. Keen, poignant agonies seemed to shoot from his neck downward through every fiber of his body and limbs. These pains appeared to flash along well-defined lines of ramification and to beat with an inconceivably rapid periodicity. They seemed like streams of pulsating fire heating him to an intolerable temperature. As to his head, he was conscious of nothing but a feeling of fulness—of congestion. These sensations were unaccompanied by thought. The intellectual part of his nature was already effaced; he had power only to feel, and feeling was torment. He was conscious of motion. Encompassed in a luminous cloud, of which he was now merely the fiery heart, without material substance, he swung through unthinkable arcs of oscillation, like a vast pendulum. Then all at once, with terrible suddenness, the light about him shot upward with the noise of a loud plash; a frightful roaring was in his ears, and all was cold and dark. The power of thought was restored; he knew that the rope had broken and he had fallen into the stream. There was no additional strangulation; the noose about his neck was already suffocating him and kept the water from his lungs. To die of hanging at the bottom of a river!—the idea seemed to him ludicrous. He opened his eyes in the darkness and saw above him a gleam of light, but how distant, how inaccessible! He was still sinking, for the light became fainter and fainter until it was a mere glimmer. Then it began to grow and brighten, and he knew that he was rising toward the surface—knew it with reluctance, for he was now very comfortable. "To be hanged and drowned," he thought, "that is not so bad; but I do not wish to be shot. No; I will not be shot; that is not fair."

He was not conscious of an effort, but a sharp pain in his wrist apprised him that he was trying to free his hands. He gave the struggle his attention, as an idler might observe the feat of a juggler, without interest in the outcome. What splendid effort!—what magnificent, what superhuman strength! Ah, that was a fine endeavor! Bravo! The cord fell away; his arms parted and floated upward, the hands dimly seen on each side in the growing light. He watched them with a new interest as first one and then the other pounced upon the noose at his neck. They tore it away and thrust it fiercely aside, its undulations resembling those of a water snake. "Put it back, put it back!" He thought he shouted these words to his hands, for the undoing of the noose had been succeeded by the direst pang that he had yet experienced. His neck ached horribly; his brain was on fire; his heart, which had been fluttering faintly, gave a great leap, trying to force itself out at his mouth. His whole body was racked and wrenched with an insupportable anguish! But his disobedient hands gave no heed to the command. They beat the water vigorously with quick, downward strokes, forcing him to the surface. He felt his head emerge; his eyes were blinded by the sunlight; his chest expanded convulsively, and with a supreme and crowning agony his lungs engulfed a great draught of air, which instantly he expelled in a shriek!

He was now in full possession of his physical senses. They were, indeed, preternaturally keen and alert. Something in the awful disturbance of his organic system *20* had so exalted and refined them that they made record of things never before perceived. He felt the ripples upon his face and heard their separate sounds as they struck. He looked at the forest on the bank of the stream, saw the individual trees, the leaves and the veining of each leaf—saw the very insects upon them: the locusts, the brilliant-bodied flies, the gray spiders stretching their webs from twig to twig. He noted the prismatic colors in all the dewdrops upon a million blades of grass. The humming of the gnats that danced above the eddies of the stream, the beating of the dragon flies' wings, the strokes of the water-spiders' legs, like oars which had lifted their boat—all these made audible music. A fish slid along beneath his eyes and he heard the rush of its body parting the water.

He had come to the surface facing down the stream; in a moment the visible world seemed to wheel slowly round, himself the pivotal point, and he saw the bridge, the fort, the soldiers upon the bridge, the captain, the sergeant, the two privates, his executioners. They were in silhouette against the blue sky. They shouted and gesticulated, pointing at him. The captain had drawn his pistol, but did not fire; the others were unarmed. Their movements were grotesque and horrible, their forms gigantic.

Suddenly he heard a sharp report and something struck the water smartly within a few inches of his head, spattering his face with spray. He heard a second report, and saw one of the sentinels with his rifle at his shoulder, a light cloud of blue smoke rising from the muzzle. The man in the water saw the eye of the man on the bridge gazing into his own through the sights of the rifle. He observed that it was a gray eye and remembered having read that gray eyes were keenest, and that all famous marksmen had them. Nevertheless, this one had missed.

A counter-swirl had caught Farquhar and turned him half round; he was again looking into the forest on the bank opposite the fort. The sound of a clear, high voice in a monotonous singsong now rang out behind him and came across the water with a distinctness that pierced and subdued all other sounds, even the beating of the ripples in his ears. Although no soldier, he had frequented camps enough to know the dread significance of that deliberate, drawling, aspirated chant; the lieutenant on shore was taking a part in the morning's work. How coldly and pitilessly—with what an even, calm intonation, presaging, and enforcing tranquillity in the men—with what accurately measured intervals fell those cruel words:

"Attention, company! . . . Shoulder arms! . . . Ready! . . . Aim! . . . Fire!"

25   Farquhar dived—dived as deeply as he could. The water roared in his ears like the voice of Niagara, yet he heard the dulled thunder of the volley and, rising again toward the surface, met shining bits of metal, singularly flattened, oscillating slowly downward. Some of them touched him on the face and hands, then fell away, continuing their descent. One lodged between his collar and neck; it was uncomfortably warm and he snatched it out.

As he rose to the surface, gasping for breath, he saw that he had been a long time under water; he was perceptibly farther down stream—nearer to safety. The soldiers had almost finished reloading; the metal ramrods flashed all at once in the sunshine as they were drawn from the barrels, turned in the air, and thrust into their sockets. The two sentinels fired again, independently and ineffectually.

The hunted man saw all this over his shoulder; he was now swimming vigorously with the current. His brain was as energetic as his arms and legs; he thought with the rapidity of lightning.

"The officer," he reasoned, "will not make that martinet's error a second time.

It is as easy to dodge a volley as a single shot. He has probably already given the command to fire at will. God help me, I cannot dodge them all!"

An appalling plash within two yards of him was followed by a loud, rushing sound, *diminuendo*, which seemed to travel back through the air to the fort and died in an explosion which stirred the very river to its deeps! A rising sheet of water curved over him, fell down upon him, blinded him, strangled him! The cannon had taken a hand in the game. As he shook his head free from the commotion of the smitten water he heard the deflected shot humming through the air ahead, and in an instant it was cracking and smashing the branches in the forest beyond.

"They will not do that again," he thought; "the next time they will use a charge   30
of grape. I must keep my eye upon the gun; the smoke will apprise me—the report arrives too late; it lags behind the missile. That is a good gun."

Suddenly he felt himself whirled round and round—spinning like a top. The water, the banks, the forests, the now distant bridge, fort and men—all were commingled and blurred. Objects were represented by their colors only; circular horizontal streaks of color—that was all he saw. He had been caught in a vortex and was being whirled on with a velocity of advance and gyration that made him giddy and sick. In a few moments he was flung upon the gravel at the foot of the left bank of the stream— the southern bank—and behind a projecting point which concealed him from his enemies. The sudden arrest of his motion, the abrasion of one of his hands on the gravel, restored him, and he wept with delight. He dug his fingers into the sand, threw it over himself in handfuls and audibly blessed it. It looked like diamonds, rubies, emeralds; he could think of nothing beautiful which it did not resemble. The trees upon the bank were giant garden plants; he noted a definite order in their arrangement, inhaled the fragrance of their blooms. A strange, roseate light shone through the spaces among their trunks and the wind made in their branches the music of Æolian harps. He had no wish to perfect his escape—was content to remain in that enchanting spot until retaken.

A whiz and rattle of grapeshot among the branches high above his head roused him from his dream. The baffled cannoneer had fired him a random farewell. He sprang to his feet, rushed up the sloping bank, and plunged into the forest.

All that day he traveled, laying his course by the rounding sun. The forest seemed interminable; nowhere did he discover a break in it, not even a woodman's road. He had not known that he lived in so wild a region. There was something uncanny in the revelation.

By nightfall he was fatigued, footsore, famishing. The thought of his wife and children urged him on. At last he found a road which led him in what he knew to be the right direction. It was as wide and straight as a city street, yet it seemed untraveled. No fields bordered it, no dwelling anywhere. Not so much as the barking of a dog suggested human habitation. The black bodies of the trees formed a straight wall on both sides, terminating on the horizon in a point, like a diagram in a lesson in perspective. Overhead, as he looked up through this rift in the wood, shone great golden stars looking unfamiliar and grouped in strange constellations. He was sure they were arranged in some order which had a secret and malign significance. The wood on either side was full of singular noises, among which—once, twice, and again—he distinctly heard whispers in an unknown tongue.

His neck was in pain and lifting his hand to it found it horribly swollen. He knew   35
that it had a circle of black where the rope had bruised it. His eyes felt congested; he

could no longer close them. His tongue was swollen with thirst; he relieved its fever by thrusting it forward from between his teeth into the cold air. How softly the turf had carpeted the untraveled avenue—he could no longer feel the roadway beneath his feet!

Doubtless, despite his suffering, he had fallen asleep while walking, for now he sees another scene—perhaps he has merely recovered from a delirium. He stands at the gate of his own home. All is as he left it, and all bright and beautiful in the morning sunshine. He must have traveled the entire night. As he pushes open the gate and passes up the wide white walk, he sees a flutter of female garments; his wife, looking fresh and cool and sweet, steps down from the veranda to meet him. At the bottom of the steps she stands waiting, with a smile of ineffable joy, an attitude of matchless grace and dignity. Ah, how beautiful she is! He springs forward with extended arms. As he is about to clasp her he feels a stunning blow upon the back of the neck; a blinding white light blazes all about him with a sound like the shock of a cannon—then all is darkness and silence!

Peyton Farquhar was dead; his body, with a broken neck, swung gently from side to side beneath the timbers of the Owl Creek bridge.

Nathaniel Hawthorne (1804–1864)

Young Goodman Brown   1835

Young Goodman Brown came forth at sunset, into the street of Salem village,° but put his head back, after crossing the threshold, to exchange a parting kiss with his young wife. And Faith, as the wife was aptly named, thrust her own pretty head into the street, letting the wind play with the pink ribbons of her cap, while she called to Goodman Brown.

"Dearest heart," whispered she, softly and rather sadly, when her lips were close to his ear, "prithee, put off your journey until sunrise, and sleep in your own bed to-night. A lone woman is troubled with such dreams and such thoughts, that she's afeard of herself, sometimes. Pray, tarry with me this night, dear husband, of all nights in the year!"

"My love and my Faith," replied young Goodman Brown, "of all nights in the year, this one night must I tarry away from thee. My journey, as thou callest it, forth and back again, must needs be done 'twixt now and sunrise. What, my sweet, pretty wife, dost thou doubt me already, and we but three months married!"

"Then God bless you!" said Faith with the pink ribbons, "and may you find all well, when you come back."

Salem village: in Massachusetts, about 15 miles north of Boston. The time of the story is the late seventeenth century.

"Amen!" cried Goodman Brown. "Say thy prayers, dear Faith, and go to bed at 5
dusk, and no harm will come to thee."

So they parted; and the young man pursued his way, until, being about to turn
the corner by the meeting-house, he looked back and saw the head of Faith still peep-
ing after him, with a melancholy air, in spite of her pink ribbons.

"Poor little Faith!" thought he, for his heart smote him. "What a wretch am I,
to leave her on such an errand! She talks of dreams, too. Methought, as she spoke, there
was trouble in her face, as if a dream had warned her what work is to be done to-night.
But no, no! 't would kill her to think it. Well; she's a blessed angel on earth; and after
this one night, I'll cling to her skirts and follow her to Heaven."

With this excellent resolve for the future, Goodman Brown felt himself justified
in making more haste on his present evil purpose. He had taken a dreary road, darkened by all the gloomiest trees of the forest, which barely stood aside to let the narrow
path creep through, and closed immediately behind. It was all as lonely as could be;
and there is this peculiarity in such a solitude, that the traveller knows not who may
be concealed by the innumerable trunks and the thick boughs overhead; so that, with
lonely footsteps, he may yet be passing through an unseen multitude.

"There may be a devilish Indian behind every tree," said Goodman Brown to
himself; and he glanced fearfully behind him, as he added, "What if the devil himself
should be at my very elbow!"

His head being turned back, he passed a crook of the road, and looking forward 10
again, beheld the figure of a man, in grave and decent attire, seated at the foot of an
old tree. He arose at Goodman Brown's approach, and walked onward, side by side
with him.

"You are late, Goodman Brown," said he. "The clock of the Old South° was striking, as I came through Boston; and that is full fifteen minutes agone."

"Faith kept me back awhile," replied the young man, with a tremor in his voice,
caused by the sudden appearance of his companion, though not wholly unexpected.

It was now deep dusk in the forest, and deepest in that part of it where these
two were journeying. As nearly as could be discerned, the second traveller was about
fifty years old, apparently in the same rank of life as Goodman Brown, and bearing a
considerable resemblance to him, though perhaps more in expression than features.
Still, they might have been taken for father and son. And yet, though the elder person
was as simply clad as the younger, and as simple in manner too, he had an indescrib-
able air of one who knew the world, and would not have felt abashed at the governor's dinner-table, or in King William's° court, were it possible that his affairs should
call him thither. But the only thing about him that could be fixed upon as remarkable,
was his staff, which bore the likeness of a great black snake, so curiously wrought, that
it might almost be seen to twist and wriggle itself like a living serpent. This, of course,
must have been an ocular deception, assisted by the uncertain light.

"Come, Goodman Brown!" cried his fellow-traveller, "this is a dull pace for the
beginning of a journey. Take my staff, if you are so soon weary."

"Friend," said the other, exchanging his slow pace for a full stop, "having kept 15

Old South: the Old South Church, in Boston, is still there.
King William: William III was King of England from 1688 to 1701; William IV was King from 1830
to 1837. Readers may choose the William that Hawthorne intends.

covenant by meeting thee here, it is my purpose now to return whence I came. I have scruples, touching the matter thou wot'st° of."

"Sayest thou so?" replied he of the serpent, smiling apart. "Let us walk on, nevertheless, reasoning as we go, and if I convince thee not, thou shalt turn back. We are but a little way in the forest, yet."

"Too far, too far!" exclaimed the goodman, unconsciously resuming his walk. "My father never went into the woods on such an errand, nor his father before him. We have been a race of honest men and good Christians, since the days of the martyrs.° And shall I be the first of the name of Brown that ever took this path and kept—"

"Such company, thou wouldst say," observed the elder person, interrupting his pause. "Well said, Goodman Brown! I have been as well acquainted with your family as with ever a one among the Puritans; and that's no trifle to say. I helped your grandfather, the constable, when he lashed the Quaker woman so smartly through the streets of Salem. And it was I that brought your father a pitch-pine knot, kindled at my own hearth, to set fire to an Indian village, in King Philip's war.° They were my good friends, both; and many a pleasant walk have we had along this path, and returned merrily after midnight. I would fain be friends with you, for their sake."

"If it be as thou sayest," replied Goodman Brown, "I marvel they never spoke of these matters. Or, verily, I marvel not, seeing that the least rumor of the sort would have driven them from New England. We are a people of prayer, and good works to boot, and abide no such wickedness."

20   "Wickedness or not," said the traveller with twisted staff, "I have a very general acquaintance here in New England. The deacons of many a church have drunk the communion wine with me; the selectmen, of divers towns, make me their chairman; and a majority of the Great and General Court are firm supporters of my interest. The governor and I, too—but these are state secrets."

"Can this be so!" cried Goodman Brown, with a stare of amazement at his undisturbed companion. "Howbeit, I have nothing to do with the governor and council; they have their own ways, and are no rule for a simple husbandman like me. But, were I to go on with thee, how should I meet the eye of that good old man, our minister, at Salem village? Oh, his voice would make me tremble, both Sabbath-day and lecture-day!"

Thus far, the elder traveller had listened with due gravity, but now burst into a fit of irrepressible mirth, shaking himself so violently, that his snakelike staff actually seemed to wriggle in sympathy.

"Ha! ha! ha!" shouted he, again and again; then composing himself, "Well, go on, Goodman Brown, go on; but, prithee, don't kill me with laughing!"

"Well, then, to end the matter at once," said Goodman Brown, considerably nettled, "there is my wife, Faith. It would break her dear little heart; and I'd rather break my own!"

---

thou wot'st: you know.

days of the martyrs: the martyrdoms of Protestants in England during the reign of Queen Mary (1553–1558).

King Philip's war (1675–1676): infamous for its cruelties, this war resulted in the suppression of Indian tribal life in New England and prepared the way for unlimited settlement of the area by European immigrants. "Philip" was the English name of Chief Metacomet of the Wampanoag Indian Tribe.

"Nay, if that be the case," answered the other, "e'en go thy ways, Goodman   25
Brown. I would not, for twenty old women like the one hobbling before us, that Faith
should come to any harm."

As he spoke, he pointed his staff at a female figure on the path, in whom Goodman Brown recognized a very pious and exemplary dame, who had taught him his
catechism in youth, and was still his moral and spiritual adviser, jointly with the minister and Deacon Gookin.

"A marvel, truly, that Goody° Cloyse should be so far in the wilderness, at nightfall!" said he. "But, with your leave, friend, I shall take a cut through the woods, until
we have left this Christian woman behind. Being a stranger to you, she might ask
whom I was consorting with, and whither I was going."

"Be it so," said his fellow-traveller. "Betake you to the woods, and let me keep
the path."

Accordingly, the young man turned aside, but took care to watch his companion, who advanced softly along the road, until he had come within a staff's length of
the old dame. She, meanwhile, was making the best of her way, with singular speed
for so aged a woman, and mumbling some indistinct words, a prayer, doubtless, as
she went. The traveller put forth his staff, and touched her withered neck with what
seemed the serpent's tail.

"The devil!" screamed the pious old lady.   30

"Then Goody Cloyse knows her old friend?" observed the traveller, confronting
her, and leaning on his writhing stick.

"Ah, forsooth, and is it your worship, indeed?" cried the good dame. "Yea, truly
is it, and in the very image of my old gossip,° Goodman Brown, the grandfather of the
silly fellow that now is. But, would your worship believe it? My broomstick hath
strangely disappeared, stolen, as I suspect, by that unhanged witch, Goody Cory,° and
that, too, when I was all anointed with the juice of smallage and cinquefoil and wolf's-
bane°—"

"Mingled with fine wheat and the fat of a new-born babe," said the shape of old
Goodman Brown.

"Ah, your worship knows the recipe," cried the old lady, cackling aloud. "So, as
I was saying, being all ready for the meeting, and no horse to ride on, I make up my
mind to foot it; for they tell me there is a nice young man to be taken into communion
to-night. But now your good worship will lend me your arm, and we shall be there in
a twinkling."

"That can hardly be," answered her friend. "I will not spare you my arm, Goody   35
Cloyse, but here is my staff, if you will."

So saying, he threw it down at her feet, where, perhaps, it assumed life, being
one of the rods which its owner had formerly lent to the Egyptian Magi.° Of this fact,
however, Goodman Brown could not take cognizance. He had cast up his eyes in

---

Goody: a shortened form of "goodwife," a respectful name for a married woman of low rank. A
"Goody Cloyse" was one of the women sentenced to execution by Hawthorne's great grandfather, Judge John Hathorne.
gossip: from "good sib" or "good relative."
Goody Cory: the name of a woman who was also sent to execution by Judge Hathorne.
smallage and cinquefoil and wolf's bane: plants especially associated with ointments made by
witches.
lent to the Egyptian Magi: see Exodus 7:10–12.

astonishment, and looking down again, beheld neither Goody Cloyse nor the serpentine staff, but his fellow-traveller alone, who waited for him as calmly as if nothing had happened.

"That old woman taught me my catechism!" said the young man; and there was a world of meaning in this simple comment.

They continued to walk onward, while the elder traveller exhorted his companion to make good speed and persevere in the path, discoursing so aptly, that his arguments seemed rather to spring up in the bosom of his auditor, than to be suggested by himself. As they went he plucked a branch of maple, to serve for a walking stick, and began to strip it of the twigs and little boughs, which were wet with evening dew. The moment his fingers touched them, they became strangely withered and dried up, as with a week's sunshine. Thus the pair proceeded, at a good free pace, until suddenly, in a gloomy hollow of the road, Goodman Brown sat himself down on the stump of a tree, and refused to go any farther.

"Friend," said he, stubbornly, "my mind is made up. Not another step will I budge on this errand. What if a wretched old woman do choose to go to the devil, when I thought she was going to Heaven! Is that any reason why I should quit my dear Faith, and go after her?"

40   "You will think better of this by and by," said his acquaintance, composedly. "Sit here and rest yourself a while; and when you feel like moving again, there is my staff to help you along."

Without more words, he threw his companion the maple stick, and was as speedily out of sight as if he had vanished into the deepening gloom. The young man sat a few moments by the roadside, applauding himself greatly, and thinking with how clear a conscience he should meet the minister, in his morning walk, nor shrink from the eye of good old Deacon Gookin. And what calm sleep would be his, that very night, which was to have been spent so wickedly, but purely and sweetly now, in the arms of Faith! Amidst these pleasant and praiseworthy meditations, Goodman Brown heard the tramp of horses along the road, and deemed it advisable to conceal himself within the verge of the forest, conscious of the guilty purpose that had brought him thither, though now so happily turned from it.

On came the hoof-tramps and the voices of the riders, two grave old voices, conversing soberly as they drew near. These mingled sounds appeared to pass along the road, within a few yards of the young man's hiding-place; but owing, doubtless, to the depth of the gloom, at that particular spot, neither the travellers nor their steeds were visible. Though their figures brushed the small boughs by the wayside, it could not be seen that they intercepted, even for a moment, the faint gleam from the strip of bright sky, athwart which they must have passed. Goodman Brown alternately crouched and stood on tiptoe, pulling aside the branches, and thrusting forth his head as far as he durst, without discerning so much as a shadow. It vexed him the more, because he could have sworn, were such a thing possible, that he recognized the voices of the minister and Deacon Gookin, jogging° along quietly, as they were wont to do, when bound to some ordination or ecclesiastical council. While yet within hearing, one of the riders stopped to pluck a switch.

"Of the two, reverend Sir," said the voice like the deacon's, "I had rather miss

jogging: riding a horse at a slow trot.

an ordination dinner than to-night's meeting. They tell me that some of our community are to be here from Falmouth and beyond, and others from Connecticut and Rhode Island; besides several of the Indian powwows,° who, after their fashion, know almost as much deviltry as the best of us. Moreover, there is a goodly young woman to be taken into communion."

"Mighty well, Deacon Gookin!" replied the solemn old tones of the minister. "Spur up, or we shall be late. Nothing can be done, you know, until I get on the ground."

The hoofs clattered again, and the voices, talking so strangely in the empty air,   45
passed on through the forest, where no church had ever been gathered, nor solitary Christian prayed. Whither, then, could these holy men be journeying, so deep into the heathen wilderness? Young Goodman Brown caught hold of a tree, for support, being ready to sink down on the ground, faint and over-burthened with the heavy sickness of his heart. He looked up to the sky, doubting whether there really was a Heaven above him. Yet, there was the blue arch, and the stars brightening in it.

"With Heaven above, and Faith below, I will yet stand firm against the devil!" cried Goodman Brown.

While he still gazed upward, into the deep arch of the firmament, and had lifted his hands to pray, a cloud, though no wind was stirring, hurried across the zenith, and hid the brightening stars. The blue sky was still visible, except directly overhead, where this black mass of cloud was sweeping swiftly northward. Aloft in the air, as if from the depths of the cloud, came a confused and doubtful sound of voices. Once, the listener fancied that he could distinguish the accent of town's-people of his own, men and women, both pious and ungodly, many of whom he had met at the communion-table, and had seen others rioting at the tavern. The next moment, so indistinct were the sounds, he doubted whether he had heard aught but the murmur of the old forest, whispering without a wind. Then came a stronger swell of those familiar tones, heard daily in the sunshine, at Salem village, but never, until now, from a cloud at night. There was one voice, of a young woman, uttering lamentations, yet with an uncertain sorrow, and entreating for some favor, which, perhaps, it would grieve her to obtain. And all the unseen multitude, both saints and sinners, seemed to encourage her onward.

"Faith!" shouted Goodman Brown, in a voice of agony and desperation; and the echoes of the forest mocked him, crying—"Faith! Faith!" as if bewildered wretches were seeking her, all through the wilderness.

The cry of grief, rage, and terror was yet piercing the night, when the unhappy husband held his breath for a response. There was a scream, drowned immediately in a louder murmur of voices fading into far-off laughter, as the dark cloud swept away, leaving the clear and silent sky above Goodman Brown. But something flutttered lightly down through the air, and caught on the branch of a tree. The young man seized it and beheld a pink ribbon.

"My Faith is gone!" cried he, after one stupefied moment. "There is no good on   50
earth, and sin is but a name. Come, devil! for to thee is this world given."

And maddened with despair, so that he laughed loud and long, did Goodman Brown grasp his staff and set forth again, at such a rate, that he seemed to fly along

powwow: a Narragansett Indian word describing a ritual ceremony of dancing, incantation, and magic.

the forest path, rather than to walk or run. The road grew wilder and drearier, and more faintly traced, and vanished at length, leaving him in the heart of the dark wilderness, still rushing onward, with the instinct that guides mortal man to evil. The whole forest was peopled with frightful sounds; the creaking of the trees, the howling of wild beasts, and the yell of Indians; while, sometimes, the wind tolled like a distant church bell, and sometimes gave a broad roar around the traveller, as if all Nature were laughing him to scorn. But he was himself the chief horror of the scene, and shrank not from its other horrors.

"Ha! ha! ha!" roared Goodman Brown, when the wind laughed at him. "Let us hear which will laugh loudest! Think not to frighten me with your deviltry! Come witch, come wizard, come Indian powwow, come devil himself! and here comes Goodman Brown. You may as well fear him as he fear you!"

In truth, all through the haunted forest, there could be nothing more frightful than the figure of Goodman Brown. On he flew, among the black pines, brandishing his staff with frenzied gestures, now giving vent to an inspiration of horrid blasphemy, and now shouting forth such laughter, as set all the echoes of the forest laughing like demons around him. The fiend in his own shape is less hideous, than when he rages in the breast of man. Thus sped the demoniac on his course, until, quivering among the trees, he saw a red light before him, as when the felled trunks and branches of a clearing have been set on fire, and throw up their lurid blaze against the sky, at the hour of midnight. He paused, in a lull of the tempest that had driven him onward, and heard the swell of what seemed a hymn, rolling solemnly from a distance, with the weight of many voices. He knew the tune. It was a familiar one in the choir of the village meeting-house. The verse died heavily away, and was lengthened by a chorus, not of human voices, but of all the sounds of the benighted wilderness, pealing in awful harmony together. Goodman Brown cried out; and his cry was lost to his own ear, by its unison with the cry of the desert.

In the interval of silence, he stole forward, until the light glared full upon his eyes. At one extremity of an open space, hemmed in by the dark wall of the forest, arose a rock, bearing some rude, natural resemblance either to an altar or a pulpit, and surrounded by four blazing pines, their tops aflame, their stems untouched, like candles at an evening meeting. The mass of foliage, that had overgrown the summit of the rock, was all on fire, blazing high into the night, and fitfully illuminating the whole field. Each pendent twig and leafy festoon was in a blaze. As the red light arose and fell, a numerous congregation alternately shone forth, then disappeared in shadow, and again grew, as it were, out of the darkness, peopling the heart of the solitary woods at once.

55   "A grave and dark-clad company!" quoth Goodman Brown.

In truth they were such. Among them, quivering to-and-fro, between gloom and splendor, appeared faces that would be seen, next day, at the council-board of the province, and others which, Sabbath after Sabbath, looked devoutly heavenward, and benignantly over the crowded pews, from the holiest pulpits in the land. Some affirm that the lady of the governor was there. At least, there were high dames well known to her, and wives of honored husbands, and widows a great multitude, and ancient maidens, all of excellent repute, and fair young girls, who trembled lest their mothers should espy them. Either the sudden gleams of light, flashing over the obscure field, bedazzled Goodman Brown, or he recognized a score of the church members of Salem village, famous for their especial sanctity. Good old Deacon Gookin had arrived, and waited at the skirts of that venerable saint, his reverend pastor. But, irreverently consorting with these grave, reputable, and pious people, these elders of the church, these chaste dames and dewy virgins, there were men of dissolute lives and women of spotted fame, wretches given over to all mean and filthy vice, and suspected even of horrid crimes. It was strange to see, that the good shrank not from the wicked, nor were the sinners abashed by the saints. Scattered, also, among their pale-faced enemies, were the Indian priests, or powwows, who had often scared their native forest with more hideous incantations than any known to English witchcraft.

"But, where is Faith?" thought Goodman Brown; and, as hope came into his heart, he trembled.

Another verse of the hymn arose, a slow and mournful strain, such as the pious love, but joined to words which expressed all that our nature can conceive of sin, and darkly hinted at far more. Unfathomable to mere mortals is the lore of fiends. Verse after verse was sung, and still the chorus of the desert swelled between, like the deepest tone of a mighty organ. And, with the final peal of that dreadful anthem, there came a sound, as if the roaring wind, the rushing streams, the howling beasts, and every other voice of the unconverted wilderness were mingling and according with the voice of guilty man, in homage to the prince of all. The four blazing pines threw up a loftier flame, and obscurely discovered shapes and visages of horror on the smoke-wreaths, above the impious assembly. At the same moment, the fire on the rock shot redly forth, and formed a glowing arch above its base, where now appeared a figure. With reverence be it spoken, the apparition bore no slight similitude, both in garb and manner, to some grave divine of the New England churches.

"Bring forth the converts!" cried a voice, that echoed through the field and rolled into the forest.

At the word, Goodman Brown stepped forth from the shadow of the trees, and 60 approached the congregation, with whom he felt a loathful brotherhood, by the sympathy of all that was wicked in his heart. He could have well-nigh sworn, that the shape of his own dead father beckoned him to advance, looking downward from a smoke-wreath, while a woman, with dim features of despair, threw out her hand to warn him back. Was it his mother? But he had no power to retreat one step, nor to resist, even in thought, when the minister and good old Deacon Gookin seized his arms, and led him to the blazing rock. Thither came also the slender form of a veiled female, led between Goody Cloyse, that pious teacher of the catechism, and Martha Carrier, who had received the devil's promise to be queen of hell. A rampant hag was she! And there stood the proselytes, beneath the canopy of fire.

"Welcome, my children," said the dark figure, "to the communion of your race! Ye have found, thus young, your nature and your destiny. My children, look behind you!"

They turned; and flashing forth, as it were, in a sheet of flame, the fiend-worshippers were seen; the smile of welcome gleamed darkly on every visage.

"There," resumed the sable form, "are all whom ye have reverenced from youth. Ye deemed them holier than yourselves, and shrank from your own sin, contrasting it with their lives of righteousness and prayerful aspirations heavenward. Yet, here are they all, in my worshipping assembly! This night it shall be granted you to know their secret deeds; how hoary-bearded elders of the church have whispered wanton words to the young maids of their households; how many a woman, eager for widow's weeds, has given her husband a drink at bedtime, and let him sleep his last sleep in her bosom; how beardless youths have made haste to inherit their father's wealth; and how fair damsels—blush not, sweet ones!—have dug little graves in the garden, and bidden me, the sole guest, to an infant's funeral. By the sympathy of your human hearts for sin, ye shall scent out all the places—whether in church, bed-chamber, street, field, or forest—where crime has been committed, and shall exult to behold the whole earth one stain of guilt, one mighty blood-spot. Far more than this! It shall be yours to penetrate, in every bosom, the deep mystery of sin, the fountain of all wicked arts, and which inexhaustibly supplies more evil impulses than human power—than my power, at its utmost!—can make manifest in deeds. And now, my children, look upon each other."

They did so; and, by the blaze of the hell-kindled torches, the wretched man beheld his Faith, and the wife her husband, trembling before that unhallowed altar.

65   "Lo! there ye stand, my children," said the figure, in a deep and solemn tone, almost sad, with its despairing awfulness, as if his once angelic nature° could yet mourn for our miserable race. "Depending upon one another's hearts, ye had still hoped that virtue were not all a dream! Now are ye undeceived!—Evil is the nature of mankind. Evil must be your only happiness. Welcome, again, my children, to the communion of your race!"

"Welcome!" repeated the fiend-worshippers, in one cry of despair and triumph.

And there they stood, the only pair, as it seemed, who were yet hesitating on the verge of wickedness, in this dark world. A basin was hollowed, naturally, in the rock. Did it contain water, reddened by the lurid light? or was it blood? or, perchance, a liquid flame? Herein did the Shape of Evil dip his hand, and prepare to lay the mark of baptism upon their foreheads, that they might be partakers of the mystery of sin, more conscious of the secret guilt of others, both in deed and thought, than they could now be of their own. The husband cast one look at his pale wife, and Faith at him. What polluted wretches would the next glance show them to each other, shuddering alike at what they disclosed and what they saw!

"Faith! Faith!" cried the husband. "Look up to Heaven, and resist the Wicked One!"

Whether Faith obeyed, he knew not. Hardly had he spoken, when he found himself amid calm night and solitude, listening to a roar of the wind, which died heavily away through the forest. He staggered against the rock, and felt it chill and damp, while a hanging twig, that had been all on fire, besprinkled his cheek with the coldest dew.

70   The next morning, young Goodman Brown came slowly into the street of Salem village staring around him like a bewildered man. The good old minister was taking a walk along the grave-yard, to get an appetite for breakfast and meditate his sermon, and bestowed a blessing, as he passed, on Goodman Brown. He shrank from the venerable saint, as if to avoid an anathema. Old Deacon Gookin was at domestic worship, and the holy words of his prayer were heard through the open window. "What God doth the wizard pray to!" quoth Goodman Brown. Goody Cloyse, that excellent old Christian, stood in the early sunshine, at her own lattice, catechising a little girl, who had brought her a pint of morning's milk. Goodman Brown snatched away the child, as from the grasp of the fiend himself. Turning the corner by the meetinghouse, he

---

once angelic nature: Lucifer, or the devil, had led the traditional revolt of the angels, and was thrown into hell as his punishment. See Isaiah 14:12–15.

spied the head of Faith, with the pink ribbons, gazing anxiously forth, and bursting into such joy at sight of him that she skipt along the street, and almost kissed her husband before the whole village. But Goodman Brown looked sternly and sadly into her face, and passed on without a greeting.

Had Goodman Brown fallen asleep in the forest, and only dreamed a wild dream of a witch-meeting?

Be it so, if you will. But, alas! it was a dream of evil omen for young Goodman Brown. A stern, a sad, a darkly meditative, a distrustful, if not a desperate man did he become, from the night of that fearful dream. On the Sabbath day, when the congregation were singing a holy psalm, he could not listen, because an anthem of sin rushed loudly upon his ear, and drowned all the blessed strain. When the minister spoke from the pulpit, with power and fervid eloquence, and with his hand on the open Bible, of the sacred truths of our religion, and of saint-like lives and triumphant deaths, and of future bliss or misery unutterable, then did Goodman Brown turn pale, dreading lest the roof should thunder down upon the gray blasphemer and his hearers. Often, awaking suddenly at midnight, he shrank from the bosom of Faith, and at morning or eventide, when the family knelt down at prayer, he scowled, and muttered to himself, and gazed sternly at his wife, and turned away. And when he had lived long, and was borne to his grave, a hoary corpse, followed by Faith, an aged woman, and children and grandchildren, a goodly procession, besides neighbors not a few, they carved no hopeful verse upon his tombstone; for his dying hour was gloom.

Katherine Mansfield (1888–1923)

Miss Brill   1920

Although it was so brilliantly fine—the blue sky powdered with gold and great spots of light like white wine splashed over the Jardins Publiques°—Miss Brill was glad that she had decided on her fur. The air was motionless, but when you opened your mouth there was just a faint chill, like a chill from a glass of iced water before you sip, and now and again a leaf came drifting—from nowhere, from the sky. Miss Brill put up her hand and touched her fur. Dear little thing! It was nice to feel it again. She had taken it out of its box that afternoon, shaken out the moth-powder, given it a good brush, and rubbed the life back into the dim little eyes. "What has been happening to me?" said the sad little eyes. Oh, how sweet it was to see them snap at her again from the red eiderdown! . . . But the nose, which was of some black composition, wasn't at

Jardins Publiques: public gardens, or public park. The setting of the story is a seaside town in France.

all firm. It must have had a knock, somehow. Never mind—a little dab of black seal-ing-wax when the time came—when it was absolutely necessary. . . . Little rogue! Yes, she really felt like that about it. Little rogue biting its tail just by her left ear. She could have taken it off and laid it on her lap and stroked it. She felt a tingling in her hands and arms, but that came from walking, she supposed. And when she breathed, some-thing light and sad—no, not sad, exactly—something gentle seemed to move in her bosom.

There were a number of people out this afternoon, far more than last Sunday. And the band sounded louder and gayer. That was because the Season had begun. For although the band played all the year round on Sundays, out of season it was never the same. It was like some one playing with only the family to listen; it didn't care how it played if there weren't any strangers present. Wasn't the conductor wearing a new coat, too? She was sure it was new. He scraped with his foot and flapped his arms like a rooster about to crow, and the bandsmen sitting in the green rotunda blew out their cheeks and glared at the music. Now there came a little "flutey" bit—very pretty!—a little chain of bright drops. She was sure it would be repeated. It was; she lifted her head and smiled.

Only two people shared her "special" seat: a fine old man in a velvet coat, his hands clasped over a huge carved walking-stick, and a big old woman, sitting upright, with a roll of knitting on her embroidered apron. They did not speak. This was dis-appointing, for Miss Brill always looked forward to the conversation. She had become really quite expert, she thought, at listening as though she didn't listen, at sitting in other people's lives just for a minute while they talked round her.

She glanced, sideways, at the old couple. Perhaps they would go soon. Last Sun-day, too, hadn't been as interesting as usual. An Englishman and his wife, he wearing a dreadful Panama hat and she button boots. And she'd gone on the whole time about how she ought to wear spectacles; she knew she needed them; but that it was no good getting any; they'd be sure to break and they'd never keep on. And he'd been so patient. He'd suggested everything—gold rims, the kind that curved round your ears, little pads inside the bridge. No, nothing would please her. "They'll always be sliding down my nose!" Miss Brill had wanted to shake her.

5   The old people sat on the bench, still as statues. Never mind, there was always the crowd to watch. To and fro, in front of the flower-beds and the band rotunda, the couples and groups paraded, stopped to talk, to greet, to buy a handful of flowers from the old beggar who had his tray fixed to the railings. Little children ran among them, swooping and laughing; little boys with big white silk bows under their chins, little girls, little French dolls, dressed up in velvet and lace. And sometimes a tiny staggerer came suddenly rocking into the open from under the trees, stopped, stared, as sud-denly sat down "flop," until its small high-stepping mother, like a young hen, rushed scolding to its rescue. Other people sat on the benches and green chairs, but they were nearly always the same, Sunday after Sunday, and—Miss Brill had often noticed—there was something funny about nearly all of them. They were odd, silent, nearly all old, and from the way they stared they looked as though they'd just come from dark little rooms or even—even cupboards!°

Behind the rotunda the slender trees with yellow leaves down drooping, and through them just a line of sea, and beyond the blue sky with gold-veined clouds.

cupboards: rooms designed for china but remodeled for a lodger; the tiniest of rooms.

Tum-tum-tum tiddle-um! tiddle-um! tum tiddley-um tum ta! blew the band.

Two young girls in red came by and two young soldiers in blue met them, and they laughed and paired and went off arm-in-arm. Two peasant women with funny straw hats passed, gravely, leading beautiful smoke-coloured donkeys. A cold, pale nun hurried by. A beautiful woman came along and dropped her bunch of violets, and a little boy ran after to hand them to her, and she took them and threw them away as if they'd been poisoned. Dear me! Miss Brill didn't know whether to admire that or not! And now an ermine toque° and a gentleman in grey met just in front of her. He was tall, stiff, dignified, and she was wearing the ermine toque she'd bought when her hair was yellow. Now everything, her hair, her face, even her eyes, was the same colour as the shabby ermine, and her hand, in its cleaned glove, lifted to dab her lips, was a tiny yellowish paw. Oh, she was so pleased to see him—delighted! She rather thought they were going to meet that afternoon. She described where she'd been—everywhere, here, there, along by the sea. The day was so charming—didn't he agree? And wouldn't he, perhaps? . . . But he shook his head, lighted a cigarette, slowly breathed a great deep puff into her face, and, even while she was still talking and laughing, flicked the match away and walked on. The ermine toque was alone; she smiled more brightly than ever. But even the band seemed to know what she was feeling and played more softly, played tenderly, and the drum beat, "The Brute! The Brute!" over and over. What would she do? What was going to happen now? But as Miss Brill wondered, the ermine toque turned, raised her hand as though she'd seen some one else, much nicer, just over there, and pattered away. And the band changed again and played more quickly, more gaily than ever, and the old couple on Miss Brill's seat got up and marched away, and such a funny old man with long whiskers hobbled along in time to the music and was nearly knocked over by four girls walking abreast.

Oh, how fascinating it was! How she enjoyed it! How she loved sitting here, watching it all! It was like a play. It was exactly like a play. Who could believe the sky at the back wasn't painted? But it wasn't till a little brown dog trotted on solemn and then slowly trotted off, like a little "theatre" dog, a little dog that had been drugged, that Miss Brill discovered what it was that made it so exciting. They were all on the stage. They weren't only the audience, not only looking on; they were acting. Even she had a part and came every Sunday. No doubt somebody would have noticed if she hadn't been there; she was part of the performance after all. How strange she'd never thought of it like that before! And yet it explained why she made such a point of starting from home at just the same time each week—so as not to be late for the performance—and it also explained why she had quite a queer, shy feeling at telling her English pupils how she spent her Sunday afternoons. No wonder! Miss Brill nearly laughed out loud. She was on the stage. She thought of the old invalid gentleman to whom she read the newspaper four afternoons a week while he slept in the garden. She had got quite used to the frail head on the cotton pillow, the hollowed eyes, the open mouth and the high pinched nose. If he'd been dead she mightn't have noticed for weeks; she wouldn't have minded. But suddenly he knew he was having the paper read to him by an actress! "An actress!" The old head lifted; two points of light quivered in the old eyes. "An actress—are ye?" And Miss Brill smoothed the newspaper

---

toque: a hat. The phrase "ermine toque" refers to a woman wearing a hat made of the fur of a weasel.

as though it were the manuscript of her part and said gently: "Yes, I have been an actress for a long time."

10   The band had been having a rest. Now they started again. And what they played was warm, sunny, yet there was just a faint chill—a something, what was it?—not sadness—no, not sadness—a something that made you want to sing. The tune lifted, lifted, the light shone; and it seemed to Miss Brill that in another moment all of them, all the whole company, would begin singing. The young ones, the laughing ones who were moving together, they would begin, and the men's voices, very resolute and brave, would join them. And then she too, she too, and the others on the benches—they would come in with a kind of accompaniment—something low, that scarcely rose or fell, something so beautiful—moving. . . . And Miss Brill's eyes filled with tears and she looked smiling at all the other members of the company. Yes, we understand, we understand, she thought—though what they understood she didn't know.

Just at that moment a boy and a girl came and sat down where the old couple had been. They were beautifully dressed; they were in love. The hero and heroine, of course, just arrived from his father's yacht. And still soundlessly singing, still with that trembling smile, Miss Brill prepared to listen.

"No, not now," said the girl. "Not here, I can't."

"But why? Because of that stupid old thing at the other end there?" asked the boy. "Why does she come here at all—who wants her? Why doesn't she keep her silly old mug at home?"

"It's her fu-fur which is so funny," giggled the. girl. "It's exactly like a fried whiting."

15   "Ah, be off with you!" said the boy in an angry whisper. Then: "Tell me, ma petite chérie—"

"No, not here," said the girl. "Not *yet*,"

On her way home she usually bought a slice of honeycake at the baker's. It was her Sunday treat. Sometimes there was an almond in her slice, sometimes not. It made a great difference. If there was an almond it was like carrying home a tiny present—a surprise—something that might very well not have been there. She hurried on the almond Sundays and struck the match for the kettle in quite a dashing way.

But to-day she passed the baker's by, climbed the stairs, went into the little dark room—her room like a cupboard—and sat down on the red eiderdown. She sat there for a long time. The box that the fur came out of was on the bed. She unclasped the necklet quickly; quickly, without looking, laid it inside. But when she put the lid on she thought she heard something crying.

Edgar Allan Poe (1809–1845)

The Cask of Amontillado 1846

The thousand injuries of Fortunato I had borne as I best could; but when he ventured upon insult, I vowed revenge. You, who so well know the nature of my soul, will not suppose, however, that I gave utterance to a threat. *At length* I would be avenged: this was a point definitively settled—but the very definitiveness with which it was resolved, precluded the idea of risk. I must not only punish, but punish with impunity. A wrong is unredressed when retribution overtakes its redresser. It is equally unredressed when the avenger fails to make himself felt as such to him who has done the wrong.

It must be understood, that neither by word nor deed had I given Fortunato cause to doubt my good-will. I continued, as was my wont, to smile in his face, and he did not perceive that my smile *now* was at the thought of his immolation.

He had a weak point—this Fortunato—although in other regards he was a man to be respected and even feared. He prided himself on his connoisseurship in wine. Few Italians have the true virtuoso spirit. For the most part their enthusiasm is adopted to suit the time and opportunity—to practice imposture upon the British and Austrian millionaires. In painting and gemmary Fortunato, like his countrymen, was a quack—but in the matter of old wines he was sincere. In this respect I did not differ from him materially: I was skilful in the Italian vintages myself, and bought largely whenever I could.

It was about dusk, one evening during the supreme madness of the carnival season, that I encountered my friend. He accosted me with excessive warmth, for he had been drinking much. The man wore motley. He had on a tight-fitting parti-striped dress, and his head was surmounted by the conical cap and bells. I was so pleased to see him, that I thought I should never have done wringing his hand.

I said to him: "My dear Fortunato, you are luckily met. How remarkably well you are looking today! But I have received a pipe of what passes for Amontillado, and I have my doubts." 5

"How?" said he. "Amontillado? A pipe? Impossible! And in the middle of the carnival!"

"I have my doubts," I replied; "and I was silly enough to pay the full Amontillado price without consulting you in the matter. You were not to be found, and I was fearful of losing a bargain."

"Amontillado!"

"I have my doubts."

"Amontillado!" 10

"And I must satisfy them."

"Amontillado!"

"As you are engaged, I am on my way to Luchesi. If anyone has a critical turn, it is he: He will tell me—"

"Luchesi cannot tell Amontillado from Sherry."

15   "And yet some fools will have it that his taste is a match for your own."

"Come, let us go."

"Whither?"

"To your vaults."

"My friend, no; I will not impose upon your good nature. I perceive you have an engagement. Luchesi—"

20   "I have no engagement;—come."

"My friend, no. It is not the engagement, but the severe cold with which I perceive you are afflicted. The vaults are insufferably damp. They are encrusted with nitre."

"Let us go, nevertheless. The cold is merely nothing. Amontillado! You have been imposed upon. And as for Luchesi, he cannot distinguish Sherry from Amontillado."

Thus speaking, Fortunato possessed himself of my arm. Putting on a mask of black silk, and drawing a *roquelaire* closely about my person, I suffered him to hurry me to my palazzo.

There were no attendants at home; they had absconded to make merry in honor of the time. I had told them that I should not return until the morning, and had given them explicit orders not to stir from the house. These orders were sufficient, I well knew, to insure their immediate disappearance, one and all, as soon as my back was turned.

25   I took from their sconces two flambeaux, and giving one to Fortunato, bowed him through several suites of rooms to the archway that led into the vaults. I passed down a long and winding staircase, requesting him to be cautious as he followed. We came at length to the foot of the descent, and stood together on the damp ground of the catacombs of the Montresors.

The gait of my friend was unsteady, and the bells upon his cap jingled as he strode.

"The pipe?" said he.

"It is farther on," said I; "but observe the white webwork which gleams from these cavern walls."

He turned toward me, and looked into my eyes with two filmy orbs that distilled the rheum of intoxication.

30   "Nitre?" he asked, at length.

"Nitre," I replied. "How long have you had that cough?"

"Ugh! ugh! ugh!—ugh! ugh! ugh!—ugh! ugh! ugh!—ugh! ugh! ugh!—ugh! ugh! ugh!"

My poor friend found it impossible to reply for many minutes.

"It is nothing," he said at last.

35   "Come," I said, with decision, "we will go back; your health is precious. You are rich, respected, admired, beloved; you are happy, as once I was. You are a man to be missed. For me it is no matter. We will go back; you will be ill, and I cannot be responsible. Besides, there is Luchesi—"

"Enough," he said; "the cough is a mere nothing; it will not kill me. I shall not die of a cough."

"True—true," I replied; "and, indeed, I had no intention of alarming you unnecessarily; but you should use all proper caution. A draught of this Medoc will defend us from the damps."

Here I knocked off the neck of a bottle which I drew from a long row of its fellows that lay upon the mould.

"Drink," I said, presenting him the wine.

He raised it to his lips with a leer. He paused and nodded to me familiarly, while his bells jingled.   40

"I drink," he said, "to the buried that repose around us."

"And I to your long life."

He again took my arm, and we proceeded.

"These vaults," he said, "are extensive."

"The Montresors," I replied, "were a great and numerous family."   45

"I forget your arms."

"A huge human foot *d'or*, in a field azure; the foot crushes a serpent rampant whose fangs are imbedded in the heel."

"And the motto?"

"Nemo me impune lacessit."

"Good!" he said.   50

The wine sparkled in his eyes and the bells jingled. My own fancy grew warm with the Medoc. We had passed through walls of piled bones, with casks and puncheons intermingling, into the inmost recesses of the catacombs. I paused again, and this time I made bold to seize Fortunato by an arm above the elbow.

"The nitre!" I said; "see, it increases. It hangs like moss upon the vaults. We are below the river's bed. The drops of moisture trickle among the bones. Come, we will go back ere it is too late. Your cough—"

"It is nothing," he said; "let us go on. But first, another draught of the Medoc."

I broke and reached him a flagon of De Grâve. He emptied it at a breath. His eyes flashed with a fierce light. He laughed and threw the bottle upward with a gesticulation I did not understand.

I looked at him in surprise. He repeated the movement—a grotesque one.   55

"You do not comprehend?" he said.

"Not I," I replied.

"Then you are not of the brotherhood."

"How?"

"You are not of the Masons."   60

"Yes, yes," I said; "yes, yes."

"You? Impossible! A Mason?"

"A Mason," I replied.

"A sign," he said.

"It is this," I answered, producing a trowel from beneath the folds of my *roque-*   65
laire.

"You jest," he exclaimed, recoiling a few paces. "But let us proceed to the Amontillado."

"Be it so," I said, replacing the tool beneath the cloak, and again offering him my arm. He leaned upon it heavily. We continued our route in search of the Amontillado. We passed through a range of low arches, descended, passed on, and descend-

ing again, arrived at a deep crypt, in which the foulness of the air caused our flambeaux rather to glow than flame.

At the most remote end of the crypt there appeared another less spacious. Its
walls had been lined with human remains, piled to the vault overhead, in the fashion
of the great catacombs of Paris. Three sides of this interior crypt were still ornamented
in this manner. From the fourth the bones had been thrown down, and lay promiscu-
ously upon the earth, forming at one point a mound of some size. Within the wall thus
exposed by the displacing of the bones, we perceived a still interior recess, in depth
about four feet, in width three, in height six or seven. It seemed to have been con-
structed for no especial use within itself, but formed merely the interval between two
of the colossal supports of the roof of the catacombs, and was backed by one of their
circumscribing walls of solid granite.

It was in vain that Fortunato, uplifting his dull torch, endeavored to pry into the
depth of the recess. Its termination the feeble light did not enable us to see.

70   "Proceed," I said; "herein is the Amontillado. As for Luchesi—"

"He is an ignoramus," interrupted my friend, as he stepped unsteadily forward,
while I followed immediately at his heels. In an instant he had reached the extremity
of the niche, and finding his progress arrested by the rock, stood stupidly bewildered.
A moment more and I had fettered him to the granite. In its surface were two iron sta-
ples, distant from each other about two feet, horizontally. From one of these depended
a short chain, from the other a padlock. Throwing the links about his waist, it was but
the work of a few seconds to secure it. He was too much astounded to resist. Withdrawing the key I stepped back from the recess.

"Pass your hand," I said, "over the wall; you cannot help feeling the nitre.
Indeed it is *very* damp. Once more let me *implore* you to return. No? Then I must positively leave you. But I must first render you all the little attentions in my power."

"The Amontillado!" ejaculated my friend, not yet recovered from his astonishment.

"True," I replied; "the Amontillado."

75   As I said these words I busied myself among the pile of bones of which I have
before spoken. Throwing them aside, I soon uncovered a quantity of building stone
and mortar. With these materials and with the aid of my trowel, I began vigorously to
wall up the entrance of the niche.

I had scarcely laid the first tier of the masonry when I discovered that the intoxication of Fortunato had in a great measure worn off. The earliest indication I had of
this was a low moaning cry from the depth of the recess. It was *not* the cry of a drunken
man. There was then a long and obstinate silence. I laid the second tier, and the third,
and the fourth; and then I heard the furious vibrations of the chain. The noise lasted
for several minutes, during which, that I might hearken to it with the more satisfaction, I ceased my labors and sat down upon the bones. When at last the clanking sub-
sided, I resumed the trowel, and finished without interruption the fifth, the sixth, and
the seventh tier. The wall was now nearly upon a level with my breast. I again paused,
and holding the flambeaux over the mason-work, threw a few feeble rays upon the
figure within.

A succession of loud and shrill screams, bursting suddenly from the throat of
the chained form, seemed to thrust me violently back. For a brief moment I hesitated—
I trembled. Unsheathing my rapier, I began to grope with it about the recess; but the
thought of an instant reassured me. I placed my hand upon the solid fabric of the cat-

acombs, and felt satisfied. I reapproached the wall. I replied to the yells of him who clamored. I reechoed—I aided—I surpassed them in volume and in strength. I did this, and the clamorer grew still.

It was now midnight, and my task was drawing to a close. I had completed the eighth, the ninth, and the tenth tier. I had finished a portion of the last and the eleventh; there remained but a single stone to be fitted and plastered in. I struggled with its weight; I placed it partially in its destined position. But now there came from out the niche a low laugh that erected the hairs upon my head. It was succeeded by a sad voice, which I had difficulty in recognizing as that of the noble Fortunato. The voice said—

"Ha! ha! ha!—he! he!—a very good joke indeed—an excellent jest. We will have many a rich laugh about it at the palazzo—he! he! he!—over our wine—he! he! he!"

"The Amontillado!" I said.   *80*

"He! he! he!—he! he! he!—yes, the Amontillado. But is it not getting late? Will not they be awaiting us at the palazzo, the Lady Fortunato and the rest? Let us be gone."

"Yes," I said, "let us be gone."

"For the love of God, Montresor!"

"Yes," I said, "for the love of God!"

But to these words I hearkened in vain for a reply. I grew impatient. I called   *85*
aloud:

"Fortunato!"

No answer. I called again:

"Fortunato!"

No answer still. I thrust a torch through the remaining aperture and let it fall within. There came forth in return only a jingling of the bells. My heart grew sick—on account of the dampness of the catacombs. I hastened to make an end of my labor. I forced the last stone into its position; I plastered it up. Against the new masonry I reerected the old rampart of bones. For the half of a century no mortal has disturbed them. *In pace requiescat!*

Mark Twain (1835–1910)

Luck[1]   1891

It was at a banquet in London in honor of one of the two or three conspicuously illustrious English military names of this generation. For reasons which will presently appear, I will withhold his real name and titles and call him Lieutenant-General Lord Arthur Scoresby, Y.C., K.C.B., etc., etc. What a fascination there is in a renowned name! There sat the man, in actual flesh, whom I had heard of so many thousands of times

---

[1]This is not a fancy sketch. I got it from a clergyman who was an instructor at Woolwich forty years ago, and who vouched for its truth. [Twain's note.]

since that day, thirty years before, when his name shot suddenly to the zenith from a Crimean battlefield,° to remain forever celebrated. It was food and drink to me to look, and look, and look at that demi-god; scanning, searching, noting: the quietness, the reserve, the noble gravity of his countenance; the simple honesty that expressed itself all over him; the sweet unconsciousness of his greatness—unconsciousness of the hundreds of admiring eyes fastened upon him, unconsciousness of the deep, loving, sincere worship welling out of the breasts of those people and flowing toward him.

The clergyman at my left was an old acquaintance of mine—clergyman now, but had spent the first half of his life in the camp and field and as an instructor in the military school at Woolwich. Just at the moment I have been talking about a veiled and singular light glimmered in his eyes and he leaned down and muttered confidentially to me—indicating the hero of the banquet with a gesture:

"Privately—he's an absolute fool."

This verdict was a great surprise to me. If its subject had been Napoleon, or Socrates, or Solomon, my astonishment could not have been greater. Two things I was well aware of: that the Reverend was a man of strict veracity and that his judgment of men was good. Therefore I knew, beyond doubt or question, that the world was mistaken about this hero: he *was* a fool. So I meant to find out, at a convenient moment, how the Reverend, all solitary and alone, had discovered the secret.

5   Some days later the opportunity came, and this is what the Reverend told me:

About forty years ago I was an instructor in the military academy at Woolwich. I was present in one of the sections when young Scoresby underwent his preliminary examination. I was touched to the quick with pity, for the rest of the class answered up brightly and handsomely, while he—why, dear me, he didn't know *anything*, so to speak. He was evidently good, and sweet, and lovable, and guileless; and so it was exceedingly painful to see him stand there, as serene as a graven image, and deliver himself of answers which were veritably miraculous for stupidity and ignorance. All the compassion in me was aroused in his behalf. I said to myself, when he comes to be examined again he will be flung over, of course; so it will be simply a harmless act of charity to ease his fall as much as I can. I took him aside and found that he knew a little of Caesar's history; and as he didn't know anything else, I went to work and drilled him like a galley-slave on a certain line of stock questions concerning Caesar which I knew would be used. If you'll believe me, he went through with flying colors on examination day! He went through on that purely superficial "cram," and got compliments too, while others, who knew a thousand times more than he, got plucked. By some strangely lucky accident—an accident not likely to happen twice in a century—he was asked no question outside of the narrow limits of his drill.

It was stupefying. Well, all through his course I stood by him, with something of the sentiment which a mother feels for a crippled child; and he always saved himself—just by miracle, apparently.

Now, of course, the thing that would expose him and kill him at last was mathematics. I resolved to make his death as easy as I could; so I drilled him and crammed him, and crammed him and drilled him, just on the line of questions which the exam-

Crimean battlefield: in the Crimean War (1853–1856), England was one of the allies that fought against Russia.

iners would be most likely to use, and then launched him on his fate. Well, sir, try to conceive of the result: to my consternation, he took the first prize! And with it he got a perfect ovation in the way of compliments.

Sleep? There was no more sleep for me for a week. My conscience tortured me day and night. What I had done I had done purely through charity, and only to ease the poor youth's fall. I never had dreamed of any such preposterous results as the thing that had happened. I felt as guilty and miserable as Frankenstein. Here was a wooden-head whom I had put in the way of glittering promotions and prodigious responsibilities, and but one thing could happen: he and his responsibilities would all go to ruin together at the first opportunity.

The Crimean War had just broken out. Of course there had to be a war, I said to myself. We couldn't have peace and give this donkey a chance to die before he is found out. I waited for the earthquake. It came. And it made me reel when it did come. He was actually gazetted to a captaincy in a marching regiment! Better men grow old and gray in the service before they climb to a sublimity like that. And who could ever have foreseen that they would go and put such a load of responsibility on such green and inadequate shoulders? I could just barely have stood it if they had made him a cornet°; but a captain—think of it! I thought my hair would turn white.

Consider what I did—I who so loved repose and inaction. I said to myself, I am responsible to the country for this, and I must go along with him and protect the country against him as far as I can. So I took my poor little capital that I had saved up through years of work and grinding economy, and went with a sigh and bought a cornetcy in his regiment, and away we went to the field.

And there—oh, dear, it was awful. Blunders?—why he never did anything *but* blunder. But, you see, nobody was in the fellow's secret. Everybody had him focused wrong, and necessarily misinterpreted his performance every time. Consequently they took his idiotic blunders for inspirations of genius. They did, honestly! His mildest blunders were enough to make a man in his right mind cry; and they did make me cry—and rage and rave, too, privately. And the thing that kept me always in a sweat of apprehension was the fact that every fresh blunder he made increased the luster of his reputation! I kept saying to myself, he'll get so high that when discovery does finally come it will be like the sun falling out of the sky.

He went right along, up from grade to grade, over the dead bodies of his superiors, until at last, in the hottest moment of the battle of _____ down went our colonel, and my heart jumped into my mouth, for Scoresby was next in rank! Now for it, said I; we'll all land in Sheol° in ten minutes, sure.

The battle was awfully hot; the allies were steadily giving way all over the field. Our regiment occupied a position that was vital; a blunder now must be destruction. At this crucial moment, what does this immortal fool do but detach the regiment from its place and order a charge over a neighboring hill where there wasn't a suggestion of an enemy! "There you go!" I said to myself; "this *is* the end at last."

And away we did go, and were over the shoulder of the hill before the insane movement could be discovered and stopped. And what did we find? An entire and unsuspected Russian army in reserve! And what happened? We were eaten up? That

10

15

cornet: the fifth ranking officer in a British cavalry troop.
Sheol: in the Hebrew Scriptures, Sheol is the region of the dead (Psalm 6:5) where worms destroy the body and the dead are alienated from God (Isaiah 14:11–19). Here, *Sheol* loosely means *Hell.*

is necessarily what would have happened in ninety-nine cases out of a hundred. But no; those Russians argued that no single regiment would come browsing around there at such a time. It must be the entire English army, and that the sly Russian game was detected and blocked; so they turned tail, and away they went, pell-mell, over the hill and down into the field, in wild confusion, and we after them; they themselves broke the solid Russian center in the field, and tore through, and in no time there was the most tremendous rout you ever saw, and the defeat of the allies was turned into a sweeping and splendid victory! Marshal Canrobert looked on, dizzy with astonishment, admiration, and delight; and sent right off for Scoresby, and hugged him, and decorated him on the field in presence of all the armies!

And what was Scoresby's blunder that time? Merely the mistaking his right hand for his left—that was all. An order had come to him to fall back and support our right; and, instead, he fell *forward* and went over the hill to the left. But the name he won that day as a marvelous military genius filled the world with his glory, and that glory will never fade while history books last.

He is just as good and sweet and lovable and unpretending as a man can be, but he doesn't know enough to come in when it rains. Now that is absolutely true. He is the supremest ass in the universe; and until half an hour ago nobody knew it but himself and me. He has been pursued, day by day and year by year, by a most phenomenal astonishing luckiness. He has been a shining soldier in all our wars for a generation; he has littered his whole military life with blunders, and yet has never committed one that didn't make him a knight or a baronet or a lord or something. Look at his breast; why, he is just clothed in domestic and foreign decorations. Well, sir, every one of them is the record of some shouting stupidity or other; and, taken together, they are proof that the very best thing in all this world that can befall a man is to be born lucky. I say again, as I said at the banquet, Scoresby's an absolute fool.

John Updike (b.1932)

A & P°

1961

In walks these three girls in nothing but bathing suits. I'm in the third checkout slot, with my back to the door, so I don't see them until they're over by the bread. The one that caught my eye first was the one in the plaid green two-piece. She was a chunky kid, with a good tan and a sweet broad soft-looking can with those two crescents of white just under it, where the sun never seems to hit, at the top of the backs of her legs.

A & P: "The Great Atlantic and Pacific Tea Company." This large grocery chain flourishes today in twenty-three states, with more than 1150 stores.

I stood there with my hand on a box of HiHo crackers trying to remember if I rang it up or not. I ring it up again and the customer starts giving me hell. She's one of these cash-register-watchers, a witch about fifty with rouge on her cheekbones and no eyebrows, and I know it made her day to trip me up. She'd been watching cash registers for fifty years and probably never seen a mistake before.

By the time I got her feathers smoothed and her goodies into a bag—she gives me a little snort in passing, if she'd been born at the right time they would have burned her over in Salem—by the time I get her on her way the girls had circled around the bread and were coming back, without a pushcart, back my way along the counters, in the aisle between the checkouts and the Special bins. They didn't even have shoes on. There was this chunky one, with the two-piece—it was bright green and the seams on the bra were still sharp and her belly was still pretty pale so I guessed she just got it (the suit)—there was this one, with one of those chubby berry-faces, the lips all bunched together under her nose, this one, and a tall one, with black hair that hadn't quite frizzed right, and one of these sunburns right across under the eyes, and a chin that was too long—you know, the kind of girl other girls think is very "striking" and "attractive" but never quite makes it, as they very well know, which is why they like her so much—and then the third one, that wasn't quite so tall. She was the queen. She kind of led them, the other two peeking around and making their shoulders round. She didn't look around, not this queen, she just walked straight on slowly, on these long white prima-donna legs. She came down a little hard on her heels, as if she didn't walk in her bare feet that much, putting down her heels and then letting the weight move along to her toes as if she was testing the floor with every step, putting a little deliberate extra action into it. You never know for sure how girls' minds work (do you really think it's a mind in there or just a little buzz like a bee in a glass jar?) but you got the idea she had talked the other two into coming in here with her, and now she was showing them how to do it, walk slow and hold yourself straight.

She had on a kind of dirty-pink—beige, maybe. I don't know—bathing suit with a little nubble all over it and, what got me, the straps were down. They were off her shoulders looped loose around the cool tops of her arms, and I guess as a result the suit had slipped a little on her, so all around the top of the cloth there was this shining rim. If it hadn't been there you wouldn't have known there could have been anything whiter than those shoulders. With the straps pushed off, there was nothing between the top of the suit and the top of her head except just *her,* this clean bare plane of the top of her chest down from the shoulder bones like a dented sheet of metal tilted in the light. I mean, it was more than pretty.

She had sort of oaky hair that the sun and salt had bleached, done up in a bun that was unraveling, and a kind of prim face. Walking into the A & P with your straps down, I suppose it's the only kind of face you *can* have. She held her head so high her neck, coming up out of those white shoulders, looked kind of stretched, but I didn't mind. The longer her neck was, the more of her there was.

She must have felt in the corner of her eye me and over my shoulder Stokesie in the second slot watching, but she didn't tip. Not this queen. She kept her eyes moving across the racks, and stopped, and turned so slow it made my stomach rub the inside of my apron, and buzzed to the other two, who kind of huddled against her for relief, and then they all three of them went up the cat-and-dog-food-breakfast-cereal-macaroni-rice-raisins-seasonings-spreads-spaghetti-soft-drinks-crackers-and-cookies aisle. From the third slot I look straight up this aisle to the meat counter, and I watched them all the way. The fat one with the tan sort of fumbled with the cookies, but on second thought she put the package back. The sheep pushing their carts down the aisle—the girls were walking against the usual traffic (not that we have one-way signs or anything)—were pretty hilarious. You could see them, when Queenie's white shoulders dawned on them, kind of jerk, or hop, or hiccup, but their eyes snapped back to their own baskets and on they pushed. I bet you could set off dynamite in an A & P and the people would by and large keep reaching and checking oatmeal off their lists and muttering "Let me see, there was a third thing, began with A, asparagus, no ah, yes, applesauce!" or whatever it is they do mutter. But there was no doubt, this jiggled them. A few houseslaves in pin curlers even looked around after pushing their carts past to make sure what they had seen was correct.

You know, it's one thing to have a girl in a bathing suit down on the beach, where what with the glare nobody can look at each other much anyway, and another thing in the cool of the A & P, under the fluorescent lights, against all those stacked packages, with her feet paddling along naked over our checkerboard green-and-cream rubber-tile floor.

"Oh Daddy," Stokesie said beside me. "I feel so faint."

"Darling," I said. "Hold me tight." Stokesie's married, with two babies chalked up on his fuselage already, but as far as I can tell that's the only difference. He's twenty-two, and I was nineteen this April.

"Is it done?" he asks, the responsible married man finding his voice. I forgot to say he thinks he's going to be manager some sunny day, maybe in 1990 when it's called the Great Alexandrov and Petrooshki° Tea Company or something.

10   What he meant was, our town is five miles from the beach, with a big summer colony out on the Point, but we're right in the middle of town, and the women generally put on a shirt or shorts or something before they get out of the car into the street. And anyway these are usually women with six children and varicose veins mapping their legs and nobody, including them, could care less. As I say, we're right in the middle of town, and if you stand at our front doors you can see two banks and the Congregational church and the newspaper store and three real-estate offices and about twenty-seven old freeloaders tearing up Central Street because the sewer broke again. It's not as if we're on the Cape;° we're north of Boston and there's people in this town haven't seen the ocean for twenty years.

The girls had reached the meat counter and were asking McMahon something. He pointed, they pointed, and they shuffled out of sight behind a pyramid of Diet Delight peaches. All that was left for us to see was old McMahon patting his mouth and looking after them sizing up their joints. Poor kids, I began to feel sorry for them, they couldn't help it.

Now here comes the sad part of the story, at least my family says it's sad, but I don't think it's so sad myself. The store's pretty empty, it being Thursday afternoon, so there was nothing much to do except lean on the register and wait for the girls to show up again. The whole store was like a pinball machine and I didn't know which tunnel they'd come out of. After a while they come around out of the far aisle, around

Great Alexandrov and Petrooshki: apparently a reference to the possibility that someday Russia might rule the United States, and might then change the names of American businesses and institutions.

the Cape: Cape Cod, the southeastern area of Massachusetts, a place of many resorts and beaches.

the light bulbs, records at discount of the Caribbean Six or Tony Martin Sings or some such gunk you wonder they waste the wax on, sixpacks of candy bars, and plastic toys done up in cellophane that fall apart when a kid looks at them anyway. Around they come, Queenie still leading the way, and holding a little gray jar in her hand. Slots Three through Seven are unmanned and I could see her wondering between Stokes and me, but Stokesie with his usual luck draws an old party in baggy gray pants who stumbles up with four giant cans of pineapple juice (what do these bums *do* with all that pineapple juice? I've often asked myself) so the girls come to me. Queenie puts down the jar and I take it into my fingers icy cold. Kingfish Fancy Herring Snacks in Pure Sour Cream: 49¢. Now her hands are empty, not a ring or a bracelet, bare as God made them, and I wonder where the money's coming from. Still with that prim look she lifts a folded dollar bill out of the hollow at the center of her nubbed pink top. The jar went heavy in my hand. Really, I thought that was so cute.

Then everybody's luck begins to run out. Lengel comes in from haggling with a truck full of cabbages on the lot and is about to scuttle into that door marked MAN-AGER behind which he hides all day when the girls touch his eye. Lengel's pretty dreary, teaches Sunday school and the rest, but he doesn't miss that much. He comes over and says, "Girls, this isn't the beach."

Queenie blushes, though maybe it's just a brush of sunburn I was noticing for the first time, now that she was so close. "My mother asked me to pick up a jar of her-ring snacks." Her voice kind of startled me, the way voices do when you see the peo-ple first, coming out so flat and dumb yet kind of tony, too, the way it ticked over "pick up" and "snacks." All of a sudden I slid right down her voice into her living room. Her father and the other men were standing around in ice-cream coats and bow ties and the women were in sandals picking up herring snacks on toothpicks off a big glass plate and they were all holding drinks the color of water with olives and sprigs of mint in them. When my parents have somebody over they get lemonade and if it's a real racy affair Schlitz in tall glasses with "They'll Do It Every Time"° cartoons sten-ciled on.

"That's all right," Lengel said. "But this isn't the beach." His repeating this   15
struck me as funny, as if it had just occurred to him, and he had been thinking all these years the A & P was a great big dune and he was the head lifeguard. He didn't like my smiling—as I say he doesn't miss much—but he concentrates on giving the girls that sad Sunday-school-superintendent stare.

Queenie's blush is no sunburn now, and the plump one in plaid, that I liked bet-ter from the back—a really sweet can—pipes up, "We weren't doing any shopping. We just came in for the one thing."

"That makes no difference," Lengel tells her, and I could see from the way his eyes went that he hadn't noticed she was wearing a two-piece before. "We want you decently dressed when you come in here."

"We *are* decent," Queenie says suddenly, her lower lip pushing, getting sore now that she remembers her place, a place from which the crowd that runs the A & P must look pretty crummy. Fancy Herring Snacks flashed in her very blue eyes.

"Girls, I don't want to argue with you. After this come in here with your shoul-ders covered. It's our policy." He turns his back. That's policy for you. Policy is what the kingpins want. What the others want is juvenile delinquency.

"They'll Do It Every Time": a syndicated daily and Sunday cartoon created by Jimmy Hatlo.

20   All this while, the customers had been showing up with their carts but, you
know, sheep, seeing a scene, they had all bunched up on Stokesie, who shook open a
paper bag as gently as peeling a peach, not wanting to miss a word. I could feel in the
silence everybody getting nervous, most of all Lengel, who asks me, "Sammy, have
you rung up the purchase?"

          I thought and said "No" but it wasn't about that I was thinking. I go through
the punches, 4, 9, GROC, TOT—it's more complicated than you think, and after you do
it often enough, it begins to make a little song, that you hear words to, in my case
"Hello (*bing*) there, you (*gung*) hap-py *pee*-pul (*splat*)!—the *splat* being the drawer flying out. I uncrease the bill, tenderly as you may imagine, it just having come from
between the two smoothest scoops of vanilla I had ever known were there, and pass
a half and a penny into her narrow pink palm, and nestle the herrings in a bag and
twist its neck and hand it over, all the time thinking.

          The girls, and who'd blame them, are in a hurry to get out, so I say "I quit" to
Lengel quick enough for them to hear, hoping they'll stop and watch me, their unsuspected hero. They keep right on going, into the electric eye; the door flies open and they
flicker across the lot to their car, Queenie and Plaid and Big Tall Goony-Goony (not that
as raw material she was so bad), leaving me with Lengel and a kink in his eyebrow.

          "Did you say something, Sammy?"

          "I said I quit."

25   "I thought you did."

          "You didn't have to embarrass them."

          "It was they who were embarrassing us."

          I started to say something that came out "Fiddle-de-doo." It's a saying of my
grandmother's, and I know she would have been pleased.

          "I don't think you know what you're saying," Lengel said.

30   "I know you don't," I said. "But I do." I pull the bow at the back of my apron
and start shrugging it off my shoulders. A couple of customers that had been heading
for my slot begin to knock against each other, like scared pigs in a chute.

          Lengel sighs and begins to look very patient and old and gray. He'd been a
friend of my parents for years. "Sammy, you don't want to do this to your Mom and
Dad," he tells me. It's true. I don't. But it seems to me that once you begin a gesture
it's fatal not to go through with it. I fold the apron, "Sammy" stitched in red on the
pocket, and put it on the counter, and drop the bow tie on top of it. The bow tie is theirs,
if you've ever wondered. "You'll feel this for the rest of your life," Lengel says, and I
know that's true, too, but remembering how he made that pretty girl blush makes me
so scrunchy inside I punch the No Sale tab and the machine whirs "pee-pul" and the
drawer splats out. One advantage to this scene taking place in summer, I can follow
this up with a clean exit, there's no fumbling around getting your coat and galoshes,
I just saunter into the electric eye in my white shirt that my mother ironed the night
before, and the door heaves itself open, and outside the sunshine is skating around on
the asphalt.

          I look around for my girls, but they're gone, of course. There wasn't anybody
but some young married screaming with her children about some candy they didn't
get by the door of a powder-blue Falcon° station wagon. Looking back in the big windows, over the bags of peat moss and aluminum lawn furniture stacked on the pave-

Falcon: a small car that had recently been introduced by the Ford Motor Company.

ment, I could see Lengel in my place in the slot, checking the sheep through. His face was dark gray and his back stiff, as if he'd just had an injection of iron, and my stomach kind of fell as I felt how hard the world was going to be to me hereafter.

Eudora Welty (b.1909)

A Worn Path

1941

It was December—a bright frozen day in the early morning. Far out in the country there was an old Negro woman with her head tied in a red rag, coming along a path through the pinewoods. Her name was Phoenix Jackson. She was very old and small and she walked slowly in the dark pine shadows, moving a little from side to side in her steps, with the balanced heaviness and lightness of a pendulum in a grandfather clock. She carried a thin, small cane made from an umbrella, and with this she kept tapping the frozen earth in front of her. This made a grave and persistent noise in the still air, that seemed meditative like the chirping of a solitary little bird.

She wore a dark striped dress reaching down to her shoe tops, and an equally long apron of bleached sugar sacks, with a full pocket: all neat and tidy, but every time she took a step she might have fallen over her shoelaces, which dragged from her unlaced shoes. She looked straight ahead. Her eyes were blue with age. Her skin had a pattern all its own of numberless branching wrinkles and as though a whole little tree stood in the middle of her forehead, but a golden color ran underneath, and the two knobs of her cheeks were illumined by a yellow burning under the dark. Under the rag her hair came down on her neck in the frailest of ringlets, still black, and with an odor like copper.

Now and then there was a quivering in the thicket. Old Phoenix said, "Out of my way, all you foxes, owls, beetles, jack rabbits, coons and wild animals! . . . Keep out from under these feet, little bob-whites. . . . Keep the big wild hogs out of my path. Don't let none of those come running my direction. I got a long way." Under her small black-freckled hand her cane, limber as a buggy whip, would switch at the brush as if to rouse up any hiding things.

On she went. The woods were deep and still. The sun made the pine needles almost too bright to look at, up where the wind rocked. The cones dropped as light as feathers. Down in the hollow was the mourning dove—it was not too late for him.

The path ran up a hill. "Seem like there is chains about my feet, time I get this far," she said, in the voice of argument old people keep to use with themselves. "Something always take a hold of me on this hill—pleads I should stay." 5

After she got to the top she turned and gave a full, severe look behind her where she had come. "Up through pines," she said at length. "Now down through oaks."

Her eyes opened their widest, and she started down gently. But before she got to the bottom of the hill a bush caught her dress.

Her fingers were busy and intent, but her skirts were full and long, so that before she could pull them free in one place they were caught in another. It was not possible to allow the dress to tear. "I in the thorny bush," she said. "Thorns, you doing your appointd work. Never want to let folks pass, no sir. Old eyes thought you was a pretty little *green* bush."

Finally, trembling all over, she stood free, and after a moment dared to stoop for her cane.

10 "Sun so high!" she cried, leaning back and looking, while the thick tears went over her eyes. "The time getting all gone here."

At the foot of this hill was a place where a log was laid across the creek.

"Now comes the trial," said Phoenix.

Putting her right foot out, she mounted the log and shut her eyes. Lifting her skirt, leveling her cane fiercely before her, like a festival figure in some parade, she began to march across. Then she opened her eyes and she was safe on the other side.

"I wasn't as old as I thought," she said.

15 But she sat down to rest. She spread her skirts on the bank around her and folded her hands over her knees. Up above her was a tree in a pearly cloud of mistletoe. She did not dare to close her eyes, and when a little boy brought her a plate with a slice of marble-cake on it she spoke to him. "That would be acceptable," she said. But when she went to take it there was just her own hand in the air.

So she left that tree, and had to go through a barbed-wire fence. There she had to creep and crawl, spreading her knees and stretching her fingers like a baby trying to climb the steps. But she talked loudly to herself: she could not let her dress be torn now, so late in the day, and she could not pay for having her arm or her leg sawed off if she got caught fast where she was.

At last she was safe through the fence and risen up out in the clearing. Big dead trees, like black men with one arm, were standing in the purple stalks of the withered cotton field. There sat a buzzard.

"Who you watching?"

In the furrow she made her way along.

20 "Glad this not the season for bulls," she said, looking sideways, "and the good Lord made his snakes to curl up and sleep in the winter. A pleasure I don't see no two-headed snake coming around that tree, where it come once. It took a while to get by him, back in the summer."

She passed through the old cotton and went into a field of dead corn. It whispered and shook and was taller than her head. "Through the maze now," she said, for there was no path.

Then there was something tall, black, and skinny there, moving before her.

At first she took it for a man. It could have been a man dancing in the field. But she stood still and listened, and it did not make a sound. It was as silent as a ghost.

"Ghosts," she said sharply, "who be you the ghost of? For I have heard of nary death close by."

25 But there was no answer—only the ragged dancing in the wind.

She shut her eyes, reached out her hand, and touched a sleeve. She found a coat and inside that an emptiness, cold as ice.

"You scarecrow," she said. Her face lighted. "I ought to be shut up for good," she said with laughter. "My senses is gone. I too old. I the oldest people I ever know. Dance, old scarecrow," she said, "while I dancing with you."

She kicked her foot over the furrow, and with mouth drawn down, shook her head once or twice in a little strutting way. Some husks blew down and whirled in streamers about her skirts.

Then she went on, parting her way from side to side with the cane, through the whispering field. At last she came to the end, to a wagon track where the silver grass blew between the red ruts. The quail were walking around like pullets, seeming all dainty and unseen.

"Walk pretty," she said. "This is the easy place. This the easy going."   30

She followed the track, swaying through the quiet bare fields, through the little strings of trees silver in their dead leaves, past cabins silver from weather, with the doors and windows boarded shut, all like old women under a spell sitting there. "I walking in their sleep," she said, nodding her head vigorously.

In a ravine she went where a spring was silently flowing through a hollow log. Old Phoenix bent and drank. "Sweet-gum makes the water sweet," she said, and drank more. "Nobody know who made this well, for it was here when I was born."

The track crossed a swampy part where the moss hung as white as lace from every limb. "Sleep on, alligators, and blow your bubbles." Then the track went into the road.

Deep, deep the road went down between the high green-colored banks. Overhead the live-oaks met, and it was as dark as a cave.

A black dog with a lolling tongue came up out of the weeds by the ditch. She   35
was meditating, and not ready, and when he came at her she only hit him a little with her cane. Over she went in the ditch, like a little puff of milkweed.

Down there, her senses drifted away. A dream visited her, and she reached her hand up, but nothing reached down and gave her a pull. So she lay there and presently went to talking. "Old woman," she said to herself, "that black dog come up out of the weeds to stall you off, and now there he sitting on his fine tail smiling at you."

A white man finally came along and found her—a hunter, a young man; with his dog on a chain.

"Well, Granny!" he laughed. "What are you doing there?"

"Lying on my back like a June-bug waiting to be turned over, mister," she said, reaching up her hand.

He lifted her up, gave her a swing in the air, and set her down. "Anything bro-   40
ken, Granny?"

"No sir, them old dead weeds is springy enough," said Phoenix, when she had got her breath. "I thank you for your trouble."

"Where do you live, Granny?" he asked, while the two dogs were growling at each other.

"Away back yonder, sir, behind the ridge. You can't even see it from here."

"On your way home?"

"No sir, I going to town."   45

"Why, that's too far! That's as far as I walk when I come out myself, and I get something for my trouble." He patted the stuffed bag he carried, and there hung down a little closed claw. It was one of the bob-whites, with its beak hooked bitterly to show it was dead. "Now you go on home, Granny!"

"I bound to go to town, mister," said Phoenix. "The time come around."

He gave another laugh, filling the whole landscape. "I know you old colored people! Wouldn't miss going to town to see Santa Claus!"

But something held old Phoenix very still. The deep lines in her face went into a fierce and different radiation. Without warning, she had seen with her own eyes a flashing nickel fall out of the man's pocket onto the ground.

50 "How old are you, Granny?" he was saying.

"There is no telling, mister," she said, "no telling."

Then she gave a little cry and clapped her hands and said, "Git on away from here, dog! Look! Look at that dog!" She laughed as if in admiration. "He ain't scared of nobody. He a big black dog." She whispered, "Sic him!"

"Watch me get rid of that cur," said the man. "Sic him, Pete! Sic him!"

Phoenix heard the dogs fighting, and heard the man running and throwing sticks. She even heard a gunshot. But she was slowly bending forward by that time, further and further forward, the lids stretched down over her eyes, as if she were doing this in her sleep. Her chin was lowered almost to her knees. The yellow palm of her hand came out from the fold of her apron. Her fingers slid down and along the ground under the piece of money with the grace and care they would have in lifting an egg from under a setting hen. Then she slowly straightened up, she stood erect, and the nickel was in her apron pocket. A bird flew by. Her lips moved. "God watching me the whole time. I come to stealing."

55 The man came back, and his own dog panted about them. "Well, I scared him off that time," he said, and then he laughed and lifted his gun and pointed it at Phoenix.

She stood straight and faced him.

"Doesn't the gun scare you?" he said, still pointing it.

"No, sir, I seen plenty go off closer by, in my day, and for less than what I done," she said, holding utterly still.

He smiled, and shouldered the gun. "Well, Granny," he said, "you must be a hundred years old, and scared of nothing. I'd give you a dime if I had any money with me. But you take my advice and stay home, and nothing will happen to you."

60 "I bound to go on my way, mister," said Phoenix. She inclined her head in the red rag. Then they went in different directions, but she could hear the gun shooting again and again over the hill.

She walked on. The shadows hung from the oak trees to the road like curtains. Then she smelled wood-smoke, and smelled the river, and she saw a steeple and the cabins on their steep steps. Dozens of little black children whirled around her. There ahead was Natchez shining. Bells were ringing. She walked on.

In the paved city it was Christmas time. There were red and green electric lights strung and crisscrossed everywhere, and all turned on in the daytime. Old Phoenix would have been lost if she had not distrusted her eyesight and depended on her feet to know where to take her.

She paused quietly on the sidewalk where people were passing by. A lady came along in the crowd, carrying an armful of red-, green- and silver-wrapped presents; she gave off perfume like the red roses in hot summer, and Phoenix stopped her.

"Please, missy, will you lace up my shoe?" She held up her foot.

"What do you want, Grandma?" 65

"See my shoe," said Phoenix. "Do all right for out in the country, but wouldn't look right to go in a big building."

"Stand still then, Grandma," said the lady. She put her packages down on the sidewalk beside her and laced and tied both shoes tightly.

"Can't lace 'em with a cane," said Phoenix. "Thank you, missy. I doesn't mind asking a nice lady to tie up my shoe, when I gets out on the street."

Moving slowly and from side to side, she went into the big building, and into a tower of steps, where she walked up and around and around until her feet knew to stop.

She entered a door, and there she saw nailed up on the wall the document that 70 had been stamped with the gold seal and framed in the gold frame, which matched the dream that was hung up in her head.

"Here I be," she said. There was a fixed and ceremonial stiffness over her body.

"A charity case, I suppose," said an attendant who sat at the desk before her.

But Pheonix only looked above her head. There was sweat on her face, the wrinkles in her skin shone like a bright net.

"Speak up, Grandma," the woman said. "What's your name? We must have your history, you know. Have you been here before? What seems to be the trouble with you?"

Old Phoenix only gave a twitch to her face as if a fly were bothering her. 75

"Are you deaf?" cried the attendant.

But then the nurse came in.

"Oh, that's just old Aunt Phoenix," she said. "She doesn't come for herself—she has a little grandson. She makes trips just as regular as clockwork. She lives away back off the Old Natchez Trace." She bent down. "Well, Aunt Phoenix, why don't you just take a seat? We won't keep you standing after your long trip." She pointed.

The old woman sat down, bolt upright in the chair.

"Now, how is the boy?" asked the nurse. 80

Old Phoenix did not speak.

"I said, how is the boy?"

But Phoenix only waited and stared straight ahead, her face very solemn and withdrawn into rigidity.

"Is his throat any better?" asked the nurse. "Aunt Phoenix, don't you hear me? Is your grandson's throat any better since the last time you came for the medicine?"

With her hands on her knees, the old woman waited, silent, erect and motion- 85 less, just as if she were in armor.

"You mustn't take up our time this way, Aunt Phoenix," the nurse said. "Tell us quickly about your grandson, and get it over. He isn't dead, is he?"

At last there came a flicker and then a flame of comprehension across her face, and she spoke.

"My grandson. It was my memory had left me. There I sat and forgot why I made my long trip."

"Forgot?" the nurse frowned. "After you came so far?"

Then Phoenix was like an old woman begging a dignified forgiveness for wak- 90 ing up frightened in the night. "I never did go to school, I was too old at the Surrender," she said in a soft voice. "I'm an old woman without an education. It was my memory fail me. My little grandson, he is just the same, and I forgot it in the coming."

"Throat never heals, does it?" said the nurse, speaking in a loud, sure voice to old Phoenix. By now she had a card with something written on it, a little list. "Yes. Swallowed lye. When was it—January—two, three years ago—"

Phoenix spoke unasked now. "No, missy, he not dead, he just the same. Every little while his throat begin to close up again, and he not able to swallow. He not get his breath. He not able to help himself. So the time come around, and I go on another trip for the soothing medicine."

"All right. The doctor said as long as you came to get it, you could have it," said the nurse. "But it's an obstinate case."

"My little grandson, he sit up there in the house all wrapped up, waiting by himself," Phoenix went on. "We is the only two left in the world. He suffer and it don't seem to put him back at all. He got a sweet look. He going to last. He wear a little patch quilt and peep out holding his mouth open like a little bird. I remembers so plain now. I not going to forget him again, no, the whole enduring time. I could tell him from all the others in creation."

95   "All right." The nurse was trying to hush her now. She brought her a bottle of medicine. "Charity," she said, making a check mark in a book.

Old Phoenix held the bottle close to her eyes, and then carefully put it into her pocket.

"I thank you," she said.

"It's Christmas time, Grandma," said the attendant. "Could I give you a few pennies out of my purse?"

"Five pennies is a nickel," said Phoenix stiffly.

100   "Here's a nickel," said the attendant.

Phoenix rose carefully and held out her hand. She received the nickel and then fished the other nickel out of her pocket and laid it beside the new one. She stared at her palm closely, with her head on one side.

Then she gave a tap with her cane on the floor.

"This is what come to me to do," she said. "I going to the store and buy my child a little windmill they sells, made out of paper. He going to find it hard to believe there such a thing in the world. I'll march myself back where he waiting, holding it straight up in this hand."

She lifted her free hand, gave a little nod, turned around, and walked out of the doctor's office. Then her slow step began on the stairs, going down.

POEMS

Matthew Arnold (1822–1888)

Dover Beach   1849

The sea is calm to-night.
The tide is full, the moon lies fair
Upon the straits:—on the French coast the light
Gleams and is gone; the cliffs of England stand,
Glimmering and vast, out in the tranquil bay.   5
Come to the window, sweet is the night air!
Only, from the long line of spray
Where the sea meets the moon-blanched land,
Listen! You can hear the grating roar
Of pebbles which the waves draw back, and fling,   10
At their return, up the high strand,
Begin, and cease, and then again begin,
With tremulous cadence slow, and bring
The eternal note of sadness in.

Sophocles long ago   15
Heard it on the Ægean, and it brought
Into his mind the turbid ebb and flow
Of human misery; we
Find also in the sound a thought,
Hearing it by this distant northern sea.   20
The Sea of Faith
Was once, too, at the full, and round earth's shore
Lay like the folds of a bright girdle furled.
But now I only hear
Its melancholy, long, withdrawing roar,   25
Retreating, to the breath
Of the night wind, down the vast edges drear
And naked shingles of the world.

Ah, love, let us be true
To one another! for the world, which seems   30
To lie before us like a land of dreams,
So various, so beautiful, so new,

Hath really neither joy, nor love, nor light,
Nor certitude, nor peace, nor help for pain;
35 And we are here as on a darkling plain
Swept with confused alarms of struggle and flight
Where ignorant armies clash by night.

Samuel Taylor Coleridge (1772–1834)

Kubla Khan   1816

In Xanadu did Kubla Kahn
A stately pleasure dome decree:
Where Alph, the sacred river, ran
Through cavern measureless to man
5   Down to a sunless sea.
So twice five miles of fertile ground
With walls and towers were girdled round:
And there were gardens bright with sinuous rills,
Where blossomed many an incense-bearing tree;
10 And here were forests ancient as the hills,
Enfolding sunny spots of greenery.

But oh! that deep romantic chasm which slanted
Down the green hill athwart a cedarn cover!
A savage place! as holy and enchanted
15 As e'er beneath a waning moon was haunted
By woman wailing for her demon lover!
And from this chasm, with ceaseless turmoil seething,
As if this earth in fast thick pants were breathing,
A mighty fountain momently was forced:
20 Amid whose swift half-intermitted burst
Huge fragments vaulted like rebounding hail,
Or chaffy grain beneath the thresher's flail;
And 'mid these dancing rocks at once and ever
It flung up momently the sacred river.
25 Five miles meandering with a mazy motion
Through wood and dale the sacred river ran,
Then reached the caverns measureless to man,
And sank in tumult to a lifeless ocean:
And 'mid this tumult Kubla heard from far
30 Ancestral voices prophesying war!

The shadow of the dome of pleasure
Floated midway on the waves;
Where was heard the mingled measure
From the fountain and the caves.
It was a miracle of rare device,   *35*
A sunny pleasure dome with caves of ice!

A damsel with a dulcimer
In a vision once I saw:
It was an Abyssinian maid,
And on her dulcimer she played,   *40*
Singing of Mount Abora.
Could I revive within me
Her symphony and song,
To such a deep delight 'twould win me,
That with music loud and long,   *45*
I would build that dome in air,
That sunny dome! those caves of ice!
And all who heard should see them there,
And all should cry. Beware! Beware!
His flashing eyes, his floating hair!   *50*
Weave a circle round him thrice,
And close your eyes with holy dread,
For he on honeydew hath fed,
And drunk the milk of Paradise.

Robert Frost (1875–1963)

Desert Places   1936

Snow falling and night falling fast, oh, fast
In a field I looked into going past,
And the ground almost covered smooth in snow,
But a few weeds and stubble showing last.

The woods around it have it—it is theirs.   5
All animals are smothered in their lairs.

I am too absent-spirited to count;
The loneliness includes me unawares.

And lonely as it is that loneliness
10 Will be more lonely ere it will be less—
A blanker whiteness of benighted snow
With no expression, nothing to express.

They cannot scare me with their empty spaces
Between stars—on stars where no human race is.
15 I have it in me so much nearer home
To scare myself with my own desert places.

Thomas Hardy (1840–1928)

Channel Firing   1914

That night your great guns unawares,
Shook all our coffins as we lay,
And broke the chancel window squares.
We thought it was the Judgment-day

5   And sat upright. While drearisome
Arose the howl of wakened hounds:
The mouse let fall the altar-crumb,
The worms drew back into the mounds,

The glebe cow drooled. Till God called, "No;
10 It's gunnery practice out at sea
Just as before you went below;
The world is as it used to be:

"All nations striving strong to make
Red war yet redder. Mad as hatters
15 They do no more for Christés sake
Than you who are helpless in such matters.

"That this is not the judgment-hour
For some of them's a blessed thing,
For if it were they'd have to scour
20 Hell's floor for so much threatening . . .

"Ha, ha. It will be warmer when
I blow the trumpet (if indeed

I ever do; for you are men,
And rest eternal sorely need)."

So down we lay again. "I wonder,   25
Will the world ever saner be,"
Said one, "than when He sent us under
In our indifferent century!"

And many a skeleton shook his head.
"Instead of preaching forty year,"   30
My neighbor Parson Thirdly said,
"I wish I had stuck to pipes and beer."

Again the guns disturbed the hour,
Roaring their readiness to avenge,
As far inland as Stourton Tower,   35
And Camelot, and starlit Stonehenge.

Robert Hayden (1913–1980)

Those Winter Sundays   1962

Sundays too my father got up early
and put his clothes on the blueblack cold,
then with cracked hands that ached
from labor in the weekday weather made
banked fires blaze. No one ever thanked him.   5

I'd wake and hear the cold splintering, breaking.
When the rooms were warm, he'd call,
and slowly I would rise and dress,
fearing the chronic angers of that house,

Speaking indifferently to him,   10
who had driven out the cold
and polished my good shoes as well.
What did I know, what did I know
Of love's austere and lonely offices?

Langston Hughes (1902–1967)

Theme for English B   1951

The instructor said,
  Go home and write
  a page tonight.
  And let that page come out of you—
5 Then, it will be true.

I wonder if it's that simple?
I am twenty-two, colored, born in Winston-Salem.
I went to school there, then Durham, then here
to this college on the hill above Harlem,
10 I am the only colored student in my class.
The steps from the hill lead down to Harlem,
through a park, then I cross St. Nicholas,
Eighth Avenue, Seventh, and I come to the Y,°
the Harlem Branch Y, where I take the elevator
15 up to my room, sit down, and write this page:

It's not easy to know what is true for you or me
at twenty-two, my age. But I guess I'm what
I feel and see and hear. Harlem, I hear you:
hear you, hear me—we two—you, me talk on this page.
20 (I hear New York, too.) Me—who?

Well, I like to eat, sleep, drink, and be in love.
I like to work, read, learn, and understand life.
I like a pipe for a Christmas present,
or records—Bessie, bop, or Bach.°

25 I guess being colored doesn't make me not like
the same things other folks like who are other races.
So will my page be colored that I write?
Being me, it will not be white.

Harlem . . . Y: places near Columbia University, in New York City.
Bessie: Bessie Smith (c. 1898–1937), American jazz singer, famed as "Empress of the Blues."
bop: a type of popular music in vogue from the 1930s through the 1960s; also called *bebop* and *rebop.*
Bach: Johann Sebastian Bach (1685–1750), German composer, considered the master of the Baroque style of music.

But it will be
a part of you, instructor.　　　　　　　　　　　*30*
You are white—
yet a part of me, as I am a part of you.
That's American.
Sometimes perhaps you don't want to be a part of me.
Nor do I often want to be part of you.　　　　*35*
But we are, that's true!
As I learn from you,
I guess you learn from me—
although you're older—and white—
and somewhat more free.　　　　　　　　　　*40*

This is my page for English B.

John Keats (1795–1821)

Bright Star　　　　　　　　　　　　1819

Bright star! would I were steadfast as thou art—
　Not in lone splendor hung aloft the night,
And watching, with eternal lids apart,
　Like Nature's patient, sleepless eremite,°
The moving waters at their priestlike task　　　　*5*
　Of pure ablution round earth's human shores,
Or gazing on the new soft-fallen mask
　Of snow upon the mountains and the moors;
No—yet still steadfast, still unchangeable,
　Pillowed upon my fair love's ripening breast,　　*10*
To feel forever its soft fall and swell,
　Awake forever in a sweet unrest,
Still, still to hear her tender-taken breath,
And so live ever—or else swoon to death.

eremite: hermit.

Irving Layton (b. 1912)

Rhine Boat Trip°   1977

The castles on the Rhine
are all haunted
by the ghosts of Jewish mothers
looking for their ghostly children

5   And the clusters of grapes
in the sloping vineyards
are myriads of blinded eyes
staring at the blind sun

The tireless Lorelei°
10   can never comb from their hair
the crimson beards
of murdered rabbis

However sweetly they sing
one hears only
15   the low wailing of cattle-cars°
moving invisibly across the land

Rhine Boat Trip: the Rhine, Germany's best-known river, is virtually synonymous with German national history.
Lorelei: a mythical shore nymph who lured passing rivermen to their doom; subject of a famous poem by Heinrich Heine (1797–1856).
cattle-cars: during the Holocaust in World War II, the Nazis crowded their victims together into cattle cars and transported them by rail to concentration and extermination camps in Germany and neighboring countries.

From *Selected Poems 1945–89/A Wild Peculiar Joy* by Irving Layton. Used by permission of the Canadian Publishers, McClelland and Stewart, Toronto.

Amy Lowell (1874–1925)

Patterns 1916

I walk down garden paths,
And all the daffodils
Are blowing, and the bright blue squills.
I walk down the patterned garden-paths
In my stiff, brocaded gown.   5
With my powdered hair and jewelled fan,
I too am a rare
Pattern. As I wander down
The garden paths.

My dress is richly figured,   10
And the train
Makes a pink and silver stain
On the gravel, and the thrift
Of the borders.
Just a plate of current fashion   15
Tripping by in high-heeled, ribboned shoes.
Not a softness anywhere about me,
Only whalebone° and brocade.
And I sink on a seat in the shade

Of a lime tree. For my passion   20
Wars against the stiff brocade.
The daffodils and squills
Flutter in the breeze
As they please.
And I weep;   25
For the lime-tree is in blossom
And one small flower has dropped upon my bosom.

And the plashing of waterdrops
In the marble fountain
Comes down the garden-paths.   30
The dripping never stops.
Underneath my stiffened gown

whalebone: used as a stiffener in tightly laced corsets.

Is the softness of a woman bathing in a marble basin,
A basin in the midst of hedges grown
35   So thick, she cannot see her lover hiding.
But she guesses he is near,
And the sliding of the water
Seems the stroking of a dear
Hand upon her.
40   What is Summer in a fine brocaded gown!
I should like to see it lying in a heap upon the ground.
All the pink and silver crumpled up on the ground.
I would be the pink and silver as I ran along the paths,
And he would stumble after,
45   Bewildered by my laughter.
I should see the sun flashing from his sword-hilt and buckles on his shoes.
I would choose
To lead him in a maze along the patterned paths,
A bright and laughing maze for my heavy-booted lover.
50   Till he caught me in the shade,
And the buttons of his waistcoat bruised my body as he clasped me,
Aching, melting, unafraid.
With the shadows of the leaves and the sundrops,
And the plopping of the waterdrops,
55   All about us in the open afternoon—
I am very like to swoon
With the weight of this brocade,
For the sun sifts through the shade.

Underneath the fallen blossom
60   In my bosom,
Is a letter I have hid.
It was brought to me this morning by a rider from the Duke.
Madam, we regret to inform you that Lord Hartwell
Died in action Thursday se'nnight°
65   As I read it in the white, morning sunlight,
The letters squirmed like snakes.
"Any answer, Madam," said my footman.
"No," I told him.
"See that the messenger takes some refreshment.

70   No, no answer."
And I walked into the garden.
Up and down the patterned paths,
In my stiff, correct brocade.
The blue and yellow flowers stood up proudly in the sun,
75   Each one.
I stood upright too,

se'nnight: i.e., a week ago (seven nights) last Thursday.

Held rigid to the pattern
By the stiffness of my gown.
Up and down I walked.
Up and down.   *80*

In a month he would have been my husband.
In a month, here, underneath this lime,
We would have broken the pattern;
He for me, and I for him,
He as Colonel, I as Lady,   *85*
On this shady seat.
He had a whim
That sunlight carried blessing.
And I answered, "It shall be as you have said."
Now he is dead.   *90*

In Summer and in Winter I shall walk
Up and down
The patterned garden-paths
In my stiff, brocaded gown.
The squills and daffodils   *95*
Will give place to pillared roses, and to asters, and to snow.
I shall go
Up and down,
In my gown.
Gorgeously arrayed,   *100*
Boned and stayed.
And the softness of my body will be guarded from embrace
By each button, hook, and lace.
For the man who should loose me is dead,
Fighting with the Duke in Flanders,°   *105*
In a pattern called a war.
Christ! What are patterns for?

Flanders: a place of frequent warfare in Belgium. The speaker's clothing (lines 5,6) suggests the time of the Duke of Marlborough's Flanders campaigns of 1702–1710. The Battle of Waterloo (1815) was also fought nearby under the Duke of Wellington. During World War I, fierce fighting against the Germans occurred in Flanders in 1914 and 1915, with great loss of life.

John Masefield (1878–1967)

Cargoes   1902

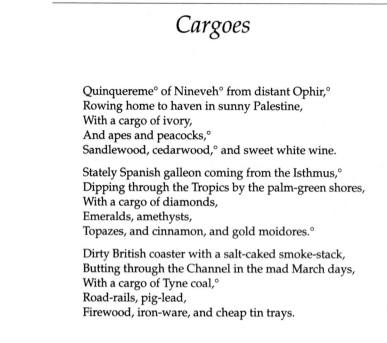

Quinquereme° of Nineveh° from distant Ophir,°
Rowing home to haven in sunny Palestine,
With a cargo of ivory,
And apes and peacocks,°
5   Sandlewood, cedarwood,° and sweet white wine.

Stately Spanish galleon coming from the Isthmus,°
Dipping through the Tropics by the palm-green shores,
With a cargo of diamonds,
Emeralds, amethysts,
10   Topazes, and cinnamon, and gold moidores.°

Dirty British coaster with a salt-caked smoke-stack,
Butting through the Channel in the mad March days,
With a cargo of Tyne coal,°
Road-rails, pig-lead,
15   Firewood, iron-ware, and cheap tin trays.

Quinquereme: the largest of the ancient ships. It was powered by three tiers of oars, and was named "quinquereme" because five men operated each vertical oar station. Two oars were each taken by two men, while the third was taken by one man alone.
Nineveh: "an exceeding great city," Jonah 3:3.
Ophir: Ophir probably was in Africa, and was known for its gold, I Kings 10:11; 1 Chron. 29:4.
apes and peacocks: I Kings 10:22, and 2 Chron. 9:21. These goods were brought to King Solomon.
cedarwood: I Kings 9:11.
Isthmus: the Isthmus of Panama.
moidores: coin in use in Portugal and Brazil during the early times of new world exploration.
Tyne coal: Newcastle upon Tyne, a coal-producing area in north England.

Reprinted with permission of The Society of Authors as the literary representative of the Estate of John Masefield.

Naomi Shihab Nye (b. 1952)

Where Children Live   1982

Homes where children live exude a pleasant rumpledness,
like a bed made by a child, or a yard littered with balloons.

To be a child again one would need to shed details
till the heart found itself dressed in the coat with a hood.
Now the heart has taken on gloves and mufflers,   5
the heart never goes outside to find something to "do."
And the house takes on a new face, dignified.
No lost shoes blooming under bushes.
No chipped trucks in the drive.
Grown-ups like swings, leafy plants, slow-motion back and forth.   10
While the yard of a child is strewn with the corpses
Of bottle-rockets and whistles,
anything whizzing and spectacular, brilliantly short-lived.

Trees in children's yards speak in clearer tongues.
Ants have more hope. Squirrels dance as well as hide.   15
The fence has a reason to be there, so children can go in and out
with the leftovers of their affection,
the roots of the tiniest grasses curl toward one another
like secret smiles.

Wilfred Owen (1893–1918)

Anthem for Doomed Youth 1920

What passing-bells° for these who die as cattle?
Only the monstrous anger of the guns.
Only the stuttering rifles' rapid rattle
Can patter out their hasty orisons.°
5   No mockeries for them from prayers or bells,
Nor any voice of mourning save the choirs—
The shrill, demented choirs of wailing shells;
And bugles calling for them from sad shires.°

What candles may be held to speed them all?
10   Not in the hands of boys, but in their eyes
Shall shine the holy glimmers of good-byes.
The pallor of girls' brows shall be their pall;
Their flowers the tenderness of patient minds,
And each slow dusk a drawing-down of blinds.

Marge Piercy (b. 1934)

A Work of Artifice 1973

The bonsai tree
in the attractive pot
could have grown eighty feet tall
on the side of a mountain
5   till split by lightning.

passing-bells: church bells that are tolled at the entry of a funeral cortège into the church cemetery.
orisons: prayers.
shires: British counties.

But a gardener
carefully pruned it.
It is nine inches high.
Every day as he
whittles back the branches   *10*
the gardener croons,
It is your nature
to be small and cozy
domestic and weak;
how lucky, little tree,   *15*
to have a pot to grow in.
With living creatures
one must begin very early
to dwarf their growth:
the bound feet,   *20*
the crippled brain,
the hair in curlers,
the hands you
love to touch.

William Shakespeare (1564–1616)

Sonnet 73: That Time of Year Thou Mayest in Me Behold 1609

That time of year thou mayest in me behold,
When yellow leaves, or none, or few do hang
Upon those boughs which shake against the cold,
Bare ruined choirs, where late the sweet birds sang.
In me thou seest the twilight of such day,   5
As after Sunset fadeth in the West,
Which by and by black night doth take away,
Death's second self that seals up all in rest.
In me thou seest the glowing of such fire,
That on the ashes of his youth doth lie,   10
As the death bed, whereon it must expire,
Consumed with that which it was nourished by.
    This thou perceiv'st, which makes thy love more strong.
    To love that well, which thou must leave ere long.

Sonnet 116: Let Me Not
to the Marriage of True Minds   1609

Let me not to the marriage of true minds
Admit impediments; love is not love
Which alters when it alteration finds
Or bends with the remover to remove.
5 O no, it is an ever fixèd mark
That looks on tempests and is never shaken;
It is the star to every wandering bark
Whose worth's unknown, although his height be taken.
Love's not Time's fool, though rosy lips and cheeks
10 Within his bending sickle's compass come;
Love alters not with his brief hours and weeks.
But bears it out even to the edge of doom:
    If this be error and upon me proved,
    I never writ, nor no man ever loved.

William Wordsworth (1770–1850)

Daffodils (I Wandered Lonely
as a Cloud)   1807 (1804)

Wordsworth's note: Written at Town-end, Grasmere. The Daffodils grew and
still grow on the margin of Ullswater, and probably may be seen to this day as
beautiful in the month of March, nodding their golden heads beside the dancing and foaming waves. [Wordsworth also pointed out that lines 21 and 22, the
"best lines," were by his wife, Mary.]

I wandered lonely as a cloud
That floats on high o'er vales and hills,
When all at once I saw a crowd,
A host, of golden daffodils;
5 Beside the lake, beneath the trees,
Fluttering and dancing in the breeze.

Continuous as the stars that shine
And twinkle on the milky way,
They stretched in never-ending line
Along the margin of a bay:
Ten thousand saw I at a glance,   10
Tossing their heads in sprightly dance.

The waves beside them danced; but they
Out-did the sparkling waves in glee:
A poet could not but be gay,
In such a jocund° company: 15
I gazed—and gazed—but little thought
What wealth the show to me had brought:

For oft, when on my couch I lie
In vacant or in pensive mood,
They flash upon that inward eye   20
Which is the bliss of solitude;
And then my heart with pleasure fills,
And dances with the daffodils.

jocund: cheerful, merry.

PLAYS

Anton Chekhov (1860–1904)

The Bear:
A Joke in One Act   1888

CAST OF CHARACTERS

Mrs. Popov. *A widow of seven months,* Mrs. Popov *is small and pretty, with dimples. She is a landowner. At the start of the play, she is pining away in memory of her dead husband.*

Grigory Stepanovich Smirnov. *Easily angered and loud,* Smirnov *is older. He is a landowner, too, and a man of substance.*

Luka. Luka *is* Mrs. Popov's *footman (a servant whose main tasks were to wait table and attend the carriages, in addition to general duties). He is old enough to feel secure in telling* Mrs. Popov *what he thinks.*

Gardener, Coachman, Workmen, *who enter at the end.*

The drawing room of Mrs. Popov's *country home.*

(Mrs. Popov, *in deep mourning, does not remove her eyes from a photograph.*)

Luka.   It isn't right madam . . . you're only destroying yourself. . . . The chambermaid and the cook have gone off berry picking; every living being is rejoicing; even the cat knows how to be content, walking around the yard catching birds, and you sit in your room all day as if it were a convent, and you don't take pleasure in anything. Yes, really! Almost a year has passed since you've gone out of the house!

Mrs. Popov.   And I shall never go out. . . . What for? My life is already ended. *He* lies in his grave; I have buried myself in these four walls . . . we are both dead.

Luka.   There you go again! Your husband is dead, that's as it was meant to be, it's the will of God, may he rest in peace. . . . You've done your mourning and that will do. You can't go on weeping and mourning forever. My wife died when her time came, too. . . . Well? I grieved, I wept for a month, and that was enough for her; the old lady wasn't worth a second more. (*Sighs.*) You've forgotten all your neighbors. You don't go anywhere or accept any calls. We live, so to speak, like spiders. We never see the light. The mice have eaten my uniform. It isn't as if there weren't any nice neighbors— the district is full of them . . . there's a regiment stationed at Riblov, such officers— they're like candy—you'll never get your fill of them! And in the barracks, never a Fri-

Slightly altered from the Bantam Press edition of *Ten Great One-Act Plays,* Morris Sweetkind, ed. (1968).

day goes by without a dance; and, if you please, the military band plays music every day. . . . Yes, madam, my dear lady: you're young, beautiful, in the full bloom of youth—if only you took a little pleasure in life . . . beauty doesn't last forever, you know! In ten years' time, you'll be wanting to wave your fanny in front of the officers—and it will be too late.

MRS. POPOV (*determined*).   I must ask you never to talk to me like that! You know that when Mr. Popov died, life lost all its salt for me. It may seem to you that I am alive, but that's only conjecture! I vowed to wear mourning to my grave and not to see the light of day. . . . Do you hear me? May his departed spirit see how much I love him. . . . Yes, I know, it's no mystery to you that he was often mean to me, cruel . . . and even unfaithful, but I shall remain true to the grave and show him I know how to love. There, beyond the grave, he will see me as I was before his death. . . .

LUKA.   Instead of talking like that, you should be taking a walk in the garden or have Toby or Giant harnessed and go visit some of the neighbors . . .

MRS. POPOV.   Ai! (*She weeps.*)   5

LUKA.   Madam! Dear lady! What's the matter with you! Christ be with you!

MRS. POPOV.   Oh, how he loved Toby! He always used to ride on him to visit the Korchagins or the Vlasovs. How wonderfully he rode! How graceful he was when he pulled at the reins with all his strength! Do you remember? Toby, Toby! Tell them to give him an extra bag of oats today.

LUKA.   Yes, madam.

(*Sound of loud ringing.*)

MRS POPOV (*shudders*).   Who's that? Tell them I'm not at home!

LUKA.   Of course, madam. (*He exits.*)

MRS. POPOV(*alone. Looks at the photograph*).   You will see, Nicholas, how much I   10
can love and forgive . . . my love will die only when I do, when my poor heart stops beating. (*Laughing through her tears.*) Have you no shame? I'm a good girl, a virtuous little wife. I've locked myself in and I'll be true to you to the grave, and you . . . aren't you ashamed, you chubby cheeks? You deceived me, you made scenes, for weeks on end you left me alone . . .

LUKA (*enters, alarmed*).   Madam, somebody is asking for you. He wants to see you. . . .

MRS. POPOV.   But didn't you tell them that since the death of my husband, I don't see anybody?

LUKA.   I did, but he didn't want to listen; he spoke about some very important business.

MRS. POPOV.   I am *not at home!*   15

LUKA.   That's what I told him . . . but . . . the devil . . . he cursed and pushed past me right into the room . . . he's in the dining room right now.

MRS. POPOV (*losing her temper*).   Very well, let him come in . . . such manners! (LUKA *goes out.*) How difficult these people are! What does he want from me? Why should he disturb my peace? (*Sighs.*) But it's obvious I'll have to go live in a convent. . . . (*Thoughtfully.*) Yes, a convent. . . .

(*Enter* SMIROV *with* LUKA).

SMIRNOV (*to* LUKA).   You idiot, you talk too much. . . . Ass! (*Sees* MRS. POPOV *and changes to dignified speech.*) Madam, may I introduce myself: retired lieutenant of the artillery and landowner, Grigory Stepanovich Smirnov! I feel the necessity of troubling you about a highly important matter. . . .

20   MRS. POPOV (*refusing her hand*).   What do you want?

SMIRNOV.   Your late husband, whom I had the pleasure of knowing, has remained in my debt for two twelve-hundred-ruble notes. Since I must pay the interest at the agricultural bank tomorrow, I have come to ask you, madam, to pay me the money today.

MRS. POPOV.   One thousand two hundred. . . . And why was my husband in debt to you?

SMIRNOV.   He used to buy oats from me.

MRS. POPOV (*sighing, to* LUKA).   So, Luka, don't you forget to tell them to give Toby an extra bag of oats.

(LUKA *goes out.*)

(*To* SMIRNOV).   If Nikolai, my husband, was in debt to you, then it goes without saying that I'll pay; but please excuse me today. I haven't any spare cash. The day after tomorrow, my steward will be back from town and I will give him instructions to pay you what is owed; until then I cannot comply with your wishes. . . . Besides, today is the anniversary—exactly seven months ago my husband died, and I'm in such a mood that I'm not quite disposed to occupy myself with money matters.

25   SMIRNOV.   And I'm in such a mood that if I don't pay the interest tomorrow, I'll be owing so much that my troubles will drown me. They'll take away my estate!

MRS. POPOV.   You'll receive your money the day after tomorrow.

SMIRNOV.   I don't want the money the day after tomorrow. I want it today.

MRS. POPOV.   You must excuse me.   I can't pay you today.

SMIRNOV.   And I can't wait until after tomorrow.

30   MRS. POPOV.   What can I do, if I don't have it now?

SMIRNOV.   You mean to say you can't pay?

MRS. POPOV.   I can't pay. . . .

SMIRNOV.   Hm! Is that your last word?

MRS. POPOV.   That is my last word.

35   SMIRNOV.   Positively the last?

MRS. POPOV.   Positively.

SMIRNOV.   Thank you very much. We'll make a note of that. (*Shrugs his shoulders.*) And people want me to be calm and collected! Just now, on the way here, I met a tax officer and he asked me: why are you always so angry, Grigory Stepanovich? Goodness' sake, how can I be anything but angry? I need money desperately . . . I rode out yesterday early in the morning, at daybreak, and went to see all my debtors; and if only one of them had paid his debt . . . I was dog-tired, spent the night God knows where—a Jewish tavern beside a barrel of vodka. . . . Finally I got here, fifty miles from home, hoping to be paid, and you treat me to a "mood." How can I help being angry?

MRS. POPOV.   It seems to me that I clearly said: My steward will return from the country and then you will be paid.

SMIRNOV.   I didn't come to your steward, but to you! What the hell, if you'll pardon the expression, would I do with your steward?

40   MRS. POPOV.   Excuse me, my dear sir, I am not accustomed to such unusual expressions nor to such a tone. I'm not listening to you any more. (*Goes out quickly.*)

SMIRNOV (*alone*).   Well, how do you like that? "A mood." . . . "Husband died seven months ago!" Must I pay the interest or mustn't I? I ask you: Must I pay, or must I not? So, your husband's dead, and you're in a mood and all that finicky stuff . . . and your steward's away somewhere; may he drop dead. What do you want me to do? Do you think I can fly away from my creditors in a balloon or something? Or should I run and bash my head against the wall? I go to Gruzdev—and he's not at home; Yaroshevich is hiding, with Kuritsin it's a quarrel to the death and I almost throw him out the window; Mazutov has diarrhea, and this one is in a "mood." Not one of these swine wants to pay me! And all because I'm too nice to them. I'm a sniveling idiot, I'm spineless, I'm an old lady! I'm too delicate with them! So, just you wait! You'll find out what I'm like! I won't let you play around with me, you devils! I'll stay and stick it out until she pays. Rrr! . . . How furious I am today, how furious! I'm shaking inside from rage and I can hardly catch my breath. . . . Damn it! My God, I even feel sick! (*He shouts.*) Hey, you!

LUKA (*enters*).   What do you want?

SMIRNOV.   Give me some beer or some water! (LUKA *exits.*) What logic is there in this! A man needs money desperately, it's like a noose around his neck—and she won't pay because, you see, she's not disposed to occupy herself with money matters! . . . That's the logic of a woman! That's why I never did like and do not like to talk to women. I'd rather sit on a keg of gunpowder than talk to a woman. Brr! . . . I even have goose pimples, this broad has put me in such a rage! All I have to do is see one of those spoiled bitches from a distance, and I get so angry it gives me a cramp in the leg. I just want to shout for help.

LUKA (*entering with water*).   Madam is sick and won't see anyone.

SMIRNOV.   Get out! (LUKA *goes.*) Sick and won't see anyone! No need to see   45
me . . . I'll stay and sit here until you give me the money. You can stay sick for a week, and I'll stay for a week . . . if you're sick for a year, I'll stay a year . . . I'll get my own back, dear lady! You can't impress me with your widow's weeds and your dimpled cheeks . . . we know all about those dimples! (*Shouts through the window.*) Semyon, unharness the horses! We're not going away quite yet! I'm staying here! Tell them in the stable to give the horses some oats! You brute, you let the horse on the left side get all tangled up in the reins again! (*Teasing.*) "Never mind" . . . I'll give you a never mind! (*Goes away from the window.*) Shit! The heat is unbearable and nobody pays up. I slept badly last night and on top of everything else this broad in mourning is "in a mood" . . . my head aches . . . (*Drinks, and grimaces.*) Shit! This is water! What I need is a drink! (*Shouts.*) Hey, you!

LUKA (*enters*).   What is it?

SMIRNOV.   Give me a glass of vodka. (LUKA *goes out.*) Oof! (*Sits down and examines himself.*) Nobody would say I was looking well! Dusty all over, boots dirty, unwashed, unkempt, straw on my waistcoat. . . . The dear lady probably took me for a robber. (*Yawns.*) It's not very polite to present myself in a drawing room looking like this; oh well, who cares? . . . I'm not here as a visitor but as a creditor, and there's no official costume for creditors. . . .

LUKA (*enters with vodka*).   You're taking liberties, my good man. . . .

SMIRNOV (*angrily*).   What?

LUKA.   I . . . nothing . . . I only . . .   50

SMIRNOV.   Who are you talking to? Shut up!

LUKA (*aside*).   The devil sent this leech. An ill wind brought him. . . . (LUKA *goes out.*)

SMIRNOV.   Oh how furious I am! I'm so mad I could crush the whole world into a powder! I even feel faint! (*Shouts.*) Hey, you!

MRS. POPOV (*enters, eyes downcast*).   My dear sir, in my solitude, I have long ago grown unaccustomed to the masculine voice and I cannot bear shouting. I must request you not to disturb my peace and quiet!

55   SMIRNOV.   Pay me my money and I'll go.

MRS. POPOV.   I told you in plain language: I haven't any spare cash now; wait until the day after tomorrow.

SMIRNOV.   And I also told you respectfully, in plain language: I don't need the money the day after tomorrow, but today. If you don't pay me today, then tomorrow I'll have to hang myself.

MRS. POPOV.   But what can I do if I don't have the money? You're so strange!

SMIRNOV.   Then you won't pay me now? No?

60   MRS. POPOV.   I can't. . . .

SMIRNOV.   In that case, I can stay here and wait until you pay. . . . (*Sits down.*) You'll pay the day after tomorrow? Excellent! In that case I'll stay here until the day after tomorrow. I'll sit here all that time . . .(*Jumps up.*) I ask you: Have I got to pay the interest tomorrow, or not? Or do you think I'm joking?

MRS. POPOV.   My dear sir, I ask you not to shout! This isn't a stable!

SMIRNOV.   I wasn't asking you about a stable but about this: Do I have to pay the interest tomorrow or not?

MRS. POPOV.   You don't know how to behave in the company of a lady!

65   SMIRNOV.   No, I don't know how to behave in the company of a lady!

MRS. POPOV.   No, you don't! You are an ill-bred, rude man! Respectable people don't talk to a woman like that!

SMIRNOV.   Ach, it's astonishing! How would you like me to talk to you? In French, perhaps? (*Lisps in anger.*) Madam, je vous prie° . . . how happy I am that you're not paying me the money. . . . Ah, pardon, I've made you uneasy! Such lovely weather we're having today! And you look so becoming in your mourning dress. (*Bows and scrapes.*)

MRS. POPOV.   That's rude and not very clever!

SMIRNOV (*teasing*).   Rude and not very clever! I don't know how to behave in the company of ladies. Madam, in my time I've seen far more women than you've seen sparrows. Three times I've fought duels over women; I've jilted twelve women, nine have jilted me! Yes! There was a time when I played the fool; I became sentimental over women, used honeyed words, fawned on them, bowed and scraped. . . . I loved, suffered, sighed at the moon; I became limp, melted, shivered . . . I loved passionately, madly, every which way, devil take me, I chattered away like a magpie about the emancipation of women, ran through half my fortune as a result of my tender feelings; but now, if you will excuse me, I'm on to your ways! I've had enough! Dark eyes, passionate eyes, ruby lips, dimpled cheeks; the moon, whispers, bated breath—for all that I wouldn't give a good goddamn. Present company excepted, of course, but all women, young and old alike, are affected clowns, gossips, hateful, consummate liars to the marrow of their bones, vain, trivial, ruthless, outrageously illogical, and as far as this is concerned (*taps on his forehead*), well, excuse my frankness, any sparrow could

---

Madam, je vous prie: Madam, I beg you.

give pointers to a philosopher in petticoats! Look at one of those romantic creatures: muslin, ethereal demigoddess, a thousand raptures, and you look into her soul—a common crocodile! (*Grips the back of a chair; the chair cracks and breaks.*) But the most revolting part of it all is that this crocodile imagines that she has, above everything, her own privilege, a monopoly on tender feelings. The hell with it—you can hang me upside down by that nail if a woman is capable of loving anything besides a lapdog. All she can do when she's in love is slobber! While the man suffers and sacrifices, all her love is expressed in playing with her skirt and trying to lead him around firmly by the nose. You have the misfortune of being a woman, you know yourself what the nature of a woman is like. Tell me honestly; Have you ever in your life seen a woman who is sincere, faithful, and constant? You never have! Only old and ugly ladies are faithful and constant! You're more liable to meet a horned cat or a white woodcock than a faithful woman!

MRS. POPOV.   Pardon me, but in your opinion, who is faithful and constant in   70
love? The man?

SMIRNOV.   Yes, the man!

MRS. POPOV.   The man! (*Malicious laugh.*) Men are faithful and constant in love! That's news! (*Heatedly*) What right have you to say that? Men are faithful and constant! For that matter, as far as I know, of all the men I have known and now know, my late husband was the best. . . . I loved him passionately, with all my being, as only a young intellectual woman can love; I gave him my youth, my happiness, my life, my fortune; he was my life's breath; I worshipped him as if I were a heathen, and . . . and, what good did it do—this best of men himself deceived me shamelessly at every step of the way. After his death, I found his desk full of love letters; and when he was alive—it's terrible to remember—he used to leave me alone for weeks at a time, and before my very eyes he flirted with other women and deceived me. He squandered my money, made a mockery of my feelings . . . and, in spite of all that, I loved him and was true to him . . . and besides, now that he is dead, I am still faithful and constant. I have shut myself up in these four walls forever and I won't remove these widow's weeds until my dying day. . . .

SMIRNOV (*laughs contemptuously*).   Widow's weeds! . . . I don't know what you take me for! As if I didn't know why you wear that black outfit and bury yourself in these four walls! Well, well! It's no secret, so romantic! When some fool of a poet passes by this country house, he'll look up at your window and think: "Here lives the mysterious Tamara, who, for the love of her husband, buried herself in these four walls." We know these tricks!

MRS POPOV (*flaring*).   What? How dare you say that to me?

SMIRNOV.   You may have buried yourself alive, but you haven't forgotten to   75
powder yourself!

MRS. POPOV.   How dare you use such expressions with me?

SMIRNOV.   Please don't shout. I'm not your steward! You must allow me to call a spade a spade. I'm not a woman and I'm used to saying what's on my mind! Don't you shout at me!

MRS. POPOV.   I'm not shouting, you are! Please leave me in peace!

SMIRNOV.   Pay me my money and I'll go.

MRS. POPOV.   I won't give you any money!   80

SMIRNOV.   Yes, you will.

MRS. POPOV.   To spite you, I won't pay you anything. You can leave me in peace!

SMIRNOV.   I don't have the pleasure of being either your husband or your fiancé, so please don't make scenes! (*Sits down.*) I don't like it.

MRS. POPOV (*choking with rage*).   You're sitting down?

85   SMIRNOV.   Yes, I am.

MRS. POPOV.   I ask you to get out!

SMIRNOV.   Give me my money . . . (*Aside.*) Oh, I'm so furious! Furious!

MRS. POPOV.   I don't want to talk to impudent people! Get out of here! (*Pause.*) You're not going? No?

SMIRNOV.   No.

90   MRS. POPOV.   No?

SMIRNOV.   No!

MRS. POPOV.   We'll see about that. (*Rings.*)

(LUKA *enters.*)

Luka, show the gentleman out!

LUKA (*goes up to* SMIRNOV).   Sir, will you please leave, as you have been asked. You musn't . . .

SMIRNOV (*jumping up*).   Shut up! Who do you think you're talking to? I'll make mincemeat out of you!

95   LUKA (*his hand to his heart*).   Oh, my God! Saints above! (*Falls into chair.*) Oh, I feel ill! I feel ill! I can't catch my breath!

MRS. POPOV.   Where's Dasha? Dasha! (*She shouts.*) Dasha! Pelagea! Dasha! (*She rings.*)

LUKA.   Oh! They've all gone berry picking . . . there's nobody at home . . . I'm ill! Water!

MRS POPOV.   Will you please get out!

SMIRNOV.   Will you please be more polite?

100   MRS. POPOV (*clenches her fist and stamps her feet*).   You're nothing but a crude bear! A brute! A monster!

SMIRNOV.   What? What did you say?

MRS. POPOV.   I said that you were a bear, a monster!

SMIRNOV (*advancing toward her*).   Excuse me, but what right do you have to insult me?

MRS. POPOV.   Yes, I am insulting you . . . so what? Do you think I'm afraid of you?

105   SMIRNOV.   And do you think just because you're one of those romantic creations, that you have the right to insult me with impunity? Yes? I challenge you!

LUKA.   Lord in Heaven! Saints above! . . . Water!

SMIRNOV.   Pistols!

MRS. POPOV.   Do you think just because you have big fists and you can bellow like a bull, that I'm afraid of you? You're such a bully!

SMIRNOV.   I challenge you! I'm not going to let anybody insult me, and I don't care if you are a woman, a delicate creature!

110   MRS. POPOV (*trying to get a word in edgewise*).   Bear! Bear! Bear!

SMIRNOV.   It's about time we got rid of the prejudice that only men must pay for their insults! Devil take it, if women want to be equal, they should behave as equals! Let's fight!

MRS. POPOV.   You want to fight! By all means!

SMIRNOV.   This minute!

MRS. POPOV.   This minute! My husband had some pistols . . . I'll go and get them right away. (*Goes hurriedly and then returns.*) What pleasure I'll have putting a bullet through that thick head of yours! The hell with you! (*She goes out.*)

SMIRNOV.   I'll shoot her down like a chicken! I'm not a little boy or a sentimen-   115
tal puppy. I don't care if she is delicate and fragile.

LUKA.   Kind sir! Holy father! (*Kneels.*) Have pity on a poor old man and go away from here! You've frightened her to death and now you're going to shoot her?

SMIRNOV (*not listening to him*).   If she fights, then it means she believes in equal-ity of rights and emancipation of women. Here the sexes are equal! I'll shoot her like a chicken! But what a woman! (*Imitates her.*) "The hell with you! . . . I'll put a bullet through that thick head of yours! . . ." What a woman! How she blushed, her eyes shone . . . she accepted the challenge! To tell the truth, it was the first time in my life I've seen a woman like that. . . .

LUKA.   Dear sir, please go away! I'll pray to God on your behalf as long as I live!

SMIRNOV.   That's a woman for you! A woman like that I can understand! A real woman! Not a sour-faced nincompoop but fiery, gunpowder! Fireworks! I'm even sorry to have to kill her!

LUKA (*weeps*).   Dear sir . . . go away!   120

SMIRNOV.   I positively like her! Positively! Even though she has dimpled cheeks, I like her! I'm almost ready to forget about the debt. . . . My fury has dimin-ished. Wonderful woman!

MRS. POPOV (*enters with pistols*).   Here they are, the pistols. Before we fight, you must show me how to fire. . . . I've never had a pistol in my hands before . . .

LUKA.   Oh dear Lord, for pity's sake. . . . I'll go and find the gardener and the coachman. . . .What did we do to deserve such trouble? (*Exit.*)

SMIRNOV (*examining the pistols*).   You see, there are several sorts of pistols . . . there are special dueling pistols, the Mortimer with primers. Then there are Smith and Wesson revolvers, triple action with extractors . . . excellent pistols! . . . they cost a minimum of ninety rubles a pair. . . .You must hold the revolver like this . . . (*Aside.*) What eyes, what eyes! A woman to set you on fire!

MRS. POPOV.   Like this?   125

SMIRNOV.   Yes, like this . . . then you cock the pistol . . . take air . . . put your head back a little . . . stretch your arm out all the way . . . that's right . . . then with this finger press on this little piece of goods . . . and that's all there is to do . . . but the most important thing is not to get excited and aim without hurrying . . . try to keep your arm from shaking.

MRS. POPOV.   Good . . . it's not comfortable to shoot indoors. Let's go into the garden.

SMIRNOV.   Let's go. But I'm giving you advance notice that I'm going to fire into the air.

MRS. POPOV.   That's the last straw! Why?

SMIRNOV.   Why? . . . Why . . . because it's my business, that's why.   130

MRS. POPOV.   Are you afraid? Yes? Aahhh! No, sir. You're not going to get out of it that easily! Be so good as to follow me! I will not rest until I've put a hole through your forehead . . . that forehead I hate so much! Are you afraid?

SMIRNOV.   Yes, I'm afraid.

MRS. POPOV.   You're lying! Why don't you want to fight?

SMIRNOV. Because . . . because you . . . because I like you.

135   MRS. POPOV (*laughs angrily*). He likes me! He dares say that he likes me! (*Points to the door.*) Out!

SMIRNOV (*loads the revolver in silence, takes cap and goes; at the door, stops for half a minute while they look at each other in silence; then he approaches* MRS. POPOV *hesitantly*). Listen. . . . Are you still angry? I'm extremely irritated, but, do you understand me, how can I express it . . . the fact is, that, you see, strictly speaking . . . (*He shouts.*) Is it my fault, really, for liking you? (*Grabs the back of a chair, which cracks and breaks.*) Why the hell do you have such fragile furniture! I like you! Do you understand? I . . . I'm almost in love with you!

MRS. POPOV. Get away from me—I hate you!

SMIRNOV. God, what a woman! I've never in my life seen anything like her! I'm lost! I'm done for! I'm caught like a mouse in a trap!

MRS. POPOV. Stand back or I'll shoot!

140   SMIRNOV. Shoot! You could never understand what happiness it would be to die under the gaze of those wonderful eyes, to be shot by a revolver which was held by those little velvet hands. . . . I've gone out of my mind! Think about it and decide right away, because if I leave here, then we'll never see each other again! Decide . . . I'm a nobleman, a respectable gentleman, of good family. I have an income of ten thousand a year. . . . I can put a bullet through a coin tossed in the air . . . I have some fine horses. . . . Will you be my wife?

MRS. POPOV (*indignantly brandishes her revolver*). Let's fight! I challenge you!

SMIRNOV. I'm out of my mind. . . . I don't understand anything . . . (*Shouts.*) Hey, you, water!

MRS. POPOV (*shouts*). Let's fight!

SMIRNOV. I've gone out of my mind. I'm in love like a boy, like an idiot! (*He grabs her hand, she screams with pain.*) I love you! (*Kneels.*) I love you as I've never loved before! I've jilted twelve women, nine women have jilted me, but I've never loved one of them as I love you. . . . I'm weak, I'm a limp rag. . . . I'm on my knees like a fool, offering you my hand. . . . Shame, shame! I haven't been in love for five years, I vowed I wouldn't; and suddenly I'm in love, like a fish out of water. I'm offering my hand in marriage. Yes or no? You don't want to? You don't need to! (*Gets up and quickly goes to the door.*)

145   MRS. POPOV. Wait!

SMIRNOV (*stops*). Well?

MRS POPOV. Nothing . . . you can go . . . go away . . . wait . . . No, get out, get out! I hate you! But—don't go! Oh, if you only knew how furious I am, how angry! (*Throws revolver on table.*) My fingers are swollen from that nasty thing. . . . (*Tears her handkerchief furiously.*) What are you waiting for? Get out!

SMIRNOV. Farewell!

MRS. POPOV. Yes, yes, go away! (*Shouts.*) Where are you going? Stop. . . . Oh, go away! Oh, how furious I am! Don't come near me!

150   SMIRNOV (*approaching her*). How angry I am with myself! I'm in love like a student. I've been on my knees. . . . It gives me the shivers. (*Rudely.*) I love you! A lot of good it will do me to fall in love with you! Tomorrow I've got to pay the interest, begin the mowing of the hay. (*Puts his arm around her waist.*) I'll never forgive myself for this. . . .

MRS. POPOV. Get away from me! Get your hands away! I . . . hate you! I . . . challenge you!

(*Prolonged kiss.* LUKA *enters with an ax, the* GARDENER *with a rake, the* COACHMAN *with a pitchfork, and* WORKMAN *with cudgels.*)

LUKA (*catches sight of the pair kissing*).   Lord in heaven! (*Pause.*)

MRS. POPOV (*lowering her eyes*).   Luka, tell them in the stable not to give Toby any oats today.

CURTAIN

Susan Glaspell (1882–1948)

Trifles   1916

CAST OF CHARACTERS

George Henderson, *county attorney*
Henry Peters, *sheriff*
Lewis Hale, *a neighboring farmer*
Mrs. Peters
Mrs. Hale

Scene. *The kitchen in the now abandoned farmhouse of John Wright, a gloomy kitchen, and left without having been put in order—unwashed pans under the sink, a loaf of bread outside the breadbox, a dish towel on the table—other signs of incompleted work. At the rear the outer door opens and the Sheriff comes in followed by the County Attorney and Hale. The Sheriff and Hale are men in middle life, the County Attorney is a young man; all are much bundled up and go at once to the stove. They are followed by two women—the Sheriff's wife first; she is a slight wiry woman, a thin nervous face. Mrs. Hale is larger and would ordinarily be called more comfortable looking, but she is disturbed now and looks fearfully about as she enters. The women have come in slowly, and stand close together near the door.*

COUNTY ATTORNEY. (*Rubbing his hands.*)   This feels good. Come up to the fire, ladies.

MRS. PETERS. (*After taking a step forward.*)   I'm not—cold.

SHERIFF. (*Unbuttoning his overcoat and stepping away from the stove as if to mark the beginning of official business.*)   Now, Mr. Hale, before we move things about, you explain to Mr. Henderson just what you saw when you came here yesterday morning.

COUNTY ATTORNEY.   By the way, has anything been moved? Are things just as you left them yesterday?

SHERIFF. (*Looking about.*)   It's just the same. When it dropped below zero last   5 night I thought I'd better send Frank out this morning to make a fire for us—no use getting pneumonia with a big case on, but I told him not to touch anything except the stove—and you know Frank.

COUNTY ATTORNEY.   Somebody should have been left here yesterday.

SHERIFF.   Oh—yesterday. When I had to send Frank to Morris Center for that man who went crazy—I want you to know I had my hands full yesterday, I knew you could get back from Omaha by today and as long as I went over everything here myself—

COUNTY ATTORNEY.   Well, Mr. Hale, tell just what happened when you came here yesterday morning.

HALE.   Harry and I had started to town with a load of potatoes. We came along the road from my place and as I got here I said, "I'm going to see if I can't get John Wright to go in with me on a party telephone." I spoke to Wright about it once before and he put me off, saying folks talked too much anyway, and all he asked was peace and quiet—I guess you know about how much he talked himself; but I thought maybe if I went to the house and talked about it before his wife, though I said to Harry that I didn't know as what his wife wanted made much difference to John—

10   COUNTY ATTORNEY.   Let's talk about that later, Mr. Hale. I do want to talk about that, but tell now just what happened when you got to the house.

HALE.   I didn't hear or see anything; I knocked at the door, and still it was all quiet inside. I knew they must be up, it was past eight o'clock. So I knocked again, and I thought I heard somebody say, "Come in." I wasn't sure, I'm not sure yet, but I opened the door—this door (*Indicating the door by which the two women are still standing*) and there in that rocker—(*Pointing to it*) sat Mrs. Wright.

(*They all look at the rocker.*)

COUNTY ATTORNEY.   What—was she doing?

HALE.   She was rockin' back and forth. She had her apron in her hand and was kind of—pleating it.

COUNTY ATTORNEY.   And how did she—look?

15   HALE.   Well, she looked queer.

COUNTY ATTORNEY.   How do you mean—queer?

HALE.   Well, as if she didn't know what she was going to do next. And kind of done up.

COUNTY ATTORNEY.   How did she seem to feel about your coming?

HALE.   Why, I don't think she minded—one way or other. She didn't pay much attention. I said, "How do, Mrs. Wright, it's cold, ain't it?" She said, "Is it?"—and went on kind of pleating at her apron. Well, I was surprised; she didn't ask me to come up to the stove, or to set down, but just sat there, not even looking at me, so I said, "I want to see John." And then she—laughed. I guess you would call it a laugh. I thought of Harry and the team outside, so I said a little sharp: "Can't I see John?" "No," she says, kind o' dull like. "Ain't he home?" says I. "Yes," says she, "he's home." "Then why can't I see him?" I asked her, out of patience. "'Cause he's dead," says she. "*Dead?*" says I. She just nodded her head, not getting a bit excited, but rockin' back and forth. "Why—where is he?" says I, not knowing what to say. She just pointed upstairs— like that (*Himself pointing to the room above*). I got up, with the idea of going up there. I walked from there to here—then I says, "Why, what did he die of?" "He died of a rope round his neck," says she, and just went on pleatin' at her apron. Well, I went out and called Harry. I thought I might—need help. We went upstairs and there he was lyin'—

COUNTY ATTORNEY. I think I'd rather have you go into that upstairs, where you 20
can point it all out. Just go on now with the rest of the story.

HALE. Well, my first thought was to get that rope off. It looked . . . (*Stops, his face twitches*) . . . but Harry, he went up to him, and he said, "No, he's dead all right, and we'd better not touch anything." So we went back down stairs. She was still sitting that same way. "Has anybody been notified?" I asked. "No," says she, unconcerned. "Who did this, Mrs. Wright?" said Harry. He said it businesslike—and she stopped pleatin' of her apron. "I don't know," she says. "You don't *know*?" says Harry. "No," says she. "Weren't you sleepin' in the bed with him?" says Harry. "Yes," says she, "but I was on the inside." "Somebody slipped a rope round his neck and strangled him and you didn't wake up?" says Harry. "I didn't wake up," she said after him. We must 'a looked as if we didn't see how that could be, for after a minute she said, "I sleep sound." Harry was going to ask her more questions but I said maybe we ought to let her tell her story first to the coroner, or the sheriff, so Harry went fast as he could to Rivers' place, where there's a telephone.

COUNTY ATTORNEY. And what did Mrs. Wright do when she knew that you had gone for the coroner?

HALE. She moved from that chair to this one over here (*Pointing to a small chair in the corner*) and just sat there with her hands held together and looking down. I got a feeling that I ought to make some conversation, so I said I had come in to see if John wanted to put in a telephone, and at that she started to laugh, and then she stopped and looked at me—scared. (*The County Attorney, who has had his notebook out, makes a note.*) I dunno, maybe it wasn't scared. I wouldn't like to say it was. Soon Harry got back, and then Dr. Lloyd came, and you, Mr. Peters, and so I guess that's all I know that you don't.

COUNTY ATTORNEY. (*Looking around.*) I guess we'll go upstairs first—and then out to the barn and around there. (*To the Sheriff*) You're convinced that there was nothing important here—nothing that would point to any motive.

SHERIFF. Nothing here but kitchen things. 25

(*The County Attorney, after again looking around the kitchen, opens the door of a cupboard closet. He gets up on a chair and looks on a shelf. Pulls his hand away, sticky.*)

COUNTY ATTORNEY. Here's a nice mess.

(*The women draw nearer.*)

MRS. PETERS (*To the other woman.*) Oh, her fruit; it did freeze. (*To the County Attorney*) She worried about that when it turned so cold. She said the fire'd go out and her jars would break.

SHERIFF. Well, can you beat the women! Held for murder and worryin' about her preserves.

COUNTY ATTORNEY. I guess before we're through she may have something more serious than preserves to worry about.

HALE. Well, women are used to worrying over trifles. 30

(*The two women move a little closer together.*)

COUNTY ATTORNEY. (*With the gallantry of a young politician.*) And yet, for all their worries, what would we do without the ladies? (*The women do not unbend. He goes to the sink, takes a dipperful of water from the pail and pouring it into a basin, washes his hands. Starts to wipe them on the roller towel, turns it for a cleaner place.*) Dirty towels! (*Kicks his foot against the pans under the sink.*) Not much of a housekeeper, would you say, ladies?

MRS. HALE. (*Stiffly.*)   There's a great deal of work to be done on a farm.

COUNTY ATTORNEY.   To be sure. And yet (*With a little bow to her*) I know there are some Dickson county farmhouses which do not have such roller towels.

(*He gives it a pull to expose its full length again.*)

MRS. HALE.   Those towels get dirty awful quick. Men's hands aren't always as clean as they might be.

35   COUNTY ATTORNEY.   Ah, loyal to your sex, I see. But you and Mrs. Wright were neighbors. I suppose you were friends, too.

MRS. HALE. (*Shaking her head.*)   I've not seen much of her of late years. I've not been in this house—it's more than a year.

COUNTY ATTORNEY.   And why was that? You didn't like her?

MRS. HALE.   I liked her all well enough. Farmers' wives have their hands full, Mr. Henderson. And then—

COUNTY ATTORNEY.   Yes—?

40   MRS. HALE. (*Looking about.*)   It never seemed a very cheerful place.

COUNTY ATTORNEY.   No—it's not cheerful. I shouldn't say she had the home-making instinct.

MRS. HALE.   Well, I don't know as Wright had, either.

COUNTY ATTORNEY.   You mean that they didn't get on very well?

MRS. HALE.   No, I don't mean anything. But I don't think a place'd be any cheerfuller for John Wright's being in it.

45   COUNTY ATTORNEY.   I'd like to talk more of that a little later. I want to get the lay of things upstairs now.

(*He goes to the left, where three steps lead to a stair door.*)

SHERIFF.   I suppose anything Mrs. Peter does'll be all right. She was to take in some clothes for her, you know, and a few little things. We left in such a hurry yesterday.

COUNTY ATTORNEY.   Yes, but I would like to see what you take, Mrs. Peters, and keep an eye out for anything that might be of use to us.

MRS. PETERS.   Yes, Mr. Henderson.

(*The women listen to the men's steps on the stairs, then look about the kitchen.*)

MRS. HALE.   I'd hate to have men coming into my kitchen, snooping around and criticising.

(*She arranges the pans under the sink which the County Attorney had shoved out of place.*)

50   MRS. PETERS.   Of course it's no more than their duty.

MRS. HALE.   Duty's all right, but I guess that deputy sheriff that came out to make the fire might have got a little of this on. (*Gives the roller towel a pull.*) Wish I'd thought of that sooner. Seems mean to talk about her for not having things slicked up when she had to come away in such a hurry.

MRS. PETERS. (*Who has gone to a small table in the left rear corner of the room, and lifted one end of a towel that covers a pan.*)   She had bread set.

(*Stands still.*)

MRS. HALE. (*Eyes fixed on a loaf of bread beside the breadbox, which is on a low shelf at the other side of the room. Moves slowly toward it.*)   She was going to put this in there. (*Picks up loaf, then abruptly drops it. In a manner of returning to familiar things.*) It's a shame about her fruit. I wonder if it's all gone. (*Gets up on the chair and looks.*) I think there's some here that's all right, Mrs. Peters. Yes—here; (*Holding it toward the window*) this is cherries, too. (*Looking again.*) I declare I believe that's the only one. (*Gets down, bottle in her hand. Goes to the sink and wipes it off on the outside.*) She'll feel awful bad after all her hard work in the hot weather. I remember the afternoon I put up my cherries last summer.

(*She puts the bottle on the big kitchen table, center of the room. With a sigh, is about to sit down in the rocking-chair. Before she is seated realizes what chair it is; with a slow look at it, steps back. The chair which she has touched rocks back and forth.*)

MRS. PETERS.   Well, I must get those things from the front room closet. (*She goes to the door at the right, but after looking into the other room, steps back.*) You coming with me, Mrs. Hale? You could help me carry them.

(*They go in the other room; reappear, Mrs. Peters carrying a dress and skirt, Mrs. Hale following with a pair of shoes.*)

MRS. PETERS.   My, it's cold in there.   55

(*She puts the clothes on the big table, and hurries to the stove.*)

MRS. HALE. (*Examining her skirt.*)   Wright was close. I think maybe that's why she kept so much to herself. She didn't even belong to the Ladies Aid. I suppose she felt she couldn't do her part, and then you don't enjoy things when you feel shabby. She used to wear pretty clothes and be lively, when she was Minnie Foster, one of the town girls singing in the choir. But that—oh, that was thirty years ago. This all you was to take in?
MRS. PETERS.   She said she wanted an apron. Funny thing to want, for there isn't much to get you dirty in jail, goodness knows. But I suppose just to make her feel more natural. She said they was in the top drawer in this cupboard. Yes, here. And then her little shawl that always hung behind the door. (*Opens stair door and looks.*) Yes, here it is.

(*Quickly shuts door leading upstairs.*)

MRS. HALE. (*Abruptly moving toward her.*)   Mrs. Peters?
MRS. PETERS.   Yes, Mrs. Hale?
MRS. HALE.   Do you think she did it?   60
MRS. PETERS. (*In a frightened voice.*)   Oh, I don't know.
MRS. HALE.   Well, I don't think she did. Asking for an apron and her little shawl. Worrying about her fruit.
MRS. PETERS. (*Starts to speak, glances up, where footsteps are heard in the room above. In a low voice.*)   Mr. Peters says it looks bad for her. Mr. Henderson is awful sarcastic in a speech and he'll make fun of her sayin' she didn't wake up.

MRS. HALE.   Well, I guess John Wright didn't wake when they was slipping that rope under his neck.

65 MRS. PETERS.   No, it's strange. It must have been done awful crafty and still. They say it was such a—funny way to kill a man, rigging it all up like that.

MRS. HALE.   That's just what Mr. Hale said. There was a gun in the house. He says that's what he can't understand.

MRS. PETERS.   Mr. Henderson said coming out that what was needed for the case was a motive; something to show anger, or—sudden feeling.

MRS. HALE. (*Who is standing by the table.*)   Well, I don't see any signs of anger around here. (*She puts her hand on the dish towel which lies on the table, stands looking down at table, one half of which is clean, the other half messy.*) It's wiped to here. (*Makes a move as if to finish work, then turns and looks at loaf of bread outside the breadbox. Drops towel. In that voice of coming back to familiar things.*) Wonder how they are finding things upstairs. I hope she had it a little more red-up° up there. You know, it seems kind of *sneaking*. Locking her up in town and then coming out here and trying to get her own house to turn against her!

MRS. PETERS.   But Mrs. Hale, the law is the law.

70 MRS. HALE.   I s'pose 'tis. (*Unbuttoning her coat.*) Better loosen up your things, Mrs. Peters. You won't feel them when you go out.

(*Mrs. Peters takes off her fur tippet, goes to hang it on hook at back of room, stands looking at the under part of the small corner table.*)

MRS. PETERS.   She was piecing a quilt.

(*She brings the large sewing basket and they look at the pieces.*)

MRS. HALE.   It's a log cabin pattern. Pretty, isn't it? I wonder if she was goin' to quilt it or just knot it?

(*Footsteps have been heard coming down the stairs. The Sheriff enters followed by Hale and the County Attorney.*)

SHERIFF.   They wonder if she was going to quilt it or just knot it!

(*The men laugh; the women look abashed.*)

COUNTY ATTORNEY. (*Rubbing his hands over the stove.*)   Frank's fire didn't do much up there, did it? Well, let's go out to the barn and get that cleared up.

(*The men go outside.*)

75 MRS. HALE. (*Resentfully.*)   I don't know as there's anything so strange, our takin' up our time with little things while we're waiting for them to get the evidence. (*She sits down at the big table smoothing out a block with decision.*) I don't see as it's anything to laugh about.

MRS. PETERS. (*Apologetically.*)   Of course they've got awful important things on their minds.

(*Pulls up a chair and joins Mrs. Hale at the table.*)

MRS. HALE. (*Examining another block.*)   Mrs. Peters, look at this one. Here, this

---

red-up: neat, arranged in order.

is the one she was working on, and look at the sewing! All the rest of it has been so nice and even. And look at this! It's all over the place! Why, it looks as if she didn't know what she was about!

(After she has said this they look at each other, then start to glance back at the door. After an instant Mrs. Hale has pulled at a knot and ripped the sewing.)

MRS. PETERS.   Oh, what are you doing, Mrs. Hale?

MRS. HALE. (*Mildly.*)   Just pulling out a stitch or two that's not sewed very good. (*Threading a needle.*) Bad sewing always made me fidgety.

MRS. PETERS. (*Nervously.*)   I don't think we ought to touch things.   80

MRS. HALE.   I'll just finish up this end. (*Suddenly stopping and leaning forward.*) Mrs. Peters?

MRS. PETERS.   Yes, Mrs. Hale?

MRS. HALE.   What do you suppose she was so nervous about?

MRS. PETERS.   Oh—I don't know. I don't know as she was nervous. I sometimes sew awful queer when I'm just tired. (*Mrs. Hale starts to say something, looks at Mrs. Peters, then goes on sewing.*) Well, I must get these things wrapped up. They may be through sooner than we think. (*Putting apron and other things together.*) I wonder where I can find a piece of paper, and string.

MRS. HALE.   In that cupboard, maybe.   85

MRS. PETERS. (*Looking in cupboard.*)   Why, here's a birdcage. (*Holds it up.*) Did she have a bird, Mrs. Hale?

MRS. HALE.   Why, I don't know whether she did or not—I've not been here for so long. There was a man around last year selling canaries cheap, but I don't know as she took one; maybe she did. She used to sing real pretty herself.

MRS. PETERS. (*Glancing around.*)   Seems funny to think of a bird here. But she must have had one, or why would she have a cage? I wonder what happened to it.

MRS. HALE.   I s'pose maybe the cat got it.

MRS. PETERS.   No, she didn't have a cat. She's got that feeling some people have   90 about cats—being afraid of them. My cat got in her room and she was real upset and asked me to take it out.

MRS. HALE.   My sister Bessie was like that. Queer, ain't it?

MRS. PETERS. (*Examining the cage.*)   Why, look at this door. It's broke. One hinge is pulled apart.

MRS. HALE. (*Looking too.*)   Looks as if someone must have been rough with it.

MRS. PETERS.   Why, yes.

(She brings the cage forward and puts it on the table.)

MRS. HALE.   I wish if they're going to find any evidence they'd be about it. I   95 don't like this place.

MRS. PETERS.   But I'm awful glad you came with me, Mrs. Hale. It would be lonesome for me sitting here alone.

MRS. HALE.   It would, wouldn't it? (*Dropping her sewing.*) But I tell you what I do wish, Mrs. Peters. I wish I had come over sometimes when *she* was here. I—(*Looking around the room*)—wish I had.

MRS. PETERS.   But of course you were awful busy, Mrs. Hale—your house and your children.

MRS. HALE.   I could've come. I stayed away because it weren't cheerful—and maybe that's why I ought to have come. I—I've never liked this place. Maybe because it's down in a hollow and you don't see the road. I dunno what it is but it's a lonesome place and always was. I wish I had come over to see Minnie Foster sometimes. I can see now—

(*Shakes her head.*)

100   MRS. PETERS.   Well, you mustn't reproach yourself, Mrs. Hale. Somehow we just don't see how it is with other folks until—something comes up.

MRS. HALE.   Not having children makes less work—but it makes a quiet house, and Wright out to work all day, and no company when he did come in. Did you know John Wright, Mrs. Peters?

MRS. PETERS.   Not to know him; I've seen him in town. They say he was a good man.

MRS. HALE.   Yes—good; he didn't drink and kept his word as well as most, I guess, and paid his debts. But he was a hard man, Mrs. Peters. Just to pass the time of day with him—(*Shivers.*) Like a raw wind that gets to the bone. (*Pauses, her eye falling on the cage.*) I should think she would 'a wanted a bird. But what do you suppose went with it?

MRS. PETERS.   I don't know, unless it got sick and died.

(*She reaches over and swings the broken door, swings it again. Both women watch it.*)

105   MRS. HALE.   You weren't raised round here, were you? (*Mrs. Peters shakes her head.*) You didn't know—her?

MRS. PETERS.   Not till they brought her yesterday.

MRS. HALE.   She—come to think of it, she was kind of like a bird herself—real sweet and pretty, but kind of timid and—fluttery. How—she—did—change. (*Silence; then as if struck by a happy thought and relieved to get back to everyday things.*) Tell you what, Mrs. Peters, why don't you take the quilt in with you? It might take up her mind.

MRS. PETERS.   Why, I think that's a real nice idea, Mrs. Hale. There couldn't possibly be any objection to it, could there? Now, just what would I take? I wonder if her patches are in here—and her things.

(*They look in the sewing basket.*)

MRS. HALE.   Here's some red. I expect this has got sewing things in it. (*Brings out a fancy box.*) What a pretty box. Looks like something somebody would give you. Maybe her scissors are in here. (*Opens box. Suddenly puts her hand to her nose.*) Why— (*Mrs. Peters bends nearer, then turns her face away.*) There's something wrapped up in this piece of silk.

110   MRS. PETERS.   Why, this isn't her scissors.

MRS. HALE. (*Lifting the silk.*)   Oh, Mrs. Peters—it's—

(*Mrs. Peters bends closer.*)

MRS. PETERS.   It's the bird.

MRS. HALE. (*Jumping up.*)   But, Mrs Peters—look at it! Its neck! Look at its neck! It's all—other side to.

MRS. PETERS.   Somebody—wrung—its—neck.

(Their eyes meet. A look of growing comprehension, of horror. Steps are heard outside. Mrs. Hale slips box under quilt pieces, and sinks into her chair. Enter Sheriff and County Attorney. Mrs. Peters rises.)

COUNTY ATTORNEY. *(As one turning from serious things to little pleasantries.)* Well, 115 ladies, have you decided whether she was going to quilt it or knot it?

MRS. PETERS. We think she was going to—knot it.

COUNTY ATTORNEY. Well, that's interesting, I'm sure. *(Seeing the birdcage.)* Has the bird flown?

MRS. HALE. *(Putting more quilt pieces over the box.)* We think the—cat got it.

COUNTY ATTORNEY. *(Preoccupied.)* Is there a cat?

(Mrs. Hale glances in a quick covert way at Mrs. Peters.)

MRS. PETERS. Well, not *now*. They're superstitious, you know. They leave. 120

COUNTY ATTORNEY. *(To Sheriff Peters, continuing an interrupted conversation.)* No sign at all of anyone having come from the outside. Their own rope. Now let's go up again and go over it piece by piece. *(They start upstairs.)* It would have to have been someone who knew just the—

(Mrs. Peters sits down. The two women sit there not looking at one another, but as if peering into something and at the same time holding back. When they talk now it is in the manner of feeling their way over strange ground, as if afraid of what they are saying, but as if they can not help saying it.)

MRS. HALE. She liked the bird. She was going to bury it in that pretty box.

MRS. PETERS. *(In a whisper.)* When I was a girl—my kitten—there was a boy took a hatchet, and before my eyes—and before I could get there—*(Covers her face an instant)* If they hadn't held me back I would have—*(Catches herself, looks upstairs where steps are heard, falters weakly)*—hurt him.

MRS. HALE. *(With a slow look around her.)* I wonder how it would seem never to have had any children around. *(Pause.)* No, Wright wouldn't like the bird—a thing that sang. She used to sing. He killed that, too.

MRS. PETERS. *(Moving uneasily.)* We don't know who killed the bird. 125

MRS. HALE. I knew John Wright.

MRS. PETERS. It was an awful thing was done in this house that night, Mrs. Hale. Killing a man while he slept, slipping a rope around his neck that choked the life out of him.

MRS. HALE. His neck. Choked the life out of him.

(Her hand goes out and rests on the birdcage.)

MRS. PETERS. *(With rising voice.)* We don't know who killed him. We don't know.

MRS. HALE. *(Her own feeling not interrupted.)* If there'd been years and years of 130 nothing, then a bird to sing to you, it would be awful—still, after the bird was still.

MRS. PETERS. *(Something within her speaking.)* I know what stillness is. When we homesteaded in Dakota, and my first baby died—after he was two years old, and me with no other than—

MRS. HALE. *(Moving.)* How soon do you suppose they'll be through, looking for the evidence?

MRS. PETERS. I know what stillness is. (*Pulling herself back.*) The law has got to punish crime, Mrs. Hale.

MRS. HALE. (*Not as if answering that.*) I wish you'd seen Minnie Foster when she wore a white dress with blue ribbons and stood up there in the choir and sang. (*A look around the room.*) Oh, I wish I'd come over here once in a while! That was a crime! That was a crime! Who's going to punish that?

135   MRS. PETERS. (*Looking upstairs.*) We mustn't—take on.

MRS. HALE. I might have known she needed help! I know how things can be— for women. I tell you, it's queer, Mrs. Peters. We live close together and we live far apart. We all go through the same things—it's all just a different kind of the same thing. (*Brushes her eyes; noticing the bottle of fruit, reaches out for it.*) If I was you I wouldn't tell her her fruit was gone. Tell her it *ain't.* Tell her it's all right. Take this in to prove it to her. She—she may never know whether it was broke or not.

MRS. PETERS. (*Takes the bottle, looks about for something to wrap it in; takes petticoat from the clothes brought from the other room, very nervously begins winding this around the bottle. In a false voice.*) My, it's a good thing the men couldn't hear us. Wouldn't they just laugh! Getting all stirred up over a little thing like a—dead canary. As if that could have anything to do with—with—wouldn't they *laugh!*

(*The men are heard coming down stairs.*)

MRS. HALE. (*Under her breath.*) Maybe they would—maybe they wouldn't.

COUNTY ATTORNEY. No, Peters, it's all perfectly clear except a reason for doing it. But you know juries when it comes to women. If there was some definite thing. Something to show—something to make a story about—a thing that would connect up with this strange way of doing it—

(*The women's eyes meet for an instant. Enter Hale from outer door.*)

140   HALE. Well, I've got the team° around. Pretty cold out there.

COUNTY ATTORNEY. I'm going to stay here a while by myself. (*To the Sheriff.*) You can send Frank out for me, can't you? I want to go over everything. I'm not satisfied that we can't do better.

SHERIFF. Do you want to see what Mrs. Peters is going to take in?

(*The County Attorney goes to the table, picks up the apron, laughs.*)

COUNTY ATTORNEY. Oh, I guess they're not very dangerous things the ladies have picked out. (*Moves a few things about, disturbing the quilt pieces which cover the box. Steps back.*) No, Mrs. Peters doesn't need supervising. For that matter, a sheriff's wife is married to the law. Ever think of it that way, Mrs. Peters?

MRS. PETERS. Not—just that way.

145   SHERIFF. (*Chuckling.*) Married to the law. (*Moves toward the other room.*) I just want you to come in here a minute, George. We ought to take a look at these windows.

COUNTY ATTORNEY. (*Scoffingly.*) Oh, windows!

SHERIFF. We'll be right out, Mr. Hale.

(*Hale goes outside. The Sheriff follows the County Attorney into the other room. Then Mrs. Hale rises, hands tight together, looking intensely at Mrs. Peters, whose eyes make a slow turn,*

team: that is, a team of horses drawing a wagon, or, more probably, a sleigh.

finally meeting Mrs. Hale's. A moment Mrs. Hale holds her, then her own eyes point the way to where the box is concealed. Suddenly Mrs. Peters throws back quilt pieces and tries to put the box in the bag she is wearing. It is too big. She opens box, starts to take bird out, cannot touch it, goes to pieces, stands there helpless. Sound of a knob turning in the other room. Mrs. Hale snatches the box and puts it in the pocket of her big coat. Enter County Attorney and Sheriff.)

COUNTY ATTORNEY. (*Facetiously.*) Well, Henry, at least we found out that she was not going to quilt it. She was going to—what is it you call it, ladies?

MRS. HALE. (*Her hand against her pocket.*) We call it—knot it, Mr. Henderson.

CURTAIN

A Glossary
of Important Terms

This glossary presents brief definitions of terms that are boldfaced in the text. Page references indicate where readers may find additional detail and illustration, together with discussions about how the concepts may be utilized in studying and writing about literature.

Accent or **beat (prosody)**, The heavy stresses or accents in lines of poetry. The number of accents or beats in a line usually dictates the meter of the line (five beats in a pentameter line, four in a tetrameter line, etc.), 170

Accented rhyme, See *heavy-stress rhyme.*

Accentual rhythm (prosody), A type of poetic rhythm that depends on heavy stresses or beats, not on regular meters, 174. See also *sprung rhythm.*

Allegory, A narrative created to parallel and illuminate a separate set of moral, philosophical, political, religious, or social situations, 128–30

Alliteration (prosody), The repetition of identical consonant sounds (most often the sounds beginning words) in close proximity (e.g., "pensive poets," "grown gray"), 168, 177

Allusion, Unacknowledged references and quotations. Authors assume that readers will recognize the original sources and relate their meaning to the new context, 130–31

Amphibrach (prosody), A three-syllable foot consisting of a light, heavy, and light stress, 173

Amphimacer or **cretic (prosody)**, A three-syllable foot consisting of a heavy, light, and heavy stress, 173

Analytical sentence outline, A scheme or plan for an essay, arranged according to topics (A, B, C, etc.) and with the topics expressed in sentences, 25–27

Analyzed rhyme, See *inexact rhyme.*

Anapaest (prosody), A three-syllable foot consisting of two light stresses climaxed by a heavy stress; also spelled *anapest,* 174

Antagonist, The person, idea, force, or general set of circumstances opposing the *protagonist;* an essential element of *plot,* 63

Archetypal/Symbolic/Mythic critical approach, An interpretive literary approach explaining literature in terms of archetypal patterns (e.g., God's creation of human beings, the sacrifice of a hero, the initiation of a young person), 273–74

Assonance (prosody), The repetition of identical vowel sounds in different words in close proximity, as in the *deep green sea*, 168, 176–77

Atmosphere or **mood,** The emotional aura invoked by a work, 91

Auditory images, References to sounds, 109

Authorial symbols, See *contextual symbols.*

Authorial voice, The voice or persona used by authors when seemingly speaking for themselves. The use of the term makes it possible to discuss a narration or presentation without identifying the ideas absolutely with those of the author. See also *speaker, point of view,* and *third-person point of view,* 73–74

Bacchius or **Bacchic (prosody),** A three-syllable foot consisting of a light stress followed by two heavy stresses, as in "a new song," 173

Ballad, Ballad Measure (prosody), A narrative poem composed of quatrains in *ballad measure,* that is, a pattern of iambic tetrameter alternating with iambic trimeter and rhyming *x-a-x-a,* 193

Beast fable, A fable featuring animals with human characteristics; see also *fable,* 130

Beat, See *accent.*

Brainstorming, The exploration, discovery, and development of details to be used in an essay, 16–17

Breve (prosody), A mark in the shape of a bowl-like half circle (˘) to indicate a light stress or unaccented syllable, 170

Cacophony (prosody), Meaning "bad sound," *cacophony* refers to words combining sharp or harsh sounds, 178

Cadence group (prosody), A coherent word group spoken as a single rhythmical unit, such as a noun phrase ("our sacred honor") or prepositional phrase ("of parting day"), 174

Caesura, caesurae (prosody), The pause(s) or juncture(s) separating phrases within lines of poetry, an important aspect of poetic *rhythm,* 174–75

Central idea, (1) The thesis or main idea of an essay. (2) The theme of a literary work, 20–23

Character, An extended verbal representation of a human being, the inner self that determines thought, speech, and behavior, 61–72

Cliché rhymes (prosody), Trite and widely used rhymes, such as *moon* and *June* or *trees* and *breeze,* 190

Climax (Greek for *ladder*), The high point of *conflict* and tension preceding the resolution of a story or play; the point of decision, of inevitability and no return. The climax is sometimes merged with the *crisis* in the consideration of dramatic and narrative structure, 55

Close reading, The detailed study of a poem or passage, designed to explain characters, ideas, style, setting, etc., 199–205

Closeup (film), A camera view of an actor's head and upper body, designed to emphasize the psychological makeup and reactions of the character being portrayed; to be contrasted with *long shot,* 210

Comparison–contrast, A technique of analyzing two or more works in order to determine similarities and differences in topic, treatment, and quality, 158–66

Complication, A stage of narrative and dramatic structure in which the major *conflicts* are brought out; the *rising action* of a *drama,* 54

Conflict, The opposition between two characters, between large groups of people, or between *protagonists* and larger forces such as natural objects, ideas, modes of behavior, public opinion, and the like. Conflict may also be internal and psychological, involving choices facing a *protagonist.* It is the essence of *plot,* 50

Consonant sounds or **consonant segments,** Consonant sounds are produced as a result of the touching or close proximity of the tongue or the lips in relation to the teeth or palate (e.g., *m, n, p, f, sh, ch*); to be compared with *vowel sounds,* 169

Contextual, private, or **authorial symbols,** A symbol that is derived not from common historical, cultural, or religious materials, but is developed within the context of an individual work, 128

Cosmic irony (irony of fate), *Situational irony* that is connected to a pessimistic or fatalistic view of life, 143

Cretic (prosody), See *amphimacer.*

Crisis, The point of uncertainty and tension—the *turning point*—that results from the *conflicts* and difficulties brought about through the complications of the *plot*. The crisis leads to the *climax*— that is, to the decision made by the protagonist to resolve the conflict. Sometimes the *crisis* and the *climax* are considered as two elements of the same stage of plot development, 54

Cultural or **universal symbols,** *Symbols* recognized and shared as a result of a common political, social, and cultural heritage; to be contrasted with *contextual symbols,* 127

Dactyl (prosody), A three-syllable foot consisting of a heavy stress followed by two lights, as in each word of the phrase *"notable quotable parables,"* 174

Dactylic or **triple rhyme (prosody),** Rhyming dactyls, 190

Deconstructionist critical approach, An interpretive literary approach that rejects absolute interpretations and stresses ambiguities and contradictions, 274–76

Dénouement (untying) or **resolution,** The final stage of plot development, in which mysteries are explained, characters find their destinies, and the work is completed. Usually the dénouement is done as speedily as possible, for it occurs after all conflicts are ended, 55

Dimeter (prosody), A line of two metrical feet, 170

Diphthong (prosody), A single meaningful sound created by the glide from one vowel to another; the three diphthongs in English are the *i* in *night*, the *oi* in *boy*, and the *au* in *house*, 169

Dipody or **syzygy (prosody),** A strong beat that creates a single foot out of two normal feet— usually iambs or trochees—so that a "galloping" or "rollicking" rhythm results, 173

Documentation, Granting recognition to the ideas and words of others, either through textual, parenthetical, or footnote references, 231

Double entendre ("double meaning"), Deliberate ambiguity, often sexual and usually humorous, 142

Double rhyme (prosody), See *trochaic rhyme.*

Drama, An individual play; also plays considered as a group; one of the three major genres of imaginative literature, 3

Dramatic irony, A special kind of *situational irony* in which a character perceives his or her plight in a limited way while the audience and one or more of the other characters understand it entirely, 143

Dramatic or **objective point of view,** A third-person *narration* reporting speech and action, but excluding commentary on the actions and thoughts of the characters, 78, 81

Dynamic character, A character who undergoes adaptation, change, or growth, unlike the *static character,* who remains constant. In a *short story*, there is usually only one dynamic character, whereas in a *novel* there may be many, 63

Economic Determinist/Marxist critical approach, An interpretive literary approach based on the theories of Karl Marx (1818–1883), stressing that literature is to be judged from an economic perspective, 271–72

Editing, See *montage.*

Enclosing setting, See *framing setting.*

End-stopped line (prosody), A line ending in a full pause, usually indicated with a period or semicolon, 175

Enjambement or **run-on line (prosody),** A line that runs over to the next line because it has no terminal pause or punctuation, 175

Epic, A long narrative poem elevating character, speech, and action, 3

Essay, A short and tightly organized written composition dealing with a topic such as a character, setting, or point of view, 15

Euphony (prosody), Meaning "good sound," *euphony* refers to word groups containing consonants that permit an easy and pleasant flow of spoken sound; to be contrasted with *cacophony*, 178

Exact rhyme (prosody), Rhyming words in which both the vowel and consonant sounds rhyme; also called *perfect rhyme.* It is important to note that rhymes result from *sound* rather than spelling; words do not have to be spelled the same way or look alike to rhyme, 189

Examination, A written or oral test or inquiry designed to discover a person's understanding and capacity to deal with a particular topic or set of topics, 247–57

Exposition, The stage of dramatic or narrative structure that introduces all things necessary for the development of the *plot*, 54

Eye rhyme or **sight rhyme (prosody),** Words that seem to rhyme because parts of them are spelled identically but pronounced differently (e.g., *bear, fear; fury, bury; stove, shove; wonder, yonder*), 192

Fable, A brief *story* illustrating a moral truth, most often associated with the ancient Greek writer Aesop, 130

Falling rhyme, Trochaic rhymes, such as *dying* and *crying*, and also dactylic rhymes, such as *flattery* and *battery*, 190

Feet, See *foot*.

Feminist critical approach, An interpretive literary approach designed to raise consciousness about the importance and unique nature of women in literature, 270–71

Fiction, *Narratives* based in the imagination of the author, not in literal, reportorial facts; one of the three major genres of imaginative literature, 3

Figurative language, Words and expressions that conform to a particular pattern or form, such as *metaphor, simile,* and *parallelism*, 3, 116

Film script, The written dramatic text on which a film is based, including directions for movement and expression, 208

Film, Motion pictures, movies, 206–218

First-person point of view, The use of an "I," or first-person, *speaker* or *narrator* who tells about things that he/she has seen, done, spoken, heard, thought, and also learned about in other ways, 77, 80, 82

Flashback, A method of narration in which past events are introduced into a present action, 55–56

Flat character, A character, usually minor, who is not individual, but rather useful and structural, static and unchanging; distinguished from *round character*, 63

Foot, feet (prosody), A measured combination of heavy and light *stresses*, such as the iamb, which contains a light and a heavy stress, 170, 171–74

Formal substitution, See *substitution*.

Formalist critical approach, See *New Critical/Formalist critical approach*.

Framing (enclosing) setting, The same features of topic or setting used at both the beginning and ending of a work so as to "frame" or "enclose" the work, 91

Freewriting, See *brainstorming*.

Graph, Graphics (spelling), Writing or spelling; the appearance of words on a page, as opposed to their actual sounds, 168

Gustatory images, References to impressions of taste, 109

Haiku, A poetic form derived from Japanese, traditionally containing three lines of 5, 7, and 5 syllables, 3

Half rhyme, See *inexact rhyme*.

Heavy-stress rhyme or **rising rhyme,** A rhyme, such as rhyming iambs or anapaests, ending with a strong stress. The rhymes may be produced with one-syllable words, such as *sky* and *fly*, or with multisyllabic words in which the accent falls on the last syllable, such as *decline* and *confine*, 190

Heptameter or **the septenary (prosody),** A line consisting of seven metrical feet, 170

Hero, heroine, The major male and female *protagonists* in a narrative or drama. The terms are often used to describe leading characters in adventures and romances, 63

Hexameter (prosody), A line consisting of six metrical feet, 170

Historical critical approach, See *Topical/Historical critical approach*.

Hovering accent, See *spondee*.

Hyperbole or **overstatement,** A rhetorical figure in which emphasis is achieved through exaggeration, 142

Iamb (prosody), A two-syllable *foot* consisting of a light stress followed by a heavy stress (e.g., *the winds*), 171

Idea or **theme,** A thought, opinion, or principle; in literature, a unifying and centralizing concept or motif, 97–106

Identical rhyme (prosody), The use of the same words in rhyming positions, such as *veil* and *veil*, or *stone* and *stone*, 192

Image, Imagery, Images are references that trigger the mind to fuse together memories of sights (*visual*), sounds (*auditory*), tastes (*gustatory*), smells (*olfactory*), and sensations of touch (*tactile*). "Image" refers to a single mental creation. "Imagery" refers to images throughout a work or throughout the works of a writer or group of writers. Images may be *literal* (descriptive and pictorial) and *metaphorical* (figurative and suggestive), 3, 107–115

Imaginative literature, Literature based in the imagination of the writer; the genres of imaginative literature are *fiction, poetry,* and *drama,* 3

Imperfect foot (prosody), A metrical foot consisting of a single syllable, either heavily or lightly stressed, 174

Inexact rhyme (prosody), Rhymes that are created from words with similar but not identical sounds. In most of these instances, either the vowel segments are different while the consonants are the same, or vice versa. This type of rhyme is variously called *slant rhyme, near rhyme, half rhyme, off rhyme, analyzed rhyme,* or *suspended rhyme,* 192

Intellectual critical approach, See *Topical/Intellectual critical approach.*

Internal rhyme, The occurrence of rhyming words within a single line of verse, 191

Irony, Broadly, a means of indirection. Language that states the opposite of what is intended is *verbal irony.* The placement of characters in a state of ignorance is *dramatic irony,* while an emphasis on powerlessness is *situational irony,* 91, 141–43

Irony of fate, See *cosmic irony.*

Irony of situation, See *situational irony.*

Journal, A notebook or word-processor file for recording responses and observations that, for purposes of writing, may be used in the development of essays, 12–15, 40

Kinesthetic images, Words describing human or animal motion and activity, 110

Kinetic images, Words describing general motion, 110

Light stress (prosody), In speech and in metrical scansion, the less emphasized syllables, as in Shakespeare's "That time of year," in which *that* and *of* are pronounced more lightly than *time* and *year,* 170

Limited point of view or **limited-omniscient point of view,** A third-person narration in which the actions and thoughts of the protagonist are the focus of attention, 79, 81

Literary research, See *research.*

Literature, Written or oral compositions that tell stories, dramatize situations, express emotions, and analyze and advocate ideas. Literature is designed to engage readers emotionally as well as intellectually, with the major genres being *fiction, poetry, drama,* and *nonfiction prose,* and with many separate subforms, 2, *passim*

Long shot (film), A distant camera view, including not only characters but also their surroundings; to be contrasted with a *closeup,* 210

Major mover, The participant in a work's action who either causes things to happen or who is the subject of major events. If the first-person narrator is also a major mover, such as the *protagonist,* that fact gives first-hand authenticity to the narration, 79

Marxist critical approach, See *Economic Determinist/Marxist critical approach.*

Mechanics of verse, See *prosody.*

Metaphor ("carrying out a change"), *Figurative language* that describes something as though it actually were something else, thereby enhancing understanding and insight, 116–25

Meter (prosody), The number of feet within a line of traditional verse, such as *iambic pentameter* referring to a line containing five *iambs,* 170–71

Metrical foot, See *foot.*

Metrics, See *prosody.*

Monometer, A line consisting of one metrical foot, 170

Montage or **editing,** The editing or assembling of the various camera "takes," or separately filmed scenes, to make a continuous film, 209

Mood, See *Atmosphere.*

Moral/Intellectual critical approach, An interpretive literary approach that is concerned primarily with content and values, 265–66

Music of poetry (prosody), See *prosody.*

Myth, Mythology, Mythos, A *myth* is a story that deals with the relationships of gods to humanity , or with battles among heroes. A myth may also be a set of beliefs or assumptions among societies. *Mythology* refers collectively to all the stories and beliefs, either of a single group or number of groups. A system of beliefs and religious or historical doctrine is a *mythos*, 3, 130

Mythic critical approach, See *Archetypal/Symbolic/Mythic critical approach.*

Narration, narrative fiction, The relating or recounting of a sequence of events or actions. While a *narration* may be reportorial and historical, *narrative fiction* is primarily creative and imaginative, 3

Narrative fiction, See *prose fiction.*

Narrator, See *speaker.*

Near rhyme, See *inexact rhyme.*

New Critical/Formalist critical approach, An interpretive literary approach based on the French practice of *explication de texte*, stressing the form and details of literary works, 267–68

Nonfiction prose, A *genre* consisting of essays, articles, and books about real as opposed to fictional occurrences and objects; one of the major *genres* of literature, 3

Novel, A long work of prose fiction, 3

Objective point of view, See *dramatic point of view.*

Octameter (prosody), A line of eight metrical feet, 170

Off rhyme, See *inexact rhyme.*

Olfactory imagery, Images referring to impressions of smell, 109

Omniscient point of view, A *third-person narrative* in which the *speaker* or *narrator*, with no apparent limitations, may describe intentions, actions, reactions, locations, and speeches of any or all of the characters, and may also describe their innermost thoughts (when necessary), 78, 81

Onomatopoeia (prosody), A blending of consonant and vowel sounds designed to imitate or suggest the activity being described, 177–78

Outline, See *analytical sentence outline.*

Overstatement, See *hyperbole.*

Parable, A short *allegory* designed to illustrate a religious truth, most often associated with Jesus as recorded in the Gospels, 3, 130

Paraphrase, A brief restatement, in one's own words, of all or part of a literary work; a précis, 225–26

Pentameter (prosody), A line of five metrical feet, 170

Perfect rhyme, See *exact rhyme.*

Phonetic, phonetics (prosody), The actual pronunciation of sounds, as distinguished from spelling or *graphics*, 168

Plausibility, See *probability.*

Plot, The plan or groundwork for a story or a play, with the actions resulting from believable and authentic human responses to a *conflict*. It is causation, conflict, response, opposition, and interaction that make a *plot* out of a series of actions, 49–61

Poem, poet, poetry, A variable literary genre of imaginative literature that is characterized by the rhythmical qualities of language. While poems may be short (including *epigrams* and *haiku* of just a few lines) or long (*epics* of thousands of lines), the essence of poetry is compression, economy, and force, in contrast with the expansiveness of prose. There is no bar to the topics that poets may consider, and poems may range from the personal and lyric to the public and discursive. A *poem* is one poetic work. A *poet* is a person who writes poems. *Poetry* may refer to the poems of one writer, to poems of a number of writers, to all poems generally, or to the aesthetics of poetry considered as an art, 2

Point of view, The *speaker, voice, narrator,* or *persona* of a work; the position from which details are perceived and related; a centralizing mind or intelligence; not to be confused with opinions or beliefs, 73–87

Point-of-view character, The central figure or *protagonist* in a *limited-point-of-view narration*, the character about whom events turn, the focus of attention in the narration, 79

Private or contextual symbols, See *Cultural symbols.*

Probability or plausibility, The standard that literature should be about what is likely, common, normal, and usual—the theory being that such literature is relevant to the majority of human beings, 66

Problem, A question or issue about the interpretation or understanding of a work, 150–57

Procatalepsis or anticipation, A rhetorical strategy whereby the writer raises an objection and then answers it, the idea being to strengthen an argument by dealing with possible objections before a dissenter can raise them, 152

Prose fiction, Imaginative prose narratives (short stories and novels) that focus on one or a few characters who undergo a change or development as they interact with other characters and deal with their problems, 3

Prosody, The sounds and rhythms of poetry, 167–88

Protagonist, The central character and focus of interest in a narrative or drama, 63

Psychological/Psychoanalytic critical approach, An interpretive literary approach stressing how psychology may be used in the explanation of both authors and literary works, 272–73

Pyrrhic (prosody), A metrical foot consisting of two unaccented syllables, 172

Quatrain, (1) A four-line stanza or poetic unit. (2) In an *English* or *Shakespearean* sonnet, a group of four lines united by rhyme, 193

Reader-Response critical approach, An interpretive literary approach based in the proposition that literary works are not fully created until readers make *transactions* with them by *actualizing* them in the light of their own knowledge and experience, 276–77

Realism or **verisimilitude,** The use of true, lifelike, or probable situations and concerns. Also, the theory underlying the use of reality in literature, 66, 90

Representative character, A *flat character* with the qualities of all other members of a group (i.e., clerks, cowboys, detectives, etc.); a *stereotype,* 64

Research, literary, The systematic use of primary and secondary sources for assistance in studying a literary problem, 219–46

Resolution, See *dénouement.*

Response, A reader's intellectual and emotional reactions to a literary work, 40–48

Rhetorical figure, See *figurative language.*

Rhetorical substitution, See *substitution.*

Rhyme, The repetition of identical or closely related sounds in the syllables of different words, most often in concluding syllables at the ends of lines, 168, 189–98

Rhyme scheme, The pattern of a poem's *rhyme,* usually indicated by assigning a letter of the alphabet to each rhyming sound, 192–93

Rhythm (prosody), The varying speed, intensity, elevation, pitch, loudness, and expressiveness of speech, especially poetry, 167

Rising rhyme, See *heavy-stress rhyme.*

Romance, (1) Lengthy Spanish and French stories of the sixteenth and seventeenth centuries. (2) Modern formulaic stories describing the growth of an enthusiastic love relationship, 3

Round character, A character who profits from experience and undergoes a change or development; usually but not necessarily the *protagonist,* 63

Run-on line, See *enjambement.*

Scan, scansion (prosody), The act of determining the prevailing *rhythm* of a poem, 170

Second-person point of view, A narration in which a second-person listener ("you") is the protagonist and the speaker is someone (e.g., doctor, parent, rejected lover, etc.) with knowledge that the protagonist does not possess or understand about his or her own actions, 77, 81, 82

Segment (prosody), The smallest meaningful unit of sound, such as the *l, uh,* and *v* sounds making up the word "love." Segments are to be distinguished from spellings, 168

Septenary, See *heptameter.*

Setting, The natural, manufactured, and cultural environment in which characters live and move, including all the artifacts they use in their lives, 88–106

Short story, A compact, concentrated work of narrative fiction that may also contain description, dialogue, and commentary. Poe used the term "brief prose tale" for the short story and emphasized that it should create a powerful and unified impact, 3

Sight rhyme, See *eye rhyme.*

Simile, A figure of comparison, using "like" with nouns and "as" with clauses, as in "the trees were bent by the wind *like actors bowing after a performance,*" 116–25

Situational irony or **irony of situation,** A type of *irony* emphasizing that human beings are enmeshed in forces beyond their comprehension and control, 142

Slant rhyme, A *near rhyme* in which the concluding consonant sounds (but not the vowels) are identical, as in "should" and "food," "slim" and "ham," 192. See also *inexact rhyme.*

Sound, The phonetics of language, collectively and separately considered, 3, 168. See also *prosody*.

Speaker, The *narrator* of a story or poem, the *point of view,* often an independent character who is completely imagined and consistently maintained by the author. In addition to narrating the essential events of the work (justifying status as the *narrator*), the speaker may also introduce other aspects of his or her knowledge and may interject judgments and opinions. Often the character of the speaker is of as much interest as the actions or incidents, 73

Spondee (prosody), A two-syllable foot consisting of successive, equally heavy accents (e.g., *slow time, men's eyes*), 172

Sprung rhythm (prosody), A method of accenting, developed by Gerard Manley Hopkins, in which major stresses are "sprung" from the poetic line, 174. See also *accentual rhythm*.

Stanza (prosody), A group of poetic lines corresponding to paragraphs in prose; the meters and rhymes are usually repeating and systematic, 193

Static character, A character who undergoes no change; contrasted with a *dynamic character*, 63

Stereotype, A character who is so ordinary and unoriginal that he or she seems to have been cast in a mold; a *representative* character, 64

Stock character, A *flat character* in a standard role with standard *traits,* such as the irate police captain, the bored hotel clerk, the sadistic criminal, etc.; a *stereotype*, 64

Stress (prosody), The emphasis given to a syllable, either strong or light, 170. See also *accent*.

Strong-stress rhythm (prosody), See *accentual rhythm*.

Structuralist critical approach, An interpretive literary approach attempting to find relationships and similarities among elements that appear to be separate and discrete, 268–70

Structure, The arrangement and placement of materials in a work, 49–61

Substitution (prosody), *Formal substitution* is the use of an actual variant foot within a line, such as an anapaest being used in place of an iamb. *Rhetorical substitution* is the manipulation of the caesura to create the effect of a series of differing feet, 175–76

Suspended rhyme, See *inexact rhyme*.

Syllable (prosody), A separately pronounced part of a word (e.g., the *sing* and *ing* parts of "singing") or, in some cases, a complete word (e.g., *the, when, flounced*), 168

Symbol, symbolism, A specific word, idea, or object that may stand for ideas, values, persons, or ways of life, 126–37

Syzygy, See *dipody*.

Tactile imagery, Images of touch and responses to touch, 109

Tetrameter (prosody), A line consisting of four metrical feet, 170

Thesis sentence or **thesis statement,** An introductory sentence that names the topics to be developed in the body of an essay, 23–24

Third-person point of view, A third-person method of narration (i.e., *she, he, it, they, them,* etc.), in which the speaker or narrator is not a part of the story, unlike the involvement of the narrator of a *first-person point of view*. Because the third-person speaker may exhibit great knowledge and understanding, together with other qualities of character, he or she is often virtually identified with the author, but this identification is not easily decided, 78–79, 81, 82. See also *authorial voice, omniscient point of view*.

Third-person objective point of view, See *dramatic point of view*.

Tone, The techniques and modes of presentation that reveal or create attitudes, 138–49

Topic sentence, The sentence determining or introducing the subject matter of a paragraph, 24

Topical/Historical critical approach, An interpretive literary approach that stresses the relationship of literature to its historical period, 266–67

Trait, traits, A typical mode of behavior; the study of major traits provides a guide to the description of character, 62

Trimeter (prosody), A line consisting of three metrical feet, 170

Triple rhyme, See *dactylic rhyme*.

Trochaic or **double rhyme,** Rhyming trochees such as *flower* and *shower*, 190–91

Trochee, trochaic (prosody), A two-syllable foot consisting of a heavy stress followed by a light stress, 171–72

Understatement, The deliberate underplaying or undervaluing of an assertion or idea to create emphasis, 142

Universal symbol, See *cultural symbol*.

Unstressed syllable, See *light stress*.

Value, values, The attachment of worth, significance, and desirability to an idea so that the idea is judged not only for its significance as thought but also for its importance as a goal, ideal, or standard, 98

Verbal irony, Language stressing the importance of an idea by stating the opposite of what is meant, 142

Verisimilitude ("like truth"), See *realism.*

Versification, See *prosody.*

Virgule (prosody), A slash mark (/) indicating the boundaries of poetic feet, 170

Visual image, Language describing visible objects and situations, 109

Vowel rhyme, The use of any vowels in rhyming positions, as in *day* and *sky,* or *key* and *play,* 192

Vowel sounds or **vowel segments,** Meaningful continuant sounds produced by the resonation of the voice in the space between the tongue and the top of the mouth, such as the *ee* in *feel,* the *eh* in *bet,* and the *oo* in *cool,* 169

Index of Authors, Directors, Topics, and Chapter Titles

Works are included alphabetically under the name of the author or director. Anonymous works, collectively authored works, and works of unknown authorship or directorship are indexed under the titles. For brief definitions of important words and terms used in the text, please consult the preceding *Glossary*.